TAKEOVERS

Attack and Survival

TAKEOVERS
ATTACK AND SURVIVAL

A Strategist's Manual

Ralph C. Ferrara
Meredith M. Brown
John H. Hall

Jonathan E. Richman
Coauthor and Editor

Christine E. Gray
Alexander M. Metviner
Coauthors

The Butterworth Group of Companies

United States
Butterworth Legal Publishers, Boston, Seattle, Austin, and St. Paul
D & S Publishers, Clearwater, Florida

United Kingdom
Butterworth & Co. (Publishers) Ltd., London and Edinburgh

Canada
Butterworth & Co. (Canada) Ltd., Toronto and Vancouver

Australia
Butterworths Pty. Ltd., Sydney, Melbourne, Brisbane, Adelaide, and Perth

New Zealand
Butterworths (New Zealand) Ltd., Wellington and Auckland

Singapore
Butterworth & Co. (Asia) Pte. Ltd., Singapore

South Africa
Butterworth Publishers (SA) (Pty) Ltd., Durban and Pretoria

ISBN 0-88063-099-X

Printed in the United States of America

TABLE OF CONTENTS

ACKNOWLEDGEMENTS

The authors wish to acknowledge the contributions of Peter L. Borowitz, Daniel M. Abuhoff, Robert E. Dozier, and Bart Schwartz to this book. They also wish to thank Thomas Carroll, Victoria Hirschland, and William J. Phillips for their contributions to Debevoise & Plimpton's ongoing research into the law of takeovers, which research has served as the foundation for this book.

The authors, coauthors, and contributors are or have been attorneys practicing with the New York and Washington offices of Debevoise & Plimpton.

INTRODUCTION

We intend in this book to demystify the takeover process for those who are not specialists in the field but who may be called upon to manage a contest for control. The book was written particularly for the corporate lawyers and officers who are expected to understand the takeover process, to control the experts, and to explain everything to the directors, executives, and employees caught up in the whirlwind. We hope, however, that this book will be useful not only to corporate counsel but also to other persons who work in the takeover field: outside counsel, investment bankers, and corporate officers interested in an overview of the legal aspects of takeovers. It is the takeover strategist's guide to attack and survival.

The federal securities laws provide the basic legal framework for takeovers, but the process also is directly affected by a panoply of other statutes, regulations, and case law, such as the Hart-Scott-Rodino Antitrust Improvements Act, the margin regulations of the Federal Reserve Board, state takeover statutes, state business judgment cases, and even some of the statutes affecting (decreasingly) regulated industries. This book provides an introduction to and a review of these and other statutes, regulations, and cases.

A takeover is simply an acquisition of control of a company in a manner that, at least initially, does not depend on negotiation. A takeover can take the form of a tender offer, a stock accumulation program, a proxy contest, or any combination of the foregoing. As a recent case stated:

> Outsider challenges to corporate management characteristically take on the dimensions of warfare. Battles are waged by proxy, in the courts and in the press. Military and Arthurian metaphors

> are applied to the various actors and their maneuvers. The costs, both public and private, are tremendous.[1]

If war is an extension of diplomacy, takeovers are an extension of negotiated corporate acquisitions and, as such, involve a variety of legal issues, including tax, securities, antitrust, general corporate law, and civil procedure. It is impossible to treat all of these issues exhaustively in a single handbook. Instead, we have attempted to focus on matters that are most likely to be central and unique to a takeover, rather than on questions (such as tax and accounting) that are of equal concern in takeovers and in negotiated acquisitions.

Substantial regulatory and legal confusion exists in the takeover area. Shifts in corporate control can occur through various means, and different maneuvers are subject to different results developed by the courts, Congress, and the responsible federal agencies. Just as it is often difficult to determine whether a corporation will be the target of a takeover bid, so, too, is it often difficult to predict precisely how the courts, the legislatures, or the regulatory agencies will react to innovative developments in the area. This handbook attempts to clarify this confusion and to shed some light on new developments and likely regulatory responses.

1. *Hubco, Inc. v. Rappaport*, 628 F. Supp. 345, 347 (D.N.J. 1985).

PART I

HISTORY OF THE WILLIAMS ACT

CHAPTER

1

BACKGROUND

Prior to the 1960s, contests for corporate control in the United States usually took the form of proxy fights, which are regulated by the Securities Exchange Act of 1934 (the "Exchange Act").[2] In the early 1960s, the cash tender offer first emerged as an effective means of obtaining corporate control, and its use since has increased dramatically. These tender offers initially were unregulated by federal or state law; an offeror could acquire an offeree without having to disclose information about itself or about its plans for the target corporation.

The use of tender offers increased throughout the 1960s because the tender offer was cheaper, less regulated, and more difficult to thwart than were other takeover strategies. In 1968, former Securities and Exchange Commission ("SEC") Chairman Manuel F. Cohen wrote in his preface to Edward Aranow and Herbert Einhorn's classic treatise on proxy contexts:

> One of the most striking phenomena of the corporate scene in recent years has been the large number of mergers and other forms of acquisitions—particularly mergers and acquisitions involving companies in different fields. Informed observers have stated that they consider the merger proxy statements prepared under the Commission's Proxy Rules to be the most useful and informative documents available in evaluating today's "conglomerate" companies. But in the very recent past, the situation has been getting away from us. Statutory mergers and proxy contests, traditional means of acquiring control of a publicly held corporation, are being supplanted to an increasing degree by cash purchases, either through tender offers or through private or open market purchases.[3]

As a result of the regulatory vacuum in the tender offer area, many abuses developed, particularly because of the secrecy in which tender offers were shrouded. Because bidders were not required to disclose information, shareholders could not make

---

2. 15 U.S.C. §§ 78a-78*lll*.

3. E.R. Aranow & H.A. Einhorn, *Proxy Contests for Corporate Control* xvii (2d ed. 1968).

informed investment decisions and thus could easily be misled by bidders. Investors consequently began to lose confidence in the securities market as control contests became more pitched and tilted against them.

In addition to being uninformed, shareholders frequently found themselves confronted with "undue pressure . . . to act hastily to accept [the offer], before management or any other group [had] an opportunity to present opposing arguments or competing offers."[4] Offerors presented partial tender offers—for less than all of the target's shares—to shareholders on a "first come, first served basis," and those shareholders who did not act hastily risked losing their chance to participate in the offer.

Shareholders also confronted substantial pressure from the target's management, which usually urged them to reject tender offers. The lack of regulation allowed management to engage in questionable defensive responses:

> If management does oppose the offer, the present lack of regulation leaves it with powerful weapons, which it may wield with impunity, provided its activities fall short of fraud. Management tactics may include making all sorts of predictions and extravagant claims. . . .[5]

For example, management or its allies often would purchase the target's securities on the open market in order to drive up the price of the company's outstanding shares, thereby making the tender offer appear less attractive to shareholders—and potentially more expensive for the bidder.[6]

---

4. *Senate Hearings on S. 510 Before the Subcomm. on Securities of the Senate Comm. on Banking and Currency*, 90th Cong., 1st Sess. 21, 35 (Mar. 21 & 22, April 4, 1967).

5. *Id.* at 196.

6. *Id.*

CHAPTER 2

LEGISLATIVE RESPONSE

In 1968, Congress enacted the Williams Act,[7] which attempted to remedy tender offer abuses by protecting shareholders of target companies. Because tender offers resemble proxy contests insofar as both devices attempt to achieve changes in corporate control, Congress conferred upon the SEC a degree of jurisdiction over tender offers similar to the authority that the Commission already exercised over proxy solicitations. Furthermore, the Williams Act imposed on bidders, and often on the target's management, certain disclosure and reporting requirements similar to those applicable in proxy contests.

The initial version of the bill was introduced in 1965 by Senator Harrison A. Williams, Jr., of New Jersey, with the co-sponsorship of Senator Thomas Kuchel, of California.[8] The bill did not focus on the need for an orderly and informed market but instead emphasized the need to restrain third-party tender offers. Nor did the bill attempt in any way to control target management's response to tender offers. In the words of Senator Williams:

> In recent years we have seen proud old companies reduced to corporate shells after white-collar pirates have seized control with funds from sources which are unknown in many cases, then sold or traded away the best assets, later to split up most of the loot among themselves. . . .
>
> The ultimate responsibility for preventing this kind of industrial sabotage lies with the management and the shareholders of the corporation that is so threatened. But the leniency of our laws places management and shareholders at a distinct disadvantage in coming to grips with the enemy.[9]

Senator Williams' message was clear: protect incumbent management.

---

7. Pub. L. 90-439, §§ 2, 3, 82 Stat. 454, 455 (July 29, 1968), amending 15 U.S.C. §§ 78m & n.

8. S. 2731, 89th Cong., 2d Sess. (1965).

9. 111 Cong. Rec. 28,257-58 (Oct. 22, 1965) (remarks of Sen. Williams).

The initial bill applied section 16 of the Exchange Act, pertaining to insider trading and short-swing profits,[10] to tender offerors. The bill also required the SEC to establish rules for the filing of official materials before a tender offer could proceed.

In 1967, Senator Williams introduced a revised bill,[11] which, with minor amendments, was passed by Congress and signed by President Johnson. The 1967 bill did not include short-swing trading rules or advance-clearance provisions. Unlike its 1965 predecessor, however, the 1967 bill did contain detailed provisions to protect shareholders from the improper conduct of the target's management and of tender offerors. Indeed, by 1967, Senator Williams had changed his objectives:

> We have taken extreme care to avoid tipping the scales either in favor of management or in favor of the person making the takeover bid. [The bill] is designed solely to require full and fair disclosure for the benefit of investors. The bill will at the same time provide the offeror and management equal opportunity to present their case.[12]

The final bill's legislative history thus reveals that Congress expressly disclaimed an intention to provide the target's management with a weapon with which to discourage takeover bids or to prevent large stock accumulations that would facilitate such attempts.[13] Under the bill's provisions,

> the Securities and Exchange Commission could specify the information to be included in any recommendation by management or others in favor or in opposition to a tender offer and could regulate the solicitation of investors by brokers and dealers who are often compensated for shares tendered as a result of their activities. It would also enable the Securities and Exchange Commission to regulate the activities of persons who

---

10. Insider trading and short-swing profits are discussed in § II.4.C., *infra.*
11. S. Rep. No. 510, 90th Cong., 1st Sess. (1967).
12. 113 Cong. Rec. 24,664 (1967) (remarks of Sen. Williams).
13. *See Rondeau v. Mosinee Paper Corp.*, 422 U.S. 49, 58-59 (1975).

> make competing tender offers or seek to influence the investor's decisions on a tender offer.[14]

The bill also attempted to guarantee to investors sufficient time to assess the disclosed information and to make a considered decision whether to tender. Shareholders no longer were to be stampeded into reaching immediate and uninformed investment decisions.

---

14. S. Rep. No. 550, 90th Cong., 1st Sess. at 9 (1967); H.R. 1711, 90th Cong., 2d Sess. at 10 (1968).

PART

II

OFFENSIVE CONSIDERATIONS

CHAPTER 1

PLANNING FOR A TAKEOVER

The bidder must carefully plan its takeover strategy. It is essential that the bidder understand the target and anticipate the possible defenses that the target may implement. Moreover, the bidder must analyze the economic effects of the acquisition, arrange financing, and consider alternative strategies to carry out the proposed takeover within the applicable regulatory framework.

A. The Bidder's Working Group

Because confidentiality and speed are so vital in the world of takeovers, the bidder should assemble a working group that is as small as possible and is expanded only on a need-to-know basis. The use of a code name often is helpful to maintain the offer's confidentiality.

A working group typically consists of the following:

- *Officers.* To insure confidentiality, the bidder should involve only a small number of its key officers in the takeover process. This group typically includes the chief executive officer, the senior financial officer (to consider the financing and the pro-forma financial effect of the acquisition), and the general counsel (to coordinate legal analysis of the target and relations with outside counsel).
- *Counsel.* In addition to regular inside and outside general counsel, bidders often rely on special takeover counsel to develop a strategy using state-of-the-art tactics and to give bidders the extra resources that they may need to act promptly. At a later stage, the bidder may need to retain local counsel in several jurisdictions if the bidder commences litigation challenging state takeover or regulatory statutes that might delay or frustrate the offer.
- *Investment banker.* An investment banker with takeover experience can help coordinate the other members of the working group, advise on takeover strategies, evaluate the target company, and help to arrange financing for the

acquisition. If the acquisition involves a tender offer, an investment banker may act as a dealer manager. Dealer managers, however, are not required by law, and hostile bids sometimes proceed without them.

- *Proxy solicitors.* If the takeover involves a proxy solicitation, the bidder should retain professional proxy solicitors.
- *Public relations firm.* If the bidder is vulnerable to public relations pressure (for example, if the bid will involve shares of the bidder's stock, or if the target might attempt to put downward pressure on the market price of the bidder's stock), the bidder should consider retaining a public relations consultant. A public relations firm might help to convince the market that the deal will be completed, thereby encouraging shareholders to tender; it also might aid the bidder in fending off the target's responses and in drafting press releases.
- *Investigator.* Finally, the bidder might wish to retain an investigator in order to uncover facts demonstrating mismanagement of the target and/or the target's directors' improper responses to the takeover.

B. Know Your Target

Before launching a takeover, a bidder should research the target company in order to explore the following matters:

- Contingent liabilities, such as environmental claims, products liability claims, unfunded pension obligations, and medical benefits liabilities.
- Loan agreements that may contain covenants that would affect plans for the financing of the acquisition. Such loans would have to be renegotiated or replaced in the aftermath of a successful tender offer.
- Major contracts, to insure that a change of control will not result in termination of the target's contractual rights.

- Charter and bylaw provisions and provisions in state corporation and takeover statutes that may impede the acquisition of control of the target or make any such acquisition prohibitively expensive. The bidder should pay particular attention to "poison pills," "fair price" amendments, staggered boards, or prohibitions of shareholder action by written consent.
- Possible antitrust obstacles that may make the acquisition impossible or require disposition of portions of the target's or the bidder's business. Analysis of these possible obstacles requires detailed study of any product and market overlap between the bidder and the target.
- The names and holdings of large shareholders and the amount of stock owned by management and management-influenced entities such as employee stock option plans ("ESOPs").
- The identity of the target's directors and senior officers. The bidder must understand the characteristics, motives, and approaches of these individuals. For instance, the CEO may be a large shareholder who is approaching retirement age and has no successor. In such a case, the target might be significantly more receptive to an acquisition proposal than might a target whose CEO is younger or has a protégé who is being groomed to take over the business.
- Employment and severance agreements (particularly "golden parachutes"). The bidder must know whether it can retain senior management once it assumes control. If the bidder does not desire to retain the target's current employees, then it must analyze the cost of changing senior management, which cost can be significantly enhanced by "golden parachutes."
- Special regulatory statutes that apply to the bidder. If the bidder engages in a regulated line of business, the bidder may need to obtain governmental approvals in connection with its acquisition of control of the target.
- Laws of foreign jurisdictions that may apply to the target. If the target has operations in other countries, the bidder may

need the approval of the relevant foreign government in order to acquire the foreign operations of the United States parent company.

- Tax attributes of the target. The bidder should determine whether the target has any desirable tax attributes, such as a net operating loss carry-forward, that the bidder may wish to preserve. If so, the desire to preserve those tax advantages may affect the structure of the acquisition. The bidder also should consider whether a taxable, as opposed to a tax-free, acquisition would be advantageous. If the transaction is taxable, the bidder should analyze the extent of taxable gain and the amount of recapture of investment and other credits.
- Accounting issues. If accountants intend to treat the acquisition as a purchase, the bidder should determine how much goodwill is involved and what effect the post-acquisition amortization of that goodwill will have on the bidder's earnings. The bidder must also investigate whether the target has audited financial statements. If the bidder is a reporting company under the Exchange Act, and if the target represents more than 10 percent of the bidder's sales, assets, or income, the bidder will need to include the target's audited financials in its own SEC filings.
- The target's team. The bidder should attempt to determine whom the target will use for advice in connection with the takeover. Identification of the target's counsel, investment bankers, accountants, and proxy solicitors will reveal the professionals whom the bidder should not approach in connection with the bid, to avoid prematurely tipping the bidder's hand to the target.

C. Consider the Bidder's Own Vulnerability

A target company might attempt to unearth unpleasant or unseemly information—such as legal problems, "sensitive" payments, and environmental issues—about the bidder and its senior management, not only by examining public records but also by retaining investigative firms. This information might be used to deter the bidder, to require additional disclosures in the bidder's SEC filings, or to turn the target's shareholders against the bidder and its offer. The bidder, therefore, should search its own house for any "skeletons in the closet" and should discuss any such skeletons with its counsel.

The bidder also should consider its own vulnerability to a counter-bid by the target. The target may employ a "Pac-Man defense" and make a bid for the bidder. Although it has been used on several occasions, the "Pac-Man defense" has fallen into disfavor in light of the criticism that accompanied Martin Marietta's counter-offer for Bendix in 1982. Nevertheless, resurrection of this tactic is always possible, and the bidder should consider its own defenses. For example, before commencing a tender offer, the bidder should insure that the target cannot acquire control of the bidder before the bidder can acquire control of the target.

The war between Bendix and Martin Marietta illustrates the importance of a bidder's preparing its defensive as well as its offensive strategy. Bendix began the battle by making a tender offer for Marietta; Marietta retaliated with a tender offer for Bendix. Even if Bendix had been successful in its tender offer, it would not have been able immediately to remove Marietta's board because, under Maryland law (which applied to Marietta), Bendix could not have acted by shareholder consent. Had Marietta succeeded in its counter-bid, however, it immediately could have removed Bendix's board and installed its own nominees. Bendix could have averted such a situation had it amended its own certificate of incorporation, before launching its tender offer for Marietta, to proscribe action by shareholder consent and to require that action be taken only at a meeting of shareholders. Such an amendment could substantially have reduced the danger of a Marietta counter-bid.[15]

---

15. *See infra* § III.4.A(1).

D. Analysis of Ways to Acquire the Target

A tender offer represents but one way to acquire a controlling interest in a target; a bidder also may acquire a substantial position in the target's stock through private transactions or open-market purchases.[16] Indeed, even if the bidder expects to make a tender offer, it first may wish to purchase some of the target's stock in the market.[17] The bidder also may wish to wage a proxy contest to achieve a shift in corporate control.[18] The merits and demerits of these different approaches must be analyzed in terms of the specific circumstances involved in each transaction.

---

16. For a discussion of open-market purchases, see *infra* § II.2.D.

17. For a discussion of the reasons for such a purchase, see *infra* § II.3.

18. For a discussion of the rules and considerations involved in proxy contests, see *infra* § II.4.E.

CHAPTER

2

THE DEFINITION OF "TENDER OFFER"

Although the Williams Act purports to regulate the making of tender offers for public companies in the United States, it does not define the term "tender offer." Similarly, when the SEC issued its rules promulgated under the Williams Act, it also failed to define "tender offer." Consequently, the judiciary has played a significant role in developing a definition of the term, based upon the purposes reflected in the Act's legislative history.

The House Report of the Committee on Interstate and Foreign Commerce, which had held hearings on the Williams Act, supplied this characterization of tender offers:

> The offer normally consists of a bid by an individual or group to buy shares of a company—usually at a price above the current market price. Those accepting the offer are said to tender their stock for purchase. The person making the offer obligates himself to purchase all or a specified portion of the tendered shares if certain specified conditions are met.[19]

Case law defines the typical or "conventional" tender offer as "a general, publicized bid by an individual or group to buy shares of a publicly-owned company, the shares of which [are] traded on a national securities exchange, at a price substantially above the current market price."[20]

When confronted with such purchases, the SEC has applied an eight-factor test to determine whether the transaction constitutes a tender offer. The test has had a checkered career in the courts, but it provides at least a useful starting point in determining what types of conventional transactions are *not* tender offers.

---

19. H.R. Rep. No. 1711, 90th Cong., 2d Sess., *reprinted in* 1968 U.S. Code Cong. & Ad. News 2811.

20. *Hanson Trust PLC v. ML SCM Corp.* 774 F.2d 47, 54 (2d Cir. 1985). *See also* H.R. Rep. No. 1711, 90th Cong., 2d Sess. 2 (1968); S. Rep. No. 550, 90th Cong., 1st Sess. 2 (1967).

A. The SEC's Eight-Factor Analysis

The SEC has proposed an eight-factor test to determine whether a purchase plan is a tender offer. The eight factors that characterize a tender offer are:

(1) An *active and widespread solicitation of public shareholders* is made for shares of an issuer;
(2) The solicitation is made for a *substantial percentage* of the issuer's stock;
(3) The offer to purchase is made at a *premium* above the prevailing market price;
(4) The terms of the offer are *firm* rather than negotiable;
(5) The offer is *contingent on the tender of a fixed minimum number* of shares and is often subject to a *ceiling* of a fixed maximum number of shares to be purchased;
(6) The offer is open for only a *limited period of time*;
(7) Offerees are subject to *pressure to sell* their stock; and
(8) *Public announcements* of an acquisition program precede or accompany the accumulation of stock.[21]

B. SEC's Proposed Rule Defining "Tender Offer"

On November 29, 1979, the SEC proposed a rule that supplied a definition of the term "tender offer." The proposed Rule 14d-1(b)(1) states:

> The term "tender offer" includes a "request or invitation for tenders" and means one or more offers to purchase or solicitations of offers to sell securities of a single class, whether or not all or any portion of the securities sought are purchased, which

---

21. *See infra* § II.2.C.

> (i) during any 45-day period are directed to more than 10 persons and seek the acquisition of more than 5% of the class of securities, except that offers by a broker (and its customer) or by a dealer made on a national securities exchange at the then current market or made in the over-the-counter market at the then current market shall be excluded if in connection with such offers neither the person making the offers nor such broker or dealer solicits or arranges for the solicitation of any order to sell such securities and such broker or dealer performs only the customary functions of a broker or dealer and receives no more than the broker's usual and customary commission or the dealer's usual and customary mark-up; or
>
> (ii) are not otherwise a tender offer under paragraph (b)(1)(i) of this section, but which (A) are disseminated in a widespread manner, (B) provide for a price which represents a premium in excess of the greater of 5% of or $2 above the current market price and (C) do not provide for a meaningful opportunity to negotiate the price and terms.

This definition contains six of the eight factors listed above. The only factors not present are (i) that the offer be contingent on the tender of a fixed number of shares, and (ii) that a public announcement of an acquisition program precede or accompany the accumulation of stock.

In proposing the rule, the SEC noted that, although many bidders comply with the various requirements of the Williams Act, many others deliberately structure purchase plans in an attempt to avoid the Act's provisions through "purported privately negotiated transactions, wide-scale solicitation of members of one family and various forms of massive open market purchase programs."[22] The SEC proposed Rule 14d-1(b)(1) to eliminate what it perceived to be abuses spawned by the lack of a definition of tender offers. The Rule has been neither adopted nor withdrawn; it has, however, received substantial criticism.

---

22. Exchange Act Release No. 16385, [1979-1980 Transfer Binder] Fed. Sec. L. Rep. (CCH) ¶ 82,374, at 82,602 (Nov. 29, 1979).

C. Judicial Response to Eight-Factor Analysis

Many courts have used the eight-factor test in considering whether a particular acquisition program constitutes a tender offer.[23] These courts have not required the presence of all eight factors in order to find that a purchase plan constitutes a tender offer; instead, they have weighed the factors according to their importance under the particular circumstances of each case.[24] But purchases of vast quantities of stock generally do not, in and of themselves, constitute a tender offer unless the eight factors are significantly present.

Other courts have refused to be guided by the eight-factor analysis. In *Brascan Ltd. v. Edper Equities Ltd.*,[25] for example, the court declined to apply the eight-factor test and questioned whether that analysis was "either a permissible or desirable interpretation of the statute." The court stated that the eight-factor analysis introduces "a crippling uncertainty in an area in which practitioners should be entitled to be guided by reasonably clear rules of the road."[26]

---

23. *See, e.g., SEC v. Carter Hawley Hale Stores, Inc.*, 760 F.2d 945, 950 (9th Cir. 1985); *Wellman v. Dickinson*, 475 F. Supp. 783, 823 (S.D.N.Y. 1979), *aff'd*, 682 F.2d 355 (2d Cir. 1982), *cert. denied*, 460 U.S. 1069 (1983); *Hoover Co. v. Fuqua Indus., Inc.*, [1979-1980 Transfer Binder] Fed. Sec. L. Rep. (CCH) ¶ 97,107, at 96,150 (N.D. Ohio June 11, 1979); *In the Matter of Paine Webber Jackson & Curtis, Inc.*, Administrative Proceedings File No. 3-6074, [1982-1983 Transfer Binder] Fed. Sec. L. Rep. (CCH) ¶ 83,310 (SEC Dec. 30, 1982); *see also Ludlow Corp. v. Tyco Laboratories, Inc.*, 529 F. Supp. 62 (D. Mass. 1981); *Kaufman & Broad, Inc. v. Belzberg*, 522 F. Supp. 35 (S.D.N.Y. 1981).

24. *See Wellman v. Dickinson*, 475 F. Supp. 783, 824 (S.D.N.Y. 1979), *aff'd*, 682 F.2d 355 (2d Cir. 1982), *cert. denied*, 460 U.S. 1069 (1983); *Hoover Co. v. Fuqua Indus., Inc.*, [1979-1980 Transfer Binder] Fed. Sec. L. Rep. (CCH) ¶ 97,107, at 96,148 (N.D. Ohio June 11, 1979).

25. 477 F. Supp. 773, 789 (S.D.N.Y. 1979). The court held that there was no tender offer where "defendant scrupulously avoided any solicitation, upon the advice of its lawyers."

26. *Id.* at 791.

More recently, in *Hanson Trust PLC v. ML SCM Corp.*,[27] the Court of Appeals for the Second Circuit rejected the eight-factor analysis, stating that "the elevation of such a list [of eight factors] to a mandatory 'litmus test' appears to be both unwise and unnecessary."[28] In the context of its discussion of the solicitation factor, the court stated that the eight factors are confusing because, as "even the advocates of the proposed test recognize, in any given case a solicitation may constitute a tender offer even though some of the eight factors are absent or, when many factors are present, the solicitation may nevertheless not amount to a tender offer because the missing factors outweigh those present." Instead of applying the eight-factor analysis, the court concluded that it could better divine the existence of a genuine tender offer by "simply look[ing] to the statutory purpose, and determining whether the Act warrants protecting the particular class of persons affected."[29] Hence, the court held that

> whether a solicitation constitutes a "tender offer" within the meaning of § 14(d) turns on whether, viewing the transaction in the light of the totality of circumstances, there appears to be a likelihood that unless the pre-acquisition filing strictures of that statute are followed there will be a substantial risk that solicitees will lack information needed to make a carefully considered appraisal of the proposal put before them.[30]

The court proceeded to hold that the instant conduct did not constitute a tender offer.

---

27. 774 F.2d 47, 56-57 (2d Cir. 1985), discussed in detail in § II.2.D., *infra*.

28. *Id.* at 57.

29. *Id.* (citing *Kennecott Copper Corp. v. Curtiss-Wright Corp.*, 449 F. Supp. 951 (S.D.N.Y.), *aff'd in relevant part*, 584 F.2d 1195 (2d Cir. 1978); *SEC v. Ralston Purina Co.*, 346 U.S. 119 (1953)).

30. *Id.*

D. Open-Market Purchases Not Considered a Tender Offer

Purchases of securities in open-market transactions or from a limited number of sophisticated investors usually do not constitute a tender offer. For instance, the Court of Appeals for the Second Circuit held in *Kennecott Copper Corp. v. Curtiss-Wright Corp.*[31] that market purchases of 9.9 percent of the target's stock were not a tender offer, even though brokers had approached the target's shareholders in making those purchases. Similarly, *Energy Ventures, Inc. v. Appalachian Co.*[32] held that a major acquisition program involving open-market purchases of 40.5 percent of the target's stock was not a tender offer.

---

31. 584 F.2d 1195 (2d Cir. 1978).

32. 587 F. Supp. 734 (D. Del. 1984). *See also Stromfeld v. Great Atl. & Pac. Tea Co.*, 484 F. Supp. 1264 (S.D.N.Y.), *aff'd without opinion*, 646 F.2d 563 (2d Cir. 1980) (purchase of 42 percent of stock from seven shareholders at substantial premium is not a tender offer: no public bid, no widespread solicitation, no high-pressure tactics, and no indication that offer was open for only a limited time); *D-Z Inv. Co. v. Holloway*, [1974-1975 Transfer Binder] Fed. Sec. L. Rep. (CCH) ¶ 94,771 (S.D.N.Y. Aug. 23, 1974) (purchases of nine percent of stock from four "highly sophisticated" institutions and 16 percent of stock in open-market transactions were not a tender offer); *Nachman Corp. v. Halfred, Inc.*, [1973-1974 Transfer Binder] Fed. Sec. L. Rep. (CCH) ¶ 94,455 (N.D. Ill. July 13, 1973) (solicitation of 40 sophisticated shareholders out of a total of 60 shareholders, who were not subjected to pressure, is not a tender offer). Certain large-scale purchases, however, have been held to constitute tender offers. In *Wellman v. Dickinson*, 475 F. Supp. 783 (S.D.N.Y. 1979), *aff'd*, 682 F.2d 355 (2d Cir. 1982), *cert. denied*, 460 U.S. 1069 (1983), for example, the purchase of approximately 34 percent of a class of a company's securities, as a result of the solicitation of approximately 33 shareholders, was deemed a tender offer, notwithstanding the absence of publicity. Similarly, *S-G Secs., Inc. v. Fuqua Inv. Co.*, 466 F. Supp. 1114 (D. Mass. 1978), held a publicly announced intention to acquire control of a target, combined with subsequent rapid accumulation of stock through open-market purchases, to be a tender offer. And in *Hoover Co. v. Fuqua Indus., Inc.*, [1979-1980 Transfer Binder] Fed. Sec. L. Rep. (CCH) ¶ 97,107 (N.D. Ohio June 11, 1979), a stock purchase offer sent by letter to over 100 Hoover family members, coupled with widespread publicity, was held to constitute a tender offer.

Three major cases—*SEC v. Carter Hawley Hale Stores, Inc.*,[33] *Hanson Trust PLC v. ML SCM Corp.*,[34] and *Crown Zellerbach Corp. v. Goldsmith*[35]—recently addressed the issue whether large-scale open-market or privately negotiated purchases constitute tender offers. All of these cases held that such purchases were not tender offers.

Carter Hawley Hale held that a company's purchase of more than 50 percent of its own shares in open-market transactions executed over a period of seven days did not constitute a tender offer within the meaning of Rule 13e-4 (governing tender offers by issuers for their own shares).

The case arose when The Limited, Inc. commenced a tender offer on April 4, 1984, for 20.3 million shares (or 55 percent) of Carter Hawley Hale ("CHH") common stock and announced that its tender offer, if successful, would be followed by a second-step merger. Although CHH's management initially did not take a public position on the offer, it sued to enjoin the bid. Finally, after 12 days of discussions, CHH announced its opposition to the tender offer, branding it " 'inadequate and not in the best interests of CHH or its shareholders.' "[36]

CHH also announced a two-part defensive plan designed to thwart the tender offer. The plan involved the placing of a substantial block of voting stock in the hands of a "white squire"—General Cinema Corporation—and the repurchasing of 15 million of the company's own shares. CHH disclosed that it already had sold to General Cinema, for $300 million, a block of one million shares of convertible preferred stock representing 22 percent of the voting rights of all outstanding shares of CHH. The proposed repurchase plan would increase General Cinema's share of CHH's total voting power to over 33 percent and thus would give General Cinema enough votes to block a change in

33. 587 F. Supp. 1248 (C.D. Cal. 1984), *aff'd*, 760 F.2d 945 (9th Cir. 1985).

34. 774 F.2d 47 (2d Cir. 1985).

35. 609 F. Supp. 187 (S.D.N.Y. 1985).

36. *SEC v. Carter Hawley Hale Stores, Inc.*, 760 F.2d 945, 946 (9th Cir. 1985) (quoting CHH press release).

corporate control, including The Limited's planned second-step merger. (CHH subsequently increased its purchase limit and acquired 17.5 million shares, or more than 50 percent of its outstanding shares.)

Pursuant to Rule 13e-1[37] (which deals with issuer repurchases during a third-party tender offer), CHH disclosed information concerning its intentions; however, CHH did not comply with Rule 13e-4,[38] which prescribes time limits and more extensive disclosure requirements applicable to issuer tender offers. When CHH acquired more than 50 percent of its outstanding shares in seven trading days, the SEC sued for injunctive relief, alleging that CHH's repurchases constituted a tender offer and that CHH had violated section 13(e)(1) of the Exchange Act[39] by failing to comply with Rule 13e-4.

Both the SEC and the district court applied the eight-factor test to determine whether CHH's repurchase plan constituted a tender offer. The SEC found all eight of the factors to be present. The district court, on the other hand, held that the plan was not a tender offer even though (*i*) the shareholders had been subjected to pressure to sell "in the sense that courts have found pressure based on the total effect of the offer on the shareholders, independent of the other indicia of a tender offer,"[40] and (*ii*) CHH had publicly announced the repurchase plan and had rapidly accumulated large amounts of securities. The court found that none of the other factors was present and denied the SEC's motion for a preliminary injunction.

The Court of Appeals for the Ninth Circuit affirmed the ruling and approved the use of the eight-factor analysis because the test provided a sufficiently flexible definition of "tender offer" that conformed with congressional intent, which was to address "the needs of the shareholders, the need to avoid giving either the target or the offeror any advantage, and the need to

---

37. 17 C.F.R. § 240.13e-1 (1986), discussed in §§ II.4.B(6)(a) and III.4.E(3)(a), *infra.*

38. *Id.* § 240.13e-4, discussed in §§ II.4.B(6)(c) and III.4.E(3)(b), *infra.*

39. 15 U.S.C. § 78m(e)(1).

40. 587 F. Supp. at 1255.

maintain a free and open market for securities."[41] The court found that only one of the eight factors was present in the transaction: CHH had made a public announcement, which had been accompanied by a rapid accumulation of a large amount of securities. But the court concluded that the market, and not CHH, had subjected the shareholders to pressure to sell. "While there certainly was shareholder pressure . . . it was largely the pressure of the marketplace and not the type of untoward pressure the tender offer regulations were designed to prohibit."[42] The court acknowledged that all of the eight factors need not be present in order for a purchase plan to be deemed a tender offer but held that CHH's repurchases had none of the traditional indicia of a tender offer.[43]

The *CHH* decision clearly adopts a narrow definition of "tender offer." The case also supports the proposition that a target company can engage in a defensive stock repurchase program without complying with the rules regulating self-tender offers.[44]

In *Hanson Trust PLC v. ML SCM Corp.*,[45] the Court of Appeals for the Second Circuit held that a bidder's purchase in privately negotiated and open-market transactions of 25 percent of the target's stock, within three hours after announcing the abandonment of a tender offer for the target, did not itself constitute a tender offer subject to regulation under the Williams Act.

On August 21, 1985, Hanson Trust announced that it would make a tender offer for any and all outstanding shares of SCM Corp. at $60 per share. SCM opposed this offer and announced that a management group had reached a preliminary agreement with Merrill Lynch, Fenner & Smith, Inc. to acquire all of SCM's shares through a $70 per share leveraged buy-out. In

41. 760 F.2d at 950.

42. *Id.* at 952.

43. *Id.*

44. For a discussion of self-tender offers, see *infra* §§ II.4.B(6)(c) and III.4.E(3)(b).

45. 774 F.2d 47 (2d Cir. 1985).

response, Hanson Trust raised its bid to $72 per share on September 3, and, on September 10, Merrill Lynch increased its own offer to $74 per share, in exchange for an option to purchase, at attractive prices, two of SCM's most valuable businesses (its "crown jewels") should any bidder other than Merrill Lynch acquire more than one-third of SCM's shares.

The next day, at 12:30 p.m., Hanson Trust announced the termination of its tender offer for SCM. Approximately 1-1/2 hours later, Hanson Trust purchased 3.1 million shares (or 25 percent) of SCM in a series of five privately negotiated transactions and in one open-market transaction.

The district court, in issuing a preliminary injunction against further purchases by Hanson Trust, ruled that the acquisitions were "a deliberate attempt to do an 'end run' around the requirements of the Williams Act."[46] The Court of Appeals reversed, however, and held that Hanson Trust's purchases did not raise the types of concerns that the Williams Act was designed to address. The court stated that, because

> the purpose of § 14(d) is to protect the ill-informed solicitee, the question of whether a solicitation constitutes a "tender offer" within the meaning of § 14(d) turns on whether, viewing the transaction in the light of the totality of circumstances, there appears to be a likelihood that unless the pre-acquisition filing strictures of that statute are followed there will be a substantial risk that solicitees will lack information needed to make a carefully considered appraisal of the proposal put before them.[47]

The court did not simply apply the eight-factor analysis to determine whether Hanson Trust's purchases constituted a tender offer. Instead, the court stated that, while the eight factors may be relevant, "the elevation of such a list to a mandatory 'litmus test' appears to be both unwise and unnecessary."[48] The court then proceeded to list seven reasons

---

46. *Id.* at 54.
47. *Id.* at 57.
48. *Id.*

why Hanson Trust's purchases, standing alone, did not amount to a tender offer. Although these reasons basically tracked the SEC's eight factors, the court also considered the number of offerees solicited and the sophistication of those offerees as important factors in determining whether a tender offer had occurred.

The court concluded that the number of shareholders solicited by Hanson Trust—six out of a total of 22,800—"was miniscule [*sic*] compared with the numbers involved in public solicitations of the type against which the Act was directed." In addition, at least five of the sellers were sophisticated market professionals who were fully informed of all materials facts by virtue of Hanson Trust's earlier disclosures concerning its tender offer.[49]

In an amicus brief, the SEC argued that Hanson Trust's purchases constituted a tender offer because they met at least four, and possibly even seven, of the eight factors. The only clearly missing factor was the purchases' contingency on the tender of a minimum number of shares.

The court rejected the SEC's argument and held that Hanson Trust did not (a) impose a general time limit for its purchases, (b) condition its purchases upon a fixed minimum acquisition, (c) pay the sellers a premium over the existing market price, (d) engage in active or widespread publicity or solicitation, or (e) subject the sellers to pressure to sell their shares except through normal market forces.[50] Nor did the court accept the SEC's theory that the purchases, which occurred immediately after Hanson Trust had announced the termination of its tender offer, constituted a de facto continuation of that offer. The court also noted that, upon terminating its offer, Hanson Trust returned all tendered shares to those SCM shareholders who had tendered.[51]

The Court of Appeals' concentration upon the sophistication of the solicited investors is problematic: although sophisticated investors arguably do not need the protections of the Williams Act, this new criterion diminishes the benefits of the Act to

---

49. *Id.*

50. *Id.* at 58.

51. *Id.* at 58-59.

investors who were not given an opportunity to sell their shares to the bidder. The denial of such an opportunity, however, probably has little practical effect on most small investors, who, needing protection from coercion and lacking detailed information, sell their securities to professional investors (usually arbitrageurs) soon after the stock is "put in play." Moreover, the court recognized that Hanson Trust already had provided investors with any information required to be disclosed by the Williams Act and that sellers therefore were in a position to make informed decisions. Had this information not been available, the court might have decided the case differently.

But *Hanson Trust* does create the danger that a bidder could adopt the following "abusive" strategy: first, either announce an intention to buy shares in a company, or purchase five percent of a company and hint that an offer for the remainder may be forthcoming, thus putting the stock in play; second, wait a few days until substantial amounts of stock have moved into the hands of professional investors; third, terminate the broad offer to all stockholders; and finally, purchase the shares from professional investors in private transactions that exclude small stockholders. This strategy could be completed in a shorter time than the 20-day minimum offering period required by the Williams Act.

Adoption of this strategy possibly could be challenged as a deceptive or manipulative practice under section 14(e) of the Exchange Act.[52] Relying on the Supreme Court's recent decision in *Schreiber v. Burlington Northern, Inc.*,[53] a shareholder might allege that a bidder who used the above technique misrepresented its intentions to shareholders by failing to disclose the plan's existence when the bidder commenced its initial tender offer. *Schreiber*, citing *Ernst & Ernst v. Hochfelder*,[54]

---

52. 15 U.S.C. § 78n(e), discussed in §§ III.2.B. and C., *infra*.

53. 472 U.S. 1, 105 S. Ct. 2458 (1985) (holding that § 14(e) of the Williams Act applies only to instances of misrepresentation or nondisclosure and that the federal securities laws do not regulate the substantive fairness of a tender offer).

54. 425 U.S. 185, 199 (1976).

defined misrepresentation as including "conduct designed to deceive or defraud investors by controlling or artificially affecting the price[s]" of securities. If the strategy in question falls within this definition of "misrepresentation," it constitutes a violation of federal law.

Another recent case, *Crown Zellerbach Corp. v. Goldsmith*,[55] also adopted a very narrow definition of the term "tender offer" by excluding open-market purchases and privately negotiated transactions from the scope of the Williams Act.

In April 1985, Sir James Goldsmith launched a tender offer for Crown Zellerbach Corp. but withdrew his bid on April 26, after purchasing 9.4 percent of the target's outstanding shares. Goldsmith continued to buy Crown Zellerbach shares on the open market and in privately negotiated transactions, however, and, by May 8, he owned 19.88 percent of the company. Goldsmith then threatened to increase his holdings beyond 20 percent, which acquisitions would trigger Crown Zellerbach's share purchase rights plan (more commonly known as a "poison pill") and cause the rights to become unredeemable.[56]

Asserting that Goldsmith's purchases constituted an illegal tender offer, Crown Zellerbach sought an injunction against further acquisitions. The court denied relief, holding that, under the eight-factor test, the purchases did not amount to a tender offer and did not violate the Williams Act. The court also noted that "the instant facts [of the case] are relatively unique and the law is unsettled."[57]

The SEC is reviewing the implications of *Carter Hawley Hale*, *Hanson Trust*, and *Crown Zellerbach* to determine whether the courts have in fact permitted bidders to make an "end run" around the SEC's disclosure requirements, particularly in the case of massive accumulations of stock immediately after the termination of a tender offer.[58] As of yet, the Commission has

---

55. 609 F. Supp. 187 (S.D.N.Y. 1985).

56. Poison pills are discussed in § III.4.B., *infra*.

57. 609 F. Supp. at 189.

58. *See* Exchange Act Release No. 23486, [Current] Fed. Sec. L. Rep. (CCH) ¶ 84,018 (July 31, 1986).

not promulgated any new guidelines or rules and has not attempted to propose a definition of "tender offer" to replace the 1979 proposal that never was adopted.

CHAPTER

3

INITIAL PURCHASES

Once a bidder has publicly announced its offer, the offeror cannot purchase shares except pursuant to the tender offer.[59] But persons considering a tender offer often accumulate stock of the target before commencing the offer, in order to acquire a "toehold" in the company. Bidders often acquire this toehold through open-market or privately negotiated block transactions, which usually are kept secret until the bidder is required to file either a Schedule 13D (because of its having acquired five percent or more of the outstanding shares of the particular class of the target's stock[60]) or a notification under the Hart-Scott-Rodino Antitrust Improvements Act ("H-S-R Act").[61]

Generally, there are advantages to acquiring an initial position in the target. First, the toehold supplies the bidder with increased leverage when dealing with the target's management. Second, the bidder might be able to purchase its initial stock position more cheaply, thus saving money that can be used to subsidize a higher price in a subsequent tender offer. Third, the initial purchase may either deter other potential bidders or increase the possibility of recouping transaction expenses (which themselves can run into millions of dollars in a sizable transaction) should a competing bidder or the target itself top the bidder's offer. (In the latter situation, the bidder often profits by selling its shares of the target to the competing bidder.) Fourth, the initial purchases permit the bidder to assert state law rights as a shareholder, including the right to demand a stockholder list and, perhaps, the right to bring a shareholder's derivative action to challenge the target's defensive maneuvers.

There may, however, be disadvantages to acquiring a toehold position. First, buying the target's shares may increase the bidder's cost and risk of loss if the deal is not consummated. Second, the acquisitions may increase the possibility of premature disclosure of the bidder's intentions. Third, the

---

59. *See* Rule 10b-13, 17 C.F.R. § 240.10b-13 (1986), discussed in II.4.B(11)(b), *infra*.

60. For a discussion of Schedule 13D, see *infra* § II.4.A.

61. For a discussion of the H-S-R Act, see *infra* § II.5.

market movement could run up the price of the target's stock, thereby increasing the price that the bidder must pay in subsequent steps of the acquisition scheme. Fourth, undertaking substantial initial purchases without the approval of the target's management might alienate management; if it perceives the purchaser as a threat, the target's management might be less willing to negotiate a friendly takeover.

CHAPTER

4

COMPLIANCE WITH THE WILLIAMS ACT

Congress adopted the Williams Act in 1968 to insure that persons who own securities that are the subject of a cash tender offer would receive meaningful information about the offer. The Act also attempts to save shareholders from being stampeded into tendering their shares and requires that tender offers remain open for a certain minimum period of time, thereby affording shareholders an opportunity to make considered investment decisions and to resist any undue pressure from the target's management or from the offeror.

The drafters of the Williams Act desired to accord similar treatment to cash tender offers and to exchange offers. Previously, bidders in cash tender offers had not been required to supply any information to shareholders, while those making exchange offers had been obliged to provide a prospectus, which contained detailed information about the transaction.

Congress also wished to treat cash tender offers like proxy contests, because both are means to achieve a change in corporate control. There thus existed no rationale either for treating tender offers and proxy contests differently or for perpetuating the exemption of cash tender offers from the federal securities laws' disclosure provisions.

A. Schedule 13D

Section 13(d) of the Exchange Act[62] attempts "to provide for full disclosure in connection with cash tender offers and other techniques for accumulating large blocks of equity securities of publicly held companies."[63] Specifically, the requirements of section 13(d) alert the marketplace to every large, rapid accumulation of securities, regardless of the technique employed,

---

62. 15 U.S.C. § 78m(d).

63. S. Rep. No. 550, 90th Cong., 1st Sess. 4; H.R. Rep. No. 1711, 90th Cong., 2d Sess. 4, *reprinted in* 1968 U.S. Code Cong. & Ad. News 2814.

that might represent a shift in corporate control.[64]

To effectuate that statutory purpose, the SEC adopted Rule 13d-1(b),[65] which requires any person who beneficially owns five percent[66] or more of the outstanding shares of a class of equity securities registered under section 12 of the Exchange Act to file with the SEC, and with each national exchange on which the target's securities are traded, certain information concerning that person's ownership. The form of the disclosure is called a Schedule 13D. This Schedule supplies information that enables investors to make informed investment decisions based upon knowledge of the person who is seeking corporate control, its plans for the target, and the likelihood of a shift in control. (The disclosure requirement also limits to less than five percent—subject to increases during the ten-day "window period"[67]—the amount of securities of a potential target that a potential bidder can legally hold without notifying the target and the SEC of its holdings.)

A person ordinarily must file a Schedule 13D within ten days after acquiring an ownership interest that equals or exceeds five percent. Pursuant to section 13(d)(5) of the Act, this requirement is relaxed for certain institutional investors (broker-dealers, banks, insurance companies, registered investment companies, registered investment advisers, and employee benefit plans subject to ERISA) whose purchases are made "in the ordinary course of [their] business and not with the purpose nor with the effect of changing or influencing the control of the issuer, nor in connection with or as a participant in any transaction having

---

64. *See Financial Gen. Bankshares, Inc. v. Lance*, [1978 Transfer Binder] Fed. Sec. L. Rep. (CCH) ¶ 96,511 (D.D.C. July 30, 1978); *GAF Corp. v. Milstein*, 324 F. Supp. 1062 (S.D.N.Y.), *aff'd in part, rev'd in part*, 453 F.2d 709 (2d Cir. 1971), *cert. denied*, 406 U.S. 910 (1972).

65. 17 C.F.R. § 240.13d-1 (1986).

66. The Williams Act originally required disclosure upon a person's attaining beneficial ownership of ten percent of any class of the target's shares. In 1970, however, Congress expanded the scope of regulation by reducing from ten to five percent the amount of equity ownership needed to trigger the disclosure requirements of §§ 13(d) and 14(d).

67. This ten-day "window period" is discussed in § II.4.A(7), *infra*.

such purpose or effect. . . ."[68] Such persons need file only a Schedule 13G (which calls for much less information than does a Schedule 13D), and they must do so only within 45 days after the end of the calendar year, rather than within ten days of reaching or exceeding the five-percent threshold. However, if such institutional investors, while owning five percent or more of the target's stock, should determine that they now hold such stock with the purpose or effect of influencing control of the target, they must file a full Schedule 13D within ten days of making that decision.[69] During that ten-day period, those persons can neither vote their previously acquired shares nor buy any additional shares of the target.[70]

1. Beneficial Ownership

A person "beneficially owns" any registered security if he either has or shares direct or indirect power to vote, sell, or determine the disposition of that security.[71] For instance, a committee that has the power to direct the voting of shares and to determine the time and means of disposition of benefits under an employee stock ownership plan will be deemed to have beneficial ownership of all shares held by the plan.[72]

All beneficially owned securities of a given class are aggregated to determine whether the owner has crossed the five-percent threshold and thus must file a Schedule 13D. Nonvoting securities, however, are not usually subject to Schedule 13D reporting, although the owner must include, when calculating his beneficial ownership for purposes of section 13(d), any voting

---

68. Rule 13d-1(b)(1)(i), 17 C.F.R. § 240.13d-1(b)(1)(i) (1986).

69. Rule 13d-3(3)(i), *id.* § 240.13d-3(3)(i).

70. Rule 13d-1(b)(3)(ii), *id.* § 240.13d-1(b)(3)(ii).

71. Rule 13d-3(a), *id.* § 240.13d-3(a).

72. *See Lanchart Indus. Inc.*, [1977-1978 Transfer Binder] Fed. Sec. L. Rep. (CCH) ¶ 81,173 (SEC March 2, 1977).

securities that he can receive by converting nonvoting securities.[73]

A person is also deemed the beneficial owner of any securities that he has the right to acquire within 60 days.[74] At times, such beneficial ownership will be imputed where a person has only a contingent right to acquire the shares. For instance, in *In the Matter of The Coca-Cola Co.*,[75] the SEC took the position that Coca-Cola beneficially owned shares of Taylor Wine because Coca-Cola had agreed to purchase a block of shares if merger negotiations were not consummated by a specified date.

2. Brokers as Beneficial Owners

The SEC has asserted that, for purposes of filing a Schedule 13D, a broker may be deemed to be the beneficial owner not only of stock held in discretionary accounts (which the customer has authorized the broker to vote according to his or her discretion) but also, in some circumstances, of stock held in customers' nondiscretionary accounts. For example, in *In the Matter of Harvey Katz*,[76] which arose out of a 1983 proxy fight for Bradford National Corporation, two brokers employed by Advest, Inc. accumulated substantial shares of Bradford together with two of their clients. These brokers also recommended that other Advest brokers and clients purchase Bradford stock. Advest's customers ultimately accumulated almost 28 percent of Bradford's shares.

The SEC concluded that the brokers belonged to a group that included their two named customers and that the group did not timely file a Schedule 13D. Brokers, reasoned the SEC, "will ordinarily be deemed to be the 'beneficial owners' of securities

73. Rule 13d-3, 17 C.F.R. § 240.13d-3 (1986). *See generally Bath Indus., Inc. v. Blot*, 427 F.2d 97 (7th Cir. 1970).

74. Rule 13d-3(d), 17 C.F.R. § 240.13d-3(d) (1986).

75. SEC Doc. No. 927.

76. Exchange Act Release No. 20893, [1984 Transfer Binder] Fed. Sec. L. Rep. (CCH) ¶ 83,618 (April 25, 1984).

held in discretionary accounts." Although it did not make a finding regarding the beneficial ownership of securities in clients' nondiscretionary accounts, the SEC cautioned:

> The Commission wishes to take this opportunity raised by the facts of this case, to remind registered representatives of broker-dealers of the need to ascertain whether they may be deemed to beneficially own common stock acquired by customers. Normally a registered representative of a broker-dealer will not be deemed to beneficially own common stock held in non-discretionary accounts of customers. However, in certain limited situations where a registered representative has or shares the *de facto* power to direct the voting or disposition of the securities in customer accounts, the registered representative may be deemed to beneficially own securities held by customers in non-discretionary accounts.[77]

3. Group Purchases

Section 13(d)'s filing requirements apply to any "person" who beneficially owns five percent or more of a class of an issuer's equity securities. Because section 13(d)(3) includes a group within the definition of "person," the filing requirements also apply to groups holding the requisite amount. For purposes of the Williams Act, a group is formed when two or more persons agree to act together to acquire, hold, vote, or dispose of securities.[78] Hence, if a group acquires five percent or more of the outstanding shares of a corporation's class of equity securities, that group must file a Schedule 13D.

The same rule applies where ownership of five percent or more results from formation of a group, even if the formation process has not entailed additional acquisitions; any group that is formed pursuant to an agreement among group members is deemed to have acquired beneficial ownership of all securities beneficially owned by each group member on the date of the

---

77. *Id.* at 86,805 (footnotes omitted).

78. *See* Rule 13d-5(b)(1), 17 C.F.R. § 240.13d-5(b)(1) (1986).

agreement.[79] Formation of a group occurs whenever individuals agree to act together for a common purpose. The requirement that a group or its members file a Schedule 13D is intended to prevent persons who agree to pool their interests from evading the disclosure requirements on the theory that each group member individually owns less than five percent of the issuer's securities.[80]

Case law indicates that some type of agreement must take place in order for a group to exist for Schedule 13D purposes.[81] The existence of a written agreement, however, is not essential to the formation of a group; circumstantial evidence of an agreement may suffice. In *Wellman v. Dickinson*,[82] for example, the court found the existence of a group, despite the lack of a written, formal agreement, because plaintiff established that the parties had reached an understanding to take concerted action. And in *Twin Fair, Inc. v. Reger*,[83] the reaching of an agreement in principle sufficed to show the formation of a group in light of the fact that the formal final agreement was almost identical to the preliminary agreement.[84]

What constitutes a preliminary agreement that triggers the reporting requirements is unclear. A shareholder's intensive efforts (including communications with other shareholders) to gather support for a takeover do not result in the creation of a

79. Likewise, the *members* of a group are considered beneficial owners of the securities owned by other members of the group. Rule 13d-5(b)(1). However, an individual who does not beneficially own any of the issuer's shares is not a member of the group for the purposes of § 13(d); such individual's assistance to a member of the group thus would not obligate him to file a Schedule 13D. *Transcon Lines v.* A.G. *Becker, Inc.*, 470 F. Supp. 356 (S.D.N.Y. 1979).

80. S. Rep. No. 550, 90th Cong., 1st Sess. (1967); H. Rep. No. 1711, 90th Cong., 2d Sess. (1968).

81. *See, e.g., Corenco Corp. v. Schiavone & Sons, Inc.*, 488 F.2d 207 (2d Cir. 1973).

82. 475 F. Supp. 783 (S.D.N.Y. 1979), *aff'd*, 682 F.2d 355 (2d Cir. 1982), *cert. denied*, 460 U.S. 1069 (1983).

83. 394 F. Supp. 156 (W.D.N.Y. 1975).

84. *See also Water & Wall Assocs., Inc. v. American Consumer Indus., Inc.*, [1973 Transfer Binder] Fed. Sec. L. Rep. (CCH) ¶ 93,943 (D.N.J. April 19, 1973).

group and need not be reported unless and until some preliminary agreement is reached.[85] One court has held that preliminary discussions alone do not establish a group.[86] The court stated:

> In general, Section 13(d) seems carefully drawn to permit parties seeking to acquire large amounts of shares in a public company to obtain information with relative freedom, to discuss preliminarily the possibility of entering into agreements and to operate with relative freedom until they get to the point where they do in fact decide to make arrangements which they must record under the securities laws. By requiring the existence of a "group," the law is designed to avoid discouraging and making risky that kind of preliminary activity.
>
> It is quite clear in this case that the parties did discuss possible arrangements. But it seems unlikely that a "group" within the meaning of Section 13(d) was formed in November when the Malsins decided not to sell their shares to the Hatleigh defendants and the Hatleigh defendants in turn told the Malsins that they did not want to make a deal with them, preferring to proceed on their own. Although defendants' decision may have been motivated by tactical considerations, it does not come close to establishing an illegal arrangement.

In *Pantry Pride, Inc. v. Rooney*,[87] the court held that a group was not formed until a proxy agreement was executed, despite the fact that discussions about a proxy contest already had occurred. Stating that section 13(d) "allows individuals broad freedom to discuss the possibility of future agreements without filing under securities laws," the court viewed the earlier discussions as preliminary, with the individuals not yet having a common goal.

Just as a pre-existing relationship is not essential to the existence of a group within the meaning of section 13(d),[88] so,

---

85. *See Calumet Indus., Inc. v. MacClure*, 464 F. Supp. 19 (N.D. Ill. 1978).

86. *Lane Bryant, Inc. v. Hatleigh Corp.*, [1980 Transfer Binder] Fed. Sec. L. Rep. (CCH) ¶ 97,529, at 97,776 (S.D.N.Y. June 9, 1980).

87. 598 F. Supp. 891, 900 (S.D.N.Y. 1984).

88. *Bayly Corp. v. Marantette*, [1982 Transfer Binder] Fed. Sec. L. Rep. (CCH) ¶ 98,834 (D.D.C. Oct. 19, 1982) (no group formed until dissidents decided to put forth a slate).

too, is a mere relationship insufficient to constitute a group. There must also be an agreement among group members to act in concert.[89] As noted above, however, a group may be formed simply by agreement among the holders of five percent or more of a class of an issuer's voting stock even if the group members do not agree to purchase additional shares but only to act together in the future to further the group's purpose. Actual affirmative acts (*e.g.*, voting, purchasing stock) are not necessary.[90]

A few cases have declined to find the formation of a group despite the existence of an agreement with respect to unspecified future action. In *Bath Industries, Inc. v. Blot*,[91] the court held that the formation of a group holding more than ten percent[92] of an issuer's securities did not trigger an obligation to file a Schedule 13D because the group had not made any purchases or sales and had no intention of trading. Similarly, in *Calumet Industries, Inc. v. MacClure*,[93] the court stated that a group was not obliged to file a Schedule 13D, even though the group had agreed to gain control of the issuer, because the group also had agreed not to acquire additional shares in furtherance of that end. The court reasoned that an agreement to solicit proxies was not an agreement to acquire, hold, or dispose of securities and thus did not require the filing of a Schedule 13D. Nor did the fact that one member of the group had purchased a few additional shares

---

89. *See Texasgulf, Inc., v. Canada Dev. Corp.*, 366 F. Supp. 374, 403 (S.D. Tex. 1973).

90. *See GAF Corp. v. Milstein*, 324 F. Supp. 1062 (S.D.N.Y.), *aff'd in part, rev'd in part*, 453 F.2d 709 (2d Cir. 1971), *cert. denied*, 406 U.S. 910 (1972); *see also Financial Gen. Bankshares, Inc. v. Lance*, [1978 Transfer Binder] Fed. Sec. L. Rep. (CCH) ¶ 96,403 (D.D.C. April 27, 1978); *National Home Prods., Inc. v. Gray*, 416 F. Supp. 1293 (D. Del. 1976).

91. 427 F.2d 97 (7th Cir. 1970).

92. Prior to 1970, the threshold ownership level that triggered § 13(d)'s reporting requirements was ten percent, not five percent.

93. 464 F. Supp. 19 (N.D. Ill. 1978).

without the knowledge of other group members necessitate the filing of a Schedule 13D.[94]

a. Management Groups

Under certain circumstances, the target's management itself may be considered a group required to file a Schedule 13D.[95] If, for example, management and a third party enter into an agreement relating to management's maintaining corporate control, and if management and the third party together own more than five percent of the company, the new group would have to comply with section 13(d)'s reporting requirements. Similarly, section 13(d) applies to a group that includes individuals other than officers and directors of a target company if that group acquires additional shares prior to a takeover and has formed a battle plan against a bidder.

But where management acts as a group that does *not* include outside participants, there is no consistent rule. *Podesta v. Calumet Industries Inc.*[96] held, in the context of a proxy fight in which management was not subject to section 14(d)'s filing requirements, that section 13(d) did apply to management if its members acted in concert to acquire shares to retain control; however, the court noted another case holding that section 13(d) did not apply to a management group that intended to sell the

94. *Calumet* appears to be inconsistent with Rule 13d-5 (adopted after the *Bath* case), which deems the process of group formation to entail the group's acquisition of the shares held by the group's individual members. *See also Advanced Computer Techniques Corp. v. Lecht*, [1982 Transfer Binder] Fed. Sec. L. Rep. (CCH) ¶ 98,795 (S.D.N.Y. Aug. 23, 1982).

95. Such groups and the transactions in which they engage must be distinguished from those discussed in § 13(d)(6)(C), which exempts from the reporting requirements any acquisition of an equity security by its issuer. This exemption, however, does not apply to an acquisition by an affiliate of the issuer, unless that affiliate is a wholly owned subsidiary of the issuer.

96. [1978 Transfer Binder] Fed. Sec. L. Rep. (CCH) ¶ 96,433 (N.D. Ill. May 9, 1978).

assets of and liquidate a company.[96a] Other cases, noting that management's shareholdings are publicly disclosed in proxy statements, have held that management, by itself, is not a group that must file a Schedule 13D. In *Warner Communications, Inc. v. Murdoch*,[97] for example, the court held that concerted action undertaken by a group in order to perpetuate management's control does not necessitate the filing of a Schedule 13D. Whether management should file a Schedule 13D thus depends, to a great extent, upon the law of the district(s) in which failure to do so may be challenged and upon the possible consequences of a ruling that a filing should have been made.[98]

b. Group Filings

A group may file one joint Schedule 13D, or each member may file individual Schedules 13D. Joint filings must disclose information pertaining to each group member. Each member of a group making a joint filing is responsible for the timely filing of the Schedule 13D and its amendments and for the accuracy of any disclosed information concerning such group member. An individual, however, is not responsible for the information concerning other members of the group unless the individual knows or has reason to know that the information pertaining to another group member is inaccurate.[99]

4. Contents of Schedule 13D

In order to fulfill the purpose of section 13(d), Schedules 13D must contain complete and accurate information. Indeed, as the

---

96a. *Id.* at 93,559-60 (citing *Scott v. Multi-Amp Corp.*, 386 F. Supp. 44 (D.N.J. 1974)).

97. 581 F. Supp. 1482, 1499 (D. Del. 1984); *see also Scott v. Multi-Amp Corp.*, 386 F. Supp. 44 (D.N.J. 1974).

98. For a discussion of Schedule 13D violations, see *infra* §§ II.4.A(5) and (6).

99. Rule 13d-1(f), 17 C.F.R. § 240.13d-1(f) (1986).

Court of Appeals for the Second Circuit observed in *GAF Corp. v. Milstein*,[100] a false statement by the bidder might cause greater damage to the proper operation of the securities market than might the absence of any statement at all.

The Schedule 13D must disclose information about the filing person's identity and background. If the filing person is a group, the Schedule must disclose the identities and employment of each member of the group.[101] The filing person must state the number of shares of the target company that it beneficially owns; its purpose in acquiring those shares; any plans or proposals to acquire or dispose of securities of the issuer; any plans for a merger, liquidation, sale of material assets, or other extraordinary corporate transaction relating either to the issuer or to any of its subsidiaries; and any contemplated change in capitalization or dividend policy, in the issuer's directors or management, or in the issuer's business or corporate structure. The filing person also must disclose any past securities law violations;[102] the source and amount of consideration for the acquisition; and the substance of any contracts, arrangements, understandings, or relationships that the filing person has with any other person concerning the issuer's securities.

With respect to any plan or proposal regarding the issuer (such as a plan to change management or to merge the company with any other entity[103]), case law holds that the plan or proposal should be disclosed if there is a reasonable likelihood of its future occurrence.[104] If a Schedule 13D does not contain any discussion of the filing person's intention to gain control of the issuer, and if

---

100. 453 F.2d 709, 710 (2d Cir. 1971), *cert. denied*, 406 U.S. 910 (1972).

101. *See SEC v. Savoy Indus., Inc.*, 665 F.2d 1310 (D.C. Cir. 1981).

102. *See Bayly Corp. v. Marantette*, [1982 Transfer Binder] Fed. Sec. L. Rep. (CCH) ¶ 98,834 (D.D.C. Oct. 19, 1982).

103. *See* Item 4 of Schedule 13D.

104. *See Sonesta Int'l Hotels Corp. v. Wellington Assocs.*, 483 F.2d 247 (2d Cir. 1973); *Otis Elevator Co. v. United Technologies Corp.*, 405 F. Supp. 960 (S.D.N.Y. 1975).

the filing person later launches a tender offer for, or negotiates a business combination with, that company, the Schedule 13D may be considered false and misleading.[105]

At the time of the Williams Act's enactment, the requirement of disclosing plans and proposals generated substantial controversy. As Professor Bromberg later wrote:

> Disclosure of plans and proposals was probably the most controversial part of the Williams Bill that passed, but it was diversely and severely opposed.
>
> For Congress to reject this nearly unanimous criticism, and to depart from a strong tradition [of nondisclosure], it must have been deeply convinced of the importance of disclosing plans.[106]

When making such disclosures, however, one should heed Judge Friendly's warning that "[i]t would be as serious of an infringement of these regulations to overstate the definiteness of the[se] plans as to understate them."[107] Similarly, another court has cautioned that "[a] person filing a Schedule 13D is not required to disclose indefinite plans or make predictions of future behavior, however tentatively phrased, which may cause the public to rely on them unjustifiably."[108]

105. *See, e.g.*, *Chromalloy Am. Corp. v. Sun Chem. Corp.*, 611 F.2d 240 (8th Cir. 1979); *Gearhart Indus., Inc. v. Smith Int'l, Inc.*, 592 F. Supp. 203 (N.D. Tex.), *aff'd in part*, 741 F.2d 707 (5th Cir. 1984); *Otis Elevator Co. v. United Technologies Corp.*, 405 F. Supp. 960 (S.D.N.Y. 1975). However, the mere possibility of a future occurrence need not be disclosed. *Chock Full O'Nuts Corp. v. Finkelstein*, 548 F. Supp. 212 (S.D.N.Y. 1982); *Vornado, Inc. v. Interstate Properties*, 470 F. Supp. 714 (S.D.N.Y. 1979).

106. Bromberg, "The Securities Law of Tender Offers," 15 N.Y.L.F. 462, 501 (1969) (footnote omitted).

107. *Electronic Specialty Co. v. International Controls Corp.*, 409 F.2d 937, 948 (2d Cir. 1969).

108. *Southeast Banking Corp. v. Adler*, [1982-1983 Transfer Binder] Fed. Sec. L. Rep. (CCH) ¶ 99,183, at 95,716 (S.D. Fla. Dec. 20, 1982).

5. Amendments to Schedule 13D

A person who has filed a Schedule 13D must file an amendment "promptly" upon the occurrence of any "material change" in the information contained in the original Schedule.[109] The SEC, however, has not definitively defined the terms "promptly" and "material change."

a. *"Material Change"*

Rule 13d-2(a) provides:

> An acquisition or disposition of beneficial ownership of securities in an amount equal to one percent or more of the class of securities shall be deemed "material" for purposes of this rule; acquisitions or dispositions of less than such amounts may be material, depending upon the facts and circumstances.

In a recent administrative action, the SEC required a filing person that had disposed of one percent of a class of securities to amend the purpose section of its previously filed Schedule 13D to reflect "that it had sold . . . shares in a specified price range and was considering making additional sales at prices within, or higher than, such price range."[110] The SEC demanded this disclosure even though the filing person had reserved the right in its initial Schedule 13D to acquire or dispose of shares of the issuer's stock "as it sees fit."

Other cases also present examples of "material changes" requiring the filing of an amendment. In *Nachman Corp. v. Halfred, Inc.*,[111] for example, the filing person, after disclosing his intent to seek control of the target, met with the target's management and suggested that the target should be dissolved

---

109. Rule 13d-2, 17 C.F.R. § 240.13d-2 (1986).

110. *In the Matter of Cooper Laboratories, Inc.*, Exchange Act Release No. 22171, [1984-1985 Transfer Binder] Fed. Sec. L. Rep. (CCH) ¶ 83,788, at 87,526 (June 26, 1985).

111. [1973-1974 Transfer Binder] Fed. Sec. L. Rep. (CCH) ¶ 94,455 (N.D. Ill. July 13, 1973).

and merged into another company. The court held that this new proposal "clearly constitute[d] a material change in the facts set forth" and that the filing person promptly should have amended his Schedule 13D.[112]

Recently, in *In the Matter of Centrust Savings Bank,*[113] the SEC charged that a federal bank regulator's directive to a savings bank to cease purchasing a target's securities constituted a material change in the savings bank's investment intentions. "Under these circumstances," ruled the SEC, "information that CenTrust had been ordered by a federal regulatory agency with supervisory authority over CenTrust to cease its purchases of MassMutual would have been material to persons making investment decisions with respect to MassMutual Securities." CenTrust thus had a duty "promptly" to disclose this information in an amendment to its Schedule 13D.

b. "Promptly"

Rule 13d-2 does not specify the exact time period within which an amendment must be filed in order to be considered "prompt." Prior to the SEC's 1985 *Cooper Laboratories* decision,[114] at least, filing persons generally tended to wait at least one week after the occurrence of a material change before amending information set forth in the original Schedule 13D. We conducted a survey of Schedule 13D amendments filed between November 16, 1984, and January 22, 1985, and found that the SEC had received more than 900 amendments, of which fewer than 25 percent had been filed within a week of the triggering event. This practice seemed well supported by case law and by SEC enforcement actions, for amendments filed five or six days after a material

112. *Id.* at 95,593.

113. Release No. 23076, [1985-1986 Transfer Binder] Fed. Sec. L. Rep. (CCH) ¶ 83,974 (March 31, 1986).

114. *In the Matter of Cooper Laboratories, Inc.*, Exchange Act Release No. 22171, [1984-1985 Transfer Binder] Fed. Sec. L. Rep. (CCH) ¶ 83,788 (June 26, 1985).

change in the Schedule 13D usually were considered to be "prompt."[115]

In the past year, however, the SEC has made clear that "promptly" means *immediately*, at least where the change requiring the amendment is important to the efficient operation of the market. The *Cooper Laboratories* ruling propounded a new standard of promptness: the prompt filing requirement would be construed flexibly, depending upon the facts and circumstances of each case. The SEC stated:

> Whether an amendment to a Schedule 13D is "prompt" must be judged, at least in part, by the market's sensitivity to the particular change of fact triggering the obligation to amend, and the effect on the market of the filing person's previous disclosures.

---

115. In *Feldman v. Simkins Indus., Inc.*, 679 F.2d 1299 (9th Cir. 1982), for example, the filing person amended its Schedule 13D on the fifth day after beginning to sell, and the day after completing sales of 14 percent of, the issuer's stock. The court held such a filing to be prompt as a matter of law. Similarly, in *D-Z Inv. Co. v. Holloway*, [1974-1975 Transfer Binder] Fed. Sec. L. Rep. (CCH) ¶ 94,771, at 96,561 (S.D.N.Y. Aug. 23, 1974), in which plaintiff contested the promptness of amendments filed five and six days after the filing person had purchased large amounts of equity securities, the district court ruled that the contention was "so piddling that it must be disregarded."

Until recently, SEC administrative proceedings and settled injunctive actions suggested that an amendment could be considered promptly filed despite the lapse of even a lengthy time period between the material change and the amendment. In *In re United States Filter Corp.*, Exchange Act Release No. 17425, [1981 Transfer Binder] Fed. Sec. L. Rep. (CCH) ¶ 82,803 (Jan. 7, 1981), which involved a settlement of an administrative proceeding, the filing person had concealed its decision to seek control for nearly one month before filing a Schedule 13D amendment. Likewise, in *SEC v. Bayswater Realty & Capital Corp.*, No. 81-3203 (D.D.C., filed Dec. 30, 1981), Litigation Release No. 9540, the filing person failed to amend its Schedule 13D until three weeks after it had entered into a contract with the issuer for the repurchase of its shares. In both cases, the amendments were considered to have been promptly filed. Other cases in which amendments were deemed promptly filed include *SEC v. Smith*, No. 83-3805 (D.D.C., filed Dec. 21, 1983) (settlement of injunctive action; filing of one amendment 46 days after triggering date, and filing of two other amendments nearly three months after triggering date), and *In the Matter of AGO Holding N.V.*, Exchange Act Release No. 18469, [1981-1982 Transfer Binder] Fed. Sec. L. Rep. (CCH) ¶ 83,097 (Feb. 4, 1982) (settlement of administrative proceeding; failure to amend for more than six months after triggering event).

> Although the promptness of an amendment to a Schedule 13D must be judged in light of all the facts and circumstances of a particular situation, "[a]ny delay beyond the time the amendment reasonably could have been filed may not be deemed to be [prompt]."[116]

The SEC ruling arose out of Cooper Laboratories' purchase of 11.1 percent of the outstanding common stock of Frigitronics, Inc., which acquisition had been reported in a Schedule 13D filed on August 20, 1984. On August 29, 1984, after the market for Frigitronics had risen by almost ten points, Cooper began selling small portions of its Frigitronics holdings. During the next five trading days, Cooper sold one percent of Frigitronics' outstanding common stock.

The SEC ruled that Cooper should have amended its Schedule 13D on September 7 to reflect these sales, September 7 being the day after Cooper's sales had crossed the one-percent threshold. Consistent with prevailing practice, Cooper had not filed an amendment until September 13, the day after it completed selling the balance of its Frigitronics holdings and seven calendar days after having sold one percent of Frigitronics' shares. When Cooper did file the amendment, Frigitronics' stock closed almost seven points below its high of the previous week. The SEC noted that "[a] prompt amendment by September 7, 1984, of items 5 and 4 of Cooper's August 20 Schedule 13D would have served the purposes of the Williams Act by alerting the market, in a timely fashion, to Cooper's sales of Frigitronics stock"[117] and concluded that "prompt" meant sooner than five business days after the event triggering Cooper's obligation to file. The SEC's conclusions were never contested, but they constituted a marked departure from earlier practice.

---

116. *In the Matter of Cooper Laboratories, Inc.*, Exchange Act Release No. 22171, [1984-1985 Transfer Binder] Fed. Sec. L. Rep. (CCH) ¶ 83,788, at 87,526 (June 26, 1985). *See* Letter from Division of Corporation Finance to Law, Weathers, Richardson & Dutcher (Feb. 13, 1976).

117. *In the Matter of Cooper Laboratories, Inc.*, Exchange Act Release No. 22171, [1984-1985 Transfer Binder] Fed. Sec. L. Rep. (CCH) ¶ 83,788, at 87,526 (June 26, 1985).

The recent SEC decision in *In the Matter of Centrust Savings Bank*[118] also involved the prompt filing requirement. On January 30, 1985, the Federal Home Loan Bank Board ("FHLBB") directed CenTrust Savings Bank to stop purchasing additional shares of MassMutual Mortgage and Realty Investors ("MMR"). CenTrust amended its Schedule 13D on February 7 to announce its intention to file an H-S-R notice[119] of its plan to increase to 35 percent its holdings of MMR shares. This 13D amendment, however, did not refer to the FHLBB's directive to cease purchasing shares of MMR. On February 21, the FHLBB directed CenTrust to divest itself of approximately two-thirds of the shares of MMR stock that it then held. CenTrust did not file an amendment disclosing the divestiture order until March 8, after MMR had announced a proposed transaction with an alternate suitor. The SEC ruled that, in light of the market's demonstrated sensitivity to changes in CenTrust's intentions, CenTrust had not promptly disclosed the information pertaining to the FHLBB orders.

6. Remedies for Noncompliance with Section 13(d)

a. Private Right of Action

Most courts have held that a shareholder who purchases or sells his shares has standing to bring an action for damages under section 13(d).[120] In addition, many (but not all) courts have allowed target companies to sue a bidder under section 13(d), especially if the target can show that it was harmed by the

118. Exchange Act Release No. 23076, [1985-1986 Transfer Binder] Fed. Sec. L. Rep. (CCH) ¶ 83,974 (March 31, 1986).

119. H-S-R notices are discussed in § II.5, *infra*.

120. *See Jacobs v. Pabst Brewing Co.*, 549 F. Supp. 1050 (D. Del. 1982). *But see Gateway Indus., Inc. v. Agency Rent A Car, Inc.*, 495 F. Supp. 92 (N.D. Ill. 1980).

alleged violation.[121] In *GAF Corp. v. Milstein*,[122] the Court of Appeals for the Second Circuit reasoned that the target should have standing under section 13(d) because, as a recipient of the information, it is in the best position to monitor the truthfulness of the bidder's filings. Similarly, the Court of Appeals for the Eleventh Circuit held in *Florida Commercial Banks v. Culverhouse*[123] that an issuer could maintain a private cause of action to seek corrective disclosure by the bidder, but not divestiture. The court concluded that shareholders, lacking the facts necessary to confirm the accuracy of the information disclosed, could not protect their own interests and that the SEC, by itself, could not police every tender offer. Affording issuers a private right of action thus would help to achieve enforcement of the securities laws.[124] Other cases have held that, before issuing a preliminary injunction in an action brought by a target, a court should consider whether the bidder caused injury to the shareholders and the investment public.[125]

However, some district courts have held that an issuer does not have an implied right of action under section 13(d), usually on the theory that that section was intended to benefit the target's shareholders, rather than the target itself.[126]

---

121. *See, e.g., Dan River Inc. v. Unitex, Ltd.*, 624 F.2d 1216 (4th Cir. 1980), *cert. denied*, 449 U.S. 1101 (1981); *General Aircraft Corp. v. Lampert*, 556 F.2d 90 (1st Cir. 1977); *GAF Corp. v. Milstein*, 453 F.2d 709 (2d Cir. 1971), *cert. denied*, 406 U.S. 910 (1972). In *Rondeau v. Mosinee Paper Corp.*, 422 U.S. 49 (1975), the Supreme Court assumed that a target had standing to sue under § 13(d) as long as the target could prove that it had been injured.

122. 453 F.2d 709 (2d Cir. 1971), *cert. denied*, 406 U.S. 910 (1972).

123. 772 F.2d 1513 (11th Cir. 1985).

124. The court in *Pabst Brewing Co. v. Jacobs*, 549 F. Supp. 1068 (D. Del. 1982), reached a similar conclusion and stated that Congress intended § 13(d) to benefit issuers as well as investors.

125. *See Mid-Continent Bancshares, Inc. v. O'Brien*, [1982 Transfer Binder] Fed. Sec. L. Rep. (CCH) ¶ 98,734 (E.D. Mo. Dec. 11, 1981); *Kirsch Co. v. Bliss & Laughlin Indus., Inc.*, 495 F. Supp. 488 (W.D. Mich. 1980).

126. *See Leff v. CIP Corp.*, 540 F. Supp. 857 (S.D. Ohio 1982); *First Alabama Bancshares, Inc. v. Lowder*, [1981 Transfer Binder] Fed. Sec. L. Rep. (CCH) ¶ 98,015 (N.D. Ala. May 1, 1981); *American Bakeries v. Pro-Met Trading Co.*, [1981 Transfer Binder] Fed. Sec. L. Rep. (CCH) ¶ 97,925 (N.D. Ill. March 27, 1981).

A bidder making a counter-tender offer may have standing to bring an action.[127] However, a district court in Michigan[128] has held that a competing bidder lacks standing under section 13(d) to seek injunctive or monetary relief.[129]

Because courts regard section 13(d) as merely a reporting requirement, they usually redress violations of that section through injunctive relief (such as by ordering curative disclosure), rather than through damages.[130] Courts also have been more willing to recognize an issuer's right to sue under section 13(d) when the issuer seeks an injunction to compel the filing of an accurate Schedule 13D rather than damages for a misleading filing. Even shareholders have been denied the right to seek damages under section 13(d).[131]

Injunctive relief is an equitable remedy, and its terms therefore depend on the nature of the violation it is designed to redress. As an initial matter, the plaintiff must show that denial of relief would irreparably injure shareholders of the issuer.[132] Congress did not intend the disclosure requirements to provide management with a weapon to prevent large accumulations of

---

127. *See McDermott, Inc. v. Wheelabrator-Frye, Inc.*, 649 F.2d 489 (7th Cir. 1980), discussed in § II.4.B(8), *infra*.

128. *Luptak v. Central Cartage Co.*, [1981 Transfer Binder] Fed. Sec. L. Rep. (CCH) ¶ 98,034 (E.D. Mich. July 30, 1979).

129. Cases have held that a tender offeror has standing to bring an injunction action against the target on behalf of the target's shareholders for violations of Rule 13e-4, which imposes disclosure requirements in the context of issuer repurchases. *See Crane Co. v. Harsco Corp.*, 511 F. Supp. 294 (D. Del. 1981); *see also ORBANCO, Inc. v. Security Bank of Oregon*, 371 F. Supp. 125 (D. Or. 1974).

130. *See, e.g., Treadway Cos. v. Care Corp.*, 490 F. Supp. 660 (S.D.N.Y.), *aff'd in part and rev'd in part*, 638 F.2d 357 (2d Cir. 1980); *Stromfeld v. Great Atl. & Pac. Tea Co.*, 484 F. Supp. 1264 (S.D.N.Y.), *aff'd without opinion*, 646 F.2d 563 (2d Cir. 1980); *Myers v. American Leisure Time Enters., Inc.*, 402 F. Supp. 213 (S.D.N.Y. 1975), *aff'd without opinion*, 538 F.2d 312 (2d Cir. 1976).

131. *See, e.g., Schnell v. Schnall*, 550 F. Supp. 650 (S.D.N.Y. 1982); *Berman v. Metzger*, [1981 Transfer Binder] Fed. Sec. L. Rep. (CCH) ¶ 97,857 (D.D.C. Feb. 9, 1981).

132. *See, e.g., General Aircraft Corp. v. Lampert*, 556 F.2d 90 (1st Cir. 1977); *Universal Container Corp. v. Horwitz*, [1977-1978 Transfer Binder] Fed. Sec. L. Rep. (CCH) ¶ 96,161 (S.D.N.Y. Sept. 6, 1977).

stock.[133] Hence, if the filing person's most recent Schedule 13D is accurate, and if shareholders thus have received the necessary information, courts generally will not issue an injunction simply because of omissions or misleading disclosures in previous filings.[134]

A court may enjoin the filing person from making further purchases of an issuer's securities until he has amended his Schedule 13D to correct any material misrepresentation or nondisclosure.[135] Courts sometimes require a "cooling-off" period after an amended Schedule 13D has been filed in order to allow adequate time for dissemination of the information to the public.[136] Alternatively, a court might enjoin the filing person from making additional stock purchases and/or proxy solicitations unless and until he offers to rescind purchases made from open-market sellers during the period between the filing of the initial Schedule 13D and the correction of the misleading disclosures.[137] Occasionally, a court will enjoin a filing person

---

133. *See Kirsch Co. v. Bliss & Laughlin Indus., Inc.*, 495 F. Supp. 488, 502 (W.D. Mich. 1980).

134. *See, e.g., Gearhart Indus., Inc. v. Smith Int'l, Inc.*, 741 F.2d 707 (5th Cir. 1984); *Chromalloy Am. Corp. v. Sun Chem. Corp.*, 611 F.2d 240 (8th Cir. 1979); *Raybestos-Manhattan, Inc. v. Hi-Shear Indus., Inc.*, 503 F. Supp. 1122 (E.D.N.Y. 1980).

135. *See, e.g., Dan River, Inc. v. Unitex, Ltd.*, 624 F.2d 1216 (4th Cir. 1980), *cert. denied*, 449 U.S. 1101 (1981); *General Steel Indus., Inc. v. Walco Nat'l Corp.*, [1981-1982 Transfer Binder] Fed. Sec. L. Rep. (CCH) ¶ 98,402 (E.D. Mo. Nov. 24, 1981); *Life Investors, Inc. v. AGO Holding, N.V.*, [1981-1982 Transfer Binder] Fed. Sec. L. Rep. (CCH) ¶ 98,356 (8th Cir. Oct. 21, 1981); *Saunders Leasing Sys., Inc. v. Societe Holding Gray D'Albion*, 507 F. Supp. 627 (N.D. Ala. 1981); *Kirsch Co. v. Bliss & Laughlin Indus., Inc.*, 495 F. Supp. 488 (W.D. Mich. 1980).

136. *See, e.g., General Aircraft Corp. v. Lampert*, 556 F.2d 90 (1st Cir. 1977); *Kirsch Co. v. Bliss & Laughlin Indus., Inc.*, 495 F. Supp. 488 (W.D. Mich. 1980); *Lane Bryant, Inc. v. Hatleigh Corp.*, [1980 Transfer Binder] Fed. Sec. L. Rep. (CCH) ¶ 97,529 (S.D.N.Y. June 9, 1980).

137. *See, e.g., General Steel Indus., Inc. v. Walco Nat'l Corp.*, [1981-1982 Transfer Binder] Fed. Sec. L. Rep. (CCH) ¶ 98,402 (E.D. Mo. Nov. 24, 1981); *Financial General Bankshares, Inc. v. Lance*, 80 F.R.D. 22 (D.D.C. 1978).

from voting any shares purchased after the filing of the misleading Schedule 13D.[138]

At least one court has declared that it may be appropriate to compel a person who has filed a false Schedule 13D to divest the stock acquired in the transaction reported in the Schedule 13D filing.[139] By acquiring a stake in the target greater than five percent, the bidder obtained a competitive advantage over any other potential offeror. Shareholders who traded based on the inaccurate Schedule 13D lost forever their opportunity to receive the premium that might have been available had the acquiror revealed its true intentions.[140] Unless divestiture were available as a form of injunctive relief, the court reasoned, an acquiror "could engage in the most deliberate form of misrepresentation in its statutory filings and when its fraud is discovered merely file corrective amendments and keep the benefits of its wrongful conduct regardless of how that conduct may continue to injure shareholders of the corporation whose stock it has acquired."[141]

b. SEC Enforcement Actions

The SEC may bring an enforcement action under section 13(d), and such an action may lead to a rescission or a divestiture order; indeed, sanctions ordered in enforcement proceedings often are more severe than those that normally would result from private suits.[142] The SEC may proceed against a tender offeror

---

138. *See Water & Wall Assocs. Inc. v. American Consumer Indus. Inc.*, [1973 Transfer Binder] Fed. Sec. L. Rep. (CCH) ¶ 93,943 (D.N.J. April 19, 1973).

139. *Hanna Mining Co. v. Norcen Energy Resources Ltd.*, 574 F. Supp. 1172, 1202-03 (N.D. Ohio 1982). For a discussion of the facts of *Hanna* in light of section 14(e), see § III.2.C(5). The SEC took this position in *Florida Commercial Banks v. Culverhouse*, 772 F.2d 1513, 1519-20 (11th Cir. 1985), but the court rejected the argument.

140. 574 F. Supp. at 1197.

141. *Id.* at 1203.

142. *See SEC v. Savoy Indus., Inc.*, 665 F.2d 1310 (D.C. Cir. 1981); *In re Gibson*, Exchange Act Release No. 18314, [1981-1982 Transfer Binder] Fed. Sec. L. Rep. (CCH) ¶ 83,068 (Dec. 7, 1981) (sanctions against attorney); *SEC v. Sun Co.*, [1979-1980 Transfer Binder] Fed. Sec. L. Rep. (CCH) ¶ 97,209 (S.D.N.Y. Dec. 19, 1979) (Consent Order). The Insider Trading Sanctions

for improper Schedule 13D filings even if a court has dismissed a private suit alleging similar claims. If the SEC was not a party to the private action and was not in privity with the parties, res judicata and collateral estoppel may not apply.[143]

Although the SEC possesses the authority to intervene in private litigation, practical experience shows that an attempt to induce the SEC to exercise that authority will rarely succeed. The SEC seldom takes an active position during a battle for corporate control; the Commission prefers to act (if at all) only after the battle has ended.[144]

7. Ten-Day Window

Under section 13(d) and Rule 13d-1, a holder of five percent of an issuer's securities can purchase additional securities during the ten days following the date on which he has reached or crossed the five-percent threshold. Therefore, subject to possible constraints under the Hart-Scott-Rodino Act's notification requirements,[145] a person can significantly increase his holdings in an issuer's equity securities before the market has had an opportunity to react to the Schedule 13D disclosures.[146]

The availability of this ten-day "window" within which the filing person can make additional purchases has been perceived

---

Act of 1984 (Pub. L. No. 98-376) amended section 15(c)(4) of the Exchange Act to permit the SEC to bring administrative proceedings for violations of the proxy and tender offer provisions of the Williams Act. *See* 15 U.S.C. § 78o(c)(4).

143. *See Susquehanna Corp.*, 44 S.E.C. 379 (1970).

144. *See, e.g., In the Matter of Centrust Savings Bank*, [1985-1986 Transfer Binder] Fed. Sec. L. Rep. (CCH) ¶ 83,974 (SEC March 31, 1986).

145. *See infra* § II.5.

146. The actual duration of the window period depends upon the day on which the purchaser reached five-percent ownership; the period may actually run for as many as 12 days. For instance, if the filing person reaches the five-percent ownership threshold on a Wednesday, the ten-day period will end on a Saturday. The SEC rules permit the acquiror to file his Schedule 13D on the next business day, which would be Monday—12 days after the acquiror reached the five-percent level.

as contrary to the disclosure purposes of the Williams Act. The SEC's Advisory Committee on Tender Offers examined the issue and recommended closing the window by providing that "[n]o person may acquire directly or indirectly beneficial ownership of more than 5% of an outstanding class of equity securities unless such person has filed a Schedule 13D and that Schedule has been on file with the Commission for at least 48 hours."[147]

The SEC supported the Advisory Committee's recommendation to close the ten-day window but did not adopt the pre-filing recommendation. Instead, the Commission has proposed that, upon acquiring five percent of the outstanding shares of a class of equity securities, the acquiror immediately must make a public announcement about the acquisition and either must file a Schedule 13D on the following day or must refrain from making further purchases until he has filed such a Schedule 13D.[148] While various bills to close the ten-day window have been introduced in Congress, none has yet reached the floor of either House.

B. Starting a Tender Offer

In order to comply with the Williams Act's requirements, an offeror must determine whether and when it has commenced a tender offer, triggering the applicable filing and substantive requirements. The bidder must bear in mind the possibility that its purchases will be held to be an unconventional tender offer. The bidder also must consider the Williams Act rules, under

---

147. Advisory Committee on Tender Offers, *Report of Recommendations* 22 (July 8, 1983).

148. *See* Statement of John S.R. Shad, SEC Chairman, Before the House Subcomm. on Telecommunications, Consumer Protection and Finance, [1983-1984 Transfer Binder] Fed. Sec. L. Rep. (CCH) ¶ 83,511 (March 28, 1984).

which a tender offer commences at 12:01 a.m. on the date that the first of the following events occurs:

- The bidder publishes an adequate long-form publication of the tender offer in a newspaper or newspapers;
- The bidder publishes a summary advertisement of the tender offer, disclosing required information, in a newspaper or newspapers;
- The bidder publishes, or sends or gives to shareholders of the target, definitive copies of tender offer materials.[149] In order to communicate with shareholders, the bidder can obtain a stockholder list from the target.[150]

These three scenarios are the most conventional ways to commence a tender offer. In addition, Rule 14d-2(b)[151] provides that a bidder will be deemed to have commenced a tender offer (and so be subject to all related filing and disclosure requirements) if the bidder publicly announces certain information: the identity of the bidder, the identity of the target, the amount and class of securities sought, and the price or range of prices being offered. Such a public announcement, however, will not constitute the commencement of a tender offer if, within five business days of that announcement, the bidder either

- publicly announces its determination not to proceed with the tender offer, or
- files a Schedule 14D-1[152] with the SEC and complies with Rule 14d-4 as to dissemination of tender offer materials, in which case the commencement date will be deemed to be the date on which the required disclosures are first published or sent or given to shareholders.

---

149. Rule 14d-2(a), 17 C.F.R. § 240.14d-2(a) (1986).
150. Rule 14d-4, discussed in § II.4.B(2), *infra.*
151. 17 C.F.R. § 240.14d-2(b) (1986).
152. *See infra* § II.4.B(2).

The SEC promulgated Rule 14d-2(b) because it realized that, absent suitable regulation, a bidder could announce its intention to make a tender offer at a particular price, and arbitrageurs could bid up and accumulate large amounts of the putative target's stock before the bidder had disseminated to shareholders any of the disclosures required by the Williams Act. Shareholders thus would be induced to sell their shares before receiving sufficient information on the basis of which to make an informed choice about a tender offer.[153]

1. Commencement and the "Bear Hug"

The manner in which the bidder begins its offer will affect the entire strategy of the acquisition. There are ways to initiate acquisition discussions without necessarily commencing a tender offer under the Williams Act. For instance, a bidder may employ a "bear hug" strategy, which involves a (more or less) "friendly" overture by the bidder to the target's management and which may be followed by a more coercive and aggressive approach if management rebuffs the embrace.

The "bear hug" usually consists of a letter to the target making an offer (either firm or subject to negotiation) to acquire the company. This overture has two primary objectives. First and foremost, the "bear hug" may serve as an opening move in a hostile game that puts pressure on the target's management in the hope that management will make a mistake. Second, the "bear hug" may be an initial step in the bidder's genuine effort to negotiate a deal.

The bidder itself may publicly disclose its letter on the theory that (if the bidder is a publicly held company) the offer is material to the bidder's own shareholders. Alternatively, the target company may feel obliged to disclose its receipt of a letter

---

153. Exchange Act Release No. 16623, 3 Fed. Sec. L. Rep. (CCH) ¶ 24,2841 (March 5, 1980); *see also* Exchange Act Release No. 34-8392, [1969-1970 Transfer Binder] Fed. Sec. L. Rep. (CCH) ¶ 77,715 (Aug. 30, 1968), *amended*, Release No. 34-16384, 44 Fed. Reg. 70326 (Jan. 7, 1979).

that amounts to a firm offer. In either case, the target's shareholders then may increase pressure on the company to consider the offer, and the target's directors may feel compelled to deal with the bidder because their fiduciary duty dictates that they act in the shareholders' best interests. Public disclosure also may attract the attention of arbitrageurs, who may buy up large amounts of the target's stock with the intention of selling out to the highest bidder in the event of a control contest.

If the *target* publicly discloses the terms of a bidder's "bear hug," a tender offer will not be deemed to have commenced, no matter what the bear hug letter says. The bidder thus can avoid complying with the formalities of the Williams Act until it chooses to begin the tender offer, while taking advantage of the pressure that the target's shareholders may exert on the target. If, however, the *bidder* confirms any disclosure by the target, this confirmation may constitute a public announcement by the bidder sufficient to trigger the five-day period prescribed in Rule 14d-2, depending on the specificity of the information concerning the bidder's tender offer intentions.[154]

To avoid the possibility of starting Rule 14d-2(b)'s five-day clock, the bidder should phrase its "bear hug" letter carefully in order not to disclose the information that constitutes the public announcement of a proposed tender offer. For example, the letter, if it is to be publicized, should not mention the term "tender offer" but instead should state that the bidder is proposing a "combination."

Must the target disclose its receipt of a firm offer? As a practical matter, the answer is generally yes. Theoretically, the target could keep silent and answer "no comment" to all inquiries, provided that (*i*) the target and its insiders abstain from trading in the company's shares and from "tipping" anyone else about the offer; (*ii*) the target is willing to answer "no comment" to inquiries from officials of stock exchanges on which the target's shares are listed; and (*iii*) the target's "no

---

154. *See* Exchange Act Release No. 16623, 3 Fed. Sec. L. Rep. (CCH) ¶ 24,284I (March 5, 1980). Rule 14d-2 is discussed in § II.4.B., *supra*.

comment" position is not inconsistent with, and does not render misleading, prior target disclosures.[155] While the confluence of these circumstances is theoretically possible, the target actually might find it difficult to maintain such a position for any length of time.

In formulating an acquisition strategy, the bidder should consider using a "bear hug" approach unless the bidder believes either that the target will summarily reject the offer or that the "bear hug" will lessen the bidder's chance of acquiring the target by giving the target time to develop and implement a defensive strategy. A surprise tender offer affords the target only a limited time (20 business days) within which to explore alternatives, and the bidder should consider the desirability of using this pressure tactic.

In short, the bidder should pursue whatever strategy increases the possibility of a negotiated acquisition, which usually will be less expensive for the bidder than will be a hostile offer. A negotiated deal also may permit the bidder to maintain good post-acquisition relationships with the target's management and employees, thus decreasing the likelihood of losing the target's key personnel. If, however, negotiation appears futile, the bidder should remember that a "bear hug" may give the target more time to prepare its defense against a subsequent hostile tender offer.

2. Disclosures upon Initiating a Tender Offer

Upon commencing a tender offer, a bidder must file with the SEC, and deliver to the target, other bidders, and the stock exchanges (or NASD) on which the target's stock is traded, a Tender Offer Statement on Schedule 14D-1. (For purposes of this

---

155. *See In the Matter of Carnation Co.*, Exchange Act Release No. 22214, [1984-1985 Transfer Binder] Fed. Sec. L. Rep. (CCH) ¶ 83,801 (July 8, 1985) (discussed in § III.2.C(6), *infra*); *cf. Gerstle v. Gamble-Skogmo, Inc.*, 478 F.2d 1281 (2d Cir. 1973); *SEC v. Falstaff Brewing Corp.*, [1977-1978 Transfer Binder] Fed. Sec. L. Rep. (CCH) ¶ 96,117 (D.D.C. Aug. 1, 1977).

Rule,[156] an issuer is not considered a bidder.[157]) The Schedule 14D-1 must be filed with the SEC and hand-delivered to the target and other bidders on the day that the tender offer commences.

The information contained in a Schedule 14D-1 resembles but goes beyond the information contained in a Schedule 13D and includes:

- the identity of the target and the addresses of its principal executive offices; the title and amount of the equity securities being sought; the consideration offered for the securities; and market information concerning such securities, including the stock's current market value.
- the identity and background of the bidder. This information will vary depending upon whether the filing person is an individual or an entity.
- a description of any past contracts, transactions, or negotiations between the bidder and the target and its affiliates. An exception exists for transactions in which the aggregate amount described is less than one percent of the target's consolidated revenues for the year in which such transactions occurred.
- the source and amount of funds or other consideration for the offer.
- the purpose of the tender offer and any plans or proposals that the bidder might have to alter the target's structure or operations. The Court of Appeals for the Second Circuit explained the reason for the disclosure of plans or proposals that are reasonably likely to occur in the future:

> A reasonable stockholder, once informed of the contingency, can then determine whether to assume the risk of its occurrence or non-occurrence in accepting or

---

156. Rule 14d-3, 17 C.F.R. § 240.14d-3 (1986).

157. For a discussion of Rule 13e-4 and the disclosure requirements applicable to issuer tender offers, see *infra* §§ II.4.B(6)(c) and III.4.E(3)(c).

> rejecting the tender offer. Where the event, if it should occur, could influence the stockholder's decision to tender, the chance that it might occur is a factor that should be disclosed to the investor for consideration in making his or her decision.[158]

- the size of the bidder's holdings in the target, and a description of any transactions involving the target's securities during the past 60 days.
- any contracts, arrangements, understandings, or relationships that the bidder has with respect to the target. This requirement attempts to provide shareholders with "meaningful disclosure concerning certain events occurring prior to the tender offer which can have a material effect on a shareholder's investment decision concerning the tender offer."[159] Such a disclosure would include an understanding relating to a subsequent merger.
- the identity of persons employed by the bidder in connection with the tender offer, and the terms of compensation for such persons.
- the financial statements of the bidder (or its parent(s)), when the financial condition of the bidder is material to a decision by the target's shareholders.
- information concerning regulatory constraints, antitrust laws, material legal proceedings relating to the tender offer, and other material information.

Should any of this information materially change, the bidder must amend the Schedule 14D-1 by filing an amendment with the SEC and delivering it to the target, other bidders, and the stock exchanges (or NASD) on which the target's shares are traded.[160]

---

158. *Sonesta Int'l Hotels Corp. v. Wellington Assocs.*, 483 F.2d 247, 251 (2d Cir. 1973).

159. Release No. 34-14699, 3 Fed. Sec. L. Rep. (CCH) ¶ 24,284H, at 17,752 (April 24, 1978).

160. Rule 14d-3(b), 17 C.F.R. § 240.14d-3(b) (1986).

The bidder also must make available to the shareholders the terms of the tender offer, through either a long-form advertisement (rarely seen these days) or a summary advertisement stating where copies of the full tender offer can be obtained. Rule 14d-6[161] details the information that the bidder must disclose to shareholders.

Tender offer materials are considered adequately disseminated to shareholders if the requisite information is published in all editions of a daily national newspaper. If the bidder elects to use a summary publication, the bidder must make available to shareholders, upon request, the full tender offer materials.[162]

Alternatively, the bidder may decide to distribute the required materials directly to the shareholders. To effect such distribution, the bidder usually can obtain a list of shareholders from the target company itself. State law often mandates that the list be open for inspection to shareholders of record.[163] In addition, the Williams Act rules grant the bidder the right to require the target either to distribute the bidder's tender offer materials to the target's shareholders, at the bidder's expense, or to turn over a shareholder list to the bidder.[164] This federal law right, however, is less valuable to the bidder than is the corresponding state law right to inspect a stockholder list because the Williams Act rules do not obligate the target actually to turn over any list to the bidder (in the event that the target elects to distribute the materials itself) and because the rules (unlike the usual state corporation statutes) do not require any disclosed list to include information about the number of shares held by each shareholder.

Regardless of the manner in which the bidder chooses to disclose information to the shareholders, the bidder promptly must inform them of any material change in that information.[165]

---

161. *Id.* § 240.14d-6.

162. *See* Rule 14d-4, *id.* § 240.14d-4 (1986).

163. *See infra* § II.4.E(3)(c)(i) (discussing how to obtain stockholder lists in proxy fights).

164. *See* Rules 14d-4 and 14d-5.

165. Rule 14d-4(c).

3. Timing Considerations

a. Period of Tender Offer

Rule 14e-1 provides that a bidder must keep its tender offer open continuously for at least 20 *business* days. This 20-day period commences with the filing of the tender offer materials and their dissemination to the target's shareholders. Mere public announcement of a tender offer does not trigger the 20-day offering period.[166]

The 20-day minimum offering period ends at midnight on the twentieth day. The bidder therefore must either provide facilities to receive shares tendered after the close of business on the twentieth business day or must conclude the offer after that date.[167]

The SEC recently amended Rule 14e-1(b)[168] to require a tender offer to remain open for at least ten days following an announced increase or decrease in the tender offer price or in the percentage of securities sought. Although the SEC's initial proposal spoke of an increase in the "amount of securities sought," the adopted version uses the term "percentage of the class of securities sought." This language change resulted from the SEC's realization that a bidder might still desire to purchase the same percentage of securities even though the amount of securities constituting that percentage has increased because of the target's issuance of additional shares.[169]

If the bidder desires to extend the offering period, it must publicly announce this extension not later than 9:00 a.m. on the next business day after expiration of the initial offer.[170] This announcement must disclose the approximate amount of securities tendered as of the time of the announcement.

---

166. *See* Exchange Act Release No. 16623, 3 Fed. Sec. L. Rep. (CCH) ¶ 24,284I, at 17,759 (March 5, 1980).

167. *Id.* at 17,758-59.

168. 17 C.F.R. § 240.14e-1(b) (1986).

169. Exchange Act Release No. 22791, [1985-1986 Transfer Binder] Fed. Sec. L. Rep. (CCH) ¶ 83,955 (Jan. 14, 1986).

170. Rule 14e-1(d), 17 C.F.R. § 240.14e-1(d) (1986).

b. *Shareholders' Withdrawal Rights*

Shareholders who tender shares to a bidder may withdraw those tendered shares at any time during the tender offer period. If the initial offering period is extended because of the announcement of another offer by another bidder, the withdrawal rights are similarly extended. In other words, withdrawal rights are now coterminous with the offering period.[171]

Under section 14(d)(5) of the Exchange Act,[172] shareholders also may withdraw tendered shares after the 60th calendar day from the commencement of a tender offer if the bidder has not yet purchased those shares. This withdrawal period is an important consideration for bidders who must obtain regulatory approvals before purchasing tendered shares.

4. Prompt Payment

Rule 14e-1(c)[173] requires that, upon terminating or withdrawing a tender offer, a bidder either must "promptly" pay the consideration offered to shareholders or must return the tendered securities. The Rule does not specify the meaning of "promptly." An SEC release[174] discussing the promptness requirement states:

> The Commission recognizes that the operation of this standard will be affected by the practices of the financial community and the following factors: current settlement, handling and delivery procedures relating to tenders made by guaranteed deliveries by appropriate institutions; procedures to cure technical defects in tenders; and the application of the Hart-Scott-Rodino Antitrust Improvements Act.

---

171. Rule 14d-7(a), *id.* § 240.14d-7(a); *see* Exchange Act Release No. 23421, [Current] Fed. Sec. L. Rep. (CCH) ¶ 84,016 (July 11, 1986).

172. 15 U.S.C. § 78n(d)(5).

173. 17 C.F.R. § 240.14e-1(c) (1986).

174. Release No. 34-16384, [1979-1980 Transfer Binder] Fed. Sec. L. Rep. (CCH) ¶ 82,373 (Nov. 29, 1978).

Several cases also have discussed this timing requirement.

In *Pryor v. United States Steel Corp.*,[175] the court stated that the question of prompt payment is one of reasonableness in light of all the circumstances. The court denied the defendant bidder's motion to dismiss a Rule 14e-1(c) claim but noted in passing that the claim was unlikely to succeed because the bidder had accepted tendered shares on a Thursday and had paid for them the following Monday. Similarly, *Caleb & Co. v. E.I. duPont de Nemours & Co.*[176] held that promptness depended upon the circumstances of the particular case and that a trial on the issue would be necessary.

Caleb also held that the bidder can *unintentionally* violate Rule 14e-1(c) and stated that "[t]he Commission in drafting the requirement for prompt payment, eliminated the requirement of a finding of scienter and exercised its authority to structure tender offers such that fraudulent or deceptive actions will be eliminated."[177] In a later decision,[178] the *Caleb* court held that violations of Rule 14e-1(c) may give rise to a private cause of action for damages. The court reasoned that shareholders are within the class intended to be protected by the prompt payment requirement even if the action in question did not involve fraud on the part of the offeror.

In *Macfadden Holdings, Inc. v. JB Acquisition Corp.*,[179] the court held that a bidder had not violated the prompt payment requirements of Rule 14e-1(c) by accepting tendered shares but deferring payment until it had obtained required regulatory approvals (from the Federal Communications Commission). Little other case law discusses Rule 14e-1(c).

---

175. 591 F. Supp. 942 (S.D.N.Y. 1984), *aff'd in part, rev'd in part on other grounds*, 794 F.2d 52 (2d Cir.), *cert. denied*, 107 S. Ct. 445 (1986).

176. 599 F. Supp. 1468 (S.D.N.Y. 1984).

177. *Id.* at 1473.

178. 615 F. Supp. 96 (S.D.N.Y. 1985).

179. 641 F. Supp. 454, 466-7 (S.D.N.Y.), *rev'd on other grounds*, 802 F.2d 62 (2d Cir. 1986).

5. Proration of Tender Offer Purchases

Section 14(d)(6) of the Williams Act[180] provides that, if a bidder makes a tender offer for less than all of the outstanding equity securities of the target (a "partial tender offer") *and* receives, during the first ten days of the offering period, tenders of more shares than were sought, the bidder must purchase the desired amount of shares on a pro rata basis from among those shares tendered during the ten-day period. The section also applies to acceptance of securities tendered within ten days after the bidder has given notice of an increase in the tender offer consideration.

In 1982, the SEC amended Rule 14d-8[181] to extend the proration period for partial tender offers from ten days to the entire period during which the offer remains open, thereby granting proration rights to shareholders who tender at any time during the offering period. Thus, Rule 14d-8 effectively prevents the bidder from purchasing tendered shares until the partial tender offer has closed (*i.e.*, not sooner than the twentieth business day after commencement), because the bidder must prorate its purchases among securities tendered throughout the entire offering period.

The SEC adopted Rule 14d-8 to afford nonprofessional investors a greater opportunity to participate in partial tender offers. Previously, such investors frequently had been excluded because they tended to have more difficulty in making and implementing decisions to tender within ten days of the commencement of the tender offer. Indeed, the SEC and commentators observed that professional arbitrageurs were raking in a disproportionate amount of the consideration in the first stage of the tender offer. The Rule thus helps partially to neutralize the coercive nature of two-tier offers (*i.e.*, a cash tender offer for fewer than all shares, followed by a merger in which the target's remaining shareholders will receive securities worth less than the cash offered in the tender offer) by

---

180. 15 U.S.C. § 78n(d)(6).

181. 17 C.F.R. § 240.14d-8 (1986).

eliminating some of the pressure on shareholders to tender their shares quickly in order to participate in the cash offer.

The Rule also allows tendering shareholders to reap the benefits of a competing offer. Under amended Rule 14d-8, if a third party launches a bid at any time before the conclusion of the initial tender offer, all shareholders who tendered pursuant to the initial tender offer receive an additional ten days within which they may withdraw their tendered shares.

Even though the SEC asserted authority under sections 14(d) and 23(a) of the Exchange Act when adopting Rule 14d-8, there remains some question whether the SEC possesses the power to adopt such a rule.[182]

6. Issuer Tender Offers

Offers by issuers for their own shares—self-tender offers—are regulated by section 13(e) of the Exchange Act.[183] Self-tender rules involve (*i*) issuer purchases, (*ii*) going private transactions, and (*iii*) issuer self-tenders.

Targets may use self-tenders to defend against hostile bids.[184] In a friendly offer, however, a self-tender may become part of the bidder's own acquisition strategy. If, for example, the bidder is a small company and cannot finance a tender offer for all of the target's stock, the bidder and the target may agree to a joint tender offer, in which the target will use its credit to finance a purchase of its own shares that the bidder is unable to buy. Bidders therefore should consider incorporating self-tenders into negotiated acquisition plans.

---

182. *See* Dissent of Commissioner John S.R. Shad, Exchange Act Release No. 19336, [1982-1983 Transfer Binder] Fed. Sec. L. Rep. (CCH) ¶ 83,306, at 85,652 (Dec. 15, 1982).

183. 15 U.S.C. § 78m(e).

184. *See infra* § III.4.E.

a. Issuer Purchases

Rule 13e-1[185] regulates an issuer's purchases of its own securities following a tender offer by a third party. Within ten business days of the commencement of a tender offer, the issuer must file a Schedule 14D-9, which states whether target management recommends acceptance or rejection of the offer or takes no position on it.[186] Rule 13e-1 supplements Rule 14d-9 by requiring that the issuer refrain from repurchasing its own equity securities once it has received notice of a tender offer by another person, unless the issuer first files a statement with the SEC and announces its repurchase intentions to its shareholders.

The issuer must disclose the title and amount of securities to be purchased, the persons or class of persons from whom they will be purchased, and the markets or exchanges to be used. The issuer also must state the purpose of the repurchase and the intended disposition of the repurchased securities. In addition, the issuer must describe the amount of funds or other consideration to be used in the repurchase as well as any transaction (including the names of any lenders) through which those funds were obtained.

b. Going Private Transactions

Rule 13e-3[187] governs going private transactions by issuers or their affiliates. The Rule applies only to (*i*) an issuer's (or affiliate's) purchase of or tender offer for its own equity securities, or (*ii*) an issuer's (or affiliate's) solicitation of proxies or mailing of information statements in connection with certain significant corporate transactions, including mergers and consolidations. Moreover, the Rule applies only if the transactions are intended, or are reasonably likely, to result in the issuer's having fewer than 300 shareholders or becoming

---

185. 17 C.F.R. § 240.13e-1 (1986).

186. Schedules 14D-9 are discussed at greater length in § III.2.A(2), *infra*.

187. 17 C.F.R. § 240.13e-3 (1986).

delisted on national securities exchanges and unquoted by any inter-dealer quotation system of a registered national securities association.[188]

Rule 13e-3 requires any issuer conducting repurchases that fall within the scope of the Rule to file a Schedule 13E-3. This Schedule discloses information that is similar to (but more extensive than) that disclosed in a Schedule 13D or 14D-1.[189] The issuer must file the Schedule 13E-3 with the SEC and must disseminate to its shareholders most of the compiled information.[190] As with Schedules 13D and 14D-1, the filing person promptly must notify the SEC and the shareholders of any material changes in the reported information.[191]

Among the disclosures called for by Schedule 13E-3 that go beyond those contained in Schedules 13D or 14D-1 and that may be difficult to answer are:

- Item 7's requirement that the filer disclose the effects of the transaction on the issuer, its affiliates (*i.e.*, controlling "insiders"), and unaffiliated security holders (*i.e.*, public investors). The instructions clearly demand a reasonably detailed discussion of benefits and detriments, quantified to the extent practicable.
- Item 8's requirement that the filer disclose whether the issuer or the affiliate reasonably believes the transaction to be fair to the unaffiliated shareholders. It is not enough either to disclaim having a belief as to fairness or to state in conclusory terms that the transaction is fair. (An affiliate obviously will be extremely reluctant to state that the transaction is unfair, because such an admission could lead to liability for breach of state law fiduciary obligations to

---

188. Rule 13e-3(a)(3).

189. Schedule 13D is discussed in § II.4.A., *supra*, and Schedule 14D in § II.4.B(2), *supra*.

190. Rule 13e-3(e)(1).

191. Rule 13e-3(e)(2).

shareholders.[192]) Item 8 requires a discussion of the material factors on which the filing person bases its belief as to fairness, including whether the consideration offered to public shareholders is fair in relation to current and historical market prices, net book value, going-concern value, liquidation prices, the per-share prices previously paid by the affiliate, any investment banker's opinions, and any firm offers by third parties to acquire the issuer. Although Item 8 purports simply to be a disclosure item, it undoubtedly affects the manner in which going-private transactions are structured and approved, because the filing person must disclose whether the transaction has been approved by a majority of the issuer's nonemployee (or "outside") directors.

- Item 9's requirement that the filer disclose whether the issuer or affiliate has received any report, opinion, or appraisal materially related to any aspect of the transaction, including its fairness. If such an opinion exists, the filer must disclose the identity of the person who rendered it, that person's qualifications, the manner in which that person was chosen, and whether the person has any material relationship with the issuer or its affiliates.

The manner of dissemination of the required Rule 13e-3 disclosures depends upon the type of transaction: in a tender offer, the information should be reported in the tender offer document; in a merger, the information should be reported in the merger proxy statement. Rule 13e-3 does provide, however, that the issuer must furnish the requisite information at least 20 days before any purchase of the issuer's shares or any meeting at which the issuer's shareholders are to vote on a going private transaction.

Different types of Rule 13e-3 transactions may require different types of disclosures. For instance, *Howing Co. v. Nationwide*

---

192. *See infra* § III.3.

Corp.[193] suggests that Rule 13e-3 demands more extensive disclosures in proxy statement transactions than in tender offers because, in the former, a minority shareholder has only the option of dissent and appraisal under state law and thus needs full disclosure as to appraisals, projections, and the like in order rationally to exercise his option.

Certain going private transactions are exempted from Rule 13e-3. For instance, the Rule does not apply to a second-step "clean-up" transaction that occurs within one year of a tender offer by or on behalf of a third-party bidder that thereafter becomes an affiliate of the issuer.[194] But a bidder may avail itself of this exemption only if the bidder previously made disclosures similar to those required by the Rule and if the unaffiliated shareholders will receive the highest consideration offered in the earlier tender offer. Rule 13e-3 also does not apply to any transaction in which the issuer's stockholders exchange their securities solely for publicly traded equity securities having substantially the same rights as those exchanged.[195]

In addition to Rule 13e-3, other rules may apply to going private transactions. For instance, although subject to the requirements of Rule 13e-3, an affiliate of an issuer may need to comply with the tender offer and proxy requirements of section 14 of the Exchange Act. The issuer also must consider any applicable state statutory and case law requirements relating to going private transactions.[196]

c. *Issuer Self-Tenders*

Rule 13e-4[197] regulates tender offers by issuers and imposes on them most of the requirements that other bidders must satisfy.[198]

---

193. 625 F. Supp. 146 (S.D. Ohio 1985).

194. Rule 13e-3(g)(1).

195. Rule 13e-3(g)(2).

196. *See generally* A. Borden, *Going Private* (1986).

197. 17 C.F.R. § 240.13e-4 (1986).

198. For a discussion of the general requirements of tender offers, see *supra* § II.4.

Just as section 13(d) does not define "tender offer," section 13(e) does not define what constitutes an issuer self-tender. The SEC and the courts use the same eight-factor analysis to evaluate both types of tender offers. Prior to 1986, there were significant differences in the timing considerations applicable to issuer as compared with third-party tender offers; recently, however, the SEC eliminated most of these disparities.[199]

Rule 13e-4 does not prescribe whether an issuer must open its self-tender offer to all shareholders. One 1985 case concluded that the Rule does not prohibit exclusionary self-tenders.[200] The SEC, however, has recently promulgated Rule 14d-10, which prohibits such offers.[201]

7. Equal Treatment of Shareholders: The Best Price and All Holders Provisions

Pursuant to section 14(d)(7) of the Exchange Act,[202] a bidder must pay the same consideration to all shareholders who tender their securities during a tender offer. Thus, if the bidder increases the consideration offered to shareholders at any time during the offering period, the bidder must pay that increased consideration to *all* tendering shareholders, even to those who tendered before the increase in consideration and whose shares the bidder already has purchased. This requirement, coupled with criticism of the discriminatory self-tender offer made by Unocal Corporation in 1985 as a defense against Mesa Petroleum's hostile tender offer,[203] led the SEC recently to promulgate Rule 14d-10.[204]

---

199. *See* Rule 13e-4; Release No. 34-22708; Release No. 34-23421 [Current] Fed. Sec. L. Rep. (CCH) ¶ 84,016 (July 11, 1986).

200. *Unocal Corp. v. Mesa Petroleum Co.*, 493 A.2d 946 (Del. 1985).

201. *See infra* § II.4.B(7).

202. 15 U.S.C. § 78n(d)(7).

203. *See infra* § III.3.B(3).

204. 17 C.F.R. § 240.14d-10.

The purpose of Rule 14d-10 is to assure equal treatment of all shareholders. The Rule prohibits a person from making a tender offer unless:

> (1) The tender offer is open to all security holders of the class of securities subject to the tender offer; and
>
> (2) The consideration paid to any security holder pursuant to the tender offer is the highest consideration paid to any other security holder during such tender offer.

The first part of the Rule is known as the "all holders" rule; the second part, as the "best price" rule. The SEC adopted a parallel amendment to Rule 13e-4, which now requires an issuer to open its own tender offer to all holders of the class of securities subject to the offer and to pay to all such shareholders the best price offered to any shareholder.[205]

The all holders rule was designed to prevent the recurrence of the discriminatory self-tender that Unocal used in fighting off Mesa's hostile bid. That offer was structured to reduce the amount of Unocal's outstanding shares and was extended to all shareholders other than Mesa. Unocal's board of directors justified the exclusion as necessary to protect those Unocal shareholders whose shares would be displaced in the proration process by Mesa's shares and who otherwise would receive inadequate consideration in the second tier of Mesa's two-tier tender offer.

Two courts addressed the legality of Unocal's gambit. The Delaware Supreme Court, in *Unocal Corp. v. Mesa Petroleum Co.*,[206] upheld the offer under Delaware law. Reversing the lower court's ruling that principles of fiduciary duty required a self-tender to be fair to all shareholders (including the raider-bidder), the court concluded that, where the hostile bidder coerces

---

205. Rule 13e-4(f)(8). Exchange Act Release No. 22199 [1984-1985 Transfer Binder] Fed. Sec. L. Rep. (CCH) ¶ 83,798 (July 1, 1985); Release 34-22791, [1985-1986 Transfer Binder] Fed. Sec. L. Rep. (CCH) ¶ 83,955 (Jan. 14, 1986).

206. 493 A.2d 946 (Del. 1985).

shareholders and has a history of seeking greenmail,[207] the business judgment rule may permit a target to make a seemingly discriminatory self-tender.[208]

In addition, a federal district court in California considered the validity of Unocal's exclusionary self-tender under the Williams Act and also concluded that there was no basis to enjoin the discriminatory transaction.[209] The court reasoned that neither the language nor the legislative history of sections 13(e) and 14(e) plainly supported Mesa's contention that the Williams Act prohibits discriminatory tender offers. Observing that the SEC had neither adopted all holders and best price rules (as of that time) nor challenged Unocal's exclusionary offer, the court inferred that the Commission believed "that such substantive rules are not authorized by the Act or that, if they are, as a matter of policy, the SEC has chosen not to require such an 'open to all' condition."[210] The court also viewed its decision not to enjoin the offer as confirming "the ability of state courts to deal with substantive issues of corporation law and corporate governance, including issues of the fairness in a corporation's treatment of its shareholders."[211]

Although it noted, in upholding Unocal's self-tender, that the SEC had not adopted a proposed all holders rule, the court observed that the Commission would lack jurisdiction to promulgate such a rule, which would constitute substantive, rather than procedural, regulation of tender offers. The view that the SEC may lack jurisdiction may be supported by the Supreme Court's recent decision in *Schreiber v. Burlington Northern, Inc.*,[212] which held that section 14(e) of the Exchange

---

207. *See infra* § II.4.F. (discussing greenmail).

208. Although the new all holders rule disallows exclusionary self-tenders, *Unocal* may still stand as precedent for other forms of exclusionary defensive tactics.

209. *Unocal Corp. v. Pickens*, 608 F. Supp. 1081 (C.D. Cal. 1985).

210. *Id.* at 1082.

211. *Id.* at 1083.

212. 472 U.S. 1, 105 S. Ct. 2458 (1985). *Schreiber* is discussed in greater detail in § III.2.B(2), *infra*.

Act provides a remedy only for misrepresentation or nondisclosure in connection with a tender offer.

The Supreme Court rejected the notion that the Williams Act could be used to regulate the substantive fairness of tender offers. In analyzing section 14(e), the Court noted that Congress, in adopting section 13(e), had stopped short of imposing substantive requirements on issuer self-tender offers;[213] indeed, if section 14(e) had been intended to provide a substantive remedy, the entire congressional regulatory scheme for self-tender offers would have been unnecessary. Thus, to the extent that either section 13(e) or 14(e) serves as the basis for the SEC's all holders requirement, *Schreiber* may limit the SEC's authority to enforce the Rule.

The Williams Act's legislative history might reinforce this view. The first version of section 13(e) authorized the SEC to adopt rules regarding issuer purchases "as necessary or appropriate in the public interest or for the protection of investors or in order to prevent such acts and practices as are fraudulent, deceptive, or manipulative."[214] In response to this proposal, numerous witnesses informed Congress that such a rule would go beyond the intended legislative purpose of fostering full and fair disclosure of material information. Hence, Congress ultimately adopted a proposal that limited the SEC's rulemaking power to defining "acts and practices which are fraudulent, deceptive, or manipulative" and to prescribing "means reasonably designed to prevent such acts and practices."

The SEC historically has adhered to a disclosure-based approach to securities regulation, leaving to state courts and legislatures the regulation of internal corporate affairs and the application of the business judgment rule. Various SEC Commissioners, as well as the SEC's Tender Offer Advisory Committee, regularly have reaffirmed this scope of authority. The all holders rule might constitute a significant intrusion by the SEC upon the traditional prerogatives of the states to

---

213. 105 S. Ct. at 2463 n.8.

214. S. 2731, 89th Cong., 2d Sess. (1965).

determine the fiduciary standards governing the fairness of tender-offer tactics.

The all holders rule also may be inconsistent with the Williams Act's policy of regulatory neutrality in tender offer battles—a principle continually reiterated in the Act's legislative history and by persons who more recently have considered federal regulation of tender offers[215]—because the new rule will limit a target's ability to use Unocal's tactics to defend against hostile tender offers. There undoubtedly will be litigation concerning the SEC's authority to adopt the Rule.

The second part of Rule 14d-10, the best price provision, seeks to insure that all shareholders who tender their shares will receive the same value in consideration for their shares, even if the bidder must offer different types of consideration to different shareholders.[216]

8. Changes in Tender Offer Terms

Certain changes in tender offer terms, such as increases in price and waiving of conditions, do not necessarily constitute the commencement of a new offer but, rather, the mere amendment of the original offer. It is possible that, at some point, changes may become so significant that a bidder must start an entirely new offer.[217] Recent SEC rule amendments, however, strongly suggest that changes in the bidder's offer usually will not

---

215. *See, e.g.*, Advisory Committee on Tender Offers, *Report of Recommendations*, Recommendation 3 (July 8, 1983).

216. Exchange Act Release No. 22198, [1984-1985 Transfer Binder] Fed. Sec. L. Rep. (CCH) ¶ 83,797, at 87,564 (July 1, 1985).

217. *See Pullman, Inc. v. McDermott, Inc.*, No. 80-C-3555 (N.D. Ill. Sept. 3, 1980) (increase in price and number of shares sought, change of intent to seek control, and addition of conditions indicated a new tender offer); *see generally* S. Lorne, *Acquisitions and Mergers: Negotiated and Contested Transactions* 4-16, 4-17 (1985). *But cf. McDermott, Inc. v. Wheelabrator-Frye, Inc.*, 649 F.2d 489 (7th Cir. 1980) (tender offeror's announcement of increase in number of shares sought is not a new tender offer and does not trigger new time periods for keeping offer open and for withdrawal rights).

constitute a new offer but will require the bidder to hold its offer open for a period of time so that investors can digest the new facts bearing on investment decisions.

An increase in the amount of consideration to be offered requires extension of the tender offer period by ten days. The SEC recently amended Rule 14e-1(b) to require a bidder to extend its tender offer when the bidder decides to increase the percentage of shares it will accept. The recent amendment is intended to give persons who have failed to tender an additional opportunity to do so if the increased size or value of the offer makes a tender economically advantageous.[218]

Prior to 1986, the SEC had indicated that any change in the composition or allocation of interests among members of an offering group might result in the commencement of a new tender offer,[219] triggering new withdrawal, proration, and expiration periods.[220] So, too, might any attempt by a bidder to purchase "significantly more" shares than the number or percent initially sought in a partial tender offer.[221]

The SEC had informally stated that a reduction in the number of shares sought in a partial tender offer, or any other material adverse change in the offering terms, might constitute the making of a new offer. The SEC also had taken the position that a bidder wishing to decrease the consideration offered in a tender offer must terminate the offer, return all tendered shares, and commence a new tender offer with a new minimum offering period.[222] However, according to a 1986 release, the SEC suggested that "a decrease in securities sought does not, in itself, constitute a new tender offer. . . ."[223]

---

218. *See* Exchange Act Release No. 22198, [1984-1985 Transfer Binder] Fed. Sec. L. Rep. (CCH) ¶ 83,798 (July 1, 1985).

219. Press release of Mesa Petroleum Corp., May 1, 1983.

220. Such periods are discussed in §§ II.4.B(3)(a) and (b), and II.4.B(5).

221. Press Release of Mesa Petroleum Corp., May 1, 1983. *But see McDermott, Inc. v. Wheelabrator-Frye, Inc.*, 649 F.2d 489 (7th Cir. 1980).

222. *See* Exchange Act Release No. 22198, [1984-1985 Transfer Binder] Fed. Sec. L. Rep. (CCH) ¶ 83,797, at 87,563 (July 1, 1985).

223. Exchange Act Release No. 22791, at 14, [1985-1986 Transfer Binder] Fed. Sec. L. Rep. (CCH) ¶ 83,955, and 87,982 (Jan. 14, 1986).

By the subsequently adopted amendment to Rule 14e-1(b), requiring extension of the offering period by ten days following a decrease in the consideration offered or the number of shares sought, the SEC made clear its belief that such decreases do not constitute a new offer, although they do require the bidder to afford investors additional time to consider their investment decisions. The new Rule, which no longer contends that the increase in shares sought constitutes the making of a new offer, brings the SEC's position more in line with the only appellate court decision on that question. In *McDermott, Inc. v. Wheelabrator-Frye, Inc.*,[224] Wheelabrator and McDermott were involved in rival tender offers for the shares of Pullman Inc. Wheelabrator increased the number of shares sought without extending the closing date of its tender offer, which was scheduled to expire at midnight on the day that the increase in shares was announced. McDermott moved in federal district court for a temporary restraining order, alleging violations of sections 13(d)-(e) and 14(d)-(f) of the Exchange Act; the court granted the motion and ordered Wheelabrator to extend its offer for 30 days and to grant Pullman shareholders 15 days within which they could withdraw any shares already tendered.

The Court of Appeals for the Seventh Circuit vacated the district court's order, stating:

> The district court's order can only rest on the proposition that the announcement of the increase in the number of shares Wheelabrator obligated itself to buy created a new tender offer, thereby triggering the time requirements of the statute and regulations attendant upon the commencement of a tender offer. We conclude that this proposition is untenable, based upon our reading of the statute and regulations thereunder. Even an increase in consideration is not treated as a new tender offer. See 17 C.F.R. § 240.14e-1(b). It is illogical to assume that when the SEC, acting under rule-making authority granted by Congress, expressly required a ten day waiting period after a change in the consideration offered, *id.*, it intended that an increase in the

224. 649 F.2d 489 (7th Cir. 1980).

> number of shares sought be the commencement of a new tender offer, triggering more extensive requirements than the SEC thought necessary for a change in the price.[225]

The court concluded that a change in the number of shares sought required the bidder to leave its offer open for some reasonable amount of time after announcement of the change; however, the court believed that the period between the entry of the district court's order and the appellate court's own decision to vacate that order constituted a reasonable lapse of time.

In its July 1986 release adopting the amendment to Rule 14e-1(b), the SEC discussed in a footnote the extra time that bidders should afford shareholders if bidders modify their offers in ways less drastic than those discussed in Rule 14e-1(b) (*i.e.*, changes in price or number of shares sought).[226] The Commission took the position that, to allow dissemination "in a manner reasonably designed to inform [shareholders] of such change[s]," the offer should remain open for a minimum of five business days from the date on which the material changes are first published, sent, or given to shareholders. If material changes affect information that approaches the significance of price and share levels, a minimum period of ten business days may be necessary to insure adequate dissemination and investor response. Moreover, five business days may not suffice when revised or additional materials become necessary because disclosure made to shareholders is found to be materially deficient. The form of dissemination may depend on the nature of the dissemination of the previously distributed materially deficient information.

9. Abandonment of Tender Offer

If a bidder decides to announce its abandonment of a tender offer, it should behave in a manner consistent with that

---

225. *Id.* at 492.

226. Exchange Act Release No. 23421, [Current] Fed. Sec. L. Rep. (CCH) ¶ 84,016, at 88,196 n.70 (July 11, 1986).

announcement. Inconsistent behavior, such as purchasing quantities of the target's stock shortly after announcing the abandonment of a tender offer, might be deemed to be an illegal continuation of the offer—illegal because the bidder did not announce an extension of the expiration period and (in the case of a partial offer) did not extend the proration period.[227]

Termination of an offer also can raise state law questions. In *Gilbert v. The El Paso Co.*,[228] for example, Burlington Northern terminated a hostile offer for 51 percent of El Paso's stock and agreed with El Paso both to start a new offer for fewer shares and to allow El Paso to grant severance contracts to senior executives. Shareholders of El Paso sued both Burlington Northern and the directors of El Paso, and the Delaware Chancery Court denied Burlington Northern's motion for summary judgment. The court concluded that, if El Paso's board of directors breached its fiduciary duty to the company's shareholders in entering into the agreement, Burlington Northern could be liable as a co-conspirator. According to the court, a bidder "may not knowingly participate in the target board's breach of fiduciary duty by extracting terms which require the opposite party to prefer its interests at the expense of its shareholders. . . ."[229]

10. Inside Information

Section 14(e) makes it illegal to engage in any fraudulent, deceptive, or manipulative act or practice in connection with a tender offer; the section also authorizes the SEC to promulgate rules to define, and to prescribe means reasonably designed to prevent, such acts or practices. Rule 14e-3[230] requires persons who have nonpublic information relating to a tender offer to

227. *But see Hanson Trust PLC v. ML SCM Corp.*, 774 F.2d 47 (2d Cir. 1985) (discussed in §§ II.2.C. and D., *supra*).

228. 490 A.2d 1050 (Del. Ch. 1984).

229. *Id.* at 1058.

230. 17 C.F.R. § 240.14e-3 (1986).

disclose that information or to abstain from trading, and it also imposes liability on certain tippers or traders of inside information relating to tender offers.

The SEC adopted Rule 14e-3 shortly after the Supreme Court decided *Chiarella v. United States*,[231] which involved trading based on material, nonpublic information concerning takeovers. Chiarella was a financial printer's employee who had deduced the names of tender offer (and merger) targets from the blank spaces or false names contained in draft takeover documents delivered to the printer. Chiarella then purchased shares in the targets and sold the stock immediately after the takeover attempts were made public. Chiarella was criminally prosecuted and convicted under section 10(b) of the Exchange Act and SEC Rule 10b-5.[232] The Court of Appeals for the Second Circuit affirmed the conviction, but the Supreme Court reversed.

The Court framed the issue as "whether a person who learns from the confidential documents of one corporation that it is planning an attempt to secure control of a second corporation violates § 10(b) . . . if he fails to disclose the impending takeover before trading in the target company's securities."[233] This case, in other words, "concern[ed] the legal effect of [Chiarella's] silence."[234]

The Court held that "a duty to disclose under § 10(b) does not arise from the mere possession of nonpublic market information"[235]; rather, section 10(b) liability arises only when nondisclosure involves a breach of a "duty to disclose arising from a relationship of trust and confidence between parties to a transaction."[236] In the absence of this affirmative duty to speak, silence is not fraudulent.

Chiarella, noted the Court, "was not a corporate insider and he received no confidential information from the target

231. 445 U.S. 222 (1980).
232. 15 U.S.C. § 78j(b); 17 C.F.R. § 240.10b-5.
233. *Id.* at 224.
234. *Id.* at 226.
235. *Id.* at 235.
236. *Id.* at 230.

company."[237] Nor could any duty arise from Chiarella's relationship with persons who sold the targets' securities, for he "had no prior dealings with them. He was not their agent, he was not a fiduciary, he was not a person in whom the sellers had placed their trust and confidence. He was, in fact, a complete stranger who dealt with the sellers only through impersonal market transactions."[238] Refusing to recognize the existence, under section 10(b), of "a general duty between *all* participants in market transactions to forgo actions based on material, nonpublic information,"[239] the Court held that Chiarella had not breached any duty to those persons from whom he had purchased securities. Chiarella's trading thus did not violate section 10(b).

Chiarella restricted the SEC's reliance on section 10(b) and Rule 10b-5 as "catch-all" weapons with which to fight insider trading. The Commission therefore promulgated Rule 14e-3 as a means of avoiding the constraints of section 10(b), as construed in *Chiarella*, and of expanding the class of persons with standing to sue users of nonpublic takeover information.

a. Rule 14e-3

Insider trading in takeover settings differs somewhat from that proscribed in cases decided before the wave of acquisitions that has swept the country during the 1980s.[240] The takeover information on which insiders rely relates directly to the price of the target's stock—there is no argument over materiality.[241] Because it is so directly and immediately valuable, such

---

237. *Id.* at 232.

238. *Id.* at 232-33.

239. *Id.* at 233 (emphasis added).

240. Fraidin, "Insider Trading: The Tender Offer Cases," in K. Bialkin & A. Matthews, *Insider Training* 343, 346 (Law Journal Seminars-Press, 1986).

241. *Id.* at 347 (commenting that news of an impending takeover unquestionably affects a stock's value, while the effect of early notice of a quarterly earnings report depends on investors' subjective evaluation of a company's overall performance).

information increases the potential profits from insider trading and, therefore, the temptation to engage in it. Moreover, unlike the older cases that tended to involve corporate information emanating from *inside* a company, the takeover cases typically turn on the use of market information (for example, word of a proposed tender offer) originating from parties *outside* the corporation.[242] Under the restrictive *Chiarella* view, however, a tender offeror and its agents, including the investment banker with whom the offeror shares confidential information about a target, owe no fiduciary duty to the target and, prior to a takeover, probably could trade in the target's shares based on nonpublic information, subject only to disclosure obligations under section 13(d).[243]

In 1980, in an effort to correct the effect of *Chiarella* in the tender offer area, the SEC adopted Rule 14e-3.[244] According to the Commission, *Chiarella* did not decide the issue whether a person could violate section 10(b) simply by trading on the basis of misappropriated or unlawfully obtained or used information, even though that person did not owe a duty directly to the shareholder from whom he purchased or to whom he sold securities.[245] The Commission thus considered itself free, through Rule 14e-3, to proscribe trading based on misappropriated or unlawfully obtained takeover information. Rule 14e-3 therefore supplements, rather than replaces, Rule 10b-5, and the SEC continues to allege violations of both rules when the conduct involved seems to fall within the proscriptions of Rule 14e-3 as well as the fiduciary duty or misappropriation theories of Rule 10b-5.[246]

---

242. *Id.* The Court in *Chiarella* recognized this distinction. *See* 445 U.S. at 233.

243. "Report of the Task Force on Regulation of Insider Trading: Part I: Regulation Under the Antifraud Provisions of the Securities Exchange Act of 1934" [hereinafter cited as "Report"], 41 Bus. Law. 223, 235 (1985).

244. 17 C.F.R. § 240.14e-3.

245. Exchange Act Release No. 17120, [1980 Transfer Binder] Fed. Sec. L. Rep. (CCH) ¶ 82,646, at 83,456, 83,458 n.37 (Sept. 4, 1980).

246. D. Langevoort, *Insider Trading Handbook* 174 (1986).

The prohibitions of Rule 14e-3 expressly apply to insiders of the target and also to any other person

> who is in possession of material information relating to such tender offer which information he knews or has reason to know is nonpublic and which he knows or has reason to know has been acquired directly or indirectly from (1) the offering person, (2) the issuer of the securities sought or to be sought by such tender offer, or (3) any officer, director, partner or employee or any other person acting on behalf of the offering person or such issuer. . . .

The release promulgating Rule 14e-3 supplies seven examples of persons to whom the Rule specifically applies:

- persons who are told by the bidder that the bidder will make a tender offer, which information is not public;
- persons who, having been delegated the duty to do so by the bidder, decide to launch a tender offer;
- the management of a target that has received a nonpublic letter from the bidder concerning a tender offer;[247]
- persons told by target management about the receipt of a nonpublic letter from a bidder concerning a tender offer;
- persons who receive material, nonpublic information from the target concerning the target's response to a tender offer;
- persons who steal, convert, or otherwise misappropriate from a bidder material, nonpublic information concerning a tender offer; and
- persons who are told about a tender offer by another person who, in turn, obtained nonpublic information about the offer from the bidder, provided that the first persons know or have reason to know that this information came indirectly from the bidder.[248]

This list, of course, is not exclusive.

---

247. *But see* the discussion on the "bear hug" strategy in § II.4.B(1), *supra*.

248. Exchange Act Release No. 17120, [1980 Transfer Binder] Fed. Sec. L. Rep. (CCH) ¶ 82,646 (Sept. 4, 1980).

Rule 14e-3 contains four specific exemptions. *First*, a person may trade in the target's shares if information about the tender offer has been publicly disclosed a reasonable time before the trading occurs.[249] *Second*, a corporation will not violate the Rule if the person making the company's investment decision concerning the target's securities has no knowledge of the material, nonpublic information *and* if the firm has implemented procedures (metaphorically termed "Chinese Walls," because they are designed to prevent the passage of such information from divisions of the company that do not trade to those that do) to insure that its employees do not violate the Rule.[250] This exclusion protects multi-service financial institutions from liability for inadvertently violating the Rule. The person seeking to rely on this exemption bears the burden of proof as to both of its elements.[251] *Third*, a broker who purchases shares on behalf of the bidder will not be held to have violated the Rule.[252] *Fourth*, a person who sells securities to the bidder will not be held to have violated the Rule.[253]

Rule 14e-3's proscriptions apply only if a bidder has taken a substantial step to commence, or has actually commenced, a tender offer. The SEC considers a person to have taken substantial steps to commence a tender offer if the bidder's board has taken a vote relating to the tender offer or if the bidder has formed a plan to make an offer. Other activities to facilitate a tender offer—such as arranging financing; preparing tender offer materials; authorizing negotiations; negotiating with a person to act as deal manager; or soliciting a dealer, forwarding agent, or depository in connection with the offer—also constitute substantial steps toward commencement of an offer.[254] This list of activities is not exclusive.

---

249. Rule 14e-3(a).

250. Rule 14e-3(b).

251. Exchange Act Release No. 17120, [1980 Transfer Binder] Fed. Sec. L. Rep. (CCH) ¶ 82,646, at 83,460 (Sept. 4, 1980).

252. Rule 14e-3(c)(1).

253. Rule 14e-3(c)(2).

254. Exchange Act Release No. 17120, [1980 Transfer Binder] Fed. Sec. L. Rep. (CCH) ¶ 82,646, at 83,458 n.33 (Sept. 4, 1980).

i. "Disclose or Abstain" Provision

A person has a duty either to disclose inside information or to abstain from trading if:

- any person has taken substantial steps to commence, or has commenced, a tender offer and another person possesses material information relating to the offer;
- the other person knows or has reason to know that the information is not public;
- the other person knows or has reason to know that the information was acquired directly or indirectly from the bidder, the issuer, or an officer, director, partner, employee, or other such person acting on behalf of the bidder or issuer; and
- the other person purchases or sells, or causes the purchase or sale of, any security sought in the tender offer, any security convertible into such security, or any option relating to such security.[255] A person can "cause" the purchase or sale of a security by recommending such a purchase or sale.

If a person who otherwise has a duty to abstain from trading still wishes to trade, he must publicly disclose the relevant nonpublic information and its source, "by press release or otherwise," "within a reasonable time prior to any purchase or sale. . . ."[256] A person who learns of nonpublic information may have a duty under the Rule to inquire as to the source of that information.

A number of cases discuss the disclose-or-abstain requirement. In *Etshokin v. Texasgulf, Inc.*,[257] the court held that Rule 14e-3 required the trader to disclose only the information on which he relied when he decided to trade; the trader was not obliged to disclose that he was contemplating a future purchase. Plaintiffs

---

255. Rule 14e-3(a); Exchange Act Release No. 17120, [1980 Transfer Binder] Fed. Sec. L. Rep. (CCH) ¶ 82,646, at 83,458 (Sept. 4, 1980).

256. Rule 14e-3(a)(3).

257. 612 F. Supp. 1220 (N.D. Ill. 1985).

had argued that defendants, who were negotiating the purchase of a block of Texasgulf stock, had a duty to disclose those negotiations to the investing public before making their purchase. The court held that requiring disclosure of an impending purchase "would be an unreasonable construction of Rule 14e-3 and an unjustified extension of existing case law."[258]

In *O'Connor & Associates v. Dean Witter Reynolds, Inc.*,[259] however, the court refused to dismiss a Rule 14e-3 claim arising from trading in options of a target before the announcement of a proposed tender offer that never actually commenced. The plaintiff had sold to two broker-dealers call options in the target before the announcement of a tender offer for that company. When the offer was announced, the price of the target's stock increased by 50 percent. The plaintiff sued the two broker-dealers, alleging that their customers had purchased the options with knowledge of the proposed tender offer.

In reaching its decision not to dismiss the claim, the court affirmed the SEC's power to adopt Rule 14e-3 and held that the Rule applied to the purchase of call options before the announcement of a proposed tender offer, even though the offer was never launched. The fact that the offer never became effective "does not change the fact that the alleged wrong relates directly to the tender offer bid."[260]

ii. Anti-Tipping Provision

Rule 14e-3(d) proscribes the communication of "material, nonpublic information relating to a tender offer to any other person under circumstances in which it is reasonably foreseeable that such communication is likely to result in a violation of this section. . . ." This anti-tipping provision applies to offerors, issuers, and their officers, directors, partners, employees, advisers, or agents, as well as to "tippees," defined as "[a]ny person in possession of material information relating to a tender

---

258. *Id.* at 1231.

259. 529 F. Supp. 1179 (S.D.N.Y. 1981).

260. *Id.* at 1192.

offer which information he knows or has reason to know is nonpublic and which he knows or has reason to know has been acquired directly or indirectly from any of the above."[261]

The Rule contains a safe harbor for communications made in good faith among the bidder, the target, and their various agents, thus alleviating concerns that the anti-tipping provision could cover participants in the tender offer who need to communicate information to each other about the offer.[262] The Rule also exempts any communications made in good faith to any person pursuant to any statutory or regulatory requirement.[263]

Certain cases have discussed the anti-tipping provision. In *Camelot Industries Corp. v. Vista Resources, Inc.*,[264] for example, the court held that a brokerage house vice president had not violated Rule 14e-3 when he recommended that a broker in his firm purchase Camelot securities, even though the vice president had reason to believe, at the time of his recommendation, that a tender offer for Camelot was imminent. The court ruled that a meeting between the bidder and Camelot, in the presence of the brokerage firm's vice president, constituted a substantial step toward the commencement of a tender offer, thereby triggering the Rule, but that any knowledge that the vice president had regarding a potential tender offer was purely conjectural, because the potential bidder had stated nothing more than its intent to purchase enough Camelot stock to insure that no one else gained control of the company. The potential bidder did not declare that it would accomplish this goal through a tender offer, and the vice president's tipping thus fell outside the scope of the Rule.

In *SEC v. Musella*,[265] however, the court held that the SEC had presented a *prima facie* case of a violation of Rule 14e-3.

---

261. Rule 14e-3(d)(2).

262. Rule 14e-3(d)(1)(i)-(ii).

263. Rule 14e-3(d)(1)(iii).

264. 535 F. Supp. 1174 (S.D.N.Y. 1982).

265. 578 F. Supp. 425 (S.D.N.Y. 1984).

Circumstantial evidence, based upon the timing of trades, suggested that the defendant had traded on nonpublic information obtained from a friend who worked at a New York law firm that was involved in the unannounced tender offers. Because the defendant was a professional in the securities market, the court concluded that he knew that law firms forbid their employees to disclose material, nonpublic information; the defendant therefore knew or should have known that he was trading on improperly obtained, nonpublic information. Similarly, in *SEC v. Wallis*,[266] the court found that a taxicab driver had violated Rule 14e-3 by trading on information concerning a planned tender offer, about which he was tipped by a law firm proofreader.

b. The Continued Vitality of Section 10(b) and Rule 10b-5 in Takeover Settings

Despite the availability of Rule 14e-3, the SEC and private litigants have not given up on section 10(b) and Rule 10b-5 in insider trading cases arising from takeovers. Under *Chiarella v. United States*, however, a possessor of nonpublic information need not disclose that information unless he has a duty to do so as a result of "a relationship of trust and confidence between parties to a transaction."[267]

The Court reiterated this position in *Dirks v. SEC*,[268] a case involving an investment analyst who had received information from corporate insiders revealing that a company was fraudulently hiding its true condition from the public. Before exposing this fraud, however, the analyst selectively tipped some of his clients to allow them to sell their shares of the subject company before the stock's value dropped. The Court held that the tippee analyst (whose duty to disclose or abstain was

---

266. [1984 Transfer Binder] Fed. Sec. L. Rep. (CCH) ¶ 91,562 (S.D.N.Y. May 31, 1984).

267. 445 U.S. 222, 230 (1980).

268. 463 U.S. 646 (1983).

derivative from that of the insider-tippers') had no duty publicly to disclose his information because the corporate insiders had not breached a fiduciary duty in attempting to reveal the fraud.[269]

In assessing the insiders' duty, the Court restated *Chiarella*'s requirement that there be a "specific relationship between the shareholders and the individual[s] trading on inside information. . . ."[270] The test for determining whether an insider has breached his fiduciary duty in disseminating nonpublic information is "whether the insider will benefit, directly or indirectly, from his disclosure. Absent some personal gain, there has been no breach of duty to stockholders."[271] The concept of "personal gain" "requires courts to focus on objective criteria, *i.e.*, whether the insider receives a direct or indirect personal benefit from the disclosure, such as a pecuniary gain or a reputational benefit that will translate into future earnings."[272]

Proof of an insider's breach of fiduciary duty does not itself suffice to establish a tippee's liability under section 10(b) unless the tippee "knows or should know that there has been a breach" by the insider-tipper of his own fiduciary duty.[273] A plaintiff therefore must prove both that the tipper breached his own fiduciary duty and personally benefited from his tipping activity *and* that the tippee knew or should have known of the insider's breach.

The Court also pointed out that lawyers and other corporate advisers can become temporary insiders:

> Under certain circumstances, such as where corporate information is revealed legitimately to an underwriter, accountant, lawyer, or consultant working for [a] corporation, these outsiders may become fiduciaries of the shareholders. The basis for recognizing this fiduciary duty is not simply that such

269. *Id.* at 666-67.
270. *Id.* at 655.
271. *Id.* at 662.
272. *Id.* at 663.
273. *Id.* at 660 (footnote omitted).

> persons acquired nonpublic corporate information, but rather that they have entered into a special confidential relationship in the conduct of the business of the enterprise and are given access to information solely for corporate purposes. . . . When such a person breaches his fiduciary relationship, he may be treated more properly as a tipper than a tippee. . . . For such a duty to be imposed, however, the corporation must expect the outsider to keep the disclosed nonpublic information confidential, and the relationship at least must imply such a duty.[274]

Chiarella and *Dirks* thus stand for the proposition that failure to disclose nonpublic information does not amount to a violation of section 10(b) unless the person using such information has an affirmative duty to disclose it. But there is more to these two cases: while not deciding the issue, the opinions of various Justices gave birth to the "misappropriation" theory of section 10(b) liability, upon which the Government has relied in "[a]lmost all" significant criminal prosecutions for insider trading in recent years.[275]

Four members of the *Chiarella* Court (Chief Justice Burger and Justices Blackmun, Brennan, and Marshall) would have applied section 10(b) to any person who "improperly obtains or converts to his own benefit nonpublic information which he then uses in connection with the purchase or sale of securities."[276] The rule thus would be that "a person who has misappropriated nonpublic information has an absolute duty to disclose that information or to refrain from trading."[277] Under this theory,

---

274. *Id.* at 655 n.14 (citations omitted).

275. Carberry & Romatowski, "Criminal Theories for Prosecution of Insider Trading," in K. Bialkin & A. Matthews, *Insider Trading* 83, 87 (Law Journal Seminars-Press, 1986). Although the Court in *Chiarella* did not rule on the validity of the misappropriation theory, four Justices indicated their approval of some form of it. *See* 445 U.S. at 238-39 (Brennan, J., concurring); *id.* at 239-43 (Burger, C.J., dissenting); *id.* at 245-46 (Blackmun and Marshall, J.J., dissenting). The Court recently discussed the misappropriation theory in favorable terms, stating: "We also have noted that a tippee may be liable if he otherwise 'misappropriate[s] or illegally obtain[s] the information.' " *Eichler v. Berner*, 472 U.S. 299, 105 S. Ct. 2622, 2630 n.22 (1985) (quoting *Dirks*).

276. *Chiarella*, 445 U.S. at 239 (Brennan, J. concurring).

277. *Id.* at 240 (Burger, C.J., dissenting).

Chiarella could have been held liable for misappropriating or converting to his own use nonpublic information conveyed to his employer by tender offerors who expected the financial printer and its employees to treat the information as confidential.[278] *Dirks* may have built on the misappropriation theory by emphasizing the requirement that an insider have received "a direct or indirect personal benefit" from the disclosure or other use of nonpublic information.[279]

The misappropriation theory, then, holds that a person who trades on the basis of inside information defrauds the source of the information, often his employer or the employer's clients. However, the person who breaches this duty by converting or otherwise misusing information need not owe any duty to a purchaser or seller of securities.

This difference poses conceptual difficulties for some commentators, because section 10(b) is supposed to apply to fraud in connection with the purchase or sale of securities.[280] The misappropriation approach punishes one who breaches a fiduciary duty in connection with his own trading and thus seems to eliminate the apparent requirement that a trading party be defrauded. (The theory does recognize, however, that the trader has defrauded the person from whom the information has been misappropriated.) Once this trading is deemed sufficient to satisfy section 10b's "in connection with" requirement, the misappropriation theory permits punishment for trading involving breaches of a broad range of duties.[281] In private

---

278. The *Chiarella* majority discussed but did not decide the merits of this theory because they did not consider it to have been presented to the jury. *Id.* at 235-36. Justice Brennan endorsed the theory but agreed that it had not been put before the jury. *Id.* at 239 (Brennan, J., concurring). Justices Blackmun and Marshall also endorsed the theory but saw no need to reach it. *Id.* at 245-46. (Blackmun and Marshall, J.J., dissenting). Only Chief Justice Burger would have affirmed the conviction on the basis of the misappropriation theory. *Id.* at 240-45 (Burger, C.J., dissenting).

279. *Dirks*, 463 U.S. at 662-63.

280. Report, *supra*, at 236-37.

281. Langevoort, "The Insider Trading Sanctions Act of 1984 and Its Effect on Existing Law," 37 Vand. L. Rev. 1273, 1295-97 (1984).

actions under section 10(b), by contrast, only those plaintiffs who have purchased or sold securities have standing to sue.[282] Because the party to whom a duty is owed under the misappropriation theory normally is not a purchaser or seller of securities, courts generally have limited the use of the theory to SEC civil enforcement actions or criminal prosecutions.

In *Walton v. Morgan Stanley & Co.*,[283] for example, investment bankers representing a potential acquiring company obtained nonpublic information from the target. The bankers later traded on that information for their firm's account, and they disclosed the information to a third company in order to induce it to make an offer for the target. In a decision issued soon after *Chiarella*, the Court of Appeals for the Second Circuit affirmed the dismissal of a derivative action brought by shareholders of the target. Because the investment bankers had obtained the nonpublic information not from a client but, rather, from the target, in arm's-length negotiations in which the target had not sought a confidentiality agreement, the court held that the bankers had not entered into a fiduciary relationship with the target and thus had no duty either to disclose or to abstain from trading.[284]

More recent cases have further clarified the restriction on standing in misappropriation cases. In *Moss v. Morgan Stanley, Inc.*,[285] a private suit for damages, the Court of Appeals for the Second Circuit refused to impose liability for insider trading on a tippee who had traded on behalf of the investment bankers who had tipped him. The bankers had learned the name of a potential target company while representing a would-be acquiror and had tipped the trader in violation of their duty to maintain the confidences of their employers and their employers' clients. The *Moss* court distinguished this case from the criminal prosecution arising out of the same events and restricted the

---

282. *Blue Chip Stamps v. Manor Drug Stores*, 421 U.S. 723 (1975).

283. 623 F.2d 796 (2d Cir. 1980).

284. *Id.* at 798-99.

285. 719 F.2d 5 (2d Cir. 1983), *cert. denied*, 465 U.S. 1025 (1984).

applicability of the misappropriation theory to criminal proceedings and, perhaps, to SEC civil enforcement actions.[286] Private plaintiffs, the court held, could demonstrate fraud only when they could show a breach of a *Chiarella-* or *Dirks*-like fiduciary duty owed directly to them.[287]

However, in *United States v. Newman*, the criminal case involving the same facts, the Court of Appeals confirmed that standing limitations vary depending on the party prosecuting the action: "When litigation under this Rule is instituted by the SEC under Section 21 or by a United States Attorney under Section 32, the court's concern must be with the scope of the Rule, not plaintiff's standing to sue."[288] Applying the misappropriation theory, the court held that the tippers had violated not only their duty to the investment bank that had employed them but also to the bank's clients, "whose takeover plans were keyed to target company stock prices fixed by market forces, not artificially inflated through purchases by purloiners of confidential information."[289] These breaches of trust constituted fraud: "By sullying the reputation of [their] employers as safe repositories of client confidences, appellee and his cohorts defrauded those employers as surely as if they took their money."[290] The tippee's involvement in this fraudulent theft of information satisfied the "in connection with" trading requirement of Rule 10b-5 because the tippee's "sole purpose in participating in the misappropriation of confidential takeover information was to purchase shares of the target companies. . . ."[291]

The Court of Appeals for the Second Circuit later decided an SEC enforcement action with facts reminiscent of those of

---

286. *Id.* at 13, 16.
287. *Id.* at 16.
288. 664 F.2d 12, 17 (2d Cir. 1981), *cert. denied*, 464 U.S. 863 (1983).
289. *Id.* at 17.
290. *Id.*
291. *Id.* at 18.

Chiarella. In *SEC v. Materia*,[292] an employee of a financial printer was charged with having traded in the stock of tender offer targets on the basis of information that he had misappropriated from his employer. Materia did not deny his actions but directly challenged the misappropriation theory. The court upheld an SEC injunction restraining Materia from further trading on misappropriated information and ordering him to disgorge unlawfully obtained profits.[293] Reiterating that it had dismissed the action in *Moss* only because the defendant had owed no duty to the plaintiffs, the court stressed that "such analysis bears only on the type of question raised in a private suit for damages; it is not relevant to an inquiry into whether the Rule was or was not contravened."[294]

The Court of Appeals for the Second Circuit further extended the misappropriation theory in *United States v. Carpenter*,[295] in which the court affirmed the convictions under Rule 10b-5 of three individuals who had made prepublication trades based on their advance knowledge of the contents of 27 "Heard on the Street" columns published in *The Wall Street Journal*. One of the defendants was R. Foster Winans, a reporter who had worked on the columns.

Defendants tried to distinguish *Newman* and *Materia* on the theory that the employees who had misappropriated information in those cases owed duties of confidentiality to their employers' clients as well as to their employers.[296] The Court of Appeals, in a two-to-one decision, rejected this attempt to limit the misappropriation theory to settings in which corporate insiders or quasi-insiders breach their fiduciary duties to persons other than their employers. Observing that the "advance knowledge of the timing and content of these publications" allowed defendants to profit from their trading, the court

---

292. 745 F.2d 197 (2d Cir. 1984), *cert. denied*, 471 U.S. 1053 (1985).

293. *Id.* at 204.

294. *Id.* at 203.

295. 791 F.2d 1024 (2d Cir. 1986), *cert. granted*, 55 U.S.L.W. 3424 (Dec. 16, 1986).

296. 791 F.2d at 1028.

declared that "such conduct constituted fraud and deceit, as it would had Winans stolen material nonpublic information from traditional corporate insiders or quasi-insiders."[297]

In recent years, the SEC has stepped up its efforts to detect and punish insider trading. From fiscal 1982 through fiscal 1985, the Commission brought 77 insider trading enforcement actions—the same number initiated from the SEC's inception in 1934 through fiscal 1981.[298] Prior to 1984, whenever the SEC successfully sought a disgorgement order in a civil case, the guilty trader simply had to return the profits gained or the losses avoided. The Insider Trading Sanctions Act of 1984 now permits the Commission to seek civil penalties of up to three times the trader's profits made or losses avoided.[299] For criminal violations of section 10(b)—or for any federal felony—committed after October 30, 1984, the maximum monetary penalty is twice the loss or gain.[300] Thus, if the SEC sues a trader, and if the Justice Department prosecutes him criminally, federal law permits the imposition of fines totalling five times his profits made or losses avoided.

Armed with these new sanctions and with automated surveillance systems instituted by the stock exchanges, the SEC has focused its resources on market experts. In November 1985, Gary Lynch, Director of the SEC's Division of Enforcement, revealed that the Commission was investigating professionals believed to have planted false takeover rumors in order to profit from the subsequent price swings. He admitted that " '[i]t is much more difficult to detect insider trading when you have someone who is trading 20 stocks a day.' "[301]

---

297. *Id.* at 1031-32.

298. Statement by John Shad, Chairman of the SEC, Before the House Energy Subcomm. on Telecommunications, Consumer Protection, and Finance, June 18, 1986, at 7.

299. 15 U.S.C. § 78u(d)(2)(A). For a complete discussion of the Act, see Langevoort, "The Insider Trading Sanctions Act of 1984 and Its Effect on Existing Law," 37 Vand. L. Rev. 1273 (1984).

300. 18 U.S.C. § 3623(e)(3) and (c)(1).

301. "SEC Probing Insider Trading by Market Professionals," *The Washington Post*, Nov. 5, 1985, at El, col. 1.

During 1986, the Commission obtained indictments and convictions that shook Wall Street and threatened to change how business is conducted there. The SEC's efforts, however, seemed to have little effect on price run-ups in the stocks of takeover targets prior to acquisition announcements. The SEC's chief economist, Gregg Jarrell, stated that he did not believe that illegal insider trading ever was a major factor in the price run-ups: " 'Ninety-five percent of it [the run-ups],' " he said, " 'is the market for information. Most of it is traders watching stocks and listening to the rumor mills, which is [sic] fed in legitimate, but highly creative ways. Insider trading is just a speck in there.' "[302]

In May 1986, the SEC brought what was until then its largest (in terms of dollar amount) insider trading case: an action against Dennis Levine, a managing director at the investment banking firm of Drexel Burnham Lambert; two Panamanian corporations that Levine had created to aid his scheme; and Bernhard Meier, a Swiss citizen and Levine's broker for trades made through a Bahamian subsidiary of a Swiss bank.[303] The Commission alleged that, since May 1980, Levine had made $12.6 million by trading in the stocks of at least 54 companies while in possession of material, nonpublic information concerning mergers, tender offers, leveraged buy-outs, and other changes in corporate control that were likely to increase the value of securities traded. At the time that the SEC brought these charges under sections 10(b) and 14(e) and Rules 10b-5 and 14e-3, Levine was 33 years old and earned more than $1 million a year in salary and bonuses.

Levine allegedly had gathered much of his information concerning pending transactions from his work at Drexel, which is the industry leader in junk bond placement. However, many of the deals from which Levine had profited had not involved corporations that his firm represented. This fact suggested that some of his information had come from arbitrageurs and others

---

302. "Spotlight on the Insiders: Wall Streeters Wonder If Levine Case Has Curbed Criminal Trading," *The Washington Post*, Sept. 21, 1986, at D1, D5.

303. *SEC v. Levine*, 86 Civ. 3726 (S.D.N.Y. May 12, 1986) (Complaint).

whom he regularly had approached to learn about market developments. Many commentators suggested that the Levine case revealed a new and discouraging Wall Street ethic of seeking quick wealth at any cost.

From the start, Levine allegedly had tried to hide his off-shore trading. He had used the code name "Mr. Diamond" and had placed his orders by collect calls from pay phones in New York. When he visited his bank in the Bahamas, he used an alias and often changed planes en route. Apparently, he never even told his wife of his trades. In testimony before the SEC in 1984, he falsely denied that he had traded in the stock of Textron, Inc. The SEC accused him of obstructing its investigation and ultimately sought emergency injunctive relief to freeze assets that it believed Levine was attempting to transfer out of the Government's reach.

On June 5, 1986, Levine entered into a consent decree with the SEC to resolve the pending civil insider trading charges.[304] Although he neither admitted nor denied the allegations, Levine agreed to disgorge $11.6 million and consented to the issuance of an administrative order barring him from the securities business for life.[305] The same day, he pleaded guilty to one count of perjury (stemming from his denial concerning his trading in Textron stock), two counts of tax evasion, and one count of trading on inside information in buying stock in the Jewel Companies.[306]

Levine had faced a possible penalty of 20 years in prison on the four counts to which he had pleaded guilty. However, because he allegedly had traded illegally in at least 54 stocks, the Wall Street community assumed that Levine had received lenient treatment in exchange for naming those who had furnished information to him. Throughout the summer, other

---

304. *SEC v. Levine*, Litigation Release No. 11117, [Current] Fed. Sec. L. Rep. (CCH) ¶ 92,761 (June 5, 1986).

305. Exchange Act Release No. 34-23300, 35 SEC Docket 1059 (June 5, 1986).

306. "Wall Street Firms Disavow Report of Insider Inquiry," *The New York Times*, June 10, 1986, at D5, col. 1.

names surfaced, including those of employees of some of the most respected firms in investment banking and arbitrage.[307]

On November 14, 1986, the SEC, widening its insider trading dragnet, brought judicial and administrative enforcement proceedings against Ivan F. Boesky, Wall Street's leading arbitrageur, for violations of the antifraud provisions of the federal securities laws arising from his trading on behalf of certain unspecified "affiliated entities" over which he had exercised investment or managerial control.[307a] The SEC alleged that Boesky, on behalf of the affiliated entities, had traded in the securities of at least seven United States companies based upon material, nonpublic information concerning tender offers, mergers, or other business combinations or extraordinary corporate transactions. The source of Boesky's inside information, according to the SEC, was Dennis Levine.

On the same day that the SEC filed its complaint in federal court in New York City, Boesky agreed to forgo a trial, to accept the entry of a judicial decree, and to pay over funds and assets to the United States Treasury. Boesky settled the SEC civil enforcement proceeding by agreeing to disgorge $50 million in trading profits and to pay another $50 million as a civil penalty. In settling a related SEC administrative proceeding, Boesky agreed to the SEC's entry of an order barring him from the securities industry for life. He also agreed to plead guilty to one unspecified criminal charge.

The SEC alleged in its complaint that for at least a one-year period—February 1985 through February 1986—Boesky had traded in the securities of at least seven companies about which Levine had provided material, nonpublic information

---

307. *Id.* Two of Levine's confederates settled SEC suits against them. *See SEC v. Wilkis*, Litigation Release No. 11145, 36 SEC Docket 50 (S.D.N.Y. July 1, 1986); *SEC v. Sokolow*, Litigation Release No. 11146, 36 SEC Docket 51 (S.D.N.Y. July 1, 1986).

307a. *SEC v. Boesky*, Litigation Release No. 11288 (SEC Nov. 14, 1986); *SEC v. Boesky*, No. 86 Civ. 8767 (S.D.N.Y. filed Nov. 14, 1986); "Big Trader to Pay U.S. $100 Million for Insider Abuses," *The New York Times*, Nov. 15, 1986, at Al, col. 6.

concerning imminent tender offers, mergers, or other significant corporate events. According to the complaint, Boesky and Levine agreed in the spring of 1985 that Boesky would pay five percent of his profits to Levine in those instances where the inside information provided to Boesky formed the initial basis for the purchase of securities by entities under Boesky's control. In those instances where the information provided by Levine was merely material to Boesky's decision to hold or to increase his holdings of a specific security, Boesky would pay Levine a lesser amount (one percent). The complaint also alleged that, in or about April 1986, Boesky and Levine had agreed that, at a future time, Boesky would pay Levine approximately $2.4 million pursuant to their compensation arrangement. Boesky had not paid Levine anything by the time Levine was sued by the SEC and arrested.

The $50 million in allegedly illegal profits that Boesky disgorged is to be applied to pay persons whom a court finds to have valid claims under the federal securities laws against Boesky or his trading entities arising from the securities transactions alleged in the complaint. If any portion of this $50 million cash payment remains after claimants have been satisfied, the remainder is to be used, pursuant to a court-approved plan, to pay persons whom the court finds to have other valid claims against Boesky or the entities over which he exercised control. The $50 million civil penalty is to be held for the benefit of the United States Treasury.

Within a week of the SEC's settlement with Boesky, the first of what ultimately may be many law suits was filed against him. Angelo Oriolo, a retired businessman who claimed that he was defrauded when he sold 100 shares of General Foods Corporation, filed a class action intended, according to Oriolo's lawyer, "to bring redress to all the public investors who sold their shares at a time when they did not have the material information that Mr. Boesky got illegally." The suit, which raises state law fraud and federal law anti-racketeering and securities claims, seeks to recover damages from Boesky's personal holdings as well as from the $50 million fund created when Boesky disgorged his illegal profits.[307b]

Another well known target of SEC investigations was W. Paul Thayer, Deputy Secretary of Defense in the first Reagan Administration and a successful businessman who had served as chairman of LTV Corp. and as a director of Anheuser-Busch Cos., Inc. ("Busch"), and Allied Corp. During 1984 and 1985, Thayer's world crumbled when the SEC accused him of tipping his associates about inside information concerning forthcoming acquisitions, of which Thayer had learned in his capacity as a corporate director. The Commission obtained a consent decree pursuant to which Thayer and the others neither denied nor admitted guilt but agreed to disgorge over $1 million in trading profits.[308]

Thayer's and an associate's elaborate attempts to impede the SEC's investigation proved more sensational. They both pleaded guilty to charges of obstructing justice and received four-year prison terms. The federal prosecutor described Thayer's behavior as "rampant obstruction of justice by an individual who served at the pinnacle of corporate and governmental power."

Thayer's troubles were not over, however, for Busch (of which Thayer had been a director) subsequently brought a private damages action against him, the other defendants, and some of their employers. Busch had made a tender offer for Campbell Taggart, Inc. ("CTI") and alleged that defendants' illegal trading had caused the price of CTI's stock to rise dramatically, thereby increasing the total cost of the CTI acquisition. In its complaint, Busch sought $80 million in compensatory damages (to be trebled under RICO).

The SEC, in a strategic move unusual at the district court level, submitted an amicus curiae brief in support of the

---

307b. *Oriolo v. Boesky*, 86 Civ. 8676 (S.D.N.Y. filed Nov. 20, 1986); "Investor Suit Filed Against Boesky," *The New York Times*, Nov. 21, 1986, at D6, col. 1.

308. *SEC v. Thayer*, Litigation Release No. 10746, 33 SEC Docket 76 (May 7, 1985).

misappropriation theory (an issue of first impression in the Fifth Circuit) and of Busch's right to sue for damages in a private action based on that theory.[309] (The SEC was advancing the latter argument for the first time.) The Commission distinguished *Moss*, which had held that defendants owed no duty to—and thus did not defraud—the shareholders of the target. In the instant case, the Commission argued, Busch had been defrauded by Thayer and his colleagues and could press a private Rule 10b-5 action as long as Busch met the statutory requirements for such an action, including that of being a purchaser or seller of securities.

The Commission also contended that the court should not apply the normal Rule 10b-5 standing requirement that a plaintiff have traded contemporaneously with those who traded on inside information. Because the fraud in a misappropriation case stems from the misuse of information, rather than from one's trading with the defendant, the SEC asserted that the fraud continues until the insider trading is discovered, as long as the fraud is causally connected with later transactions by the defrauded party. In August 1986, the district court denied defendants' motion for summary judgment and ruled that the complaint stated claims upon which relief could be granted under Rule 10b-5.[310]

In a similar action, Litton Industries has sued Dennis Levine and his associates, claiming that defendants' insider trading in the stock of Itel Corporation artificially inflated the price of that stock and caused Litton to spend extra money to take over that company.[310a] At the time of the takeover, Levine had been working in the mergers and acquisitions department of Lehman Brothers, which Litton had hired as its adviser for the Itel deal.

---

309. Memorandum of the SEC, Amicus Curiae, *Anheuser-Busch Cos., Inc. v. Thayer*, CA3-85-0794-R (N.D. Tex).

310. *Anheuser-Busch Cos., Inc. v. Thayer*, CA3-85-0794-R (N.D. Tex. Aug. 19, 1986).

310a. *Litton Indus., Inc. v. Lehman Bros. Kuhn Loeb Inc.*, 86 Civ. 6447 (S.D.N.Y. filed Aug. 20, 1986).

11. Other Rules

a. *Rule 10b-4*

Rule 10b-4,[311] which the SEC promulgated pursuant to the Exchange Act's general antifraud provision, proscribes "short tendering" by persons responding to a partial tender offer. The Rule forbids a person to tender a security unless he owns the security (or an equivalent security) both at the time of tender and at the end of the proration period. A person is deemed to own a security only to the extent that he has a net long position in that stock.

The Rule attempts to prevent investors from tendering, in a partial tender offer, more shares than they actually own, in the hope of increasing the number of their shares that the bidder actually will accept after proration. *SEC v. Weisberger* describes the effects of such a ploy:

> When a proration in fact occurs, the short tender acts to the detriment of each individual shareholder who tenders only the shares he actually owns; were no shares short tendered a greater number of those shares legally tendered would be purchased by the offeror. On a larger scale the practice leads to the disruption of the trading market in the security tendered following expiration of the tender offer as persons purchase the security to cover their short positions. Thus, a short tender results in both a manipulation of the normal pro rata requirements and a disruption of the securities markets, irrespective of the method of tender.[312]

Rule 10b-4 applies both to persons tendering securities for their own account and to those tendering securities for the account of others. Persons acting in an agency capacity are forbidden to tender securities unless they either possess the securities or reasonably believe that their principal owns the

---

311. 17 C.F.R. § 240.10b-4 (1986).

312. [1974-1975 Transfer Binder] Fed. Sec. L. Rep. (CCH) ¶ 95,108, at 97,942 (S.D.N.Y. 1975).

securities or their equivalent and will deliver them. Borrowed securities are not owned for purposes of the Rule.[313] The term "tender" is defined as the delivery, guarantee of delivery, or any other method of acceptance of a tender offer.

Rule 10b-4 also prohibits "hedged tendering," a practice whereby an investor either tenders securities to more than one tender offeror or sells his securities in the open market and also tenders them to the bidder. By hedging, the investor attempts to sell that portion of his securities that he estimates will not be accepted by the partial tender offeror once proration has occurred. Of course, if the shareholder withdraws tendered securities from the initial tender offer, he may retender them in a second offer or sell them in the open market.

Judicial interpretation of Rule 10b-4 has been minimal. The early case of *SEC v. Weisberger*[314] suggested that simple negligence sufficed to constitute a violation of the Rule and that scienter need not be proved, at least in the context of an SEC enforcement proceeding. However, the Supreme Court implicitly overruled *Weisberger* in *Aaron v. SEC*,[315] which held that the SEC must establish scienter in a civil enforcement action to enjoin violations of section 10(b) and Rule 10b-5 (but need not establish scienter in an action to enjoin violations of section 17).

Another early case, *Bache & Co. v. International Controls Corp.*,[316] established a *de minimis* exception to Rule 10b-4, holding that the Rule did not apply to a short tender of "minor proportions" where the tendering person did not act with specific intent to defraud. Bache & Co., on behalf of its clients, had tendered 30,649 shares to a bidder and then discovered that it had short-tendered 148 shares because of an error caused by duplicate customer orders. The next day, Bache purchased

---

313. *Amswiss Int'l Corp.* (SEC No Action Letter) (available July 9, 1973).

314. [1974-1975 Transfer Binder] Fed. Sec. L. Rep. (CCH) ¶ 95,108 (S.D.N.Y. 1975).

315. 446 U.S. 680 (1980).

316. 324 F. Supp. 998 (S.D.N.Y. 1971), *aff'd*, 469 F.2d 696 (2d Cir. 1972).

sufficient shares to cover its short tender. When Bache brought a contract action against the bidder based on the latter's failure to purchase the tendered shares, the court did not permit the bidder to assert a Rule 10b-4 defense and held the bidder liable for rejecting the broker-dealer's tender.

b. Rule 10b-13

Rule 10b-13[317] provides that, from the time a tender offer is publicly announced until the time it expires, a tender offeror may not directly or indirectly purchase or arrange to purchase, other than pursuant to the tender offer, securities that are the subject of that offer. This Rule, which attempts to prevent manipulation of the market during a tender offer, prohibits the offeror from making either open-market or privately negotiated purchases until the tender offer is concluded or withdrawn.

The mere filing of a Schedule 13D disclosing an intention to acquire control of a company, possibly through a tender offer, usually is not considered a public announcement of a tender offer for purposes of Rule 10b-13.[318] The Rule does not preclude the conversion of previously owned securities into the subject security. Purchases made before public announcement of the tender offer do not violate the Rule, even if the purchaser had already decided to make the offer.[319] But purchase agreements scheduled to close during the offering period will violate the Rule, even if the agreements were made before public announcement of the offer.

---

317. 17 C.F.R. § 240.10b-13 (1986).

318. *Jewelcor, Inc.*, [1974-1975 Transfer Binder] Fed. Sec. L. Rep. (CCH) ¶ 80,014 (SEC Sept. 11, 1974). *But see United Brands Co.*, [1972-1973 Transfer Binder] Fed. Sec. L. Rep. (CCH) ¶ 79,268 (SEC Dec. 19, 1972) (public announcement that corporations may conduct exchange offer for $80 million in convertible debentures triggers Rule 10b-13, precluding the purchase of $10 million of such securities in open-market and privately negotiated transactions).

319. *Sunshine Mining Co. v. Great Western United Corp.*, [1977-1978 Transfer Binder] Fed. Sec. L. Rep. (CCH) ¶ 96,049 (D. Idaho April 22, 1977); *Heine v. Signal Cos.*, [1976-1977 Transfer Binder] Fed. Sec. L. Rep. (CCH) ¶ 95,898 (S.D.N.Y. March 4, 1977).

C. Section 16 of the Exchange Act

Section 16 of the Exchange Act[320] attempts to deter controlling persons ("insiders") from engaging in unfair trading practices. The section defines insiders as officers or directors of an issuer or as beneficial owners of ten percent or more of the issuer's equity securities. Once a tender offeror beneficially owns ten percent of the target's securities, it becomes an insider for purposes of section 16.

1. Section 16(a)

Section 16(a) of the Exchange Act and the SEC's ancillary rules require insiders to report any acquisition or sale of the issuer's securities. Such persons must file a Form 3 with the SEC within ten days of becoming insiders. The Form 3 is a simple document that discloses the amount and type of ownership interest that the insider holds in the issuer's securities. Section 16(a) also requires insiders to file a Form 4 upon any subsequent change in their beneficial ownership of the issuer's securities. This form must be filed within ten days after the end of any month in which such change in beneficial ownership occurred.

Insiders must file the Forms 3 and 4 with the SEC and with the exchange on which the issuer's securities are traded. If the securities are traded on more than one exchange, the issuer may select one exchange to receive the Forms.

Although the Exchange Act does not define "beneficial ownership," the Rules offer some guidelines. Rule 16a-2(b)[321] states that a person beneficially owns securities that he "has the right to acquire through the exercise of presently exercisable options, warrants or rights or through the conversion of presently convertible securities." Cases have held that the

320. 15 U.S.C. § 78p.

321. 17 C.F.R. § 240.16a-2(b) (1986).

ten-percent threshold requirement is computed by assuming "full dilution" of the underlying securities as a result of the exercise of conversion rights.[322]

Section 16(a)'s reporting requirements attempt to subject changes in beneficial ownership (which may indicate shifts in corporate control) to public scrutiny. The requirements also cause insiders to provide certain information needed to trigger the more draconian remedies of section 16(b).

2. Section 16(b)

Section 16(b)[323] seeks to deter improper trading and speculative abuse by requiring insiders to disgorge all profits earned in short-term transactions involving the issuer's securities. The disgorgement requirement does not depend on any wrongdoing by the insider. Section 16(b) applies to all persons who must disclose beneficial ownership under section 16(a), although reporting under section 16(a) will not necessarily lead to potential liability under section 16(b).[324]

Liability under section 16(b) arises whenever an insider makes "any purchase and sale, or any sale and purchase, of any equity security of [the] issuer . . . within any period of less than six months, unless such security was acquired in good faith in connection with a debt previously contracted. . . ." The insider

---

322. *See Foremost-McKesson, Inc. v. Provident Secs. Co.*, 423 U.S. 232 (1976); *Chemical Fund, Inc. v. Xerox Corp.*, 377 F.2d 107 (2d Cir. 1967).

323. 15 U.S.C. § 78p(b).

324. *Whittaker v. Whittaker Corp.*, 639 F.2d 516, 526 (9th Cir.), *cert. denied*, 454 U.S. 1031 (1981), held that an insider should be found liable under § 16(b) "only following a determination by the trial court not simply that the requirements of beneficial ownership were met for purposes of the § 16(a) reporting requirement, but that actual rewards of ownership were sufficiently present to warrant attributing the stock to the insider for purposes of § 16(b)." Likewise, *Colan v. Monumental Corp.*, 713 F.2d 330 (7th Cir. 1983), states that "we must [not] blindingly apply § 16(b) to every person who falls within the ambit of § 16(a)." However, one still must read § 16(b) in light of § 16(a) in order to determine who is liable under § 16(b).

must disgorge any profits realized from such short-term transactions, and those profits "shall inure to and be recoverable by the issuer, irrespective of any intention on the part of such [insider] in entering into such transaction of holding the security purchased or of not repurchasing the security sold for a period exceeding six months." For purposes of determining the existence of a short-term transaction within the meaning of the statute, any purchase can be matched with any sale within a six-month period.

The Exchange Act, however, does not adequately define when a sale and purchase will be deemed to have occurred. Cases suggest that the terms "purchase" and "sale," regardless of their meanings in other contexts, shall be construed under section 16(b) in a way that will effectuate the purposes of that section,[325] and courts tend to conclude that a transaction falls within section 16(b) only if the conduct at issue possibly can lead to insiders' abuse of nonpublic information.[326] According to *Bershad v. McDonough*, "[a]pplicability of this section may depend upon the factual circumstances of the transaction and whether the insider is 'purchasing' or 'selling the security.' "[327] Even a firm commitment to buy, without a fixed price, does not itself necessarily constitute a purchase under section 16(b).[328]

---

325. *See Bershad v. McDonough*, 428 F.2d 693, 696 (7th Cir. 1970), *cert. denied*, 400 U.S. 992 (1971) (although the parties considered the transaction to be the granting of an option, court considered it a sale of securities for purposes of § 16(b)); *cf. SEC v. National Secs., Inc.*, 393 U.S. 453, 467 (1969) (discussing definition of purchase and sale to effectuate the purposes of the Exchange Act in the context of § 10(b)).

326. *See Blau v. Lamb*, 363 F.2d 507, 518 (2d Cir. 1966), *cert. denied*, 385 U.S. 1002 (1967) (holding § 16(b) inapplicable where common stock was converted to its economic equivalent in preferred stock, where there was no change of investment position, and where there was no opportunity for gain or speculative trading); *Blau v. Lehman*, 286 F.2d 786, 792 (2d Cir. 1960), *aff'd*, 368 U.S. 403 (1962) (finding § 16(b) liability where common stock was exchanged for preferred stock, leading to speculative abuse).

327. 428 F.2d 693, 697 (7th Cir. 1970), *cert. denied*, 400 U.S. 992 (1971).

328. *See Booth v. Varian Assocs.*, 334 F.2d 1 (1st Cir. 1964), *cert. denied*, 379 U.S. 961 (1965) (in determining which of two dates was the date of "purchase," court selected the date more likely to lead to speculative abuse).

Likewise, the date on which title passes might not control over purchase and sale dates to which the parties have stipulated.[329]

Case law under section 16(b) suggests that a sale or purchase will result only when all conditions to the transaction have been satisfied. Thus, an insider acquires stock for purposes of section 16(b) only when he has "incurred an irrevocable liability" to take and pay for the stock and when his "rights and obligations become fixed."[330] *Portnoy v. Revlon, Inc.*,[331] for example, held that neither a letter of intent to merge nor a merger agreement, both of which were subject to conditions, constituted a sale of shares by insiders. And the Court of Appeals for the Seventh Circuit held that, when a corporate insider became committed to acquire stock and paid for it, he purchased the stock for purposes of the Exchange Act even though the stock was subject to resale restrictions for five years.[332]

In *Heublein, Inc. v. General Cinema Corp.*,[333] the Court of Appeals for the Second Circuit confronted the issue whether a "sale" for section 16(b) purposes occurred when a hostile bidder automatically exchanged the target shares that it had acquired for shares of the white knight with which the target had merged. According to Supreme Court precedent, only " 'unorthodox' transactions" (such as the merger of a target into a white knight)

---

329. *Morales v. Reading & Bates Offshore Drilling Co.*, 392 F. Supp. 41, 44 (N.D. Okla. 1975) (holding that no purchase occurs within the meaning of § 16(b) until the purchaser assumes irrevocable liability, which arises not when he simply proceeds in a plan to exercise an option and takes collateral steps but only when he actually purchases the options).

330. *Blau v. Ogsbury*, 210 F.2d 426 (2d Cir. 1954).

331. 650 F.2d 895 (7th Cir. 1981).

332. *See Freeman v. Decio*, 584 F.2d 186, 200 (7th Cir. 1978); *see also Stella v. Graham-Paige Motors Corp.*, 232 F.2d 299 (2d Cir.), *cert. denied*, 352 U.S. 831 (1956) (holding that no purchase occurred within meaning of § 16(b) because purchase contract provided that the buyer could terminate the agreement if he were unable to obtain financing); *Lewis v. Realty Equities Corp. of N.Y.*, 396 F. Supp. 1026 (S.D.N.Y. 1975) (holding that transaction resembled an option and that purchase therefore occurred only upon exercise of the option, at which time rights and obligations became fixed).

333. 722 F.2d 29 (2d Cir. 1983), *cert. denied*, 465 U.S. 1066 (1984).

even permit debate as to whether there has been a "sale" subject to strict section 16(b) liability.[334] The *Heublein* court refused to conclude that the bidder's tactics were "beyond reproach, moral or legal."[335] However, the court held that a strict liability statute such as section 16(b) does not apply to

> the *class* of cases of which the present case is representative, where (1) an atmosphere of suspicion, if not hostility, characterizes relations between the two corporations, (2) the exchange of shares is "involuntary" in that it is effectuated pursuant to a merger over which the investing corporation exercised no control or influence, and (3) there is no likelihood of access to material inside information. . . .[336]

By contrast, a district court recently permitted a successor corporation to sue under section 16(b) for short-swing profits earned by a company that had aggressively threatened its predecessor with a hostile takeover and effectively greenmailed its eventual white knight acquiror.[337] Because the bidder voluntarily elected a cash-for-stock transaction within six months, it faced strict liability. The court declared that "the lack of actual insider knowledge and the resulting lack of actual insider abuse is only relevant in those section 16(b) claims that involve unorthodox transactions."[338]

Persons who are neither officers nor directors of an issuer have no reporting obligation under section 16(a) until such time as they become owners of more than ten percent of a class of equity securities registered under section 12 of the Exchange Act; nor need they comply with section 16(a) once their ownership slips below the ten-percent level (although they must file a Form 4 disclosing that decrease in holdings). Because the last sentence of

---

334. *See Kern County Land Co. v Occidental Petroleum Corp.*, 411 U.S. 582, 593-95 (1973) (footnote omitted).

335. 722 F.2d at 31.

336. *Id.* (emphasis in original).

337. *Bunker Ramo-Eltra Corp. v. Fairchild Indus., Inc.*, 639 F. Supp. 409 (D. Md. 1986).

338. *Id.* at 417-18.

section 16(b) (which states that the provision "shall not be construed to cover any transaction where [a ten-percent beneficial] owner was not such both at the time of the purchase and sale, or the sale and purchase of the security involved") is usually read literally, section 16(b) does not apply to beneficial owners who have but "one leg in" a registered security. Hence, the Supreme Court has held that a purchase that puts the beneficial owner over the ten-percent mark does not count as a purchase for purposes of section 16(b); only those purchases made subsequent to the purchase that made the person a ten-percent holder can be matched with subsequent sales occurring within six months and resulting in profit.[339]

3. Exemptions from Section 16(b) Liability

The SEC's Rule 16b-7[340] exempts from section 16(b) liability the acquisition and disposition of shares pursuant to a merger or consolidation of companies where 85 percent or more of the assets or securities of one company is owned by the other company. The rationale for this exemption is that "such transactions are relatively of minor importance to shareholders . . . , do not present significant opportunities to insiders to profit by advance information concerning the merger . . . [and] do not significantly alter in an economic sense the type of security that the insider held prior to the transaction."[341] Rule 16b-7 typically applies when a company reincorporates in a different state or reorganizes its corporate structure. No Action Letters discussing Rule 16b-7(a)(3) tend to deal with situations in which a holding company is superimposed on an existing corporation.

Also exempt from section 16(b) is "[a]ny acquisition or disposition of an equity security involved in the conversion of an equity security" that, by its terms or the terms of the corporate

---

339. *Foremost-McKesson, Inc. v. Prudent Secs. Co.*, 423 U.S. 232 (1976).

340. 17 C.F.R. § 240.16b-7 (1986).

341. Exchange Act Release No. 18114, 46 Fed. Reg. 48,147 (Sept. 24, 1981).

charter, is convertible into another equity security of the same issuer.[342] In addition, transactions involving the deposit or withdrawal of securities under a voting trust or deposit agreement may, under certain circumstances, be exempt.[343]

4. Amount of Liability

The amount recoverable from an insider under section 16(b) is limited to the profit that the insider realized from the short-term transaction(s) at issue. Because section 16(b) attempts to "squeeze all possible profits" out of short-swing transactions, courts usually calculate those profits by matching a purchase (or sale) with any sale (or purchase) that occurs within a six-month period.[344] Nevertheless, it often is difficult to determine the amount of profit realized for section 16(b) purposes.

The Exchange Act does not define the term "profit"; most courts therefore have applied to the term the ordinary meaning of "gain" and "the excess of the price received over the price paid for goods sold."[345] As *Stella v. Graham-Paige Motors Corp.*[346] held, "[t]o determine 'actual' profit, 'actual' cost must be sought—at least to the extent of ascertaining whether any profit resulted from the sale."

---

342. Rule 16b-9, 17 C.F.R. § 240.16b-9 (1986).

343. *See* Rule 16b-8, *id.* § 240.16b-8.

344. *See Smolowe v. Delendo Corp.*, 136 F.2d 231 (2d Cir.), *cert. denied*, 320 U.S. 751 (1943) (discussing the matching of the lowest purchase price with the highest sale price within a six-month period).

345. *See Heli-Coil Corp. v. Webster*, 352 F.2d 156, 167 (3d Cir. 1965) (holding that director who converted debentures into common stock when each debenture was substantially the economic equivalent of the common stock did not realize a profit at such time; however, the director did realize a profit on the subsequent sale of the common stock within six months).

346. 259 F.2d 476, 479 (2d Cir. 1958), *cert. denied*, 359 U.S. 914 (1959) (holding that corporation that sold stock within six months of acquisition did not realize profit on sale; although corporation used certain cost figures for income tax returns and SEC filings, court permitted corporation to use other cost figures to show no profit under § 16(b)).

Many cases hold that, where a person converts stock into or exchanges stock for other stock, and where there is no market value for the converted or exchanged stock at the time of such conversion or exchange, the stock may be valued by looking to the market price of the stock or interest received.[347] Similarly, the value of stock that is not traded can be equated with the value of the assets delivered in exchange for that stock.[348]

Where stock is acquired for property, either tangible or intangible, the cost of the stock should be computed by reference to the value of the assets delivered in exchange. According to *Marquette Cement Manufacturing Co. v. Andreas,* "[t]he law is clear that the purchase price in a short-swing transaction is the value of the consideration given up for the newly acquired stock."[349]

D. Tender Offer Methods

In addition to acquiring a toehold position in the target and resolving any questions involving section 13(d) of the Exchange Act, a prospective tender offeror must make certain decisions concerning takeover strategy. If it desires to acquire all of the shares of the target, the offeror must first decide whether to launch a cash tender offer for all shares or whether to make a partial offer for only a certain percentage of the outstanding

---

347. *B.T. Babbitt, Inc. v. Lachner,* 332 F.2d 255, 258 (2d Cir. 1964) (holding that no profit was realized when preferred stock with no market value was converted into common stock, and that preferred stock exchanged was worth only the market value of the common stock received).

348. *Stella v. Graham-Paige Motors Corp.,* 259 F.2d 476 (2d Cir. 1958), *cert. denied,* 359 U.S. 914 (1959). The court also held that recoverable profit should be calculated by matching the costs of the stock acquired by exchange with the highest market price of the common stock on the date of disposition by conversion, and not with the average price on that date. *See also Blau v. Lamb,* 242 F. Supp. 151 (S.D.N.Y. 1965), *aff'd in part, rev'd in part,* 363 F.2d 507 (2d Cir. 1966), *cert. denied,* 385 U.S. 1002 (1967) (discussing § 16(b) profits).

349. 239 F. Supp. 962, 967-68 (S.D.N.Y. 1965).

shares and to follow up with a merger on terms less advantageous to the target's shareholders (a "two-tier, front-end-loaded tender offer"). Each method has its advantages and disadvantages, and the target must consider the relevant federal and state securities and corporation laws in determining how to proceed.

1. Cash Tender Offers for All Shares

A cash tender offer for all of the target's shares may allow a bidder to obtain control of a target without having to defend against claims of coercion and possible unfairness to shareholders that the target might raise if the bidder were to proceed by means of a two-tier, front-end-loaded offer.[350] Such claims occasionally lead courts to uphold a target's defensive measures, to the chagrin of the bidder.

Prior to the 1986 amendments to the tender offer rules, a 100 percent cash offer had a time advantage over a partial offer, because the 100 percent bidder could commence purchasing tendered securities as soon as the 15-day withdrawal period for those securities expired, while the maker of a partial offer could not purchase shares until the twentieth business day—the date on which the offer expired. This difference resulted from the fact that a partial offeror must purchase shares on a pro rata basis, and proration continues throughout the offering period. The 1986 amendments, however, eliminated this time advantage for 100 percent offers by making the withdrawal right period for all offers coterminous with the offering period.

More important are the certainty and quantifiability of all-cash offers. Shareholders who tender their shares in response to such an offer know the amount of money that they will receive and the number of shares that they will be able to unload. Courts thus might look less favorably on the target management's defensive measures than they might in the case of

350. Two-tier offers are discussed in § II.4.D(2), *infra*.

a partial or two-tier offer, which can be characterized as unfair to the target's shareholders.

An all-cash tender offer—unlike an exchange offer,[351] in which securities constitute all or part of the consideration (requiring the filing of a registration statement)—permits the bidder to keep its plans secret and to avoid affecting the market for the target's securities before the offer is launched. Secrecy is of particular importance to a bidder planning a hostile tender offer because the success of such an offer will depend, in part, on the surprise it generates. Secrecy accords the bidder flexibility in deciding when—or whether—to make the offer, and it limits the time available to the target to implement defensive measures or to locate a white knight.

The SEC recently adopted Form S-4, which simplifies the disclosure requirements for exchange offers by applying the principles of integrated disclosure[352] to disclosures made in the context of mergers and exchange offers. Thus, Form S-4 requires the same level of disclosure about the target or the bidder as would be required if each company were filing a Form S-1, S-2, or S-3, as appropriate.[353] The new form, however, still does not

---

351. Exchange offers are discussed in § II.4.D(3), *infra*.

352. Integrated disclosure simplifies disclosure requirements under the Securities Act and the Exchange Act by reducing overlaps in filings while still requiring the provision of meaningful, nonduplicative information. *See* Special Report, 1982 Integrated Disclosure Adoptions, Fed. Sec. L. Rep. (CCH) No. 956 (March 11, 1982).

353. A Form S-1 is the basic long-form registration statement generally used by registrants not qualified to use one of the other forms. The S-1 is generally used either by issuers that are filing a registration statement for the first time or by small public companies. If the registrant has filed under the Exchange Act for at least three years, it may use a Form S-2, which is less descriptive than a Form S-1 and incorporates certain Exchange Act filings by reference. A registrant may use a Form S-3 if the registrant (a) has reported under the Exchange Act for three years and (b) has either (i) $150 million or more of voting stock held by non-affiliates or (ii) $100 million of voting stock held by non-affiliates and has an annual trading volume of three million shares. A Form S-3 is much less detailed than the other forms and incorporates much information by reference. There are numerous other registration forms that can be used in specific situations.

allow a bidder to preserve precommencement secrecy with respect to its exchange offer.

In adopting Form S-4, the SEC specifically accepted its Tender Offer Advisory Committee's Recommendation 11, which urged application of the principles of integrated disclosure to business combinations. The SEC, however, specifically rejected the Advisory Committee's Recommendation 12, which would have permitted an exchange offer to commence on a preliminary registration statement's date of filing, rather than on its date of effectiveness, thus putting exchange offers on the same timetable as cash tender offers. An exchange offer therefore remains an inadequate means of launching a secret, hostile tender offer, because the prospective bidder must file a preliminary registration statement—which is a matter of public record—well before commencing the exchange offer.

Although the 100 percent cash tender offer involves a maximum payout of cash to acquire the equity interest in the target, a cash offer can involve lower transaction costs than can other forms of takeovers because it does not require the bidder to incur the additional expenses associated with preparing and distributing registration statements covering the bidder's securities. Unlike a bidder who must file a registration statement, the cash offeror seeking all of the target's outstanding shares need not fully describe its business or provide pro forma financial statements.

The bidder also might find it advantageous to pay cash for an acquisition to avoid diluting its own equity through the issuance of additional equity securities. But some of the target's larger shareholders with a low tax basis in their shares might find a cash tender offer less attractive than a tax-free merger involving the bidder's securities, because the sale of shares in a cash offer inevitably is a taxable transaction.

2. Two-Tier Offers

A two-tier offer is a tender offer with two different prices: a higher price for shares tendered immediately (the "front end"), and a lower price for shares purchased for cash or securities in a subsequent merger (the "back end").

The two-tier offer has many of the same advantages and disadvantages as does the any and all tender offer. But although some strategists have concluded that the two-tier offer is tactically superior to the any and all offer, two-tier offers have not been widely used in recent years.

Commentators who favor two-tier offers stress their offensive and defensive advantages over 100 percent cash offers. An article by Lawrence Lederman[354] concludes that two-tier offers are more likely to succeed because the front-end price attracts professional investors who will tender their shares for an assured profit, rather than wait and tender later to a white knight, which might not be able to consummate its offer. Lederman further observes that, if the price of the first tier of the two-tier offer exceeds the overall price for the any and all offer, the two-tier offer will prevail even though the any and all offer might be economically superior, because shareholders will be attracted by the first tier's higher price and by the greater possibility of the two-tier offer's consummation.

For example, assume that a bidder holding five percent of a target's stock, which trades at $15 per share, makes a two-tier tender offer for 47.5 percent of the outstanding shares. If the first-tier price is $30 and the second tier is $20, the blended price for the offer is $25 per share. Also assume that the target finds a white knight to launch, shortly before the initial bidder's offer expires, an all-cash tender offer at $28 per share, conditioned on the acquisition of at least 50 percent of the target's securities. Lederman concludes that the initial bidder may prevail in this battle, even though its offer (which has a blended price of $25 per share) is economically inferior to the white knight's offer (priced at $28 per share), because the bidder's first tier tempts shareholders with the possibility of receiving $30 per share. Shareholders therefore will tender to the bidder, rather than to the white knight, because the bidder's offer will end first and because no one can be sure whether the white knight will receive a sufficient number of shares to meet the offer's minimum.

---

354. Lederman, "Tender Offer Bidding Strategy," 17 Rev. of Sec. Reg. 917 (April 18, 1984).

Moreover, Lederman notes, the true value of the first tier of a two-tier offer actually is higher than the blended value of the two tiers because many of the outstanding shares generally are not tendered in the first tier. The withholding of these shares increases the proportion of tendered shares that the bidder will accept in the first tier, thereby increasing the value of that tier's effective price and further encouraging shareholders to participate in the first tier.

There are, however, disadvantages to two-tier offers. They are harder to understand than are across-the-board offers, and they may be perceived as coercive (in that shareholders may feel obliged to tender rather than to miss the chance to participate in the higher front end). This apparent coerciveness may cause courts to be more receptive to targets' defensive measures.[355]

The second stage of a two-tier offer also can raise questions about the majority stockholder's fulfillment of its fiduciary duty to the minority shareholders who are being divested of their holdings in a cash-out merger. One can argue, however, that there is no breach of fiduciary duty if (a) the bidder does not control the target prior to the initial tender offer, (b) both steps are carefully disclosed in the offer, and (c) all shareholders have a pro rata opportunity to participate in the offer and to receive the blended value of the two steps.

State, rather than federal, law governs issues pertaining to fiduciary duties involved in cash-out mergers. Not many cases deal with two-tier offers; however, an increasing number of decisions has discussed squeeze-out mergers, which are analogous to the second step of a two-tier offer. In *Weinberger v. UOP, Inc.*,[356] one of the most important cases discussing a majority stockholder's fiduciary duties to minority shareholders in the context of a squeeze-out merger following a partial tender offer, the Delaware Supreme Court held that a parent

---

355. Until the 1986 amendments to the tender offer rules, another disadvantage related to timing: the partial tender offeror could not buy any tendered shares until the expiration of the offer. This problem now affects *all* tender offers, not just partial ones.

356. 457 A.2d 701 (Del. 1983).

corporation negotiating an acquisition of its partly owned subsidiary owes a duty of fair dealing to the subsidiary and its minority shareholders and that the parent does not fulfill this duty when its directors, some of whom also are directors of the subsidiary, participate in negotiations on behalf of the subsidiary while considering only the interests of the parent. The court stated:

> When directors of a Delaware corporation are on both sides of a transaction, they are required to demonstrate their utmost good faith and the most scrupulous inherent fairness of the bargain. . . . The requirement of fairness is unflinching in its demand that where one stands on both sides of a transaction, he has the burden of establishing its entire fairness, sufficient to pass the test of careful scrutiny by the courts.[357]

The court divided fairness into fair dealing and fair price. Fair dealing

> embraces questions of when the transaction is timed, how it is initiated, structured, negotiated, disclosed to the directors, and how the approvals of the directors and stockholders were obtained. The latter aspect of fairness relates to the economic and financial considerations of the proposed merger: assets, market value, earnings, future prospects, and any other elements that affect the intrinsic or inherent value of a company's stock.[358]

To determine the fairness of a transaction, "[a]ll aspects of the issue must be examined as a whole since the question is one of entire fairness."[359]

In adopting the fairness test, the Delaware Supreme Court expressly overruled *Singer v. Magnavox Co.*[360] and its progeny, which had held that a majority shareholder may not force a cash-out merger on minority shareholders absent a business

---

357. *Id.* at 710 (citations omitted).

358. *Id.* at 711.

359. *Id.*

360. 380 A.2d 969 (Del. 1977).

purpose for the merger.[361] Furthermore, *Weinberger* held that minority shareholders who object to a cash-out merger may avail themselves only of an appraisal remedy, except in situations where such a remedy would be inadequate because of alleged fraud, misrepresentation, self-dealing, deliberate waste of corporate assets, or "gross and palpable overreaching."[362] In such cases, "the Chancellor's powers are complete to fashion any form of equitable and monetary relief as may be appropriate, including rescissory damages."[363]

Although the court did liberalize the formula for determining appraisal value, *Weinberger* nevertheless may limit significantly the remedies available to dissenting minority shareholders in cash-out mergers. Only those dissenters who comply with various statutory requirements before the merger's consummation may seek appraisal. If these shareholders perfect their appraisal rights, they may not be able to seek injunctive relief against the parent because they will be unable to show irreparable harm. If the dissenters fail to perfect their appraisal rights, they may be able to bring an action against the parent corporation based on self-dealing or unfairness, but, if they lose their suit, they will not be entitled to appraisal.

In *Joseph v. Shell Oil Co.*,[364] however, a Delaware court applied *Weinberger* and declined to dismiss a claim by minority shareholders alleging overreaching by a parent corporation that planned to conduct a short-form merger with its partly owned subsidiary. The court found that plaintiffs had raised sufficient allegations of overreaching to create a reasonable doubt as to the adequacy of an appraisal remedy.

The *Joseph* court previously had granted a preliminary injunction against a two-tier tender offer by a majority shareholder of Shell Oil Company because the parent had been on both sides of the transaction and had violated its fiduciary

---

361. *Weinberger*, 457 A.2d at 715.

362. *Id.* at 714.

363. *Id.*

364. 482 A.2d 335 (Del. Ch. 1984); 498 A.2d 1117 (Del. Ch. 1985).

duty to minority shareholders.[365] The court found that the plaintiffs had met their burden of establishing a reasonable probability that the defendants neither had offered a fair price to the minority shareholders for their shares of Shell nor had fully and accurately disclosed all pertinent facts.

The court noted that tender offerors generally are not required to offer a fair price because shareholders usually can determine for themselves whether the price is fair and whether to tender. A different situation exists, however, when the offeror owes a fiduciary duty to the offerees but nevertheless structures its offer in a way that results both in an unfair price and in a likelihood that unwary minority stockholders will not learn of the unfairness.[366] The court found that the defendants had breached their fiduciary duty to the minority shareholders because they had retained an appraiser to determine a fair price for the shares but had not supplied to the appraiser complete information about the value of those shares.[367]

---

365. 482 A.2d 335 (Del. Ch. 1984).

366. *Id.* at 341.

367. In another case applying the *Weinberger* fairness standard, the Delaware Supreme Court held that Getty Oil Company had acted fairly when negotiating the acquisition of the minority interest in Skelly Oil Company. *Rosenblatt v. Getty Oil Co.*, 493 A.2d 929 (Del. 1985). Getty had acquired the minority interest in Skelly through an exchange offer for Getty's own securities. The court held that, because Getty, "as majority shareholder of Skelly, stood on both sides of this transaction, [Getty] bore the initial burden of establishing its entire fairness." *Id.* at 937. However, the approval of the merger by an informed vote of a majority of the minority shareholders shifted "the burden of proving the unfairness of the merger entirely to the plaintiffs." *Id.* But Getty nevertheless retained the burden of showing complete disclosure of all material facts relevant to the vote. The court found that Getty had dealt fairly with Skelly's minority shareholders and had fully disclosed all material information. *But cf. Kahn v. United States Sugar Corp.*, No. 7313 (Del. Ch. Dec. 10, 1985) (holding that defendants breached fiduciary duty by failing to disclose all material information about coercive tender offer and that company's controlling shareholders had conflict of interest with respect to setting offering price).

3. Exchange Offers

An exchange offer is a tender offer in which a bidder offers securities, instead of cash, as consideration for tendered shares. An exchange offer, which must be registered with the SEC under the Securities Act of 1933, becomes public upon the filing of a preliminary prospectus for the registration, but many weeks may elapse before the registration statement is declared effective and the bidder can commence its offer.

Exchange offers also are subject to broader disclosure requirements than are cash offers. For example, an exchange offeror must fully describe the businesses of the bidder and the target and must provide a complete set of pro forma financial statements. These disclosure requirements, and the waiting period before the offer becomes effective, account for the relatively infrequent use of hostile exchange offers, as compared with hostile cash tender offers.

Nevertheless, hostile exchange offers do make an occasional appearance. In April 1985, for example, Turner Broadcasting System made a hostile exchange offer for all outstanding shares of CBS. For each share of CBS stock, Turner offered a package consisting of a senior note, a senior debenture, various zero-coupon notes, a subordinated debenture, one share of preferred stock, and a fractional share of common stock.[368]

4. Bust-Up Takeovers and Group Bids

In recent years, a number of bidders have made tender offers with the intention of selling off pieces of the target, rather than of obtaining control of the company in order to operate it as an ongoing business enterprise. Bidders that adopt this strategy believe that the pieces of the target are more valuable when sold separately than is the target as a single entity. A recent, highly

---

368. *Turner Broadcasting System, Inc. v. CBS, Inc.*, 627 F. Supp. 901 (N.D. Ga. 1985).

publicized example of this "bust-up" technique was Pantry Pride's bid for Revlon.[369]

A "group bid" is similar to a bust-up takeover because it often involves the division of the target into two or more pieces after a successful tender offer. A group of bidders may launch a group bid when the group as a whole desires to purchase the entire target, although each individual bidder is attracted by only a segment of the company. The bidders therefore join together for the sole purpose of making the tender offer and acquiring control; if they prevail in their quest, they carve up the target and go their separate ways. Occasionally, the group assembles during a tender offer that is conditioned upon the assembly of such a group.[370] Alternatively, a group may assemble before or during a pending tender offer in order to finance the offer[371] or to increase the threat of a takeover, thus enhancing the possibility of obtaining greenmail.[372]

The group bid presents various issues under the Williams Act. Any group that owns or acquires five percent or more of an equity security must report that ownership as a group on Schedule 13D. Changes in group membership and group goals require additional filings.[373] If a bidder begins a tender offer and subsequently forms a group to finance the offer, assembling that group might cause changes in the tender offer and might require the bidder to terminate the offer and commence a new one. At the very least, the bidder would have to amend its tender offer disclosures.

Because group members frequently have different interests, group bids, by their very nature, can create a number of

---

369. *See Revlon, Inc. v. MacAndrews & Forbes Holdings, Inc.*, 506 A.2d 173 (Del. 1986).

370. The bids by Anderson Clayton and others for Norton Simon, and the bids by Roy M. Huffington and others for ENSTAR Corporation, serve as good examples of this procedure.

371. An example is the Mesa Petroleum bid for Gulf.

372. The Steinberg-Disney deal illustrates this point. Greenmail is discussed in § III.4.F., *infra*.

373. For a more extensive discussion of Schedule 13D, see *supra* § II.4.A.

potential problems. In a hostile bid, for example, the group might not have an opportunity to scrutinize the target's financial affairs until after the bid's conclusion. The group might find it difficult to divide the company as planned, once the offer has succeeded. Some group members might cede control to one member while other group members might not wish to do so, in part because all members would remain liable for the leader's actions during the tender offer. A group might have trouble reacting with the requisite speed in a hostile tender offer. Finally, the group bid might be more vulnerable to litigation because of the greater number of parties involved and because of fiduciary questions raised by the group's agreement to sell a target's asset to one group member at a specified price before the group owns all of the target's stock.[374]

E. Proxy Contests

1. Advantages and Disadvantages

This book thus far has concentrated on hostile takeovers effectuated through the acquisition of the target's securities by means of tender offers, market accumulations, or block purchases. An alternative to such takeovers—indeed, the principal means before tender offers gained in popularity during the 1970s—is a proxy contest. To wage a proxy contest, the "bidder" solicits proxies for the election of its own slate of candidates as directors of the target; if the bidder's candidates win, a change in control of the target occurs.

Unlike a tender offer, a proxy contest does not require the bidder to buy additional shares of the target in order to obtain control of the company. (It is elementary, however, that the bidder's likelihood of success increases in direct proportion to

---

374. *See generally* Green & Dupler, "Group Bid Becomes Important Acquisition Tactic," *Legal Times*, Jan. 21, 1985, at 20.

the size of the bidder's (and its allies') holdings in the target.) The bidder thus may save some of the enormous amount of money needed to effect a takeover, although proxy contests themselves inherently involve substantial transaction costs. A bidder must expect to spend in excess of $1 million to wage a proxy contest for even a small public company.

In contrast with a tender offer, a proxy contest does not award to the victor the economic benefits associated with ownership of the target's publicly held equity. If the successful bidder and its nominees on the target's board of directors can increase the target's profitability, the bidder will benefit only to the extent of its equity ownership in the target. The public shareholders will receive the remaining benefit.

Because of this inability to reap the economic benefits of equity ownership through a proxy contest, the bidder usually will proceed through a tender offer or stock accumulation if the bidder can finance such means—unless special considerations dictate otherwise. One such consideration relates to the preservation of a target's net operating loss ("NOL") carryover. A target's NOL carryover for any year will be limited, and may be lost, if, at any point during a three-year period, the bidder and other holders of five percent of the target's stock increase their ownership in the target by at least 50 percent.[375]

Since 1984, bidders have transformed proxy fights, which traditionally had been lengthy election battles for control of corporate boards, into quick and direct appeals designed to enlist shareholder support for the bidders' ultimate goals. By soliciting proxies for a slate of officers pledged to sell a valuable corporate asset or to implement a corporate strategy resisted by incumbent management, a bidder can simultaneously expedite a tender offer and force a target's management to take the unwelcome steps—sometimes including extraordinary corporate transactions such as divestiture or liquidation—that the new officers would take if elected.

An example of this technique was the Clore/Gulf Resources proxy contest in 1982. During an 18-day period, Allen E. Clore,

---

375. 26 U.S.C. § 382(a).

a British investor, waged a proxy fight to win control of Gulf Resources and Chemical Corporation. The effort cost him only $1.5 million beyond what he had previously paid in "creeping up" on Gulf Resources by buying a 15-percent block of its stock. Clore successfully promoted the election of 12 of the company's 14 directors by having his nominees promise to consider a "redeployment of some or all" of the company's assets.

Bust-up proxy contests remained popular in 1986 despite the prevalence of junk bond financing for tender offers. Bidders used the tactics in fights for control of, among others, Leaseway Transportation Corporation, Fruehauf Corporation, and CTS Corporation. In the Leaseway situation, for example, about three weeks before Leaseway's annual meeting, family members and their friends who controlled roughly 30 percent of Leaseway's stock commenced a proxy fight against the company's candidates for directors. To bolster their election efforts, the insurgents promised, if elected, to sell the company. The Leaseway board responded—apparently out of fear that institutional shareholders would shift their support to the dissidents in order to receive a quick profit from the sale—by committing itself to the sale of the company. The incumbents won reelection, but their victory was a Pyrrhic one that depended on their pledge to sell Leaseway.

Special considerations may arise if the bidder seeks to acquire control of a regulated company such as a broadcasting company. The Federal Communications Commission ("FCC") has taken the position that a proxy contest for control of a company that itself controls radio, television, or common-carrier licenses does not result in a substantial change in control of the target as long as such change is not accompanied by a substantial change in the ownership of the target. As a result of this interpretation, a bidder waging a proxy contest for control of a broadcasting company can seek a streamlined form of FCC approval, and the process can be completed within a few weeks. By contrast, a bidder making a tender offer for, or otherwise acquiring, a controlling stock position in such a target must obtain "long-form" FCC approval—a process that often requires a month to complete—although the bidder may decide to proceed by using a voting trust arrangement, which will not give the bidder voting control of the FCC-regulated target but will require the bidder to obtain only short-form FCC approval.[376]

2. Filing Requirements

a. *Schedule 13D*

As discussed above, a "person" who acquires more than five percent of any class of registered equity securities of a target must file a Schedule 13D within ten days after making such acquisition. The term "person" includes a "group" acting "for the purposes of acquiring, holding, or disposing of securities" of the target.[377] If the bidder and disenchanted target shareholders agree to act together as a group to try to replace existing target management, the group constitutes a "person" and is deemed to have acquired beneficial ownership of all shares owned by the individual members of the group.[378] Case law recognizes, however, that disgruntled shareholders may hold preliminary discussions about their grievances and may explore the possibility of joint action without being deemed to have formed a reportable group.[379]

---

376. Tender Offers and Proxy Contests, FCC No. 86-87 (March 17, 1986).

377. Exchange Act § 13(d)(3), 15 U.S.C. § 78m(d)(3). For a more extensive discussion of Schedule 13D, see *supra* § II.4.A.

378. Rule 13d-5(b)(1), 17 C.F.R. § 240.13d-5(b)(1) (1986) (when two or more persons agree to act together for the purpose of acquiring, holding, voting, or disposing of an issuer's equity securities, the group thus formed shall be deemed, as of the date of such agreement, to have acquired beneficial ownership, for purposes of §§ 13(d) and 13(g) of the Act, of all equity securities of that issuer beneficially owned by any such persons).

379. *See, e.g.*, *Storer Communications, Inc. v. Coniston Partners*, 85 Civ. 2694 (S.D.N.Y. April 30, 1985); *Pantry Pride, Inc. v. Rooney*, 598 F. Supp. 891 (S.D.N.Y. 1984) (no "group" was formed for a proxy contest until members actually executed a proxy contest agreement, even though they had had earlier discussions about proxy contests; court noted that § 13(d) allowed individuals broad freedom to discuss the possibilities of future agreements without having to file under the securities laws); *Lane Bryant, Inc. v. Hatleigh*

Once a group has been formed, the required Schedule 13D filing must include information concerning the identity of the group's members, the means by which the group financed its purchase(s) of its shares of the target, and the group's plans and intentions for the target.[380]

b. Schedule 14B

The dissidents may not make any solicitation for the election or removal of any directors unless they file, at least five business days (or such shorter period as the SEC may authorize on a showing of good cause) before making any such solicitation, a Schedule 14B on behalf of each "participant" in the solicitation. This Schedule must be filed with the SEC and with each national securities exchange on which the target's shares are registered.[381] If the information contained in the Schedule 14B changes in any material way, the filers must "promptly" amend the Schedule.[382]

The term "participant," as used in Rule 14a-11, includes a director of the issuer; a nominee for whose election proxies are solicited; a committee or group that solicits proxies; any member of such a committee or group; anyone who engages in organizing, directing, or arranging the financing of such committee or group; any person who contributes more than $500 to finance the solicitation of proxies; and any person (other than a bank, broker, or dealer acting in the ordinary course of business) who lends money to finance or induce the purchase, sale, holding, or voting of securities by a participant or by others. Any person who solicits proxies also is a "participant." The term "participant" does not include a hired proxy solicitor;

Corp., [1980 Transfer Binder] Fed. Sec. L. Rep. (CCH) ¶ 97,529 (S.D.N.Y. June 9, 1980); *Cook United, Inc. v. "Stockholders Protective Committee of Cook United, Inc.,"* [1979 Transfer Binder] Fed. Sec. L. Rep. (CCH) ¶ 96,875 (S.D.N.Y. May 21, 1979).

380. For a more complete discussion, see *supra* § II.4.A(3).

381. Rule 14a-11(c), 17 C.F.R. § 240.14a-11(c) (1986).

382. Rule 14a-11(c)(5).

a person performing ministerial or clerical duties; a person employed by a participant as an attorney, an accountant, or an advertising, public relations, or financial adviser, or one whose activities are limited to the performance of his duties in the course of such employment; or any person who is an officer, director, or employee of a participant but who is not otherwise a participant.[383]

Disclosures demanded by Schedule 14B closely resemble those called for by Schedule 13D; indeed, the latter Schedule derived from the former. Unlike Schedule 13D, however, Schedule 14B also requires disclosure of any material interest that the participant may have in any transaction with the issuer, any agreements as to future employment with the issuer, the circumstances under which the participant agreed to become a participant, and the amount of the participant's contributions in excess of $500. The proxy rules require solicitors of proxies to summarize, in the proxy statement sent to shareholders, much of the information contained in the Schedule 14B.[384]

c. *Schedule 14A Proxy Statements*

A person generally may not make a proxy solicitation unless he concurrently furnishes or has previously furnished to each solicitee a written proxy statement containing the information specified in Schedule 14A.[385] In addition, the solicitor must file the proxy statement in preliminary form (together with a $500 filing fee[386]) with the SEC at least ten days (or such shorter period as the SEC may authorize) before the date on which the solicitor intends to send definitive copies of the statement to shareholders.[387]

---

383. Rule 14a-11(b).
384. Rule 14a-11(c)(6); Schedule 14A, Item 4(b).
385. Rule 14a-3(a), 17 C.F.R. § 240.14a-3(a) (1986).
386. Rule 14a-6(i), *id.* § 240.14a-6(i).
387. Rule 14a-6(a).

Participants in a proxy contest may solicit shareholders without sending them a full proxy statement if the participants have (A) filed their Schedules 14B, (B) do not provide the shareholders with a form of proxy before furnishing them with the written proxy statement, and (C) include in their soliciting materials at least a summary of specified Schedule 14B disclosures.[388] This ability to make an early solicitation is useful if the dissident group knows that management is about to call a shareholders' meeting but does not know when that meeting will be held or what matters management will submit to the shareholders.

The bidder ordinarily must file preliminary copies of its pre-proxy statement materials with the SEC at least five business days before the materials are to be used.[389] The bidder also must file final copies with the SEC, and with the exchanges on which the issuer's securities are listed, not later than the day on which such materials are first sent to shareholders.[390]

d. *What Is a Solicitation?*

The term "solicitation" includes not only requests to execute or not to execute a proxy but also any communication to shareholders "under circumstances reasonably calculated to result in the procurement withholding or revocation of a proxy."[391] Cases have held that the solicitation of an agreement to form a stockholders' committee is not a "solicitation" within the meaning of the proxy rules.[392] Nor does a preliminary exploration of shareholders' attitudes toward management fall within the rules.[393]

---

388. Rule 14a-11(d).

389. Rule 14a-11(e).

390. Rule 14a-6(c).

391. Rule 14a-1(f)(iii), 17 C.F.R. § 240.14a-1(f)(iii) (1986).

392. *Calumet Indus., Inc. v. MacClure*, 464 F. Supp. 19 (N.D. Ill. 1978).

393. *D-Z Inv. Co. v. Holloway*, [1974-1975 Transfer Binder] Fed. Sec. L. Rep. (CCH) ¶ 94,771 (S.D.N.Y. Aug. 23, 1974).

The rules governing the filing of proxy materials do not apply to certain kinds of solicitations, including:

- Solicitations not made on behalf of the issuer, where the total number of persons solicited is not more than ten;
- Solicitations made by a person with respect to securities held in his own name or in that of his nominee, if the person merely impartially requests proxies or instructions;
- Solicitations made by a person with respect to securities of which he is the beneficial owner;
- Solicitations made by means of an advertisement that merely names the target, identifies the proposal to be acted on by shareholders, and states where copies of proxy materials may be obtained;[394] and
- The furnishing of proxy voting advice by an adviser to a person with whom he has a business relationship, if the adviser furnishes financial advice in the ordinary course of his business, discloses to the recipient any significant relationship with the other side, receives no special remuneration for furnishing the advice, and is not giving the advice on behalf of a participant.[395]

e. *Subsequent Proxy Materials*

In addition to filing preliminary proxy materials, the dissidents must file with the SEC preliminary copies of additional solicitation materials. These materials must be filed at least two business days before they are to be sent to shareholders, unless the SEC authorizes otherwise upon a showing of good cause.[396]

The rules also require the filing of definitive copies of proxy materials no later than the date on which they first are sent to shareholders.[397] Copies of any written instructions for personal

---

394. Rule 14a-2(a).
395. Rule 14a-2(b)(2).
396. Rule 14a-6(b), 17 C.F.R. § 240.14a-6(b) (1986).
397. Rule 14a-6(c).

solicitations are to be filed at least five business days (unless the SEC shortens the period) before the materials are given to shareholders.[398]

Final copies of press releases and speeches must be filed not later than the day on which they are made public or otherwise used.[399] Preliminary copies of such materials, other than reprints or reproductions, need not be filed.

3. Strategic Considerations

a. Six Fundamental Questions for Insurgents

Any bidder contemplating a proxy contest must consider the following six questions:

1. How much stock do the bidder and its allies own?
2. How much stock do management and its allies own?
3. How many shares (or what percentage) of the outstanding stock are likely to be voted at the meeting?
4. How can the bidder discredit the target's present management?
5. How can the target's present management discredit the bidder?
6. How much time does the bidder have?

b. Development of Issues Against Management

In addition to performing the basic fact-gathering needed for any takeover, a bidder considering a proxy contest must obtain information about the number of shares likely to be voted at the stockholders' meeting. Such information is important because directors will be elected by a majority of the shares voted at the meeting, and not by a majority of the outstanding shares. This

---

398. Rule 14a-6(d).

399. Rule 14a-6(g), 17 C.F.R. § 240.14a-6(g) (1986).

distinction could make a difference, depending on the sources of the insurgents' prospective votes.

The bidder also must gather information concerning its own slate of nominees, including the nominees' business experience, a list of the companies with which they are affiliated, litigation in which they are involved, conflicts of interest that they might have with the company, and any other "skeletons" that the target might exploit. Use of a questionnaire may help to gather this information (as well as the information that must be reported in Schedules 13D, 14A, and 14B).

When developing issues against target management and its performance, the bidder must recognize that shareholders more likely will vote for a bidder that promises them an immediate economic reward than for a bidder that simply claims that its candidates would be better directors than would management's nominees. Shareholders usually favor a known over an unknown evil—and money over both.

Various economic issues may attract shareholders' attention. For instance, shareholders might eagerly support a proposal to liquidate an undervalued, asset-rich company if such liquidation would yield a large economic return; similarly, they might leap at a plan to spin off a subsidiary whose business is unrelated to that of the parent, if the bidder can show (or at least argue) that the two businesses will command greater value when traded separately than when traded under one corporate roof. Odyssey Partners successfully advanced this spin-off issue in its proxy contest for Trans World Corporation.[400] If the target is a closed-end investment company, a proposal for open-ending the target (causing shares to be redeemable at net asset value) may be attractive if the target's shares have traded at a discount from net asset value. Finally, if the company has adopted a "poison pill" rights plan,[401] a proposal to redeem those rights in connection with a tender offer by the bidder or any other company at a

---

400. *See Trans World Corp. v. Odyssey Partners*, 561 F. Supp. 1315 (S.D.N.Y. 1983).

401. Poison pill rights are discussed in § III.4.B., *infra*.

higher than specified price per share may become an economic issue.

The bidder also may develop noneconomic issues, such as management's poor performance, measured by company earnings or dividends; management's failure to keep promises; management's self-dealing and conflicts of interest (as reflected in the "Certain Transactions" portion of the target's proxy statements); management's integrity; and management's compensation.

The bidder should take all possible measures to investigate and present thoroughly and accurately the facts underlying proxy statement allegations in order to guard against defamation charges, defend against possible litigation, and expedite the SEC's review of the proxy materials. It is extremely desirable for the bidder to include in its SEC filing package annotated copies of all preliminary proxy materials identifying the background for each factual allegation against management.

c. *Orchestration of Campaign*

i. **Obtaining a Shareholder List**

A bidder contemplating a proxy contest should attempt (in its capacity as a stockholder) to obtain a shareholder list as soon as possible and should press its state law right to do so. While Rule 14a-7[402] requires the target to mail out the bidder's (or other insurgents') proxy materials, the bidder would be well advised to obtain its own copy of the shareholder list and send out the materials on its own. Reliance on Rule 14a-7 permits the target to control, to some extent, the timing of the mailing and prevents the bidder from collecting information about the number of shares that each stockholder owns.

In framing a request to the target, the bidder should ask not only for the list of shareholders but also for the computer tapes, instructions for using the computer tapes, depository listings (*i.e.*, what brokerage firms hold how many shares of the total

---

402. 17 C.F.R. § 240.14a-7 (1986).

number of shares held by Cede & Co.), and a list of NOBOs (that is, the "non-objecting beneficial owners"—beneficial owners of stock, held of record by brokers or other nominees, who do not object to furnishing their names to the issuer so that the issuer can mail proxy statements and other communications to them directly). The Delaware courts generally allow an insurgent to obtain access to all materials available to management in communicating with shareholders, not just to the record list of stockholders.

State statutes typically require a shareholder to state a "proper purpose" for inspecting a shareholder list,[403] but a "proper purpose" generally includes any purpose related to the stockholder's position as a stockholder.[404]

The following are some commonly accepted "proper purposes" for obtaining stockholder lists under state inspection statutes:

- soliciting proxies for any purpose;[405]
- purchasing additional stock;[406]
- contacting other stockholders to oppose any corporate action;[407]
- facilitating litigation instituted by the stockholder and inviting other stockholders to join in the suit against the corporation or its management;[408] and
- facilitating tender offers.[409]

---

403. *See, e.g.*, Del. Code Ann. tit. 8, § 220(b) (1983).

404. *Id.*

405. *See, e.g.*, *Hatleigh Corp. v. Lane Bryant, Inc.*, 428 A.2d 350 (Del. Ch. 1981); *Credit Bureau of St. Paul, Inc. v. Credit Bureau Reports, Inc.*, 290 A.2d 689 (Del. Ch.), *aff'd*, 290 A.2d 691 (Del. 1972); *Kerkorian v. Western Air Lines, Inc.*, 253 A.2d 221 (Del. Ch.), *aff'd*, 254 A.2d 240 (Del. 1969).

406. *See, e.g.*, *Western Pac. Indus., Inc. v. Liggett & Myers, Inc.*, 310 A.2d 669 (Del. Ch. 1973).

407. *Susquehanna Corp. v. General Refractories Co.*, 250 F. Supp. 797, 801-02 (E.D. Pa.), *aff'd*, 356 F.2d 985 (3d Cir. 1966).

408. *Sivin v. Schwartz*, 22 A.D.2d 822, 254 N.Y.S.2d 914, 916 (2d Dep't 1964).

409. *Crane Co. v. Anaconda Co.*, 39 N.Y.2d 14, 382 N.Y.S.2d 707, 346 N.E.2d 507 (1976).

This list, of course, is not exhaustive.

Once a shareholder requests access to the stockholder list, the corporation bears the burden of demonstrating that the shareholder's stated purpose is improper. This allocation of burdens differs from that of common law, under which the stockholder always bore the burden of proof. It also differs from the allocation of burdens applicable to a shareholder's demand to inspect other books and records of the corporation. In such cases, the stockholder bears the burden of proving that he has a "proper" purpose for inspecting those records.[410]

Although the stockholder need not *prove* that he has a proper purpose for seeking access to the shareholder list, he nevertheless must *state*, in the demand, his purpose for requesting to see the list. This purpose, however, may be stated with considerable generality. For example, courts have consistently held sufficient a purpose described as the "solicitation of proxies," without further explanation as to the issue upon which the shareholders will vote.[411]

While the stated purpose may be quite general, however, it must not be *too* general. In *Northwest Industries, Inc. v. B.F. Goodrich Co.*,[412] the Delaware Supreme Court held that the purpose requirement in section 220 of the Delaware Code demands more "than a mere statement of intent to communicate with other stockholders"; it requires a statement of the purpose of the communication. This statement must be sufficiently specific to enable management or a court to determine whether there is a reasonable relationship between that purpose and the interests of the stockholder. In *Shamrock Associates v. The Dorsey Corp.*,[413] the court held that the stated purpose—"to permit [the stockholder] to communicate with other stockholders . . . on

410. *See* Del. Gen. Corp. L. § 220(c); *Skoglund v. Ormand Indus. Inc.*, 372 A.2d 204 (Del. Ch. 1976).

411. *See, e.g.*, *Credit Bureau of St. Paul, Inc. v. Credit Bureau Reporter, Inc.*, 290 A.2d 689 (Del. Ch.), *aff'd*, 290 A.2d 691 (Del. 1972); *Kerkorian v. Western Air Lines, Inc.*, 253 A.2d 221 (Del. Ch.), *aff'd*, 254 A.2d 240 (Del. 1969).

412. 260 A.2d 428, 429 (Del. 1969).

413. No. 7678 (Del. Ch. July 24, 1984).

matters related to their interest as stockholders, including without limitation, with regard to the Board of Directors and individual members thereof and possible solicitation of other stockholders . . . as is necessary and appropriate to effect a change in the composition of the Board of Directors"—was too general. The court noted that the statement did not include any reference to an impending event such as a tender offer or a stockholders' meeting.

The target may resist the demand for inspection by attacking the bidder's (or other stockholder's) standing to make that demand. For example, the corporation may argue that the stockholder is not a stockholder of record or (if the applicable state law requires the requesting stockholder either to have held stock for a prescribed period or to own a minimum percentage of stock) that the stockholder either has not held his stock for a long enough period or does not own the requisite percentage of stock. The corporation also may contend that the stockholder obtained his stock by fraud or has defective title to the stock and thus is not qualified to make the demand.[414]

In addition, the target may attack the legitimacy of the bidder's alleged purpose for demanding inspection. Given the broad range of acceptable purposes, this attack probably will fail, unless the shareholder's purpose is unduly vague (as in *Shamrock Associates*[415]) or is meant only to promote one of the following:

- mere communication;[416]
- harassment;[417]
- curiosity;[418]

---

414. *Kerkorian v. Western Air Lines, Inc.*, 253 A.2d 221 (Del. Ch.), *aff'd*, 254 A.2d 240 (Del. 1969).

415. *Shamrock Assocs. v. The Dorsey Corp.*, No. 7678 (Del. Ch. July 24, 1984).

416. *Northwest Indus., Inc. v. B.F. Goodrich Co.*, 260 A.2d 428 (Del. 1969).

417. *CM & M Group, Inc. v. Carroll*, 453 A.2d 788 (Del. 1982).

418. *Id.*

- speculative or commercial use of the stockholder list;[419] or
- political or philosophical ends.[420]

If the shareholder provides one proper purpose for demanding to inspect the stockholder list, the corporation may not rely on, and a court may not consider, the fact that the shareholder also might have listed other, improper purposes.[421] Moreover, in order to defeat a demand for inspection, the corporation must prove the impropriety of the purpose stated in the demand.[422] No other purpose is relevant, even if such other purpose is in fact the shareholder's primary purpose for obtaining the list. Indeed, as long as the stockholder states a proper purpose, the target may not even question him in a deposition about any secondary purpose or motive.[423]

It is not a defense to a demand for inspection that the stockholder making the request is a competitor of the corporation.[424] The mere possibility that a shareholder might misuse any information obtained through the inspection does not itself constitute a sufficient reason to limit the stockholder's right of inspection.

ii. Letters to Shareholders

Bidders typically send several letters to shareholders during the course of a proxy contest, and the bidder should remember this fact in planning its strategy. The first letter thus should not be a long one; the bidder should save substantive information for

---

419. *White v. Jacobsen Mfg. Co.*, 293 F. Supp. 1358, 1359-60 (E.D. Wis. 1968).

420. *National Consumer's Union v. National Tea Co.*, 14 Ill. App. 3d 186, 302 N.E.2d 118 (1973).

421. *See CM & M Group, Inc. v. Carroll*, 453 A.2d 788 (Del. 1982); *Skouras v. Admiralty Enters., Inc.*, 386 A.2d 674 (Del. Ch. 1978); *Skoglund v. Ormand Indus., Inc.*, 372 A.2d 204 (Del. Ch. 1976).

422. *Mite Corp. v. Heli-Coil Corp.*, 256 A.2d 855, 858 (Del. Ch. 1969).

423. *General Time Corp. v. Talley Indus., Inc.*, 240 A.2d 755, 756 (Del. 1968).

424. *See, e.g., E.L. Bruce Co. v. State*, 144 A.2d 533 (Del. 1958); *Skouras v. Admiralty Enters., Inc.*, 386 A.2d 674 (Del. Ch. 1978); *Skoglund v. Ormand Indus., Inc.*, 372 A.2d 204 (Del. Ch. 1976).

later letters, which can develop at greater length the theme articulated in the initial letter. The final letter typically serves as a brief recapitulation of the main arguments expounded in the earlier letters.

All letters sent to shareholders should be as readable as possible and should be printed in type larger than that used for prospectus boilerplate. Bold-faced type and italics are often used, and indented "bullet" paragraphs may be visually effective.

A bidder often finds, however, that its efforts to make its "fight letters" readable are undercut by SEC comments concerning the proxy materials. The SEC requires many arguable matters to be "opinionized," so that they read: "In our opinion, management has failed to keep its promises," or "We submit that the claim against management is. . . ."

Bidders usually try to send to the shareholders the last proxy that the shareholders will have time to return. Many shareholders return more than one proxy, and, in such cases, it is the final one that counts.

CHAPTER 5

HART SCOTT RODINO ANTITRUST IMPROVEMENTS ACT

The Hart-Scott-Rodino Antitrust Improvements Act of 1976 ("H-S-R Act") was enacted to supply the United States antitrust agencies (the Federal Trade Commission ("FTC") and the Antitrust Division of the Department of Justice) with advance information about significant transactions so that those agencies can adequately review the anticompetitive effects of proposed mergers and acquisitions prior to their consummation. Before the enactment of the H-S-R Act, companies often were able to conclude major anticompetitive transactions without the antitrust agencies' learning, until too late, of the combinations. Presented with such *faits accomplis*, the agencies had difficulty in enforcing the antitrust laws.

The H-S-R Act provides:

> Except as exempted . . . no person shall acquire, directly or indirectly, any voting securities or assets of any other person, unless both persons (or in the case of a tender offer, the acquiring person) file notification . . . under this section and the waiting period . . . has expired, if [the jurisdictional standards are met].[425]

If the Act applies to a tender offer, the bidder need not make its H-S-R filings before it begins its offer. However, the bidder must file a premerger notification form and must observe a waiting period before acquiring shares of the target, so that the enforcement agencies can review the legality of the acquisition under the antitrust laws. This waiting period may have a critical effect on a tender offer's timing, even if the acquisition itself raises no substantive antitrust issues. Accordingly, the bidder should consider the applicability of the H-S-R Act and its requirements in formulating a takeover strategy.

---

425. 15 U.S.C. § 18a(a). The H-S-R Act amended the Clayton Act by adding § 7A, codified as 15 U.S.C. § 18a.

A. Jurisdictional Standards

The H-S-R Act and the premerger notification rules (the "Rules")[426] generally require the reporting of all mergers and acquisitions that satisfy the following standards:

- *In commerce.* One of the persons involved is engaged in United States commerce or in an activity affecting United States commerce.[427]
- *Size of persons.* The transaction is between persons with minimum sizes of $100 million and $10 million, respectively, in gross assets or, for manufacturing companies, sales;[428] and
- *Size of transaction.* As a result of the transaction, the acquiring person will hold (not acquire) *either* (A) more than $15 million of the acquired person's voting securities and assets *or* (B) 50 percent or more of the voting securities (or contractual control) of an issuer that, together with all entities it controls, has annual sales or gross assets of $25 million or more.[429]

The acquiring and acquired "persons" include not only the particular corporations involved but also all related entities under common control. "Control" is defined as ownership of 50 percent or more of an issuer's voting securities or, alternatively, the contractual power to designate a majority of an issuer's board of directors.[430]

---

426. 16 C.F.R. Parts 801, 802, and 803 (1986).
427. 15 U.S.C. § 18a(a)(1); Rules 801.1(1), 801.3.
428. 15 U.S.C. § 18a(a)(2); Rule 801.1(j).
429. 15 U.S.C. § 18a(a)(3); Rule 802.20.
430. Rule 801.1(b).

B. Premerger Notification Form

Completing the premerger notification form takes some time, but the information required should be reasonably accessible. The form (currently 16 pages in length) calls for a description of the parties and the acquisition, current financial data, and a breakdown of dollar revenues according to the Standard Industrial Classification ("SIC") codes. Most companies must submit annual SIC code information to the Bureau of the Census and, therefore, should have this information at hand.

The filer of a premerger notification form also must attach all reports prepared for the purpose of analyzing an acquisition's effects on competition and relevant markets. Accordingly, those persons who are likely to prepare such reports should be aware of this requirement when an acquisition is proposed, so that they will avoid exaggerating an acquisition's potential impact in terms of market shares.

C. Waiting Periods

If an acquisition falls within the scope of the H-S-R Act, the bidder should file its premerger notification form as soon as it announces the tender offer and notifies the target of the bid.[431] The Act imposes a 30-day waiting period (15 days in the case of a cash tender offer) before the acquiror may accept tendered shares for payment.[432] If an acquisition raises antitrust concerns, the enforcement agencies may extend the waiting period by requesting additional information, in which case the waiting period will not expire until 20 days (ten days in the case of a cash

431. *See* Rule 803.5.

432. Rule 803.10(b)(1). The target must also file a premerger notification form within 15 days after the acquiring person files its own form (ten days in the case of a cash tender offer), but lateness of the target's filing does not affect the waiting period. Rule 801.30(b).

tender offer) after the requested information has been provided.[433]

A bidder may request early termination of the waiting period.[434] Such requests have been more freely granted in recent years, especially when there is a compelling business reason for the transaction or when the acquisition does not appear, on its face, to pose any threat to competition (as is the case when the acquiring and acquired persons have no revenues in the same SIC code). Early termination, however, is granted at the discretion of the enforcement agencies, and a bidder should not assume that the agencies will accede.

D. Exemptions to the H-S-R Act

There are a number of exemptions to the H-S-R Act, including exemptions for acquisitions supervised by government agencies, acquisitions by underwriters, and foreign acquisitions.[435] The exemptions most likely to be of use in planning and making a tender offer are those applicable to investments, convertible voting securities, and acquisition vehicles.

1. Investment Exemption

The investment exemption is an exception to the $15 million reporting threshold for acquisitions of voting securities: it permits a person to acquire up to ten percent of an issuer's voting securities—regardless of the value of those holdings—as long as the acquisition is "solely for the purpose of investment."[436] Under the Rules, an investor who purchases

---

433. Rule 803.10(b)(2).

434. Rule 803.11(c).

435. *See generally* Rule 802.

436. Rule 802.9.

voting securities "solely for the purpose of investment" "has no intention of participating in the formulation, determination or direction of the basic business decisions of the issuer."[437]

The investment exemption does not apply to a tender offer, because a tender offeror clearly is seeking control of the target. But the exemption may cover initial purchases, made before the bidder has decided whether or not to make a tender offer. It is not unusual for purchasers to seek a minority position in a variety of potential targets, and such purchasers often reach the $15 million size of transaction threshold before holding five percent of the issuer's shares—the threshold for reporting under the securities laws.[438] The H-S-R Act requires public disclosure of these holdings once they reach the $15 million level, but only if the investment exemption does not apply.

Entitlement to the investment exemption rests on a purchaser's subjective intent, and the enforcement agencies are sensitive to the potential for the exemption's abuse. In the Statement of Basis and Purpose for the H-S-R Act and Rules, the FTC stated that a purchaser's asserted investment intent may be challenged on the basis of objective factors.[439] In fact, the only two instances of sanctions imposed under the H-S-R Act have been for abuse of this exemption.

---

437. Rule 801.1(i)(1).

438. *See supra* § II.4.A. (discussing § 13(d) of the Exchange Act).

439. The FTC declared:

> [M]erely voting the stock will not be considered evidence of an intent inconsistent with investment purpose. However, certain types of conduct could be so viewed. These include but are not limited to: (1) nominating a candidate for the board of directors of the issuer; (2) proposing corporate action requiring shareholder approval; (3) soliciting proxies; (4) having a controlling shareholder, director, officer or employee simultaneously serving as an officer or director of the issuer; (5) being a competitor of the issuer; or (6) doing any of the foregoing with respect to any entity directly or indirectly controlling the issuer.

43 Fed. Reg. 33,465 (1978).

One such case, *United States v. Coastal Corporation*,[440] arose out of the unsuccessful attempt by Coastal Corporation to take over the Houston Natural Gas Corporation ("HNG"). Coastal, which already held $15 million worth of HNG stock, purchased an additional 75,500 shares on January 19, 1984 and, relying on the investment exemption, made no premerger notification filing until January 27, when it announced a tender offer for HNG. Following an FTC investigation, the Department of Justice sued Coastal for its failure to file a premerger notification form for the January 19 purchase. The parties ultimately entered into a consent decree, pursuant to which Coastal was fined $230,000—the maximum fine of $10,000 for each day between January 19 and February 11 (the effective date of its eventual filing) during which Coastal was in violation of the H-S-R Act. In addition, Coastal was required to divest itself of the 75,500 shares illegally acquired on January 19.

More recently, the Department of Justice instituted an action against Weeks Petroleum Ltd., Bell Resources Ltd. (Weeks' parent), and M.R.H. Holmes A Court (chairman of Bell Resources Ltd.), relating to Weeks' acquisition of shares of Asarco Incorporated.[441] Weeks' holdings of Asarco shares reached the $15 million mark on November 21, 1984, but, relying on the investment exemption, Weeks continued to purchase shares without filing a premerger notification form. By February 19, 1985, Weeks owned five percent of Asarco; by February 28, Weeks' holdings reached ten percent. On March 8, 1985, Weeks filed a premerger notification form for additional purchases and reported that it would acquire between 25 and 49.9 percent of Asarco. Six days later, Weeks amended its Schedule 13D to state that these additional "purchases could be made with a view toward acquiring control of [Asarco]."[442]

---

440. No. 84-1675 (D.D.C. August 30, 1984).

441. *United States v. Bell Resources Ltd.*, No. 85-6202 (S.D.N.Y. Aug. 9, 1985).

442. *Asarco, Inc. v. Holmes A Court*, 611 F. Supp. 468, 470 (D.N.J. 1985) (motion for preliminary injunction against Asarco's issuance of new series of preferred shares). For a discussion of Schedule 13D, see *supra* § II.4.A.

The enforcement agencies rejected Weeks' invocation of the investment exemption and sought the maximum penalty of $10,000 for each day between November 21, 1984, when Weeks' holdings reached $15 million, and April 7, 1985, when the premerger filing became effective. On March 17, 1986, the parties agreed to a proposed consent decree fining the defendants $450,000.

Coastal and *Weeks* were extreme cases: the defendants belied their claims that purchases were made "solely for the purpose of investment" by seeking control soon after making such purchases. The enforcement actions thus were appropriate.

There are indications in *Coastal*, however, that the FTC takes an unduly narrow view of the investment exemption. In its letter agreement settling the action against Coastal, the FTC suggested that the investment exemption is limited to "purchases of voting securities made with the intention of holding the stock as a passive investment" and does not apply when the purchaser's intent "include[s] the possibility of acquiring control."[443] This restrictive interpretation might not be supported by the H-S-R Act, the Rules, or the objective factors listed in the Statement of Basis and Purpose. Perhaps a purchaser that views a future takeover attempt merely as one of many possibilities should be entitled to rely on the exemption. Once a tender offer emerges as a more likely course of action, however, the acquiror probably should file a premerger notification form before making further purchases.

---

443. Letter from Barbara A. Clark, acting for Timothy J. Muris, Director, Bureau of Competition, FTC, to George L. Brundrett, Senior Vice President and General Counsel of Coastal (February 10, 1984). Similarly, in reviewing the purchase of shares of The Trane Company by O'Connor & Associates, the FTC stated that the investment exemption is available only to "passive investors." Letter from Thomas J. Campbell, Director, Bureau of Competition, FTC, to Michael N. Sohn, Arnold & Porter (August 19, 1982).

2. Convertible Securities

The acquisition of convertible, nonvoting securities is expressly exempt from the filing requirements of the H-S-R Act until such securities are converted to voting securities. Options and warrants for voting securities receive similar treatment: their acquisition is not reportable, but their exercise is.[444]

These exemptions could become a factor in a control battle between bidders. The initial bidder generally has an advantage over subsequent bidders (including any white knight solicited by the target) because its waiting period under the H-S-R Act is likely to expire first. The target can shift this balance of power, however, by selling to another bidder convertible voting securities, options, or warrants that are not covered by the Act. Although such sales would not give the purchaser immediate control of the target, they might render the acquisition unattractive to the initial bidder or to other bidders.

3. Acquisition by an Acquisition Vehicle

Transactions made through newly formed acquisition vehicles often escape the reporting requirements of the H-S-R Act by virtue of the acquisition vehicles' failure to meet the size of persons threshold. A "person's" size generally is determined by that person's last regularly prepared balance sheet. Because a newly formed entity has no regularly prepared balance sheet, it must evaluate its assets on the basis of the capital contributed to the entity upon its formation. The FTC staff has concluded, however, that assets contributed for consideration in a proposed acquisition should not be taken into account in calculating a new entity's size.

There is some logic to this position. Funds contributed for an acquisition simply flow through a newly formed entity and have no effect on its preacquisition competitive significance.

444. Rules 801.32, 802.31.

Moreover, a contrary interpretation would render the size of person test meaningless: any time an acquisition by a newly formed entity met the $15 million size of transaction test, it also would necessarily meet the $10 million size of person test.

The FTC's view, however, has created a substantial gap in the H-S-R Act's coverage. As long as a newly formed entity does not have $10 million in assets (exclusive of the consideration for a proposed acquisition) and is not controlled by any other person with $10 million in assets, it may be used to effect a substantial acquisition that escapes reporting under the Act.

The FTC widened this gap in the H-S-R Act's coverage in a ruling concerning the acquisition of Phillips Petroleum Company by Mesa Partners, a general partnership formed by three companies, including a subsidiary of Mesa Petroleum Co. In 32 separate transactions, Mesa Partners acquired a total of 8,980,000 shares (about 5.8 percent) of Phillips for approximately $383 million. Mesa Partners never filed a premerger notification form on the theory that, except for money flowing through the entity in order to acquire Phillips shares, the partnership never had assets of $10 million. Phillips complained to the FTC that Mesa Partners had more than $10 million in assets in the form of Phillips voting securities, but the FTC decided in Mesa Partners' favor, reasoning that a person's prior possession of a target's securities has no bearing on an acquisition's anticompetitive potential.

Thus, the current state of the law is as follows: where an acquisition vehicle (i) is not controlled, (ii) does not have a regularly prepared balance sheet, (iii) does not have $10 million in sales, and (iv) does not have $10 million in assets (exclusive both of cash to be used as consideration in the acquisition and of any voting securities of the target), the acquisition vehicle will not meet the size of person test, and the acquisition need not be reported under the H-S-R Act.

These requirements are most easily met when the acquisition vehicle is a partnership. Under the H-S-R Act, a partnership is not subject to control by any other entity and, regardless of the interests of its partners, will not be considered part of a larger person for purposes of the size of person test. Moreover, the formation of a partnership is not a reportable event. Thus, an acquiror can make a substantial acquisition through a newly formed partnership without filing a premerger notification form.

If the acquisition vehicle is a corporate joint venture, applicability of the H-S-R requirements will depend on the interests of the parties forming the venture. If a single person holds 50 percent or more of the voting securities of the joint venture, the venture will be included within that person for purposes of the size of person test, and the acquisition probably will be reportable. Moreover, the formation of a corporate joint venture must be reported if the size of transaction test and a special size of person test are met.[445] Conversely, if no participant in a corporate joint venture receives either a 50 percent interest or voting securities valued at more than $15 million (the size of transaction test for the joint venture's formation), neither the formation of, nor an acquisition by, the joint venture need be reported.

The H-S-R Rules prohibit the use of devices to evade filing requirements, and an acquisition vehicle created to escape the H-S-R Act's coverage might be considered such a device.[446] The FTC has acknowledged, however, that creation of acquisition vehicles is often justified by tax and other business considerations, and, in most circumstances, the use of such vehicles should be defensible.[447]

The enforcement agencies realize that many acquisitions go unreported because they are accomplished through newly formed entities. In 1985, the FTC reported new Rules that would apply the H-S-R reporting requirements to a holder of a

445. The formation of a corporate joint venture meets the size of person test if (i) one of the parties forming the joint venture is a $100 million person, another party is a $10 million person, and the joint venture has assets of $10 million, or (ii) two parties forming the joint venture are $10 million persons and the joint venture has assets of $100 million. Rule 801.40.

446. Rule 801.90.

447. 50 Fed. Reg. 38,744 (1985).

minority interest in an acquisition vehicle if the holder's pro rata interest in the acquisition meets the size of transaction standard. The FTC invited public comment in the fall of 1985 and, after reviewing the responses, decided to reconsider the proposed Rules. It is unclear whether the FTC will abandon its proposals or resubmit them in revised form.

CHAPTER

6

JUNK BOND FINANCING OF TENDER OFFERS

A. Junk Bond Financing

During the last few years (particularly before the Federal Reserve Board's interpretation of the margin requirements' application to leveraged acquisitions of publicly traded stock[448]), high yield corporate bond financing, more commonly referred to as junk bond financing, has emerged as a particularly attractive means of acquiring a company whose stock is considered to be undervalued. Junk bonds simply are bonds of less than investment grade. Junk bond financing of tender offers involves the use of a highly leveraged shell company that the bidder funds with a minimal amount of cash. The bulk of the shell's capital derives from a combination of privately placed, high coupon debt instruments and bank financing (sometimes coupled with preferred stock). After completing the acquisition, the bidder often either sells the assets of the target (a "bust-up" takeover) and retires the debt instruments with the proceeds or restructures the company to meet its increased debt burden.

Junk bonds usually have a rate of return that is three to four percentage points higher than is the typical rate of return on corporate bonds of investment grade. However, junk bonds also have a default rate that is 20 times higher than that on all corporate bonds: during the past ten years, junk bonds' default rate was 1.6 percent per year, as compared with 0.08 percent for all corporate bonds. The real rate of loss, however, is closer to one percent, because issuers of junk bonds often pay back some of the principal and interest.[449]

Carl Icahn's 1985 bid for Phillips Petroleum provides a classic example of the use of junk bonds. Icahn, who owned a 4.8 percent interest in Phillips, threatened to make a two-tier tender offer for the company at $55 per share if the company did not raise to $55 its buy-back offer to shareholders. Icahn intended to pay for the first tier (consisting of 51 percent of Phillips'

---

448. *See infra* § II.6.B.

449. *See* Altman & Nammacher, *The Default Rate Experience on High Yield Corporate Debt* (March 1985) (a study conducted for Morgan Stanley & Co.).

securities) with cash and for the second tier with securities purportedly valued at $55. Although Phillips doubted that Icahn could obtain the financing necessary to complete the offering, Icahn demonstrated that he had commitments from investors for the purchase of $1.5 billion in junk bonds and that, if necessary, he could raise an additional $2.7 billion.[450] These investors conditioned their commitment to purchase the junk bonds upon the success of the tender offer, and Icahn agreed to pay a commitment fee if the bonds were not issued.

Some commentators criticize the current craze for junk bonds because such financing results in significantly higher leveraging of companies acquired in hostile tender offers. Although bidders assert that companies generally do not make sufficient use of the debt market, their critics equate the increase in leveraging with the market trends that occurred before the stock market crash of 1929 and argue that increased debt may result in more bankruptcies in the future.

Drexel Burnham Lambert Inc., the industry leader in the placement of junk bonds, has contended that junk bonds are not a new phenomenon. According to Drexel, more than 85 percent of the debt securities issued by publicly held companies in the United States with assets in excess of $25 million would fall below investment grade if rated and hence would be considered junk bonds. Drexel further noted that only 12 percent of the $14 billion raised through public high yield bond issues in 1984 was issued in connection with acquisitions or leveraged buy-outs; by contrast, mergers and acquisitions in 1984 consumed $122 billion in cash, bank borrowings, and internal cash flow.[451]

Junk bond financing of takeovers frequently occurs through private placements, although bidders also have sold junk bonds to the public. Public offerings may raise the issue whether the bidder adequately has disclosed all material information

---

450. *See* "Many Sign Up in Phillips Bid," *The New York Times*, Feb. 21, 1985, at D1, col. 3.

451. Corporate Finance Briefing, Drexel Burnham Lambert Inc., Washington, D.C. (May 8, 1985).

concerning its acquisition intentions—in particular, whether there has been adequate disclosure of the intended use of proceeds, whether the prospectus speaks generally of possible acquisitions, and whether, soon after the public offering, the bidder intends to start a tender offer for a particular target.[452]

B. The Margin Requirements

Section 7 of the Exchange Act[453] limits the amount of credit that may be used to finance any transaction involving non-exempt securities. Sections 7(a) and (b) authorize the Federal Reserve System's Board of Governors (the "FRB") to promulgate rules regulating the amount of credit that may be used in transactions in which securities are offered as collateral to secure a loan.

In January 1986, the FRB adopted a new interpretation of Regulation G,[454] the margin rule applicable to lenders other than banks and brokers. Regulation G (like Regulation U, the margin requirement applicable to banks) applies only to loans made for the purpose of buying "margin securities," and only if the loan is directly secured by margin securities. The first requirement is satisfied in the case of most tender offers for shares of large, publicly traded companies. The second question was the subject of the FRB's interpretation: is a loan made to a shell company, to finance a tender offer, deemed to be indirectly secured by the target's shares and thus subject to margin rules?

Under the interpretation, the FRB considers a loan to a shell company with no significant business function other than to acquire and hold the stock of a public company, and with substantially no assets other than the margin stock to be acquired through a tender offer, to be indirectly secured by the

---

452. *See Revlon, Inc. v. Pantry Pride, Inc.*, 621 F. Supp. 804 (D. Del. 1985) (denying preliminary injunction).

453. 15 U.S.C. § 78g.

454. 12 C.F.R. § 207 (1986).

shares to be acquired in the tender offer. The loan therefore is subject to the margin requirements, even in the absence of any express restrictions on the shell's ability to dispose of the target's shares. This presumption that the loan is indirectly secured by margin stock does not apply, however, if there is evidence that lenders could rely in good faith on assets other than margin stock as collateral, as would be the case, for example, if the debt securities were guaranteed by the shell company's parent or by another company with substantial nonmargin stock assets or cash flow.

The FRB's interpretation of Regulation G provides for two exceptions. First, the presumption does not apply if the acquiring company and the target have entered into a merger agreement before loaned funds are advanced. Thus, loans made to finance a tender offer as the first step of a negotiated leveraged buy-out are exempt from the margin rules. Second, the presumption does not apply if the loan is conditioned on the bidder's acquiring the minimum number of shares needed under applicable state law to effect a merger (*i.e.*, a short-form merger) between the bidder and the target without the approval of the target's shareholders or directors. Because a merger is likely to take place promptly in either of these two situations, the FRB believes that the lenders reasonably could be presumed to be relying on the target's assets, rather than on the stock acquired in the tender offer, for repayment of the loan.

The FRB's interpretation also considers a case in which an operating company with substantial assets or cash flow seeks to acquire a significantly larger target by means of a tender offer through a new shell subsidiary. In such a case, the acquiror might finance the tender offer through two sources: a bank loan to the shell company secured by the target's shares but in compliance with the margin restrictions of Regulation U[455] (*i.e.*, the loan does not exceed 50 percent of the value of the target's shares to be acquired), or an unsecured borrowing by the shell company backed up by a guarantee from the parent company.

---

455. 12 C.F.R. § 221 (1986).

The FRB will not presume a loan guaranteed by the parent company to be indirectly secured by the target's shares because the bidder's parent has substantial assets or cash flow; the existence of such assets or cash flow suggests that lenders who have received a guarantee from the parent may be relying on the parent's assets, rather than on the target's shares, to insure repayment of the loan.

Under the FRB's interpretation of Regulation G, it is difficult for a bidder without significant assets or operations to make a loan-financed bid for a public company except pursuant to a merger agreement with the target. This difficulty is exacerbated by the fact that the FRB's interpretation of when a loan is indirectly secured applies not only to non-bank loans (subject to Regulation G) but also to bank loans (subject to Regulation U).

To circumvent these new margin requirements, bidders that are not operating companies may seek to finance tender offers by issuing preferred stock or other equity securities, rather than by borrowing. Bidders also may seek to finance offers through public sales of bonds. The FRB's interpretation does not state that publicly offered debt securities are subject to the margin requirements, and the notice accompanying the final interpretation indicates that, unless and until the FRB formally amends Regulation G, bidders may continue to rely on FRB staff opinions to the effect that publicly offered debt securities are not subject to the margin regulations if the public offering is bona fide. But the notice raises an interpretative question as to whether a registered offering is in fact a public offering if the securities are sold in such large minimum amounts (as in Pantry Pride's junk bond offering to finance its bid for Revlon, where the minimum purchase was $2.5 million) that the sale in practice resembles a private placement.

CHAPTER

7

CONFLICTS OF INTEREST AND CONFIDENTIAL INFORMATION

Banks often acquire confidential information concerning companies with which they have commercial relationships. When such a bank is approached by a bidder to assist in financing the acquisition of one of the bank's customers, the bank is subject to potential liability for using inside information relating to the target in connection with its participation in the acquisition. A bank that discloses to a potential bidder material, nonpublic information concerning a target-client could be liable as a tipper under the anti-fraud provisions of the Exchange Act and also could be liable for breaching its fiduciary duties to its customer.

A bank must guard against even internal use of nonpublic information acquired from a client because such information could give the bank an improper competitive advantage. Some banks have established "Chinese Walls" and other protections to insure that decisionmakers will not use confidential material in determining whether to finance a tender offer.

Most courts that have considered the matter have declined to enjoin a target's bank from financing a bidder's tender offer for the target. In *Washington Steel Corp. v. TW Corp.*,[456] for example, the Court of Appeals for the Third Circuit reversed a preliminary injunction and held that a bank had not breached its fiduciary duty to a target-client by participating in a tender offer for the target. The target argued that the bank owed it a fiduciary duty because the target had given to the bank a study projecting the target's future earnings. Furthermore, the target asserted that the bank's participation in the takeover attempt constituted a *per se* breach of the bank's fiduciary duty to its customer.

The court rejected such a *per se* rule as well as the target's contention that the bank had breached its fiduciary duty by using the financial study received from the target. The court noted the absence of any allegation that the bank had tipped information to the bidder and found that the bank had not used the information in deciding whether to loan money for the

---

456. 602 F.2d 594 (3d Cir. 1979).

takeover bid. More importantly, the court stated that, even if the bank had used this information, the bank still would not have breached any duty: "We do not believe that a bank violates any duty it may owe to one of its borrowers when it uses information received from that borrower in deciding whether or not to make a loan to another prospective borrower."[457] A rule prohibiting banks from using all available information in determining whether to make a loan either might compel banks to enter blindly into transactions that may hurt the banks' depositors or might discourage banks from lending money. The court observed, however, that its decision was limited to situations in which a bank used customer information internally, within its commercial lending department. Supplying this inside information to other departments, such as the bank's trust department, could result in a violation of section 10(b) of the Exchange Act.

In *American Medicorp, Inc. v. Continental Illinois National Bank and Trust Co.*,[458] which also dealt with a bank's use of customer information, another court declined to enjoin a bank from lending money to a bidder to finance a tender offer for a customer of the bank. The target contended that the bank's loan was a *per se* breach of the bank's fiduciary duty to the target because the target had supplied the bank with confidential information during the course of their commercial relationship. As in *Washington Steel Corp.*, the court declined to adopt such a *per se* rule and held that the target had not established that a bank would breach any duty either by using confidential information in deciding whether to make a loan or by revealing that information to a third party.[459]

---

457. *Id.* at 603.

458. 475 F. Supp. 5 (N.D. Ill. 1977).

459. *Id.* at 10; *see also Harnischfeger Corp. v. Paccar, Inc.*, 474 F. Supp. 1151 (E.D. Wis.), *aff'd without opinion*, 624 F.2d 1103 (7th Cir. 1979); *cf. Walton v. Morgan Stanley & Co.*, 623 F.2d 796 (2d Cir. 1980) (receipt of confidential information from a target by a financial adviser does not, in and of itself, change the nature of the arm's-length relationship between the parties, and the financial adviser did not breach its fiduciary duty by using the information to advise a bidder for the target).

In its package of proposed legislation submitted to Congress in 1980, the SEC recommended amendments to the Williams Act that would have required five-percent shareholders and tender offerors to disclose information when financing their acquisitions with loans from banks that had prior business dealings with the target.[460] The SEC proposals attempted to diminish the possibility that banks would use information acquired from the target in a manner that would conflict with the target's interests.

After considering a variety of approaches to the issue, including a prohibition on loans by banks in connection with any acquisition of their customers' securities, the SEC determined that the disclosure by a lending bank of a possible conflict of interest provided adequate protection to the public. The SEC's proposal would have required a bidder to disclose the name of its lending bank if that bank had had a prior commercial relationship with the target. The SEC also proposed legislation that would have prohibited any lender of money for a tender offer from tipping any nonpublic information learned from a target.

As of yet, none of the above proposals has been adopted.

---

460. Securities and Exchange Commission Report on Tender Offer Laws (Comm. Print March 1980).

CHAPTER

8

FRAUDULENT CONVEYANCE ISSUES

One popular method of acquiring a company is through a leveraged buy-out ("LBO"), in which, in essence, the acquiror uses the target company's credit to back up the borrowing of the funds needed to buy out the public's shares and to refinance any of the target's debt that may need refinancing. While LBOs traditionally have taken the form of mergers in which lenders have had direct access to the target's assets, mergers take much longer to consummate than do tender offers and thus are more vulnerable to competing bids. Consequently, more and more LBOs have taken place in two steps: a tender offer followed by a merger.

Because the LBO acquisition vehicle may itself have little borrowing capacity, the initial tender offer sometimes is structured as a joint tender offer by the LBO acquisition vehicle and the target. This structure accords lenders direct access to the target's credit.

If the tender offer phase of a two-step LBO succeeds and the bidder subsequently merges with the target, the target will assume the bidder's debts by operation of law. This assumption of debts (or the borrowings by the target, if the initial tender offer is in part by the target or if the LBO is a one-step merger) may lead to questions whether, under the law of fraudulent conveyances, the target has obtained fair consideration (or reasonably equivalent value) in the transaction or whether the transaction has rendered the target insolvent.

Typically, the transaction does not result in the target's receiving fair consideration in exchange for its borrowing money or for use of its credit. The LBO dramatically reduces the target's stockholders' equity, and the funds generated by the acquisition are paid not to creditors but to stockholders.

Under most state and federal (the Bankruptcy Code) fraudulent conveyance statutes, if a company makes any transfer or incurs any obligation without receiving fair consideration, the creditors of that company may sue to invalidate any such transfer or obligation if the company was insolvent or in a precarious financial condition (as defined in the applicable statute) at the time of the transaction or if that transaction rendered the company insolvent or financially unstable. Thus, any payment of cash or issuance of subordinated debt by a financially impaired target to its stockholders pursuant to a tender offer or other LBO transaction may be deemed, for purposes of fraudulent conveyance statutes, to have been made without fair consideration, because the transaction did not provide fair value to the target from the perspective of its prior creditors. Accordingly, the target's creditors could sue under state law (or, in the event of subsequent bankruptcy proceedings, the debtor or bankruptcy trustee could sue under state or federal law) to invalidate and recapture from stockholders any such cash payment or debt issuance, if the transaction left the target insolvent under the tests prescribed in the applicable statutes.

Under some circumstances, the target's creditors could sue the lender that loaned money to the bidder to purchase the shares held by the target's public stockholders, and the debts owed to the lender could be subject to subordination. For instance, if one views the takeover as a purchase of the publicly held shares followed by the target's upstream guarantee of the acquiring corporation's debt, the bidder's creditors would become beneficiaries of the disguised upstream guarantee, and obligations incurred by the financially impaired target could be subordinated as fraudulent conveyances.

Because of the fraudulent conveyance risk, LBO tender offer materials often (and LBO proxy statements always) disclose the possibility that the transaction may pose fraudulent conveyance questions. When GAF made a tender offer for Union Carbide, for example, GAF's tender offer materials contained the following disclosure:

> (f) Potential Creditor Claims. It may be contended that, due to the proposed merger of Purchaser into the Company, the Shareholders who tender their Shares pursuant to the Offer could be potentially liable to the Company's creditors for the payment received by them pursuant to the offer on the theory that the Company would be rendered insolvent, or left with unreasonably small capital with which to continue its business. It is also possible that creditors of the Company on a similar theory may seek to impede or enjoin sales of the Company's business segments referred to in Section 10 and described in Section 12, or the application of the proceeds of such sales to the repayment of acquisition indebtedness. GAF believes that the theory will not be warranted by the facts. This conclusion is based on, among

> other things, (i) an analysis of what will be the fair salable value of the Company's assets immediately after such merger; (ii) an estimate of the Company's probable liability on its existing debts, as they become absolute and mature; and (iii) projections as to the Company's earnings, cash flow, and working capital positions over the years following such merger. Based, among other things, upon these analyses and projections, GAF has concluded that, after the proposed merger of Purchaser into the Company, the Company will be solvent and have sufficient capital with which to conduct its business.

While such disclosures are unusual (and may not be necessary) in hostile tender offers by third parties that are not shells, these disclosures are customary in negotiated LBO disclosure documents.

Fraudulent conveyance questions may arise not only under the Bankruptcy Code[461] but also under the Uniform Fraudulent Conveyance Act, which has been adopted by 26 states, including New York. Several other states have other statutes pertaining to fraudulent transfers.

---

461. 12 U.S.C. § 548.

CHAPTER

9

STRATEGIC LITIGATION

A bidder that launches a tender offer must be prepared to litigate a variety of issues; the bidder's counsel and senior management thus should address litigation strategies, and the impact of litigation on the tender offer, before the offer begins. Advance preparation is necessary to minimize the possibility that litigation will block or delay the offer (thereby making it less competitive) or result in the release of sensitive corporate information.

A general litigation strategy should take into account the bidder's overall corporate interests. In addition, counsel must prepare to confront the legal issues that are likely to arise. Tender offer litigation tends to be fast-paced, leaving counsel with little time to research issues once the war has commenced.

A bidder's litigation strategy generally includes three components: preparing to resist the target's attack, suing to challenge state takeover statutes, and selecting a relatively favorable forum.

A. Preparing to Resist the Target's Attack

Litigation attorneys should be key members of the bidder's team. In addition to anticipating legal challenges that the target may mount, counsel should review drafts of the offer or proxy materials for possible disclosure problems or other legal issues upon which the target might seize in an attempt to enjoin or delay the offer.

As soon as they can identify possible bases for legal challenges, litigation counsel should prepare drafts of memoranda to oppose such attacks. These memoranda can be used either as the basis for oral or written presentations to administrative agencies investigating antitrust or regulatory issues or as court papers filed to resist motions for preliminary injunctive relief. Draft briefs should address not only the merits of the particular questions but also other reasons why preliminary injunctive relief is not warranted: the standards for injunctive relief, the extraordinary nature of injunctive relief, the harm to the bidder should an injunction be issued, the adequacy of money damages should a court subsequently determine the bid to be somehow improper, etc.

If the bidder can identify the forum that the target is likely to select, the bidder should consider retaining local counsel, both to obtain help in immediately resisting motions for preliminary injunctive relief and to prevent the target from hiring such counsel. The bidder should insure that the prospective local counsel have no ties to the target.

Litigation counsel also should assemble and review all of the bidder's documents that the target is likely to request in discovery. This review will enable the bidder both to identify troublesome issues in advance, so that it might make appropriate disclosures in its offering materials (thereby precluding claims of inadequate disclosure), and to respond promptly to the target's predictable request for expedited discovery. The bidder's inability to comply with an expedited discovery schedule could, in an extreme case, delay the injunction hearing and the bidder's timetable, thereby affording the target more time to take defensive steps or to find a white knight.

Once a bid is launched, the bidder's litigation attorneys might find it advisable to identify themselves to the target's counsel (if the identity of the target's counsel is known) in order to make it more difficult for the target to obtain a temporary restraining order on an *ex parte* basis.

B. Suing to Challenge State Takeover Statutes

If the bidder's tender offer will involve states with takeover statutes[462] that either the target or the state authorities might invoke to slow down or block the takeover, the bidder's litigation counsel should consider filing suit in federal district court in those states to obtain declarations of the statutes'

---

462. *See infra* § III.5. (discussing state takeover statutes).

unconstitutionality and injunctions against their enforcement. Such suits could contend that the state statutes are preempted by the Williams Act or that they impose an impermissible burden on interstate commerce.

In *Edgar v. MITE Corp.*,[463] the Supreme Court invalidated an Illinois statute on Commerce Clause grounds. Since that decision, various courts have invalidated many other state takeover statutes. Some statutes passed in response to *MITE*, however, have been upheld.[464]

Bidders suing to enjoin application of state takeover statutes typically file suit in federal court immediately upon commencing a hostile bid and before the target (or the state regulatory authority) can bring an action in state court to enforce the statutes, because the prior commencement of the bidder's federal suit reduces the risk that the federal court might decline to enjoin enforcement of the state statute on the basis either of the Anti-Injunction Act[465] (which, with specified exceptions, requires a federal court not to enjoin a pending state action) or of principles of abstention or comity. In *Icahn v. Blunt*,[466] for example, the federal district court, in enjoining enforcement of the Missouri takeover statute as applied to Carl Icahn's proposed takeover of TWA, noted that Icahn had commenced his federal action to invalidate the statute one day before a state court claim had been amended to seek enforcement of the statute.

In addition, the court held that Icahn's suit fell within the Anti-Injunction Act's exception for stays expressly authorized by act of Congress, because Icahn claimed that the Missouri statute violated his civil rights under 42 U.S.C. § 1983. Citing the

---

463. 457 U.S. 624 (1982).

464. *See Cardiff Acquisitions, Inc. v. Hatch*, 751 F.2d 906 (8th Cir. 1984) (upholding certain aspects of Minnesota's Corporate Takeovers Act); *Agency Rent-A-Car, Inc. v. Connolly*, 686 F.2d 1029 (1st Cir. 1982) (upholding provision of Massachusetts statute). *But see APL Ltd. Partnership v. Van Dusen Air, Inc.*, 622 F. Supp. 1216 (D. Minn. 1985), *vacated as moot*, No. 85-5346 (8th Cir. Nov. 25, 1986) (enjoining application of portions of Minnesota statute); *Icahn v. Blunt*, 612 F. Supp. 1400 (W.D. Mo. 1985) (enjoining application of portions of Missouri statute).

465. 28 U.S.C. § 2283.

466. 612 F. Supp. 1400 (W.D. Mo. 1985).

important federal policy questions raised by the bidder's suit, the court declined to abstain under *Younger v. Harris*[467] and its progeny, which hold that a federal court should not enjoin a state court proceeding commenced after the filing of the federal case but before substantive proceedings on the merits have begun in the federal suit. Similarly, the court declined to abstain under *Railroad Commission of Texas v. Pullman Co.*[468] and subsequent cases holding that a federal court should refrain from deciding unsettled questions of state law where resolution of such issues by a state court might obviate the need for a federal court to decide the plaintiff's federal claims. The *Blunt* court ruled that Icahn's suit did not raise unsettled state law questions that a state court could resolve through a narrowing construction of the statute; in the court's view, the state statute was clearly unconstitutional.

C. Choice of Forum

The target is likely to elect to sue the bidder in a "home town" forum where the judge may be more sympathetic to the target's allegations concerning the bidder's conduct. The target has a wide choice of forums for federal claims based on alleged violations of the Williams Act or proxy rules: it may sue in any district in or to which the tender offer or proxy materials were mailed, on the theory that the wrong occurred (at least in part) in such district.[469]

To guard against the possibility of ending up with a pro-target, home town judge, the bidder should consider filing suit against

---

467. 401 U.S. 37 (1971).

468. 312 U.S. 496 (1941).

469. *See* Exchange Act § 27, 15 U.S.C. § 78aa (suit to enjoin any violation of Exchange Act, or of rules promulgated thereunder, may be brought in any district in which "any act or transaction constituting the violation occurred"); *Warren v. Bokum Resources Corp.*, 433 F. Supp. 1360 (D.N.M. 1977) (jurisdiction exists over bidder in district into which the bidder mailed the allegedly unlawful tender offer).

the target in a more neutral (or favorable) forum, if there is a basis for such a suit (for example, a misleading press release by the target). If it succeeds in filing such a suit, the bidder may be able to cause subsequent litigation commenced by the target to be transferred (as related litigation) to the bidder's chosen forum.

PART

III

DEFENSIVE CONSIDERATIONS

CHAPTER 1

PLANNING CONSIDERATIONS FOR REBUFFING HOSTILE TENDER OFFERS

Tender offers move extraordinarily fast. There is no time for leisurely contemplation of strategic alternatives. Immediate action and reaction are the orders of the day.

Because the target may have very little time for organization and planning once a hostile bidder announces an unsolicited tender offer, advance preparation is essential. The target must remember, however, to conform its ultimate responses to the specific circumstances of a particular offer.

The following sections discuss various elements of a program of preparation, including the creation of a working group to deal with all phases of a tender offer; the allocation of responsibilities to members of that group; the preparation—before an offer is made—of the target's officers and directors; the institution of an "early warning" stock watch program to insure maximum advance notice of an impending tender offer or other stock acquisition scheme; the analysis of the company's shareholders; the commencement of advance research that could prove helpful in a takeover fight; the possible amendment of the target's certificate of incorporation and bylaws; and the adoption of a shareholder rights plan (or "poison pill") or of other potentially useful measures to assure that the target will be in the best position to evaluate a tender offer and to respond appropriately, should the target's directors determine that the offer is not in the best interests of the company's shareholders.

A. Creation of Working Group and Assignment of Responsibilities

1. The Working Group

Virtually no company is immune to a takeover attempt. A target might not learn of a bidder's unwanted attention until the offeror publicly announces the offer, at which point it may already be too late to begin to assemble a defense team and to formulate a defensive strategy. Accordingly, every company should make arrangements for a tender offer defense team as part of its overall long-term planning. The team should include:

- *Officers.* A small group of three to five key corporate officers are critical members of the team. The group should be small enough to insure secrecy and allow for quick assembly, and it probably should include the company's chief executive officer, vice president for finance, secretary, and shareholder/investor-relations manager.
- *Directors.* The target's directors will play an important role in determining the company's response to a tender offer and thus must be kept informed and available for quick decisionmaking.
- *Counsel.* The team also should include both in-house and outside general counsel as well as special tender offer counsel. (Counsel should identify local counsel in jurisdictions where the target is incorporated or does business so that the company can respond to offensive litigation wherever it arises.[470]) Because tender offers proceed at a frenzied pace, it is essential that the target retain experienced tender offer counsel. Counsel must be prepared to advise the target's directors of their responsibilities under federal and state securities and corporation laws and to develop and implement various defensive measures, including litigation, which plays a major role in many hostile tender offer battles. In addition, counsel can help the potential target install various protective measures before a tender offer is ever launched.[471]
- *Investment banker.* Involvement of an experienced and reputable investment banker is vital in assisting a target to understand its strengths and weaknesses and in assessing the adequacy of an unsolicited tender offer. Because these assessments must be accurate and quickly obtainable, it is important to have an ongoing relationship with an investment banker that is familiar with the potential target and its prospects and has a rapport with the company's officers. The investment banker also may act as team

---

470. *See supra* § II.9.

471. *See infra* § III.4.A. (discussing protective measures).

manager, supervising the other participants on the team. Moreover, a friendly investment banker may be able to inform the target of market information and alert the company to possible rumors of an impending tender offer.

- *Public relations firm.* A media campaign often constitutes an important element in a target's defense against a hostile takeover attempt, particularly if the bidder is proceeding by way of a proxy fight or a tender offer using the bidder's own securities. While counsel and the investment banker must shape key press releases (given the legal constraints and financial strategies involved in a takeover contest), a public relations firm can be essential in handling the media campaign.
- *Proxy solicitors.* The target may find it necessary to engage professional proxy solicitors, should a proxy fight constitute part of the takeover battle.
- *Accountants.* Accountants should be available to respond rapidly to questions relating to the structuring of alternative transactions.
- *Financial printer.* A target will find it necessary quickly to produce and distribute a variety of documents—letters to shareholders, SEC filings, etc.—during the course of a hostile tender offer. It thus can be helpful to a target to have an ongoing relationship with a financial printer who will be sensitive to the company's needs and capable of printing large quantities of documents on very short notice, although any good financial printer should be able to meet these requirements.

2. Responsibilities

- *Working group list.* The company's general counsel or secretary should compile and maintain a current list of the names, addresses, and telephone numbers (including home and weekend numbers) of the team members. Such a directory will facilitate rapid communication with and assembly of the working group. The target should be able to convene a meeting of its board of directors on 24 to 48 hours' notice. (Counsel should review the target's bylaws to make sure that a meeting can be quickly called.)

- *Periodic meetings.* Members of the working group should hold periodic meetings to insure that everyone is aware of the latest developments and has the latest information in order to respond promptly, should a response become necessary.
- *Press contacts.* The company should carefully coordinate all press contacts and should insure that only a single spokesperson will communicate with the press in the event that a tender offer is made.

B. Preparation of Officers and Directors

1. Preparation of Officers

The target should advise its officers concerning how to respond to unsolicited approaches. If the company has decided to pursue a policy of independence, officers should realize that the best way to avoid misunderstandings is to reject firmly and unequivocally all unsolicited advances. Thus, an officer (or director) who wishes to convey the idea that the company has no desire to be acquired should not respond "It depends on the price" if asked whether he or she would be interested in pursuing takeover discussions.

Officers also should be advised to make no response whatsoever to unsolicited offers, other than to assemble the company's working group immediately. The target must be very careful about its initial public comments concerning the offer: the SEC has adopted various regulations governing comments by target companies,[472] and the target should avoid violating these regulations. Any such violation could give the potential acquiror a basis for filing suit against the target and thereby controlling the choice of forum. Normally, the target should

472. *See infra* § III.2.A.

issue no press release or statement other than a "stop-look-and-listen" statement, which may announce the calling of a special board meeting to consider the offer and may ask shareholders not to take any action pending further word from the company. Under SEC rules, the target must inform its shareholders, within ten business days of the making of an offer, of its position (or lack thereof) concerning that offer.

2. Preparation of Directors

The company's attorneys and investment bankers should make periodic presentations to the board to familiarize directors with their obligations in the event of a tender offer. The board should review company policy with respect to engaging in acquisition discussions and responding to inquiries. The directors also should understand the importance of centralization of information: all inquiries, however informal, should be reported to the target's chief executive officer, both to prevent the dissemination of conflicting signals and to enable the company rapidly to respond to what could become a fast-paced hostile tender offer.

C. Overview of Pre-Tender Offer Defensive Measures

In addition to assembling a defense team to cope with future hostile tender offers, a potential target can take a number of defensive measures that either will serve as preemptive strikes against future offers or will better prepare the target to oppose such offers. A potential target should undertake these measures before a hostile tender offer is launched against it.

1. Assessing Vulnerability

A potential target should assess its own desirability and vulnerability as a takeover candidate. Various characteristics historically have been associated with supposedly typical target companies: weak management, widespread stock ownership with small management holdings, significant holdings by institutional investors, broadly distributed stock ownership, low market value in comparison with book or liquidation value, and limited outstanding debt. In recent years, however, these alleged hallmarks of vulnerability have not appeared consistently in target companies, and many large companies with good earnings ratios, solid employee and shareholder relations, and strong management have been the victims of hostile tender offers. Many bidders have been examining potential targets as would a leveraged buy-out sponsor, focusing on the existence of underutilized cash flow.

2. Early Warning Systems

A potential target should develop an advance warning system that will enable it to identify takeover threats before they materialize. Of great importance is a stock watch program, to determine and follow the trading patterns of the company's securities and to spot any aberrations.

In connection with a stock watch program, the target should take the following steps:

- *Security.* The target should insure the security of its shareholder list and review the extent of access to that list.
- *Specialist.* The target should check frequently with a specialist concerning trading in the company's shares. Having a good relationship with a specialist is often the best way promptly to obtain information about any unusual market activity.
- *Transfers.* The target should insure that its transfer agents promptly prepare and deliver transfer sheets and advise the company of all large transfers or other unusual movements.
- *Charts.* The target should prepare and maintain charts of daily volume and price to facilitate detection of unusual activity.

- *Contacts with Street.* The target should maintain contacts with banks, mutual funds, insurance companies, investment bankers, and investment advisers to pick up and track down rumors concerning potential takeover threats.
- *SEC filings.* The target should employ a service to monitor all SEC filings made by any third party with respect to the company. These filings, such as Schedules 13D, may indicate that a tender offer for the company's securities is being planned. Although Schedule 13D filers are required to mail copies of the filing to the subject company, such delivery can take several days, and, in the world of tender offers, time is a precious commodity. The target or its monitoring service also should review section 13(f) filings made by large institutional investors, who must report their positions in the target's stock. A number of organizations offer watch services for nominal fees and inform their clients of filings on the very day that those filings occur.
- *Coordinator.* The target should designate an officer who will have both ongoing responsibility for the stock watch program and the duty to alert the working group and initiate action upon detection of a possible takeover threat. This officer also should serve as the clearinghouse for all relevant information obtained outside the scope of the formal program.

Various proxy solicitation firms have begun offering "shark watch" programs to monitor trading, filings, market rumors, and other matters relating to clients' securities. There is some controversy concerning the incremental benefits of these programs; however, the programs may be useful simply because they allow the target to conserve internal resources for other purposes.

3. Shareholder List Analysis and Shareholder Relations

Management should analyze its shareholder list to identify principal shareholders, facilitate communication, and gain a greater understanding of shareholder needs. (For example, knowledge of shareholders' bases for tax purposes may helpmanagement to determine whether shareholders would prefer a taxable or a tax-free transaction.) Advance work in shareholder public relations will lay the foundation for later contacts and can help both to bolster the company's image and to increase shareholders' receptiveness to the company's comments and recommendations, particularly if a potential acquiror launches a proxy fight or an exchange offer rather than a cash tender offer. Efforts undertaken before the advent of a takeover bid also can improve the machinery for contacting shareholders and disseminating information.

Shareholder list analysis involves the compilation and maintenance, to the extent practicable, of the following information concerning each shareholder who owns more than a specified number of shares: (*a*) the number of shares held at past record dates; (*b*) the approximate tax bases of those shares (based on market prices at the time that the shares were acquired); (*c*) the shareholder's voting record; (*d*) any special relationship that the shareholder might have with the company (as employee, retired employee, customer, supplier, etc.); (*e*) any contacts or possible contacts that the shareholder might have with management; (*f*) any known connection that the shareholder might have with a potential acquiror; and (*g*) whether the shares at issue are held by a trust or other fiduciary and, if so, the terms and restrictions contained in the instruments relating to those shares.

The company should attempt to perform several other analyses as well. First, it should analyze periodically the geographic distribution of its shareholders. Second, it should analyze the largest publicly identifiable shareholders, which most likely are large institutions (banks, mutual funds, etc.), and should develop data as to their percentage ownership of shares. Contacts with these large shareholders should be cultivated assiduously. Third, the company should determine the number of shares held by its employee benefit plans and should analyze the instruments governing those plans to ascertain whether, in the event of a tender offer, the shares may be tendered or may be sold to an alternative suitor. Fourth, the company should review how many shares are held by management.

The company also should try to discover the identity of the beneficial owners of securities held in street name. Management often can obtain these owners' names by including shareholder response cards in the company's annual reports. Learning the identity of these shareholders not only helps management to ascertain shareholders' concerns; it also speeds up the process of contacting shareholders during any hostile control battle.

4. Advance Research

Because speed and efficiency are so critical once a hostile takeover attempt has commenced, a potential target should undertake and keep current the research and other work necessary to provide information that might be needed if a tender offer should materialize. Advance research may include the following areas of inquiry.

a. Company Background

The target should compile, review, and update background information relating to the company in order both to determine whether legal or other defenses exist against an undesirable offer and to be in a position promptly to seek an alternative business transaction, if necessary. Relevant background information includes:

- *Certificate of incorporation and bylaws.* The company and its counsel should analyze any restrictions imposed by the certificate of incorporation and the bylaws.[473]

473. *Cf. infra* §§ III.1.C(5),(6) and III.4.A. (discussing possible amendments that the company might make to those documents).

- *Loan agreements.* The company and its counsel should examine loan agreements and other instruments relating to the borrowing of money to see whether they contain restrictive covenants that may relate to possible defensive maneuvers in the event of a takeover. Counsel should look for, among other things, restrictions on liquidations, distributions, sales of assets, and purchases by the company of its own shares.
- *Brokers' reports.* The company should review recent financial analyses of the company by brokerage firms, investment advisers, etc. Such analyses can be valuable in identifying the company's strengths and weaknesses as perceived by the Wall Street community.
- *Business lines.* The company should review information concerning its line(s) of business and its market share in each business line. This information takes time to assemble, and it may be of critical importance should the company and its counsel decide to seek judicial or administrative relief from a takeover bid on antitrust grounds.
- *Interested companies.* The company should compile a history of any recent expressions of interest in the company by any other company. This information may help either to identify a potential acquiror or to suggest possibilities for a defensive merger that may be more beneficial to the potential target and its shareholders. The company should realize, however, that advance contact with potential alternative suitors may lead to undesirable misunderstandings.
- *Tax position.* The company's accountants should review the tax consequences to the company of a tender offer, merger, or asset disposition to determine, among other things, (i) whether the company has tax loss carry-forwards that could be jeopardized in certain transactions or that could enhance the value of other transactions, and (ii) whether the company has assets that could be stepped up in a premium transaction, and, if so, what recaptures would accompany those step-ups.

- *Preparation by investment banker.* The company should keep current a due diligence file and an analysis of off-balance-sheet values and should discuss these materials with its investment banker, to facilitate prompt preparation of an offering memorandum.

b. Regulatory Matters

The company and its counsel should review any applicable regulatory schemes to determine whether any agency or commission must approve any change in control. Relevant considerations may include the following:

- *Location of assets.* The company should consider whether any of its assets are located in a foreign jurisdiction that requires governmental approval of either a change in control or an acquisition of a significant stock position (*e.g.*, the Investment Canada Act).
- *Nature of business.* The company should consider whether it (or any of its subsidiaries) engages in one or more lines of business involving significant governmental regulation and whether it must obtain governmental approval of either a change in control or an acquisition of a significant stock position (*e.g.*, insurance, banking, public utility, common carrier).
- *Nature of customers.* The company should consider whether it provides goods or services to the United States Government or to foreign countries and whether a change in control either might adversely affect the company's competitive position or might result in termination of important contracts. These considerations may be especially critical if the potential acquiror is a foreign enterprise.

c. *State Takeover Statutes*

The potential target also should investigate the existence and terms of any state takeover statutes that might apply to a takeover bid. These statutes might require an offeror to give advance notice before making a tender offer and to leave the offer open for a stated period of time; they also might provide for hearings before regulatory authorities concerning disclosures in a proposed tender offer.

The Supreme Court's 1982 decision in *Edgar v. MITE Corp.*,[474] which declared the Illinois Business Takeover Act unconstitutional, has substantially weakened the vitality of state takeover statutes to the extent that they purport to regulate offers made to residents of other states. In light of that ruling, a number of states have revised their statutes.

Some states, including Pennsylvania and Maryland, have written the equivalent of fair price provisions into their statutes. The Ohio statute (and a number of similar statutes) requires, among other things, the approval of a majority of the shares held by the target's disinterested shareholders before an acquiror may obtain, by tender offer or otherwise, 20 percent or more of the target's outstanding shares. This statute recently was struck down on constitutional grounds in *Fleet Aerospace Corp. v. Holderman*.[475] New York imposes a flat five-year ban against mergers between a target and a 20-percent shareholder absent approval by the target's directors before the 20-percent threshold is crossed.[476]

All of these state statutes apply only to target companies organized under the laws of the relevant state. Thus, for a company to obtain the benefits of any given statute, it must be incorporated, or must reincorporate, in that particular state. Reincorporation requires shareholder action: typically, approval

---

474. 457 U.S. 624 (1982).

475. 796 F.2d 135 (6th Cir. 1986), *appeal docketed*, No. 86-344, 55 U.S.L.W. 3175 (U.S. Sept. 2, 1986).

476. N.Y. Bus. Corp. L. § 912.

of the company's merger into a new company organized under the laws of the desired state. The benefits of such reincorporation, however, are unclear, because the constitutionality of many of these state statutes has not yet been tested. Many experts believe that the most far-reaching of these statutes will not withstand constitutional scrutiny.[477]

5. Charter Amendments

A potential target might make itself less attractive to corporate raiders by amending its charter in such a way as to make it more difficult for a hostile acquiror to change control of the target even after purchasing a majority of the target's shares. Such charter amendments include the imposition of supermajority voting provisions, requiring the votes of 66-2/3 or 80 percent of the target's shareholders before a merger can be effected; the classification of directors' terms, theoretically delaying for two years the obtaining of effective control of the board by majority shareholders; the adoption of fair price provisions, which require supermajority support for completing the second step of a two-step tender offer; the placing of limitations on special shareholder meetings and shareholder action by consent (*i.e.*, without a meeting of shareholders); the increasing of the number of the target's authorized shares, thereby enhancing defensive flexibility during a takeover battle; the creation of "blank check" preferred stock, which can be issued to thwart a takeover bid; the adoption of cumulative voting, which might permit management to compete more effectively with an antagonistic holder of a large (but minority) position in the company's common stock (but which would help the holder of a relatively small percentage of stock and would have little effect against the holder of a majority of stock); the adoption of anti-greenmail provisions, prohibiting the payment of a significant premium over market price to a significant shareholder absent

---

477. State takeover statutes are discussed in greater detail in § III.5, *infra.*

approval of some percentage of the target's shareholders as a whole; and the granting of authority to the board to consider noneconomic factors—such as a proposed acquisition's impact not only on the company's shareholders but also on its employees, customers, and suppliers as well as on the communities in which the company's facilities are located—in evaluating a takeover bid.[478]

None of these "shark repellents" is a "showstopper"; indeed, many hostile takeovers in recent years have involved targets whose charters have contained most of the provisions discussed above. Nevertheless, shark repellents may have some deterrent effect, particularly against smaller, ill-financed bidders.

In submitting such charter amendments for shareholder approval, management must take care fully to disclose the effects that the amendments might have on the corporation. An SEC study, for example, has shown a three-percent decline in the economic value of New York Stock Exchange companies that have adopted both fair price amendments and supermajority provisions.[479] Moreover, the adoption of certain provisions such as board classification and supermajority voting can affect corporate governance even absent a takeover bid.

Before proposing any charter amendments, the company should carefully evaluate the likelihood that the shareholders will vote to adopt them. A proxy solicitation firm can assist in assessing particular institutional investors' likely reaction to particular proposed amendments. Proposals that are not adopted could send signals to potential acquirors that the company's shareholders might look sympathetically upon an acquisition proposal. The company also should remember that a number of these amendments, while discouraging unsolicited tender offers, might also reduce the board's flexibility to act in the aftermath of a tender offer.

---

478. These and other "shark repellent" charter amendments are discussed in greater detail in § III.4.A., *infra.*

479. *See* Sec. Reg. & L. Rep. (BNA) vol. 16, no. 44, at 1746 (Nov. 9, 1984).

A potential target incorporated in a state that does not permit certain defensive charter amendments might consider reincorporating itself in a state with more flexible corporate laws, such as Delaware. The company should be aware, however, that, although Delaware law grants the target's board great leeway in responding to a hostile bid, it also might increase the target's vulnerability to a takeover attempt unless the target adopts protective charter amendments. The famous Bendix-Martin Marietta battle illustrates the difficulties that an unprotected target can experience under Delaware law: the hostile bidder, Bendix, was vulnerable to a counter-offer by the target, Martin Marietta, because Bendix' charter (and applicable Delaware law) permitted the holder of a majority of Bendix' shares to take immediate action by written consent, without having to call a shareholders' meeting. Such action was not possible under Maryland law, however, with respect to Marietta. Thus, Marietta would find it easier to gain control over Bendix than would Bendix over Marietta.[480]

6. Bylaw Amendments

If the company's bylaws permit the board of directors to amend the bylaws without obtaining shareholder approval, the board might consider inserting "shark repellent" amendments in the bylaws themselves, without going through the more elaborate process of amending the certificate of incorporation (with shareholder approval). The company must bear in mind that state corporation law may provide that shareholders always are free to amend bylaws; accordingly, the company might wish to propose a charter amendment requiring a supermajority vote of shareholders to amend the bylaws.

Possible bylaw amendments (if permitted by applicable state law) might include the following:

---

480. *See infra* §§ III.2.B(1) and III.4.I. (discussing the Bendix-Marietta battle).

- *Calling of special meetings.* The company might wish to allocate only to the president and a majority of the board of directors the authority to call a special meeting of shareholders. This limitation would increase the difficulty of waging a proxy fight against management or of taking control of the company with less than a majority of shares. If such an amendment were coupled with a charter amendment requiring written consent of all of the company's shareholders in order to take action without a meeting, a would-be acquiror would find it difficult promptly to change the composition of the board and to assert effective control even after acquiring 51 percent of the company's shares.
- *Notice of shareholders' business.* The company could amend the bylaws to require that any shareholder who wishes to bring any business before a meeting must give written notice of the matter at issue within a reasonable period (*e.g.*, 60 to 90 days) before that meeting. A similar provision could apply to shareholder nominees for election as directors. These amendments might help the company in dealing with a large, aggressive shareholder or, at least, would limit the time during which the company would be exposed to a proxy fight. The provisions also could help to insure that shareholders would hear both sides (and not just the bidder's arguments) before voting.
- *Consent procedure.* If the bylaws authorize the board to establish a record date for such business as the taking of actions by written consent, the board could amend the bylaws to require that any shareholder desiring to act by consent notify the board and request the board to set a record date. The amendment then could require the board to set a record date that would give management a reasonable opportunity to react to the proposed transaction and, if desirable, to solicit proxies in opposition. A related amendment could fix a date (*e.g.*, 30 days after the mailing of proxy materials) for determining whether the proposed action received the approval of a majority of shares. Under section 228 of the Delaware corporation statute, if the board

has not established a record date, that date shall be deemed to be the date on which the first written consent is signed. Thus, a significant minority shareholder might be able to solicit consents and then spring a *fait accompli* on the board, which would have no time to solicit opposing proxies.[481]

7. Structural Changes

Before confronting an unwanted tender offer, a potential target might consider a number of possible changes in the company's structure that either would make the company less attractive to raiders or would put the company in a better position to resist an offer that it determines not to be in the best interests of the shareholders. These structural changes include placing "crown jewels"—the company's most desirable assets—in free-standing subsidiaries, to facilitate their rapid sale or spin-off; insuring that indentures and loan agreements do not restrict spin-offs, self-tender offers, or recapitalizations; developing a plan of liquidation; arranging for adequate financing to permit reverse tender offers, preemptive strikes against raiders, and self-tender offers; implementing a program for periodic repurchases of company stock; issuing company stock to a "white squire" (a friendly third party that will hold the shares and vote in accordance with management's wishes) or an employee stock option plan; effecting a leveraged buy-out; recapitalizing the company to increase the debt-to-equity ratio; creating two classes of stock, one with higher voting rights (but restrictions on transfer), the other with lower voting rights (but freely tradeable); and adopting "golden parachutes" for top management. The implementation of these and other structural defenses *before* a raider strikes will assist the board in establishing that it approved the measures after careful consideration

481. These and other forms of "shark repellents" are discussed in greater detail in § III.4.A., *infra*.

consistent with the directors' fiduciary obligations to the shareholders.[482]

8. Poison Pills

A potential target might also elect to issue "poison pills" to deter unwanted tender offers. Poison pills, which are one of the newest and most fashionable defensive techniques, are intended to deter hostile offers by making the cost of such bids prohibitive. While the pills may tend to discourage bidders from proposing weak offers, however, they do not appear to operate as a total bar to takeovers—and are not intended to do so.

Poison pills come in different packages but contain essentially similar toxins. The most common form of pill is a "call" plan, pursuant to which a company declares to shareholders a dividend of a right to buy (or "call") shares of the issuer. An example illustrates how call plans work.

Assume a target with 10,000,000 shares of outstanding common stock that trade at $50 per share. The target may choose to distribute one right for every share of outstanding common stock. The distribution is effected as a dividend, without shareholder approval. Each right entitles the holder to purchase a share of common (or of a new series of preferred) for $150 per share. The rights trade with the common shares and are not initially exercisable; indeed, no one would even wish to exercise a right to pay $150 for shares trading at $50. Thus, the rights presumably have no present market value, and each unit of common-plus-right probably is worth only $50 (unless the market price is affected by the very fact that the rights have been issued).

The toxic feature of the pill, however, lies elsewhere. In the event that a hostile tender offer is announced, the purchase rights become detachable from the common shares. If the bidder

---

482. These and other structural changes are discussed in greater detail in § III.4., *infra*.

acquires more than a threshold amount (typically 20 to 30 percent) of the target's stock and then seeks to consummate a merger, the rights agreement requires that the holder of each outstanding right, or pill, thereafter be entitled to purchase $300 worth of the offeror's stock for $150. The offeror thus would suffer severe dilution of its equity if it attempted to gain complete control of the target.

The rights issuer's board retains control of the poison through its authority to redeem the rights for a nominal amount (*e.g.*, five cents per right) typically until (or for a limited period of time after) someone acquires at least the threshold percentage of the target's stock. It is this redemption power that encourages the bidder to negotiate with the board.

With a pill in place, the takeover scenario might play out as follows. A bidder might offer to effect a friendly merger with the target, paying $600,000,000 (or $60 per share) to buy the 10,000,000 outstanding shares currently trading at $50 per share. If the target's board rebuffs the bidder's friendly overtures, the bidder must decide whether to pursue a hostile tender offer, in which case it would have to address the poison pills that would become detachable from the common shares upon the making of that hostile offer. The bidder would need to determine the necessity of following its tender offer with a merger to eliminate any minority interest not wiped out through the tender offer. If the bidder would be willing to live indefinitely (or for the ten-year life of the rights) with the minority interest, the bidder could simply ignore the pills, for their poison typically would be activated only by the clean-up merger or by certain kinds of self-dealing transactions. But many successful bidders would not wish to suffer the existence of a minority interest in their newly acquired company. A bidder that wishes to get rid of the minority would have to buy up as many of the detachable rights as possible prior to the merger, to prevent the pills from becoming poisonous during and after the merger.

The bidder might attempt to negate the rights by making its tender offer for both common stock and rights and by conditioning its obligation to purchase *any* securities on the tender of, for example, at least 95 percent of the rights. The problem with this approach, however, is obvious: every rights holder will know that, upon a subsequent merger, his right will be worth far more than he would be paid for it up front, during the tender offer; he therefore will have a strong incentive to withhold his rights, hoping—probably in vain—that other, less calculating holders will tender sufficient rights to satisfy the bidder's minimum. (It is true, however, that such "sophisticated" holders might risk outsmarting themselves: if the bidder truly has no desire to effect a subsequent merger, and if the tender offer fails because the bidder's minimum tender conditions have not been met, the holders will have deprived themselves of the tender offer price even though, had they tendered, the pills would have remained untriggered and the rights might have had little or no value.)

The bidder also could condition its tender offer on elimination of the rights, either through redemption by the target's board or through judicial invalidation. If the target's board has not come up with better alternatives for shareholders as the end of the tender offer approaches, and if most shareholders have shown their approval of the offer by tendering their shares, the target's directors may be under heavy pressure to redeem the rights. Failure to do so may expose the directors to shareholder suits if the bidder withdraws its offer and the price of the target's stock falls back to its pre-bid levels.

The adoption of a poison pill plan might also affect the initial tender offer price. A bidder that was willing, in the absence of a pill, to pay $600,000,000 in cash to effect a friendly merger might reduce that sum by the maximum amount of dilution it could afford to suffer in a subsequent merger. If the bidder conditioned its offer on obtaining 95 percent (9,500,000) of the 10,000,000 outstanding rights, it still would face exposure to as many as 500,000 outstanding rights at the time of the subsequent merger. These rights, each of which would give a holder $150 worth of "free" shares of the bidder, would dilute the bidder's equity by as much as $75,000,000. The bidder thus would not be willing to pay more than $525,000,000 for 100 percent of the common and 95 percent of the rights and consequently might wish either to reduce its tender offer price to protect against this dilution or to make a tender offer with two prices—$600,000,000 if the board redeems the rights, but $525,000,000 if the rights are not redeemed. Again, this strategy would tend to pressure the target's board to redeem the rights, unless the board can come up with a better alternative (*e.g.*, recapitalization or a white knight merger) for the shareholders.

Users (and victims) of poison pills should realize, however, that pills tend *not* to be "showstoppers," guaranteed to scare away or defeat hostile offerors. Rather, pills far more often constitute negotiating tools that the target may be able to use to obtain better offers or friendlier bidders.[483]

9. Defensive Acquisitions

Another tactic available to a potential target is to make "defensive acquisitions" by acquiring other companies that would render the target a less eligible takeover candidate. Acquiring companies in certain regulated industries, such as banks and savings and loan associations, could help to discourage a hostile bid: many bidders depend on speedy hit-and-run tactics and will be unwilling to endure the months of regulatory review that might be needed to obtain approval to acquire a regulated company or its parent.

The potential target might also consider diversification into business areas occupied by potential acquirors. Such overlapping diversification could expand the grounds for antitrust challenges to takeover attempts.

Acquisitions and diversifications, however, are probably becoming outmoded defensive devices as antitrust enforcement declines and deregulation becomes more widespread. Nevertheless, the mere specter of governmental intervention or regulatory problems may allow the target to place a lower value on a hostile offer, on the theory that the offer is conditioned on government approval and may never be consummated.[484]

---

483. Poison pills are discussed in greater detail in § III.4.B., *infra*.

484. Defensive acquisitions and related measures are discussed in greater detail in § III.4.D. and K., *infra*.

Regardless of the defensive tactic(s) selected, the target fully should realize the dangers of placing too much faith in prepackaged responses. Overpreparation might induce in the target's management a false sense of security and a blindness to the realities of a threatening situation or an actual hostile offer. As one commentator has observed, a "black book" that purports to contain all the answers

> may restrict tactics that a target utilizes, and target management will argue about deviations from the recommended procedures. In addition, canned responses may create a "credibility gap" which reflects on the good faith of a management which slavishly employs them. Thus, the risk of embarrassment in a litigation or a state proceeding resulting from the use of such releases may outweigh their utility.[485]

Thus, planning, while important, should never replace fresh analysis of the actual, real-life offer and of the possible responses to such an offer. Management always owes a fiduciary duty to the target's shareholders, and it must fulfill that duty in the context of business realities, not of theoretical boardgames.

---

485. 1 A. Fleischer, Jr., *Tender Offers: Defenses, Responses, and Planning* 5-6 (1983) (footnote omitted).

CHAPTER 2

WILLIAMS ACT REGULATION OF TENDER OFFER RESPONSES

The Williams Act and the regulations promulgated thereunder impose three principal obligations on a target responding to a tender offer. First, the target must announce to its shareholders, within ten business days after a tender offer has been made, its position regarding that offer. Second, the target must insure that its disclosures are not materially misleading and do not omit any material information. Third, the target must itself comply with tender offer regulations if it makes a counter tender offer or a self-tender offer in response to a hostile bid.

Part III of this book discusses the response and disclosure requirements as they relate to tender offer targets. Part II, above, discusses tender offer regulations applicable to bidders and counter-offerors.

A. Target Response

Exchange Act Rule 14e-2 provides that a target must inform its shareholders of its position on a tender offer within ten business days after that offer has been made. In making this communication to its shareholders, the target also must file a Schedule 14D-9 with the SEC. Should the target wish to communicate immediately with its shareholders on a more informal basis, it may send to them a "stop-look-and-listen" letter.

1. "Stop-Look-and-Listen" Letters

Rule 14d-9(e)[486] prescribes the contents of "stop-look-and-listen" letters. These letters may do no more than request that shareholders "defer making a determination whether to accept or reject [the] tender offer until they have been advised of the subject company's position with respect" to that offer in the

---

486. 17 C.F.R. § 240.14d-9(e) (1986).

ten-day letter.[487] In other words, the "stop-look-and-listen" letter asks the shareholders simply to refrain from making any immediate decisions with respect to the securities and to await further word from management about the offer. The letter also must (*a*) identify the offer by the bidder, (*b*) state that the target's board or management is considering the offer, and (*c*) state that, on or before a specified date (which, under Rule 14e-2, must be within ten business days after the offer's commencement date), the target will advise the shareholders whether the company recommends acceptance or rejection of the offer, expresses no opinion on and remains neutral toward the offer, or is unable to take any position.[488]

It is foreseeable that litigation may arise from "stop-look-and-listen" letters. A hostile offeror might allege that the target violated Rule 14d-9 by communicating with shareholders (to dissuade them from tendering) without complying with the Rule. Management, by contrast, will characterize the communication as simply a "stop-look-and-listen" letter and will invoke Rule 14d-9(e), which expressly exempts such letters from the disclosure requirements.

2. Announcement of Target's Position on Offer

Rule 14e-2 provides:

> (a) *Position of subject company.* As a means reasonably designed to prevent fraudulent, deceptive or manipulative acts or practices within the meaning of section 14(e) of the Act, the subject company, no later than 10 business days from the date the tender offer is first published or sent or given, shall publish, send or give to security holders a statement disclosing that the subject company:
>
> (1) Recommends acceptance or rejection of the bidder's tender offer;

487. Rule 14d-9(e)(4).
488. Rule 14d-9(e)(1)-(3).

> (2) Expresses no opinion and is remaining neutral toward the bidder's tender offer; or
>
> (3) Is unable to take a position with respect to the bidder's tender offer. Such statement shall also include the reason(s) for the position (including the inability to take a position) disclosed therein.
>
> (b) *Material change.* If any material change occurs in the disclosure required by paragraph (a) of this section, the subject company shall promptly publish or send or give a statement disclosing such material change to security holders.[489]

According to Rule 14d-9(f), this Rule 14e-2 statement sent by the target to its shareholders constitutes "a solicitation or recommendation within the meaning of this section and section 14(d)(4) of the Act"[490]—*i.e.*, a statement that must be preceded or accompanied by a disclosure statement on Schedule 14D-9.

Rule 14d-9, which implements section 14(d)(4), provides that any person who makes a solicitation or recommendation subject to the Rule shall file with the SEC eight copies of a Tender Offer Solicitation/Recommendation Statement on Schedule 14D-9 "as soon as practicable on the date such solicitation or recommendation is first published or sent or given to security holders. . . ."[491] The target also must hand-deliver a copy of the Schedule 14D-9 to the bidder making a tender offer for the target's securities and must notify any exchange on which the class of securities at issue is registered and listed for trading.[492]

The Schedule 14D-9 sets forth information roughly comparable to that contained in the bidder's Schedule 14D-1[493] and also contains the target's recommendation to shareholders concerning the tender offer. The target must explain the *reasons* for its recommendation; "[c]onclusory statements such as '[t]he

---

489. 17 C.F.R. § 240.14e-2 (1986).

490. 17 C.F.R. § 240.14d-9(f) (1986).

491. *Id.* § 240.14d-9(a) (1986).

492. *Id.* § 240.14d-9(a)(2).

493. *See supra* § II.4.B(2) (discussing Schedule 14D-1).

tender offer is in the best interest of shareholders,' will not be considered sufficient disclosure. . . ."[494]

Litigation involving Rule 14d-9, as it applies to targets' responses to tender offers, has covered a number of different issues, including (*a*) the duty to file a Schedule 14D-9, (*b*) the contents of the Schedule, (*c*) the curative effect, if any, of disclosure by the bidder, and (*d*) remedies for misstatements.

a. *Duty to File Schedule 14D-9*

Unless a target's communication to its shareholders about a tender offer constitutes merely a bland statement of the "stop-look-and-listen" variety, the target has a duty to file a Schedule 14D-9. As soon as the target's management attempts to inform stockholders of its opinion about the merits—or lack thereof—of a tender offer, Rule 14d-9 applies.

In *Cauble v. White*,[495] for example, on the very day that plaintiff announced a tender offer for the target's shares, the target's president sent a letter to all shareholders labeling the $41 offering price " 'quite a surprise to our management' " and stating: " 'The book value of our stock is now $41.00 per share and the realistic potential value of our stock, based on our earnings and the growth of our area, would be $100.00 per share.' "[496] The court held that the target should have complied with Rule 14d-9 because the letter amounted to a recommendation by management not to tender.[497] "[I]t is reasonable to assume," wrote the court, "that a shareholder could be deterred from tendering his stock at $41.00 per share in the face of a potential valuation of the same stock at $100.00 per share."

494. 17 C.F.R. § 240.14d-101, Item 4(b) (1986). For a detailed discussion of the form and contents of Schedule 14D-9, see 17 C.F.R. § 240.14d-101 (1986).

495. 360 F. Supp. 1021 (E.D. La. 1973).

496. *Id.* at 1025-26.

497. *Id.* at 1028-29.

The duty to comply with Rule 14d-9 arises even if the communication relates to a proposed tender offer that has neither been actually made to shareholders nor filed with the SEC. Such a situation arose in *Applied Digital Data Systems, Inc. v. Milgo Electronic Corp.*[498] Applied Digital Data Systems ("ADDS") had proposed a tax-free merger with Milgo Electronic; when Milgo rejected the offer, ADDS publicly announced that it intended to make an exchange offer directly to Milgo's shareholders. The next day, Milgo issued a press release stating that " 'the revised proposal appears to be even less favorable to our shareholders than the exchange offer that was turned down last week by the unanimous decision of the Milgo board.' "[499] During the ensuing litigation, ADDS alleged that Milgo had violated sections 14(d) and 14(e) of the Williams Act and Rule 14d-9 when it issued the press release without filing the requisite materials with the SEC; Milgo contended that the regulations apply only when an offeror actually has made an offer to shareholders, or at least has filed it with the SEC, and not when, as here, the offeror merely has announced its intention to make an offer in the future.[500]

The court granted ADDS' request for a preliminary injunction, ruling that a target's duties under Rule 14d-9 arise as soon as an imminent tender offer is publicly announced, even if the offeror has not yet filed with the SEC or solicited shareholders. "Indeed," observed the court,

> it would be anomalous were sections 14(d) and 14(e) not applicable to the offeror or target corporation once a public announcement of an imminent tender or exchange offer was made, for numerous misstatements, omissions and half-truths could be promulgated with relative impunity until the offer was actually filed with and approved by the SEC. Although the shareholders might not in the pre-offer period be faced with a present decision whether to exchange their stock in the target

---

498. 425 F. Supp. 1145 (S.D.N.Y. 1977) (Weinfeld, J.).

499. *Id.* at 1148-49 (quoting press release).

500. *Id.* at 1151.

> corporation, statements and actions of the target corporation and the offeror during this period clearly have the capacity to affect any future decision and should thus fall within the purview of the statute.[501]

b. *Contents of Schedule 14D-9*

Rule 14d-101[502] prescribes the minimum contents of a Schedule 14D-9.

1. The Schedule must state the title and class of equity securities to which the statement relates and the name and address of the subject company's principal executive offices. (Item 1.)
2. The Schedule must identify the tender offer to which the statement relates as well as the name and address of the bidder. (Item 2.)
3. The Schedule must identify the person filing the statement and describe any material agreements or understandings and any actual or potential conflict of interest between the filer (or its affiliates) and either the subject company or the bidder (including the executive officers, directors, or affiliates of either entity). The target thus must disclose the existence of, among other things, severance or "golden parachute" arrangements with its executives. If the filer is the subject company itself, however, the Schedule 14D-9 need not describe any material agreements or understandings between the subject company (or any affiliate) and any executive officer or director of that company if such (or similar) information has been disclosed in any proxy statement, report, or other communication sent within one year of the Schedule's filing date to the then-current shareholders and has been filed with the SEC. Should the filer avail itself of this exception, the filer's solicitation or recommendation to shareholders must refer specifically to

---

501. *Id.* at 1154.
502. 17 C.F.R. § 240.14d-101 (1986).

any such prior proxy statement, report, or other communication, the pertinent portion(s) of which must be filed as an exhibit to the Schedule 14D-9. (Item 3.)

4. The Schedule must specifically state the nature of any solicitation or recommendation being made to the target's shareholders, as well as the reason(s) for the position taken. Conclusory statements will not satisfy the filer's obligation to provide a statement of reason(s). (Item 4.)
5. The Schedule must identify any person(s) employed, retained, or to be compensated by the filer (or by any person on its behalf) to make solicitations or recommendations to security holders. The filer also must describe the terms of any such employment, retainer, or compensation arrangement. (Item 5.)
6. The Schedule must describe, with respect to the securities listed in Item 1, any transactions in those securities effected during the previous 60 days by the filer of the statement (or by any executive officer, director, affiliate, or subsidiary of the filer). The Schedule also must state whether any such persons or entities "presently intend to tender to the bidder, sell or hold securities of the class of securities being sought by the bidder which are held of record or beneficially owned by such persons." (Item 6.)
7. If the filer of the Schedule is the subject company, the Schedule must state whether any negotiations relating to the tender offer are intended or underway, if such negotiations relate to or would result in (*a*) an extraordinary transaction, such as a merger or reorganization, involving the subject company or any subsidiary; (*b*) a purchase, sale, or transfer of a material amount of assets by the subject company or any subsidiary; (*c*) a tender offer for or other acquisition of securities by or of the subject company; or (*d*) any material change in the subject's present capitalization or dividend policy. The Schedule also must describe any other transaction, board resolution, agreement in principle, or signed contract made in response to the tender offer if such transaction, resolution, agreement, or contract relates to or would result in any of the above eventualities. (Item 7.)

The degree of disclosure required may vary, depending on the stage of any negotiations that might be in progress. As the SEC recently pointed out:

> The "Instruction" to Item 7(a) recognizes that negotiations can occur prior to an agreement in principle and allows target companies to withhold the "possible terms of any transaction or the parties thereto . . . if in the opinion of the Board of Directors of the subject company such disclosure would jeopardize continuation of such negotiations." But Item 7(a) does not relieve the target company of the duty to disclose the fact of negotiations. The Instruction specifically requires that "[i]n such an event, disclosure that negotiations are being undertaken or are underway and are in the preliminary stages will be sufficient." Once those negotiations ripen into an agreement in principle, it becomes an event required to be disclosed under Item 7(b).[503]

8. The Schedule must furnish any other additional information necessary to prevent the required statements from being materially misleading. (Item 8.)
9. The filer must provide as exhibits a copy of (*a*) any written solicitation or recommendation published, sent, or given to shareholders and referred to in Item 4; (*b*) any written instructions or other materials furnished to any persons making oral solicitations or recommendations to shareholders on behalf of the filer; and (*c*) any contract, agreement, arrangement, or understanding referred to in Item 3. (Item 9.)

Litigation over the contents of Schedule 14D-9 frequently relates to the issues of disclosure of management's self-interest or of management's basis for finding the tender offer inadequate.

---

503. *In the Matter of Revlon, Inc.*, Exchange Act Release No. 23320, [Current] Fed. Sec. L. Rep. (CCH) ¶ 84,006, at 88,146 (June 16, 1986). *See also infra* § III.2.C(6) (discussing the duty to disclose negotiations).

i. Management's Self-Interest

The issue of management's self-interest arose, for example, in *Scott v. Multi-Amp Corp.*,[504] a proxy solicitation case, in which plaintiff shareholders of Multi-Amp sued to enjoin defendant directors from using management's proxy statement and from consummating a proposed sale of Multi-Amp assets to MUL Company, an acquisition vehicle organized by the defendant "inside" directors. Plaintiffs alleged, among other things, that the proxy statement had failed to disclose the business associations of James Berick, a Multi-Amp director and stockholder who was not part of the "inside" group, and defendant Lerner, chairman of the board and chief executive officer of Multi-Amp and also an MUL stockholder. Berick was at once a partner in the firm of Burke, Hahn & Berick, which had served as Multi-Amp's general counsel; a trustee and officer of the Lerner-controlled Realty Refund Trust; and a director and vice president of Realty's adviser, Refund Advisors, Inc., also controlled by Lerner.

The court held the omission of these associations material, and in violation of section 14(a) of the Exchange Act[505] and Rule 14a-9(a)[506], because a shareholder might have considered the withheld information important in deciding how to vote.[507] Berick's position was considered unusually sensitive because of what the proxy statement termed "inherent conflicting interests" among Lerner and other members of the inside group and because the board had approved the proxy statement and MUL transaction at the first meeting that Berick and the only other "independent" director had attended. The court also noted that, in a letter dated nine days before the date of the proxy statement, the SEC had instructed the company to set forth "the affiliation of the parties involved. . . ." The court ordered

504. 386 F. Supp. 44 (D.N.J. 1974).

505. 15 U.S.C. § 78n(a).

506. 17 C.F.R. § 240.14a-9(a).

507. 386 F. Supp. at 66. *But cf. TSC Indus., Inc. v. Northway*, 426 U.S. 438, 449 (1976) (enunciating a somewhat different materiality standard), discussed in § III.2.C(2), *infra*.

defendants to send to Multi-Amp shareholders a "supplemental letter" transmitting the information concerning Berick.

In *Oscar Gruss & Son v. Natomas Co.*,[508] however, the court rejected an allegation that a tender offer target had failed to disclose material information concerning management's self-interest. The dispute arose amidst a flurry of competing tender offers for Thermal Power Company. Thermal and Natomas Company had entered into an agreement in principle providing for a merger between the two companies through an exchange of Thermal and Natomas shares. Thereafter, two other companies also attempted to gain control of Thermal. During the bidding war, the market price of Thermal's stock fluctuated between $7 and $16 per share, until Natomas finally prevailed with a tender offer of $20 per share.

Plaintiff, seeking to represent a class of Thermal shareholders who had sold their holdings on the market at less than $20 per share, claimed that defendants had violated section 10(b) of the Exchange Act and Rule 10b-5 through various manipulative practices. Several of plaintiff's allegations focused on a press statement and a letter sent to Thermal stockholders, in which materials Thermal allegedly had failed to disclose, among other things, that many of the Thermal shares held by Thermal management had extremely low tax bases and that Thermal's president was to receive an employment contract with Natomas in the event of consummation of the merger.

The court granted summary judgment for defendants, holding the omissions immaterial as a matter of law "in light of the circumstances of the case."[509] "Both the low tax bases of directors' shares and negotiations for the retention of existing management," the court declared, "are common aspects of merger agreements. Omission of neither fact rises to the level of a violation of § 10(b) on the facts of this case."[510]

---

508. [1977-1978 Transfer Binder] Fed. Sec. L. Rep. (CCH) ¶ 96,258 (N.D. Cal. Dec. 17, 1976).

509. *Id.* at 92,702.

510. *Id.*

ii. Basis for Deeming Offer Inadequate

In announcing to shareholders its position on the tender offer, and in stating any such recommendation as part of the Schedule 14D-9 requirements, the filer must provide the *reasons* that led to the formulation of any solicitation or recommendation. Conclusory statements about the "best interests of the shareholders" will not satisfy the SEC's requirements; the filer must specify *why* it reached its conclusions. Allegations of a bid's inadequacy frequently focus on the offer's price or conditions or on its allegedly coercive two-tier structure. Of course, a myriad of other issues also can arise in litigation involving Schedule 14D-9.

c. *Curative Effect of Disclosure by Offeror*

Tender offers can generate a substantial (and often bewildering) amount of communication between the offeror or the target and the target's shareholders. Shareholders inevitably receive letters from bidder and target; they also may read newspaper advertisements and receive telephone calls from professional proxy solicitors.

Given this flood of information, there may be time for the offeror to comment on or rebut statements made or filed by the target's management. This process sometimes enables the shareholders to obtain reasonably accurate and complete disclosure even if, for whatever reason, the target's own submissions were inadequate. Because the *raison d'être* of Rule 14d-9 is to insure that shareholders receive full disclosure, some courts have declined to impose sanctions for violations of the Rule if disclosure by the bidder "cured" those violations and provided shareholders with the necessary information. Not all courts, however, have accepted this principle.

d. Remedies for Misstatements

Courts have ordered a number of different remedies when issuers have misstated information in communications to shareholders and the SEC. Some courts have granted preliminary or permanent injunctions against further misconduct; others have ordered the issuer to correct the misstatements; still others have awarded damages to the bidder.

B. Lack of a Federal Substantive Remedy Under Section 14(e)

Section 14(e) of the Williams Act provides that

> [i]t shall be unlawful for any person to make any untrue statement of a material fact or omit to state any material fact necessary in order to make the statements made, in the light of the circumstances under which they were made, not misleading, or to engage in any fraudulent, deceptive, or manipulative acts or practices, in connection with any tender offer or request or invitation for tenders, or any solicitation of security holders in opposition to or in favor of any such offer, request, or invitation.[511]

The section also empowers the SEC to promulgate rules and regulations "reasonably designed" to prevent fraudulent, deceptive, or manipulative practices.

Pursuant to this legislative mandate, the SEC has adopted rules designed to effect the purposes of the Act. These rules are essentially procedural, regulating the offering process: they prescribe minimum waiting periods, require the offeror to treat all tendering shareholders equally, impose rules governing extensions of offers, regulate the manner in which the target communicates with its shareholders, etc.

---

511. 15 U.S.C. § 78n(e).

Over the years, however, tender offer litigants have attempted to derive from these procedural rules a *substantive* federal law governing acquisition-related corporate strategies. A few courts accepted the gambit and held that certain practices, even if fully disclosed in accordance with SEC rules, could themselves be so inherently fraudulent, deceptive, or manipulative as to violate the Williams Act. The majority of courts, however, read the Act more narrowly and refused to divine from that legislation a substantive federal law governing fully disclosed corporate maneuvers, even when those maneuvers affected the outcome of a tender offer as well as the market price of a corporation's shares.

The issue came to a head in June 1985, with the Supreme Court's decision in *Schreiber v. Burlington Northern, Inc.*[512] *Schreiber* held that the "manipulative acts" referred to in section 14(e) of the Williams Act necessarily involve misrepresentation or nondisclosure. Where such acts have been fully disclosed to shareholders (and do not violate other express provisions of the Act), section 14(e) will not authorize a federal court "to oversee the substantive fairness of tender offers. . . ."[513]

A target thus may not invoke section 14(e) as a possible remedy for suspect tactics that are fully and accurately disclosed. Pre-*Schreiber* cases allowing such judicial supervision of the marketplace probably are no longer good law. To understand the full meaning of *Schreiber*, however, one must understand the history of cases addressing the existence of a substantive remedy under section 14(e).

1. Pre-*Schreiber* Cases

The issue of a substantive remedy under section 14(e) first exploded in *Mobil Corp. v. Marathon Oil Co.*,[514] which arose out

512. 472 U.S. 1, 105 S. Ct. 2458 (1985).

513. 105 S. Ct. at 2464.

514. 669 F.2d 366 (6th Cir. 1981), *cert. denied*, 455 U.S. 982 (1982).

of the epic battle for control of Marathon Oil. On October 30, 1981, Mobil announced its intention to purchase up to 40 million outstanding shares of Marathon's common stock for $85 per share in cash, with a follow-up merger to buy up the remaining shares. The offer was conditioned on Mobil's receiving at least 30 million tendered shares, just over one-half of those outstanding.

Marathon's directors were dissatisfied with Mobil's offer and determined to seek a more attractive merger candidate. Negotiations ensued between Marathon and several other companies, including Allied Industries, Gulf Oil, and United States Steel. On November 18, United States Steel made a proposal, to be acted upon that very day: the company offered $125 per share for 30 million shares of Marathon and proposed a follow-up merger with U.S.S. Corporation ("USS"), a subsidiary of United States Steel. There were two conditions to the offer, however: USS required (a) an immediately exercisable and irrevocable option to purchase ten million authorized but unissued shares of Marathon common stock at $90 per share and (b) an option to purchase Marathon's 48% interest in oil and mineral rights in the lucrative Yates Field for $2.8 billion, the option to be exercisable only if USS' tender offer did not succeed and if a third party (such as Mobil) gained control of Marathon. USS thus insisted on two classic devices to "lock up" a deal against competition from third parties: a discount purchase of a substantial portion (here, 17 percent) of the target's shares and a right to buy the target's "crown jewel"—one of its most valuable assets. (Indeed, both Gulf Oil and Allied had conditioned their willingness to make a tender offer for Marathon's shares upon assurances that they would have an option to buy Marathon's interest in the Yates Field.)

Marathon's directors voted to recommend the USS offer to the shareholders, and Marathon, U.S. Steel, and USS executed a formal merger agreement that same day. Mobil then filed suit in federal court to enjoin exercise of the stock and Yates Field options as well as any purchase of shares pursuant to the USS tender offer. Mobil alleged that the two options constituted a "lock-up" arrangement designed to defeat competitive offers and thus amounted to a "manipulative" practice "in connection with a tender offer," in violation of section 14(e) of the Williams Act. The district court entered a temporary restraining order, whereupon Mobil announced a new tender offer, for at least 30 million shares at $126 per share in cash, conditioned on invalidation of the lock-up options. The court ultimately denied Mobil's request for a preliminary injunction, finding an insubstantial likelihood that Mobil would prevail on the merits of its section 14(e) claim. Mobil appealed, and the Court of Appeals for the Sixth Circuit reversed.

The Court of Appeals began its analysis with the observation that a "manipulative" device, within the meaning of section 14(e), is one that "affect[s] . . . the market for, or price of, securities by *artificial* means, i.e., means unrelated to the natural forces of supply and demand."[515] The "lock-up" options at issue constituted proscribed "manipulative" devices because they "not only artificially affect, but for all practical purposes completely block, normal healthy market activity and, in fact, could be construed as expressly designed solely for that purpose."[516] The blockage of normal market activity resulted from the fact that the option created "an artificial price ceiling" of $125 per share in the market for Marathon's common shares because no other bidder could top the USS offer.[517] No potential offeror (Mobil included) would be willing to offer a competitive price for a Marathon stripped of its "crown jewel"; nor could any other offeror (Mobil included) afford to offer a higher price per share, because USS, with its discounted purchase of 17 percent of Marathon, would end up paying less for every dollar rise in the bid than would a disfavored offeror such as Mobil. (Every extra dollar per share would cost USS $30 million and Mobil $47 million.[518]) Thus, the "lock-up" options rendered the success of the USS offer a *fait accompli* and thereby artificially manipulated

515. *Id.* at 374 (emphasis added).

516. *Id.*

517. *Id.* at 375.

518. *Id.*

the value of Marathon's shares by preventing competitive bidding.

Defendants ascribed a more narrow meaning to section 14(e), arguing that the statute "requires full disclosure and nothing more."[519] The Court of Appeals rejected this limited construction of the term "manipulative":

> It may be that the Marathon shareholders in this case have now been fully informed that their management granted USS the Yates Field option and the stock option. They may now understand fully how these options deter any tender offers higher than $125 per share. Yet, they have no real alternative to accepting the USS offer, because Mobil's offer of $126 is conditional upon the invalidity of the options, and there is and could be no other comparable tender offer as long as the "lock-up" options remain in effect. The artificial ceiling on the price of their shares at $125 is manipulation to which they must submit whether it is disclosed to them or not, since in not tendering their shares to USS they risk being relegated to the "back end" of USS's takeover proposal and receiving only $90 per share.[520]

"In short," concluded the court, "to find compliance with section 14(e) solely by the full disclosure of a manipulative device as a *fait accompli* would be to read the 'manipulative acts and practices' language completely out of the Williams Act."[521]

Mobil, then, announced the proposition that certain types of "lock-ups" or other tender offer maneuvers could violate section 14(e) even if those arrangements were fully disclosed. The issue became whether those devices artificially affected or manipulated the tender offer market for the target's shares.

The *Mobil* decision sent shock waves through investment circles. In the immediate aftermath of the ruling, it seemed that almost anything that a target's management might do to avoid a hostile takeover could result in a charge—and even a finding—of manipulation. But virtually every court to consider the issue

519. *Id.* at 376.

520. *Id.* at 376-77.

521. *Id.* at 377.

since *Mobil* read section 14(e)'s "manipulative acts and practices" more narrowly than did the Court of Appeals for the Sixth Circuit. One of the most important and most celebrated post-*Mobil* decisions is *Martin Marietta Corp. v. Bendix Corp.*,[522] in which the district court decisively rejected the *Mobil* ruling and squarely construed section 14(e) as strictly a disclosure provision.

The Martin Marietta-Bendix dispute was an extraordinarily bloody battle featuring the use of the "Pac-Man" defense, which the court characterized as an " 'I'll eat you before you eat me' " gambit.[523] The tale began on August 25, 1982, when Bendix (which owned just under five percent of Marietta's common stock) announced a tender offer for approximately 44.5 percent of Marietta's common stock at $43 per share. On September 7, Bendix increased its offer to $48 per share and, on September 10, announced that it would purchase up to 55 percent of Marietta's common stock.

On August 30, however, five days after Bendix announced its tender offer for Marietta, Marietta countered with a tender offer for approximately 50.3 percent of Bendix' common stock at $75 per share (the "Pac-Man" defense). Marietta also announced that, should the tender offer succeed, the company would acquire all untendered Bendix shares through a squeeze-out merger, granting the remaining Bendix shareholders 1-2/3 shares of Marietta for each share of Bendix.

Bendix sued for injunctive relief, claiming, among other things, that the Marietta offer was "manipulative" within the meaning of section 14(e) in that (*a*) the offer constituted a "scorched earth" tactic deliberately designed to thwart Bendix' tender offer for Marietta and (*b*) the "front-end loaded" nature of the "two step" proposal pressured Bendix shareholders into tendering to Marietta.[524] Bendix thus accused Marietta of manipulating both the Bendix and the Marietta tender offers.

---

522. 549 F. Supp. 623 (D. Md. 1982).

523. *Id.* at 625.

524. *Id.* at 627.

The court rejected both claims of manipulation. Starting with the claim relating to the Bendix offer, the court subdivided the argument into two components: (*i*) the claim that a successful "scorched earth" offer by Marietta would nullify the Bendix offer by divesting Bendix of the financial benefits of any victory and (*ii*) the claim that the Marietta offer inhibited Bendix from purchasing Marietta shares.

As to the first of these contentions, the court held that the Williams Act in general, and section 14(e) in particular, do not accord an offeror "any rights to the 'fruits' of its tender offer."[525] The court read the Supreme Court's opinion in *Piper v. Chris-Craft Industries, Inc.*[526] as limiting the scope of section 14(e) to protecting the target's shareholders, rather than conferring any substantive rights on either the offeror or the offeree. Thus, Marietta's "scorched earth" policy did not violate section 14(e) merely because it would divest Bendix of financial benefits or thwart its attempt to complete a takeover.[527]

As to the second contention, that Marietta's offer interfered with the consummation of Bendix' offer, the court noted that the point was moot, because Bendix had, in fact, completed its offer for Marietta. However, the court also observed that, even if the issue were not moot, Bendix would not have a federal remedy under section 14(e) insofar as Bendix sought to challenge the substantive fairness of Marietta's aggressive response. "Section 14(e)," wrote the court, "is solely a disclosure provision. Congress has not authorized the federal judiciary to scrutinize the substantive fairness of tender offers as long as adequate disclosure is made."[528] Thus, according to the court's reading of the case law and legislative history, "any 'scorched earth' tender offer is 'manipulative' under Section 14(e) only if misrepresentations or omissions have been made about it."[529]

---

525. *Id.* at 627.
526. 430 U.S. 1 (1977).
527. 549 F. Supp. at 627-28.
528. *Id.* at 628.
529. *Id.*

The court then proceeded to find that Marietta adequately had disclosed pertinent information.[530]

This approach also disposed of the claim of manipulation asserted against Marietta's own tender offer. The fact that the structure of the two-tier, front-ended-loaded offer might have "coerced" tenders by Bendix shareholders did not amount to a violation of section 14(e), for "Section 14(e) is violated only in instances of deception. If the counter offer is in fact 'coercive,' it would only be because its two tier structure is revealed all too well."[531]

In reading section 14(e) as strictly a disclosure provision, the *Marietta* court directly confronted the Sixth Circuit's decision in *Mobil Corp. v. Marathon Oil Co.*[532] The court characterized *Mobil* as "an exceptionally strained interpretation" of the Supreme Court's ruling in *Santa Fe Industries, Inc. v. Green*[533] (which had narrowly construed the term "manipulation" as used in section 10(b) of the Exchange Act) and quoted *Santa Fe*'s holding that " 'the cases do not support the proposition . . . that a breach of fiduciary duty by majority stockholders, without any deception, misrepresentation, or nondisclosure, violates the statute. . . .' "[534] The court therefore declined to adopt the Sixth Circuit's construction of section 14(e).

Mobil and *Martin Marietta* might be considered as representing the two ends of the pre-*Schreiber* spectrum of views on the meaning of section 14(e) and the availability of federal law to regulate the substantive fairness of tender offer activities. The *Mobil* court assumed relatively broad authority to evaluate tender offer terms and responses; the *Marietta* court expressly rejected *Mobil* and construed the Williams Act as providing a remedy only for improper disclosure. Other courts tended to line up behind the *Marietta* position, some repudiating *Mobil* and others simply distinguishing it.

---

530. *Id.* at 631-33.

531. *Id.* at 630.

532. 669 F.2d 366 (6th Cir. 1981), *cert. denied*, 455 U.S. 982 (1982).

533. 430 U.S. 462 (1977).

534. 549 F. Supp. at 630 (quoting *Santa Fe Industries, supra*, 430 U.S. at 476).

2. *Schreiber*

The conflict in the federal courts regarding the meaning of section 14(e) finally reached the Supreme Court in 1985, in *Schreiber v. Burlington Northern, Inc.*[535] The suit arose out of Burlington Northern's takeover of El Paso Gas. Initially, Burlington had made a tender offer for 25.1 million shares of El Paso at $24 per share. El Paso management had opposed the offer, but shareholders had responded favorably, fully subscribing the offer by its deadline.

Instead of accepting the tendered shares, however, Burlington rescinded its offer after negotiations with El Paso management and announced a new offer for only 21 million shares at $24 per share. Burlington also agreed to recognize "golden parachute" contracts between El Paso and four of its senior officers.

Because the new offer was greatly oversubscribed, Burlington accepted the tendered shares on a pro rata basis. This proration had the effect of diminishing the payment to those shareholders who had tendered during the first offer (which had sought an additional 4.1 million shares). Relying on section 14(e), a shareholder filed suit on behalf of herself and similarly situated shareholders, claiming that the withdrawal of the initial offer and the substitution of the second one together constituted a "manipulative" distortion of the market for El Paso stock. The district court dismissed the suit for failure to state a claim, and the Court of Appeals for the Third Circuit affirmed, holding that the alleged manipulation did not involve misrepresentation and thus did not violate section 14(e).[536] The Supreme Court granted certiorari and affirmed.

The *Schreiber* Court rejected the Sixth Circuit's approach in *Mobil* and the proposition that section 14(e) "is directed at purposes broader than providing full and true information to investors."[537] Instead, the Court held that "the term

---

535. 472 U.S. 1, 105 S. Ct. 2458 (1985).

536. *Schreiber v. Burlington Northern, Inc.*, 568 F. Supp. 197 (D. Del. 1983), *aff'd*, 731 F.2d 163 (3d Cir. 1984), *aff'd*, 472 U.S. 1, 105 S. Ct. 2458 (1985).

537. 105 S. Ct. at 2461 & n.3.

'manipulative' as used in § 14(e) requires misrepresentation or nondisclosure. It connotes 'conduct designed to deceive or defraud investors by controlling or artificially affecting the price of securities.' . . . Without misrepresentation or nondisclosure, § 14(e) has not been violated."[538] Because the complaint did not allege that any misrepresentation, nondisclosure, or deception had accompanied the cancellation of the first offer, no cognizably "manipulative" conduct had occurred.

In reaching its decision concerning the meaning of the term "manipulative" in section 14(e), the Court considered the statutory language and its analogue in section 10(b) of the Exchange Act. The Court also examined the provision's purpose and legislative history. The Court read section 14(e) as an antifraud provision, whose sole purpose was to insure the full disclosure to shareholders of all material information that they would need to evaluate the merits and demerits of a tender offer. "Nowhere in the legislative history," continued the Court, "is there the slightest suggestion that § 14(e) serves any purpose other than disclosure, or that the term 'manipulative' should be read as an invitation to the courts to oversee the substantive fairness of tender offers; the quality of any offer is a matter for the marketplace."[539]

Indeed, the Court expressed concern about the dangers that a broader reading of the section could pose:

> Inviting judges to read the term "manipulative" with their own sense of what constitutes "unfair" or "artificial" conduct would inject uncertainty into the tender offer process. An essential piece of information—whether the court would deem the fully disclosed actions of one side or the other to be "manipulative"—would not be available until after the tender offer had closed. This uncertainty would directly contradict the expressed Congressional desire to give investors full information.[540]

---

538. *Id.* at 2465 (quoting *Ernst & Ernst v. Hochfelder*, 425 U.S. 185, 199 (1976)).

539. *Id.* at 2464 (footnote omitted).

540. *Id.* at 2464-65.

In light of *Schreiber*, a target seeking to thwart a hostile tender offer may no longer invoke section 14(e) as a means of attacking the substantive fairness of that offer. (Nor, of course, may any other party use that provision to assert a similar claim.) Section 14(e) provides a cause of action only for improper or incomplete disclosure; absent misrepresentation, nondisclosure, or deception, it cannot be used as a basis for involving a court in the maneuverings of the offeror or offeree. A plaintiff wishing to bring judicial scrutiny to bear on the substantive terms of an offer or on tender offer tactics unrelated to disclosure must rely on state law and not on section 14(e).

This emphasis on state law also had emerged in the Supreme Court's earlier decision in *Piper v. Chris-Craft Industries, Inc.*[541] In holding that a tender offeror, suing in its capacity as a bidder, did not have standing to sue for damages under section 14(e), the Court observed that a frustrated bidder could pursue its grievances through a cause of action "under common-law principles of interference with a prospective commercial advantage."[542] *Piper*'s and *Schreiber*'s restriction of the scope of federal law remedies thus has helped to highlight state law causes of action such as tortious interference with contractual relations, as the bitter Pennzoil-Texaco battle well illustrates.[543]

3. The Post-*Schreiber* Era

The *Schreiber* decision leaves unanswered several important questions. First, the Court did not decide whether a private cause of action exists under section 14(e). The Court expressly declined to decide this issue in *Piper v. Chris-Craft Industries, Inc.*[544] and *Rondeau v. Mosinee Paper Corp.*[545] and did not even

541. 430 U.S. 1 (1977).
542. *Id.* at 40-41.
543. *See infra* § III.4.N.
544. 430 U.S. 1 (1977).
545. 422 U.S. 49 (1975).

address it in *Schreiber.* Given, however, *Schreiber's* heavy reliance on section 10(b) of the Exchange Act and on Rule 10b-5 promulgated pursuant to that Act, it appears likely that the Court would continue to analogize section 14(e) to section 10(b) when called upon to decide the issue and would uphold the existence of a private right of action under section 14(e), as have the lower courts that have considered the question.

Second, the Court declined to determine whether scienter—the intent to deceive, defraud, or manipulate—constitutes a necessary element of a cause of action under section 14(e). Again, however, *Schreiber*'s reliance on section 10(b) and Rule 10b-5 suggests that the Court would find a scienter requirement in section 14(e).

Third, *Schreiber* might implicitly raise questions about the continuing vitality of certain rules adopted by the SEC under section 14(e). If section 14(e) exists only to insure proper disclosure to shareholders, does the SEC, pursuant to its power to promulgate rules implementing the Williams Act, have authority to promulgate, for example, Rule 14e-1, which requires that tender offers remain open for 20 days and be extended for ten days upon an increase in the offered consideration? These requirements arguably do not relate to the disclosure purposes of the Williams Act and might therefore be invalid. Similar questions might apply to the SEC's "all holders" and "best price" rules.[546]

The "problem" probably is more theoretical than real, for *Schreiber* noted that Congress intended other parts of the Williams Act—sections 13(e) and 14(d)—to insure "that investors will possess additional time within which to take advantage of the disclosed information."[547] Moreover, the Court acknowledged that the Act gives the SEC "latitude to regulate nondeceptive activities as a 'reasonably designed' means of preventing manipulative acts."[548] Such "nondeceptive acts"

546. *See supra* § II.4.B(7).
547. 105 S. Ct. at 2463.
548. *Id.* at 2464 n.11.

arguably could include the offeror's election to leave open its offer for a certain period of time.

Nevertheless, the SEC's authority has come under some scrutiny in light of *Schreiber.* On October 3, 1985, Congressman Timothy E. Wirth, chairman of the House Subcommittee on Telecommunications, Consumer Protection, and Finance, wrote a letter to SEC Chairman John S.R. Shad, asking him to comment on various aspects of tender offer regulation. In particular, Congressman Wirth observed that *Schreiber* "appears to place substantial limitations on the Commission's rulemaking authority, as well as the Commission's enforcement program" under section 14(e) and has limited application of that section to claims involving disclosure, rather than substantive fairness. Congressman Wirth asked the SEC to report on the decision's implications and on the SEC's continuing ability to provide for fairness to shareholders.[549]

The SEC has insisted that its authority remains unimpaired by *Schreiber.* Testifying before Congressman Wirth's subcommittee on October 24, 1985, Chairman Shad asserted that *Schreiber* did not confine the SEC's power under section 14(e) to adopting rules relating solely to disclosure. The Supreme Court, said Chairman Shad,

> recognized the Congressional intention to provide broader authority to the Commission. The Commission has the authority to proscribe conduct that is not in itself fraudulent, deceptive or manipulative, but that may lead to such conduct, or is so related to such conduct that its prohibition constitutes a means reasonably designed to prevent it.[550]

Chairman Shad also observed that two post-*Schreiber* decisions involving the validity of rules promulgated under section 14(e)

---

549. Letter from Timothy Wirth to John Shad at 4 (Oct. 3, 1985).

550. *Developments in Corporate Takeovers: Can the SEC Protect Shareholders Under Current Law?, Hearings Before the Subcomm. on Telecommunications, Consumer Protection, and Finance of the House Committee on Energy and Commerce,* 99th Cong., 1st Sess. (Oct. 24, 1985) (testimony of SEC Chairman John S.R. Shad).

have upheld the rules based on the authority asserted by the SEC.[551] In addition, Chairman Shad noted that the SEC has rulemaking power under sections 3(b), 10(b), and 23(b) and that *Schreiber* did not affect such authority.

C. Section 14(e) as a Federal Disclosure Remedy

Although there may remain some hope that serious structural abuses introduced into a particular contest for control may be actionable under the federal antifraud provisions, the Supreme Court's decision in *Schreiber* appears to have foreclosed resort to section 14(e) to remedy a lack of substantive fairness in takeovers. However, the Court's ruling left untouched the availability of relief under that section for misrepresentation or nondisclosure. Section 14(e) serves as the Williams Act's general antifraud provision and provides, in a takeover context, a remedy equivalent to that provided by the SEC's Rule 10b-5 in connection with other purchases or sales of securities.[552] Section 14(e)'s proscription of fraudulent or manipulative conduct in the context of a takeover applies, of course, both to the bidder and to the target.

The elements of a cause of action under section 14(e) are similar to those required by Rule 10b-5, except that, under section 14(e), the alleged violation must have occurred "in connection with" a tender offer, rather than in connection with a purchase or sale of securities.[553] The target (or bidder) plaintiff must show that the alleged fraud, misrepresentation, or manipulation concerned a material matter and probably must

---

551. *See L.P. Acquisition Co. v. Tyson*, 772 F.2d 201 (6th Cir. 1985); *Caleb & Co. v. E.I. duPont de Nemours & Co.*, 615 F. Supp. 96 (S.D.N.Y. 1985).

552. *See, e.g., Vaughn v. Teledyne, Inc.*, 628 F.2d 1214 (9th Cir. 1980); *Smallwood v. Pearl Brewing Co.*, 489 F.2d 579 (5th Cir.), *cert. denied*, 419 U.S. 873 (1974).

553. *See, e.g., Electronic Specialty Co. v. International Controls Corp.*, 409 F.2d 937 (2d Cir. 1969).

prove that the defendant acted with scienter. Depending on the nature of the conduct at issue, the plaintiff might also need to demonstrate reliance on the defendant's conduct and harm caused by that reliance.

Like remedies under Rule 10b-5, remedies under section 14(e) seek to redress the defendant's failure to make full and adequate disclosure. Accordingly, a section 14(e) suit probably will not be a permanent block to a tender offer. Even if the target is able to convince a court that the bidder has inadequately disclosed material information, the plaintiff is likely to obtain, in all but the most egregious cases, nothing more than an injunction ordering the dissemination of curative disclosure before the bidder can buy tendered shares. This limited remedy in large part explains the decline in importance of much of the section 14(e) litigation by targets in recent years. Nevertheless, a target and its counsel may decide that the possibility of buying additional time to look for alternatives justifies the cost and disruption of suing under section 14(e).

1. Standing

As a threshold matter, it is necessary to determine who may invoke section 14(e) and the remedies available under the Williams Act. Several classes of plaintiffs have standing to sue under section 14(e). These classes include:

(i) The target company itself, where the target seeks *injunctive* relief against a bidder.[554]

---

554. *See, e.g., Butler Aviation Int'l, Inc. v. Comprehensive Designers, Inc.*, 425 F.2d 842 (2d Cir. 1970); *Electronic Specialty Co. v. International Controls Corp.*, 409 F.2d 937 (2d Cir. 1969); *E.H.I. of Fla., Inc. v. Insurance Co. of N. Am.*, 499 F. Supp. 1053 (E.D. Pa. 1980), *aff'd*, 652 F.2d 310 (3d Cir. 1981).

(ii) A non-tendering shareholder, even though such a shareholder would lack standing under Rule 10b-5 (because there has been no "purchase or sale" of a security).[555]

(iii) A bidder, in an action for *injunctive* relief.[556] An offeror, however, does *not* have standing under section 14(e) to sue for *damages* (unless it sues in its capacity as a shareholder). The Supreme Court held in *Piper v. Chris-Craft Industries, Inc.*[557] that the sole purpose of section 14(e) is to protect *investors* confronted with a tender offer and that bidders—the class regulated by the statute—are not intended beneficiaries of the legislation.

2. Materiality

Section 14(e) applies, by its terms, only to an "untrue statement of a *material* fact" or to an omission "to state any *material* fact necessary in order to make the statements made, in the light of the circumstances under which they are made, not misleading. . . ."[558] In *TSC Industries, Inc. v. Northway, Inc.*[559] a case involving a proxy solicitation, the Supreme Court held that a fact is material if there is a substantial likelihood that reasonable shareholders would consider the fact important in deciding how to vote. The plaintiff must show a substantial likelihood that, under the circumstances, an omitted fact would

---

555. *See, e.g.*, *Electronic Specialty Co. v. International Controls Corp.*, 409 F.2d 937 (2d Cir. 1969); *Hundahl v. United Benefit Life Ins. Co.*, 465 F. Supp. 1349 (N.D. Tex. 1979); *Petersen v. Federated Dev. Co.*, 416 F. Supp. 466 (S.D.N.Y. 1976); *McCloskey v. Epko Shoes, Inc.*, 391 F. Supp. 1279 (E.D. Pa. 1975).

556. *See, e.g.*, *Great Western United Corp. v. Kidwell*, 577 F.2d 1256 (5th Cir. 1978), *rev'd on other grounds*, 443 U.S. 173 (1979); *Whittaker Corp. v. Edgar*, 535 F. Supp. 933 (N.D. Ill. 1982); *Weeks Dredging & Contracting, Inc. v. American Dredging Co.*, 451 F. Supp. 468 (E.D. Pa. 1978); *Humana, Inc. v. American Medicorp, Inc.*, [1977-1978 Transfer Binder] Fed. Sec. L. Rep. (CCH) ¶ 96,286 (S.D.N.Y. Jan. 5, 1978).

557. 430 U.S. 1 (1977).

558. 15 U.S.C. § 78n(e) (emphasis added).

559. 426 U.S. 438, 449 (1976).

have assumed actual significance in a reasonable shareholder's deliberations and that such a shareholder would have viewed disclosure of that fact as significantly altering the "total mix" of available information. This standard of materiality applies as well to actions under section 14(e) of the Williams Act.[560]

The materiality standard, as expounded by the Supreme Court in *TSC Industries* and applied in takeover cases, does not demand a showing that a shareholder would have *changed* his or her decision concerning a tender offer on the basis of undisclosed information. Instead, the plaintiff need show only that the undisclosed fact(s) would have been important in the decisionmaking process.[561]

Courts are less likely strictly to construe the materiality requirement in the context of takeovers (and proxy contests) than in other contexts because, in a heated takeover battle (as in a proxy contest), both sides generally have a full and equal opportunity to present their views to shareholders and to the public.[562] As the Court of Appeals for the Second Circuit observed:

> Congress intended to assure basic honesty and fair dealing, not to impose an unrealistic requirement of laboratory conditions that might make the new statute a potent tool for incumbent management to protect its own interests against the desires and

---

560. *See, e.g.*, *Flynn v. Bass Bros. Enters., Inc.*, 744 F.2d 978 (3d Cir. 1984); *Bell v. Cameron Meadows Land Co.*, 669 F.2d 1278 (9th Cir. 1982); *Staffin v. Greenberg*, 672 F.2d 1196 (3d Cir. 1982).

561. *See, e.g.*, *Kramas v. Security Gas & Oil, Inc.*, 672 F.2d 766 (9th Cir.), *cert. denied*, 459 U.S. 1035 (1982); *Riggs Nat'l Bank v. Allbritton*, 516 F. Supp. 164 (D.D.C. 1981).

562. *See, e.g.*, *Flynn v. Bass Bros. Enters., Inc.*, 744 F.2d 978 (3d Cir. 1984); *Seaboard World Airlines, Inc. v. Tiger Int'l, Inc.*, 600 F.2d 355 (2d Cir. 1979); *Chem-Nuclear Systems, Inc. v. Waste Management, Inc.*, [1982 Transfer Binder] Fed. Sec. L. Rep. (CCH) ¶ 98,759 (W.D. Wash. July 16, 1982); *cf. Blanchette v. Providence & Worcester Co.*, 428 F. Supp. 347 (D. Del. 1977); *Broder v. Dane*, 384 F. Supp. 1312 (S.D.N.Y. 1974).

> welfare of the stockholders. These considerations bear on the kind of judgment to be applied in testing conduct—of both sides—and also on the issue of materiality.[563]

Not surprisingly, the question of materiality has been much litigated. Frequently recurring issues include the materiality of the bidder's financial condition, of earnings projections, and of possible harm to the target resulting from the bidder's acquisition of control.

a. Bidder's Financial Condition

In *Prudent Real Estate Trust v. Johncamp Realty, Inc.*,[564] the Court of Appeals for the Second Circuit confronted the issue of the materiality of omitted information concerning the bidder's financial condition. The case involved a tender offer by Johncamp for any and all shares of Prudent. Johncamp itself was owned by a complex chain of interlocking interests, many of which provided funds for the Prudent bid. Prudent sued to block the offer, claiming, among other things, that Johncamp had failed to disclose any financial information about some of its parent and sibling companies.

The Court of Appeals reviewed the history of the SEC rule requiring disclosure of the financial condition of bidders and concluded that Johncamp had not disclosed sufficient financial information. Applying the *TSC Industries* test of materiality, the court weighed the importance to shareholders of receiving financial information about the bidder:

> It is true that, in the case of an "any and all" offer such as that here at issue, a stockholder who has firmly decided to tender has no interest in the financial position of the offeror other than its ability to pay—a point not here at issue—since he will have severed all financial connections with the target. It is also true

---

563. *Electronic Specialty Co. v. International Controls Corp.*, 409 F.2d 937, 948 (2d Cir. 1969).

564. 599 F.2d 1140 (2d Cir. 1979).

> that in the case of such an offer, there is less reason for him to seek to eliminate the risk of being partly in and partly out by selling to arbitrageurs, usually at a price somewhere between the previous market and the offered price, than where the offer is for a stated number or percentage of the shares (with or without the right to accept additional shares) or is conditioned on a minimum number being obtained. Still, the shareholder of the target company faces a hard problem in determining the most advantageous course of action, a problem whose difficulty is enhanced by his usual ignorance of the course other shareholders are adopting. If the bidder is in a flourishing financial condition, the stockholder might decide to hold his shares in the hope that, if the offer was only partially successful, the bidder might raise its bid after termination of the offer or infuse new capital into the enterprise. *Per contra*, a poor financial condition of the bidder might cause the shareholder to accept for fear that control of the company would pass into irresponsible hands.[565]

The court thus held that the bidder should have fully disclosed its financial condition, despite the fact that the entities whose financial condition was not disclosed were supplying only 20 percent of the financing for the tender offer and that another principal financier was "a company of substance," as shown by its annual reports and other financial statements.

Prudent Real Estate involved a tender offer for any and all shares of the target; thus, it was at least arguable that the shareholders had no interest in the bidder's financial condition other than, perhaps, in the bidder's ability to pay for tendered shares. Where the offer is for less than all of the target's shares, however, the bidder's finances become particularly important, because shareholders cannot be assured that they will be able to unload all of their shares during the tender offer.

Such a situation arose in *Life Investors, Inc. v. AGO Holding, N.V.*,[566] in which Life Investors sought to enjoin a tender offer by AGO, a Dutch company, which had disclosed "only a three-sentence summary" of its worldwide revenues, assets, and net

---

565. *Id.* at 1147.

566. [1981-1982 Transfer Binder] Fed. Sec. L. Rep. (CCH) ¶ 98,356 (8th Cir. Oct. 21, 1981).

income.[567] The district court denied the injunction and declared AGO's lack of disclosure immaterial because (*i*) AGO's offer was financed internally, rather than through outside loans; (*ii*) no party challenged AGO's ability to pay for the tendered stock; and (*iii*) AGO already owned 41 percent of the target and thus already had effective control. The Court of Appeals for the Eighth Circuit disagreed (although it observed that "these factors are properly considered in determining materiality").[568]

Noting that AGO had sought only 15 percent of the target's stock, an amount sufficient to give AGO operating control of the company despite the existence of a 44-percent minority, the Court of Appeals held that

> [t]hese facts make it likely that Life Investors' stockholders will be intensely interested in how AGO has run its own business. If AGO was purchasing all the stock, a stockholder would have relatively little concern for the bidder's financial condition. Where, as here, the partial offer means that a substantial minority will necessarily remain, the shareholder must weigh staying with the company and the bidder as part of a minority bloc, a decision in which the bidder's financial condition may be quite significant. . . . AGO's financial condition could be very important to shareholders who might desire to either hold all their shares in the hope existing management and directors will continue to have operating control, or hold some and tender some in anticipation of gain from AGO's acquiring operating control, or tender all shares because of the imminent transfer of such control. . . . The partial tender offer, combined with its purpose of obtaining immediate operating control, weigh heavily in favor of finding that the offeror's financial condition is material.[569]

Also important were the "broad disclosure goals of the Williams Act" and the fact that AGO, as a foreign company, was not

567. *Id.* at 92,195.
568. *Id.*
569. *Id.*

subject to the routine financial disclosures required by the SEC.[570]

Disclosure rules, of course may apply to individuals as well as to companies. When Paul Kalmanovitz and Irwin Jacobs, through a corporate entity of which they were the largest shareholders, launched a partial tender offer for Pabst Brewing Company, the two investors were required (*i*) to disclose their personal net worth (or to state that it was at least $250 million), (*ii*) to state the value of the assets securing a loan that Kalmanovitz had taken to help finance the bid, and (*iii*) to state the amount of a personal loan to Jacobs by his bank.[571] The court found that Kalmanovitz and Jacobs together constituted "the primary motivating force behind the formation and capitalization of" the two companies that technically were involved in the tender offer; that the bidder was organized solely for the purpose of making the offer; and that Kalmanovitz and Jacobs intended to borrow money to fund the bidder and to use personal assets to repay the loans. The court therefore held information about the investors' personal finances to be material because

> there is a substantial likelihood that reasonable shareholders of Pabst would consider the disclosure important in deciding whether or not to tender their shares. When confronted with such a decision, a reasonable shareholder would want to know whether the individuals who are the primary motivating forces behind the consummation of the tender offer will have sufficient resources to pay their debtors. For example, the shareholder would want to know whether the individuals are so financially strapped as to raise the probability that they will be pressured into a compromising position in order to avoid default; or whether they have sufficient capital to permit them to make decisions based on the merits of the transaction and be able to fulfill their fiduciary obligations.[572]

---

570. *Id.*

571. *Pabst Brewing Co. v. Kalmanovitz*, 551 F. Supp. 882, 892 (D. Del.), *aff'd sub nom. Jacobs v. Pabst Brewing Co.*, 707 F.2d 1392 (3d Cir. 1982).

572. 551 F. Supp. at 893.

Not surprisingly, courts have considered misrepresentations of (rather than failure to disclose) financial conditions to be misstatements of material facts. In *Butler Aviation International, Inc. v. Comprehensive Designers, Inc.*,[573] the district court enjoined Comprehensive Designers' ("CDI's") tender offer for Butler because CDI had misrepresented corporate earnings and inflated the price of its shares through inaccurate press releases and undisclosed changes in accounting practices. The court had no difficulty in determining these misrepresentations to be material within the meaning of section 14(e).

b. *Projections*

Less clear, however, is the answer to the question whether the bidder must disclose mere projections of *future* corporate earnings and performance. Courts have taken somewhat different approaches to this question, often relying on the type of projections at issue.

Vaughn v. Teledyne, Inc.,[574] for example, involved an issuer tender offer and an allegation that Teledyne improperly had failed to disclose estimates of its operating companies' sales and earnings for the upcoming fiscal year, which estimates had been prepared solely for internal corporate use. The court observed that "[t]he SEC does not require a company to disclose financial projections"[575] and refused to reverse the grant of summary judgment for Teledyne on plaintiffs' disclosure claim. "It is just good general business practice," held the court, "to make such projections for internal corporate use. There is no evidence, however, that the estimates were made with such reasonable certainty even to *allow* them to be disclosed to the public."[576] Nor had plaintiffs adduced "specific evidence" suggesting why the projections were material. But the court did note previous

573. 307 F. Supp. 910 (S.D.N.Y. 1969), *aff'd*, 425 F.2d 842 (2d Cir. 1970).

574. 628 F.2d 1214 (9th Cir. 1980).

575. *Id.* at 1221.

576. *Id.* (emphasis added).

decisions holding that "partial disclosure of financial projections makes them material facts and that an individual may be liable under Rule 10b-5 if those projections thereafter are not disclosed completely and accurately."[577]

Fisher v. Plessey Co. Ltd.[578] illustrates what might be a slightly different judicial approach to the disclosure and materiality issues. *Fisher*, like *Vaughn*, also involved a tender offer by an issuer to buy back its own securities. The offer commenced on March 18, 1980, almost at the end of Plessey's fiscal year, which closed on March 29, 1980. Plessey's tender offer documents contained no information relating to the company's fourth-quarter and year-end 1979-80 results; nor did they include Plessey's predictions for those two periods or its forecasts for the first two quarters of fiscal 1980. Plessey contended, however, that it had no obligation to disclose projections or other figures that had not yet been verified and put in final form.

The district court denied Plessey's motion for summary judgment on claims relating to the nondisclosure of the fourth-quarter and fiscal 1979 year-end financials. Rejecting Plessey's assertion that "there was no undue delay in publishing the figures pursuant to [the company's] normal reporting procedures," the court held that

> the real issue is whether the figures were calculable with substantial certainty before that point and whether they were material and thus should have been disclosed. . . . Although Plessey cannot be expected to publish raw, unverified data, neither can it, under the circumstances of this case, take refuge behind the business judgment rule if preliminary earnings reports were available and substantially verified.[579]

(The court appears to have been swayed, in part, by the fact that Plessey became aware of the undisclosed financial information while making a tender offer for the securities of its wholly owned

---

577. *Id.* at n.7.
578. 559 F. Supp. 442 (S.D.N.Y. 1983).
579. *Id.* at 449-50 (footnote omitted).

subsidiary: "it can hardly be disputed that a corporation has a greater obligation to make known material inside information during the pendency of a tender offer for its own securities than it does in the routine operation of the business."[580])

But the court granted defendants' motion for summary judgment on the claims relating to the nondisclosure of predictions of fourth-quarter and year-end figures and of projections for the following two quarters. Characterizing the claims as seeking disclosure "not of fact but of conjecture, albeit highly competent conjecture," the court held that, "[w]hile a company may give such a projection, so long as it sets forth its basis, . . . it is not required to do so."[581] Thus, under *Fisher*, certain non-final figures may, under certain circumstances, be material and subject to disclosure, but other, more conjectural projections may not be.

Nondisclosure claims may also arise with respect to estimates or projections concerning assets of the target, rather than of the bidder. In *Flynn v. Bass Brothers Enterprises, Inc.*,[582] for example, plaintiffs claimed that Bass, which had made a tender offer for National Alfalfa Dehydrating and Milling Company, should have disclosed a projected valuation of National Alfalfa's shares and land holdings. These estimates had been made neither by the target nor by the bidder but, rather, by a third party that itself had once been interested in buying shares of National Alfalfa. The court denied plaintiffs' and defendants' motions for summary judgment, holding that the duty to disclose and the materiality of the valuations were issues for the trier of fact. But the court rejected the bidder's claim that, as a matter of law, it was not obliged to disclose the valuations.

The suit proceeded to trial, and, at the close of plaintiffs' case, the district court granted defendants' motion for a directed verdict. The Court of Appeals for the Third Circuit affirmed, ruling that the valuation reports (*i*) had not been prepared by

580. *Id.* at 449.

581. *Id.* at 451.

582. 456 F. Supp. 484 (E.D. Pa. 1978), *aff'd*, 744 F.2d 978 (3d Cir. 1984).

experts, (*ii*) "had no adequately demonstrated basis in fact," and (*iii*) had been prepared as "selling" documents, to encourage financing of a proposed acquisition, rather than to present a neutral appraisal of the company.[583]

The Court of Appeals went further, however, and articulated a new "law for disclosure of soft information as it is to be applied from this date on."

> Henceforth, the law is not that asset appraisals are, as a matter of law, immaterial. Rather, in appropriate cases, such information must be disclosed. Courts should ascertain the duty to disclose asset valuations and other soft information on a case by case basis, by weighing the potential aid such information will give a shareholder against the potential harm, such as undue reliance, if the information is released with a proper cautionary note.
>
> The factors a court must consider in making such a determination are: the facts upon which the information is based; the qualifications of those who prepared or compiled it; the purpose for which the information was originally intended; its relevance to the stockholders' impending decision; the degree of subjectivity or bias reflected in its preparation; the degree to which the information is unique; and the availability to the investor of other more reliable sources of information.[584]

Thus, in the Third Circuit, courts will apply a case-by-case balancing approach in deciding whether "soft information" such as appraisals, projections, and valuations must be disclosed.

The Court of Appeals for the Sixth Circuit, however, has expressly rejected the Third Circuit's rule. In *Starkman v. Marathon Oil Co.*[585] and *Radol v. Thomas*,[586] two of the myraid lawsuits spawned by the battle for control of Marathon,[587] the

583. *Flynn v. Bass Bros. Enters., Inc.*, 744 F.2d 978, 989 (3d Cir. 1984).
584. *Id.* at 988 (footnote omitted).
585. 772 F.2d 231 (6th Cir. 1985), *cert. denied*, 106 S. Ct. 1195 (1986).
586. 772 F.2d 244 (6th Cir. 1985), *cert. denied*, 106 S. Ct. 3272 (1986).
587. *See supra* § III.2.B(1) (discussing the facts of the takeover struggle).

court confronted the claim that Marathon and United States Steel (the winning bidder) had violated section 10(b) of the Exchange Act and section 14(e) of the Williams Act by failing to disclose internally and externally prepared asset appraisals and five-year earnings and cash-flow projections relating to Marathon. The appraisals at issue were two reports, prepared, respectively, by Marathon's vice president (John Strong) and its investment banker (First Boston) as "selling documents" or "presentation pieces" to attract the interest of friendly prospective purchasers and thus to save the company from falling prey to a hostile bidder making an inadequate offer.

The Court of Appeals affirmed the district court's rulings for defendants and set forth its own standard governing disclosure of soft information:

> [A] tender offer target must disclose projections and asset appraisals based upon predictions regarding future economic and corporate events only if the predictions underlying the appraisal or projection are substantially certain to hold. An example is when the predictions in fact state a fixed plan of corporate activity. If a target chooses to disclose projections and appraisals which do not rise to this level of certainty, then it must also inform the shareholders as to the basis for and limitations on the projected realizable values.[588]

Under this standard, the court continued,

> Marathon plainly had no duty to disclose the Strong and First Boston reports, because these reports contained estimates of the value of probable, potential and unexplored oil and gas reserves which were based on highly speculative assumptions regarding the path of oil and gas prices, recovery rates and the like over a period of thirty to fifty years. Disclosure of such estimated values could well have been misleading without an accompanying mountain of data and explanations. There is no reported case actually holding that disclosure of appraised values of oil and gas reserves is required, and several which agree with our decision that such disclosure is not required.

---

588. *Starkman v. Marathon Oil Co.*, 772 F.2d 231, 241 (6th Cir. 1985), *cert. denied*, 106 S. Ct. 1195 (1986) (footnote omitted).

> Similarly, Marathon had no duty to disclose the five-year earnings and cash flow projections given to Steel and First Boston. This information does not rise to the level of substantial certainty triggering a duty to disclose.[589]

In formulating its new rule, the court criticized, and declined to follow, the balancing approach adopted by the Court of Appeals for the Third Circuit.

> By its very nature, . . . this sort of judicial cost-benefit analysis is uncertain and unpredictable, and it moreover neglects the role of the market in providing shareholders with information regarding the target's value through competing tender offers. Our approach, which focuses on the certainty of the data underlying the appraisal or projection, ensures that the target company's shareholders will receive all essentially factual information, while preserving the target's discretion to disclose more uncertain information without the threat of liability, provided appropriate qualifications and explanations are made.[590]

The materiality of, and the concomitant duty to disclose, projections and estimates thus depend largely on the facts of each case and on the law of the relevant jurisdiction(s) in which nondisclosure might be challenged. Claims of this sort might well prove effective against a bidder that has disclosed insufficient information; the target-plaintiff must remember, however, that the bidder probably is not obligated to disclose data or estimates that are too hypothetical.

c. *Possible Harm to Target from Change in Control*

"Material" information may also include information showing possible harm to the target resulting from the bidder's acquisition of control. A number of courts have required offerors to disclose information concerning a possible or probable loss of significant tax exemptions. In *Prudent Real Estate*

---

589. 772 F.2d at 242 (footnote omitted).

590. *Id.*

Trust v. Johncamp Realty, Inc.,[591] the Court of Appeals for the Second Circuit held that the bidder had not sufficiently disclosed the tax consequences that would flow from the target's loss of its status as a real estate investment trust. The court required fuller disclosure of these consequences—but did not insist that the bidder "attempt to *quantify* the effect of loss of REIT status."[592]

Inadequate disclosure of tax consequences also figured in *Commonwealth Oil Refining Co. v. Tesoro Petroleum Corp.*,[593] in which the target, Commonwealth Oil ("Corco"), claimed that the bidder, Tesoro Petroleum, had failed to make full disclosure of the potential impact of a successful bid on Corco's tax exemption under the Puerto Rican Industrial Incentive Act. Tesoro's offering statement had informed shareholders that Corco could lose the exemption if its shares were transferred without the prior written approval of the Governor of Puerto Rico and that forfeiture of the exemption "could have a material adverse effect" on Corco.[594] To this level of disclosure, the court responded:

> When told that the success of Tesoro's efforts might have a "materially adverse" effect on Corco, a reasonable shareholder may well ask, "How material is material?" When told that in 1974 the Puerto Rico tax exemption resulted in a saving to Corco of $29,220,501, the shareholder is far better able to understand the consequences of his decision to tender or not and can intelligently choose between the two alternatives.[595]

The court therefore ordered Tesoro to disclose the actual dollar amounts potentially at risk. "Having chosen to make the Commonwealth shareholders aware of the possible adverse consequences of a . . . Tesoro bid," the court declared,

---

591. 599 F.2d 1140 (2d Cir. 1979).
592. *Id.* at 1148-49 (emphasis added).
593. 394 F. Supp. 267 (S.D.N.Y. 1975).
594. *Id.* at 276.
595. *Id.* at 277.

> the offeror could not stop there. Rather, it was obligated to make full and complete disclosure of all relevant and material facts bound up with the tax exemption . . . so as to afford the stockholders sufficient predicate for a knowledgeable and enlightened decision. In short, the initial disclosure necessitates the further disclosure and the contents of the original offering statement renders [sic] any contrary contention without merit.[596]

(The court expressly noted that it was not required to decide whether omission of *all* references to the tax issue would have constituted a material omission. However, the court added, "given the conflicting legal opinions presented on this undeniably material issue, we do not doubt that such an omission would have presented serious and substantial questions."[597])

Courts also have required disclosure of other types of possible harm. *Grumman Corp. v. LTV Corp.*,[598] for example, involved possible adverse effects on the target's business opportunities. LTV, which sought to acquire Grumman, had a subsidiary, Vought, through which it engaged in business in the aerospace industry and competed with Grumman in the design, development, and production of military aircraft, commercial aircraft components and sub-assemblies, and other aerospace products. Both Grumman and Vought were competing for the multi-billion-dollar contract to build the Navy's VTX missile. Grumman, as prime contractor, formed a team with Beech and Link Corporations to bid on the project; Vought was teamed with Northrop Corporation. The agreement between Northrop and Vought contained a clause pledging that LTV, Vought's parent, would not undertake to support any other bidder for the VTX contract. Thus, it appeared that LTV could not seek to advance the interests of Grumman, the company for which LTV was making a tender offer.

---

596. *Id.* at 278.

597. *Id.*

598. 527 F. Supp. 86 (E.D.N.Y.), *aff'd on other grounds*, 665 F.2d 10 (2d Cir. 1981).

LTV's offering statement, however, contained no information about the competition between Vought and Grumman for the VTX contract; nor did it disclose the existence of the Vought-Northrop noncompetition agreement. The court found that "[t]he consequences to Grumman and to its employees if Grumman must withdraw from the competition are, to say the least, serious, considering the costs involved in making the bid and the possible loss of the contract."[599] Accordingly, the court held the failure to disclose the agreement to be a material omission.

But there are levels of speculation at which hypothetical impacts on a target's business will not be deemed material, as *Sunshine Mining Co. v. Great Western United Corp.*[600] illustrates. The case involved a tender offer for Sunshine by Great Western, a company controlled by the Hunt family. In fighting the unwelcome bid, Sunshine appears to have argued that Great Western failed to disclose a potential conflict of interest between the Hunts, who traded heavily in the silver market, and Sunshine, which produced silver. The court found no evidence that the Hunts could affect any market by acquiring control of Sunshine and rejected the target's disclosure claims.

An appropriate postscript to the above cases is the admonition that "[c]ourts should tread lightly in imposing a duty of self-flagellation on offerors with respect to matters that are known as well, or almost as well, to the target company; some issues concerning a contested tender offer can safely be left for the latter's riposte."[601] Nor will courts usually require the offeror or, for that matter, the offeree "to publicly admit to misconduct"—provided that the party discloses "all material *facts* relating to the party's actions, including those that might relate to misconduct."[602]

599. *Id.* at 104.

600. [1977-1978 Transfer Binder] Fed. Sec. L. Rep. (CCH) ¶ 96,049 (D. Idaho April 22, 1977).

601. *Missouri Portland Cement Co. v. Cargill, Inc.*, 498 F.2d 851, 873 (2d Cir.), *cert. denied*, 419 U.S. 883 (1974) (footnote omitted).

602. *Warner Communications, Inc. v. Murdoch*, 581 F. Supp. 1482, 1490 (D. Del. 1984) (emphasis added).

d. *Reasons for the Offer*

As long as the bidder's offering materials (or the target's defensive materials) disclose all relevant and material *facts*, it usually is not necessary for the bidder (or the target) to disclose its subjective *motives* in making (or fighting) the offer.[603] In *Bucher v. Shumway*,[604] for example, plaintiffs attacked two separate tender offers by the Signal Companies and Gulf & Western Industries for Signal common stock by claiming, among other things, that defendants had failed to disclose the transaction's "true" purpose, which allegedly was to entrench Signal's management and to deprive Signal's shareholders of competing offers that threatened management's control. Relying on a number of cases rejecting causes of action based on failure to disclose motives for "true" purposes of specific transactions, the court dismissed the claim and held that, "[t]he facts relating to the agreement [between the two offerors] having been disclosed, the fairness of the terms of the transaction is at most a tangential concern of the securities laws."[605]

Federal claims of failure to disclose "true" purposes thus are unlikely to succeed as long as the offeror (or target) has disclosed the objective facts from which the allegedly illicit purpose may be inferred. But the plaintiff may be able to attack the purpose under state law by alleging that the decisionmakers breached their fiduciary duty to the shareholders.[606]

e. *Disparity of Treatment*

If a target has two or more classes of shareholders, and if the offeror treats those classes unequally, the offeror must disclose this disparity of treatment because it "is generally of great

---

603. *See, e.g.*, *Rodman v. Grant Found.*, 608 F.2d 64, 71 (2d Cir. 1979).

604. [1979-1980 Transfer Binder] Fed. Sec. L. Rep. (CCH) ¶ 97,142 (S.D.N.Y. Oct. 11, 1979).

605. *Id.* at 96,300-01 (footnote omitted).

606. *See infra* § III.3.

importance to the disfavored shareholder. . . ."[607] The solicitation materials in *SEC v. Texas International Co.* were found to be materially misleading because they stated that the offer to one group of creditors was worth more than the offer to another group of creditors on a per-share basis but neglected to inform shareholders that the share distributions to the two groups were unequal. The court held that the offers more properly should have been evaluated on a dollar-per-claim basis, under which the first group actually would receive less than would the second group.

f. Intention to Exercise Control

Courts generally consider material a bidder's intention to exercise control over a target and require the bidder to disclose any such intention. When Gulf & Western Industries ("G&W") made a tender offer for shares of Great Atlantic & Pacific Tea Company ("A&P"), an A&P shareholder sued G&W under the Williams Act, claiming that G&W had failed to disclose its intention to acquire a controlling position in A&P or at least to influence A&P's management and policies. Plaintiff also alleged that G&W had failed to inform A&P shareholders that the acquisition of A&P shares would likely cause antitrust problems for both G&W and A&P because of G&W's holdings in other companies.[608] The Court of Appeals for the Second Circuit held that "[t]he intention to exercise control over a target company and the knowledge of antitrust violations that might result from acquisition of the tendered stock are normally both matters of importance to prospective tenderors. . . ."[609]

---

607. *SEC v. Texas Int'l Co.*, 498 F. Supp. 1231, 1251 (N.D. Ill. 1980).

608. *Lowenschuss v. Kane*, 520 F.2d 255, 267 (2d Cir. 1975).

609. *Id.* at 268; *see also Otis Elevator Co. v. United Technologies Corp.*, 405 F. Supp. 960 (S.D.N.Y. 1975) (offeror illegally withheld information concerning plan to merge target with offeror where merger plan was not inchoate but was highly developed and clearly adopted by offeror's management).

3. Scienter

Ever since the Supreme Court's decision in *Ernst & Ernst v. Hochfelder*[610] revolutionized the law of liability for securities fraud under section 10(b), it has been clear that a private cause of action for damages will not lie "in the absence of any allegation of 'scienter'—intent to deceive, manipulate, or defraud."[611] The Supreme Court has not yet decided whether a Williams Act plaintiff must make a similar showing, but a number of lower courts have ruled that liability under section 14(e) depends upon a demonstration of scienter.[612]

Because the scienter requirement evolved in cases brought under section 10(b), it is appropriate to examine those cases to determine the meaning of "scienter" as it applies to Williams Act suits. The Supreme Court, in *Hochfelder*, observed that

> the term "scienter" refers to a mental state embracing intent to deceive, manipulate, or defraud. In certain areas of the law recklessness is considered to be a form of intentional conduct for purposes of imposing liability for some act. We need not address here the question whether, in some circumstances, reckless behavior is sufficient for civil liability under § 10(b) and Rule 10b-5.[613]

Predictably, a battle has raged about the question whether—and under what circumstances—recklessness can satisfy *Hochfelder*'s scienter requirement. But one point does seem settled: "*Hochfelder* clearly eliminates negligence as a possible basis for a finding of liability. . . ."[614] Indeed, even allegations of

---

610. 425 U.S. 185 (1976).

611. *Id.* at 193 (footnote omitted).

612. *See, e.g.*, *Smallwood v. Pearl Brewing Co.*, 489 F.2d 579, 606 (5th Cir.), *cert. denied*, 419 U.S. 873 (1974); *Chris-Craft Indus., Inc. v. Piper Aircraft Corp.*, 480 F.2d 341, 362-63 (2d Cir.), *cert. denied*, 414 U.S. 910 (1973); *S-G Secs., Inc. v. The Fuqua Inv. Co.*, 466 F. Supp. 1114 (D. Mass. 1978); *A&K R.R. Materials, Inc. v. Green Bay & Western R.R. Co.*, 437 F. Supp. 636, 641-42 (E.D. Wis. 1977).

613. 425 U.S. at 194 n.12.

614. *Stokes v. Lokken*, 644 F.2d 779, 783 (8th Cir. 1981).

gross negligence "fall short of the state of mind that § 10(b) and Rule 10b-5 require."[615]

Scienter, then, imports actual knowledge or, perhaps, recklessness. One would expect a concept such as "actual knowledge" to require no explanation; in fact, it usually gets none. But the apparent clarity of this seemingly subjective standard has not prevented at least one court from allowing a jury to determine the existence of "actual knowledge" from "the defendant's irresponsible and reckless disregard of the truth" or from evidence showing that "the defendant had or should have had actual knowledge of the fraudulent scheme."[616] True, this case was decided before the Supreme Court handed down *Hochfelder,* a factor that might well affect the case's precedential value.

The actual knowledge requirement probably stems from the idea that liability under section 10(b) should import a finding of evil intent, or bad faith, on the part of the defendant, for "[t]here is no indication that Congress intended anyone to be made liable for [manipulative and deceptive] practices unless he acted other than in good faith."[617] Other courts frequently have acknowledged this construction of section 10(b).[618]

---

615. *Id.* at 784; *see also* McLean *v. Alexander*, 599 F.2d 1190, 1198 (3d Cir. 1979) ("negligence—whether gross, grave or inexcusable—cannot serve as substitute for scienter," although recklessness can); *Mansbach v. Prescott, Ball & Turben*, 598 F.2d 1017, 1025 (6th Cir. 1979) (negligence not enough for liability).

616. *Saltzman v. Zern*, 407 F. Supp. 49, 56 (E.D. Pa. 1976) (footnote omitted).

617. *Ernst & Ernst v. Hochfelder*, 425 U.S. 185, 206 (1976).

618. *See, e.g., Stokes v. Lokken*, 644 F.2d 779, 784 (8th Cir. 1981) (quoting *Hochfelder* and finding that defendant's actions "cannot be regarded as so reckless that an inference of bad faith might reasonably be made"); *Wertheim & Co. v. Codding Embryological Sciences, Inc.*, 620 F.2d 764, 766 (10th Cir. 1980) (no liability exists if defendant acted in good faith, without intent to deceive); *Stern v. American Bankshares Corp.*, 429 F. Supp. 818, 828 (E.D. Wis. 1977) (unwitting participant not liable as aider-abettor); *United States Steel and Carnegie Pension Fund, Inc., v. Orenstein*, [1976-1977 Transfer Binder] Fed. Sec. L. Rep. (CCH) ¶ 95,680, at 90,340 (S.D.N.Y. Aug. 4, 1976) (defendant bank acted in good faith in dealings with plaintiffs).

Nevertheless, recklessness has often been held to satisfy section 10(b)'s scienter requirement; the same is true for cases brought under section 14(e).[619] While it would be too much to expect the courts to have evolved a uniform definition of "recklessness," a surprising number of opinions have adopted the language of an Oklahoma federal district court opinion, *Franke v. Midwestern Oklahoma Development Authority:*

> In the context of an omissions case, reckless conduct may be defined as a highly unreasonable omission, involving not merely simple, or even inexcusable, negligence, but an extreme departure from the standards of ordinary care, and which presents a danger of misleading buyers or sellers that is either known to the defendant or is so obvious that the actor must have been aware of it.[620]

Franke framed its definition of "recklessness" in the context of omissions, but courts borrowing the definition have applied it as well in cases involving misrepresentations. Cases in the Second, Third, Fifth, Seventh, and Eleventh Circuits have followed *Franke*'s language.[621]

---

619. *See, e.g., Pryor v. United States Steel Corp.*, 591 F. Supp. 942, 956 (S.D.N.Y. 1984), *aff'd in part, rev'd in part,* 794 F.2d 52 (2d Cir.), *cert. denied,* 107 S. Ct. 445 (1986) ("Under the law of this circuit, the scienter requirement does not mean that plaintiff must prove intent to defraud; a showing that defendants had knowledge of the falsity of their statements or reckless disregard for the truth is sufficient.") (footnote omitted); *A&K R.R. Materials, Inc. v. Green Bay & Western R.R. Co.*, 437 F. Supp. 636, 642 (E.D. Wis. 1977).

620. 428 F. Supp. 719, 725 (W.D. Okla. 1976), *remanded on other grounds sub nom. Cronin v. Midwestern Okla. Dev. Auth.*, 619 F.2d 856 (10th Cir. 1980).

621. *See, e.g., Broad v. Rockwell Int'l Corp.*, 642 F.2d 929, 961-62 (5th Cir.) (en banc), *cert. denied,* 454 U.S. 965 (1981) (adopting *Franke* definition for both omissions and misrepresentations but changing the defined term to "severe recklessness"); *McLean v. Alexander*, 599 F.2d 1190, 1197 (3d Cir. 1979) (expressly approving *Franke* formula in context of both misstatements and omissions); *Rolf v. Blyth, Eastman Dillon & Co.*, 570 F.2d 38, 47 (2d Cir.), *cert. denied,* 439 U.S. 1039 (1978); *Sanders v. John Nuveen & Co.*, 554 F.2d 790, 793 (7th Cir. 1977), *cert. denied,* 450 U.S. 1005 (1981) (recklessness is "closer to being a lesser form of intent than merely a greater degree of ordinary negligence"—"not just a difference in degree, but also in kind"); *In re N. Am. Acceptance Corp. Secs. Cases*, 513 F. Supp. 608, 625-26 (N.D. Ga. 1981); *Lake v.*

Other courts have chosen to formulate their own definitions of "recklessness." The Court of Appeals for the Sixth Circuit, for example, has explicated the term as "highly unreasonable conduct which is an extreme departure from the standards of ordinary care. While the danger need not be known, it must at least be so obvious that any reasonable man would have known of it."[622] A footnote helpfully adds that "the standard falls somewhere between intent and negligence."[623]

There is yet a third line of cases, one that purports to follow the *Franke* test but, in explicating it, probably changes it in a subtle but significant respect. *Sundstrand Corp. v. Sun Chemical Corp.*[624] begins its analysis by setting out the *Franke* definition, which the court views as " 'equivalent to willful fraud.' "[625]

> Indeed, the *Franke* definition of recklessness should be viewed as the functional equivalent of intent. . . . Under this definition, the danger of misleading buyers must be actually known or so obvious that any reasonable man would be legally bound as knowing, *and* the omission must derive from something more egregious than even "white heart/empty head" good faith.[626]

One footnote (directly preceding the underscored "and") labels the first part of the test "objective," while another footnote (at the end of the quotation) categorizes the second part as

---

Kidder, Peabody & Co., [1978 Transfer Binder] Fed. Sec. L. Rep. (CCH) ¶ 96,509, at 93,974 (N.D. Ind. May 22, 1978) (recklessness "requires a showing substantially the same as actual knowledge at least in terms of the ready availability of material facts and blatant affirmative acts in total derogation [of] or indifference to the knowledge shown to be at hand").

622. *Mansbach v. Prescott, Ball & Turben*, 598 F.2d 1017, 1025 (6th Cir. 1979).

623. *Id.* at n.36; *see also Wertheim & Co. v. Codding Embryological Sciences, Inc.*, 620 F.2d 764, 767 (10th Cir. 1980) (following Seventh Circuit's definition of recklessness as coming closer to being a lesser form of intent than merely a greater degree of ordinary negligence); *Tucker v. Janota*, [1979 Transfer Binder] Fed. Sec. L. Rep. (CCH) ¶ 96,701, at 94,716 (N.D. Ill. Nov. 1, 1978) (recklessness is wanton ignorance of readily available evidence of fraud).

624. 553 F.2d 1033 (7th Cir.), *cert. denied*, 434 U.S. 875 (1977).

625. *Id.* at 1045 (emphasis added).

626. *Id.* (footnotes omitted).

"subjective," based on *Hochfelder*'s requirement of more than " 'inexcusable negligence.' " "Thus if a trial judge found, for example, that a defendant genuinely forgot to disclose information or that it never came to his mind, etc., this prong of the *Franke* test would defeat a finding of recklessness even though the proverbial 'reasonable man' would never have forgotten."[627] This subjective prong probably does not inhere in the *Franke* that test, and the Seventh Circuit most likely has gone beyond *Franke* in focusing on the defendant's *actual* state of mind.

Regardless of the applicable definition of "actual knowledge" or "recklessness," it seems clear that a plaintiff need not show that the defendant had a *specific* intent to induce a shareholder to act in a certain way. A *general* intent to deceive should suffice to establish liability. Thus, as the court stated in *In re Commonwealth Oil/Tesoro Petroleum Corp. Securities Litigation*, "[w]hat section 14(e) requires is simply a misleading statement or omission of a material fact made with intent to deceive in connection with a tender offer. It does not require that a stockholder be misled in the way that the alleged wrongdoer intended."[628]

As a footnote to the scienter requirement, it is worth remembering that the rule arose in the context of actions for *damages*; indeed, the Supreme Court expressly stated in *Hochfelder* that it "need not consider the question whether scienter is a necessary element in an action for *injunctive* relief under § 10(b) and Rule 10b-5."[629] The question also remains unresolved with respect to injunction actions under section 14(e).[630] At least one court, however, has enjoined a tender offer based on violations of section 14(e)'s disclosure requirements even though the material misstatements and omissions at issue

627. *Id.* at n.20.

628. 467 F. Supp. 227, 244 (W.D. Tex. 1979).

629. 425 U.S. at 194 n.12 (emphasis added).

630. *See Applied Digital Data Sys., Inc. v. Milgo Elec. Corp.*, 425 F. Supp. 1145, 1157 n.41 (S.D.N.Y. 1977).

"may have been inadvertent."[631] Injunctive relief thus might be available even without a showing of scienter.

4. Causation/Reliance

A plaintiff asserting a section 14(e) claim based on alleged misrepresentation must show not only that the misrepresentation was material and made with scienter but also that he or she *relied* upon the misrepresentation and that it caused the harm at issue. In *Pryor v. United States Steel Corp.*,[632] for example, plaintiff brought a class action seeking damages allegedly sustained during the acquisition of Marathon Oil by United States Steel and its subsidiary, U.S.S., Inc. U.S.S. had made an offer for 30 million shares of Marathon at $125 per share, with the proviso that, if more than 30 million shares were tendered and not subsequently withdrawn, U.S.S. would purchase shares pro rata, according to the number of shares tendered on or before the proration date of November 28, 1981, later extended to December 4, 1981. Because tendering Marathon shareholders could withdraw their tendered shares until the offer expired on January 6, 1982, however, the actual number of shares in the proration pool—and, hence, the proportion of each tendering shareholder's shares that would be bought for cash—did not become fixed until that date.

On December 8, defendants publicly announced that they had received approximately 54 million tendered shares—well in excess of the 30 million that they had undertaken to purchase. Later that month, defendants made two more announcements, stating that approximately 51 million shares had been tendered. When the offer expired in January 1982, defendants purchased 30 million of the tendered shares and, on January 11, issued a

---

631. *Blanchette v. Providence & Worcester Co.*, 428 F. Supp. 347, 357 (D. Del. 1977).

632. 591 F. Supp. 942 (S.D.N.Y. 1984), *aff'd in part, rev'd in part*, 794 F.2d 52 (2d Cir.), *cert. denied*, 107 S. Ct. 445 (1986).

final press release stating that 53,880,360 Marathon shares had been accepted for proration.

Based on this pattern of announcements, plaintiff claimed that defendants either had accepted for inclusion in the proration pool approximately three million shares that had not been duly and validly tendered on or before the December 4, 1981 proration date or had intentionally made false and misleading statements concerning the number of shares to be accepted for proration. Acceptance of these "extra" shares reduced from 58.8 percent to 55.6 percent the pro rata percentage of plaintiff's shares that defendants purchased. Thus, instead of purchasing 882 of plaintiff's 1,500 tendered shares at $125 per share, defendants bought only 834 shares.

Plaintiff further claimed that he (and other similarly situated Marathon shareholders) had relied on defendants' misrepresentations in calculating how many shares would be returned unpurchased after proration and that he had based his investment decisions on this information. Expecting the market price for returned and unpurchased shares to be significantly lower than the $125-per-share tender offer price, plaintiff and the class allegedly attempted to reduce their losses by engaging in various hedging and options transactions and short sales. Had they known that an even larger percentage of their shares would be returned unpurchased, plaintiff and the class allegedly would have included those extra shares in their market transactions.

The court found plaintiff's complaint to be "particularly sketchy in the area of reliance and injury."[633]

> The Complaint totally fails to allege the details of plaintiff's hedging transactions, including the type of hedging transactions plaintiff engaged in, how many shares were included in the transactions, precisely when the transactions took place, what specifically caused plaintiff's financial losses, what specifically plaintiff would have done to prevent those losses had he had the

633. 591 F. Supp. at 959.

> correct information, and whether he was actually able to cut his losses with respect to the shares he did hedge on.[634]

The court therefore held the amended complaint "not sufficiently specific in the areas of reliance, injury and causation to satisfy Rule 9(b)" of the Federal Rules of Civil Procedure (requiring that, "[i]n all averments of fraud or mistake, the circumstances constituting fraud or mistake shall be stated with particularity").[635] However, the court granted plaintiff an opportunity to amend his complaint.[636]

The *Pryor* case addressed the issues of reliance and causation in the context of a claim of intentional *misrepresentation*. Where the complaint alleges not misrepresentation but, rather, *nondisclosure* of material facts, the plaintiff need not proffer direct proof of reliance. Instead, the plaintiff generally need prove only that the omitted facts were material in that a reasonable investor would be likely to have considered them important in making investment decisions. One court, in a case involving alleged nondisclosures, expressly drew this distinction between misrepresentation cases and nondisclosure cases:

> The distinction between materiality and reliance is one of degree. . . . The inquiry as to materiality in the tender offer context is whether there exists a substantial likelihood that a reasonable shareholder would consider a particular fact important in deciding what to do with his stock. . . . The element of reliance essentially concerns whether the misrepresentation or omission actually induced the plaintiff himself to act differently than he would have acted in his investment decision.
>
> In general, a plaintiff must demonstrate both materiality and reliance in securities fraud cases. The violations alleged by plaintiffs here, however, arise from nondisclosure of material facts. In such situations the Supreme Court has held that "positive proof of reliance is not a prerequisite to recovery. All that is necessary is that the facts withheld be material. . . . *This obligation*

634. *Id.* (footnotes omitted).

635. *Id.*

636. The Court of Appeals upheld the substance of plaintiff's legal challenge. *See Pryor v. United States Steel Corp.*, 794 F.2d 52, 55-56 (2d Cir.), *cert. denied*, 107 S. Ct. 445 (1986).

> *to disclose and this withholding of a material fact establish the requisite element of causation in fact.*"[637]

It would be a mistake, however, to believe that reliance always may be presumed from materiality in a case involving an alleged failure to disclose material information. As the Court of Appeals for the Seventh Circuit held,

> neither *Mills v. Electric Auto-Lite Co.*, 396 U.S. 375 . . . (1970), nor *Affiliated Ute* abolished the reliance requirement, but "[r]ather . . . held that in cases in which reliance is possible, and even likely, but is unduly burdensome to prove, the resulting doubt would be resolved in favor of the class the statute was designed to protect."[638]

"The *Mills-Ute* presumption," continued the court, "is essentially a rule of judicial economy and convenience, designed to avoid the impracticality of requiring that each plaintiff shareholder testify concerning the reliance element. . . . However, when the logical basis on which the presumption rests is absent, it would be highly inappropriate to apply the *Mills-Ute* presumption."[639]

In *Panter*, the court found "no logical basis" for applying the presumption where the bidder withdrew its tender offer before plaintiffs had had an opportunity to decide whether or not to tender their shares. Because plaintiffs never faced the critical decision whether to tender, the court concluded that they never had relied on the alleged deception and thus could not sue the target (which allegedly had thwarted the offer) under section 14(e). The Court of Appeals for the Second Circuit reached the same conclusion on similar facts in *Lewis v. McGraw*.[640]

---

637. *Berman v. Gerber Prods. Co.*, 454 F. Supp. 1310, 1324 (W.D. Mich. 1978) (emphasis in original) (quoting *Affiliated Ute Citizens v. United States*, 406 U.S. 128, 153 (1972)).

638. *Panter v. Marshall Field & Co.*, 646 F.2d 271, 284 (7th Cir.), *cert. denied*, 454 U.S. 1092 (1981) (quoting *Lewis v. McGraw*, 619 F.2d 192, 195 (2d Cir.), *cert. denied*, 449 U.S. 951 (1980)).

639. *Id.*

640. 619 F.2d 192, 195 (2d Cir.), *cert. denied*, 449 U.S. 951 (1980).

5. "In Connection With"

Section 14(e) applies to misrepresentations or nondisclosures of material facts made "in connection with any tender offer or request or invitation for tenders. . . ." The "in connection with" requirement generally receives little attention when the offeror has publicly announced and formally commenced a takeover bid. Where the offeror has engaged in less definitive conduct, however, the "in connection with" requirement may cause some concern to a target (or any other plaintiff) seeking to rely on section 14(e).

The fact that a material misrepresentation or omission may have *preceded* the public announcement and formal commencement of a takeover does *not* necessarily mean that the alleged misconduct falls outside the ambit of section 14(e), as *Hanna Mining Co. v. Norcen Energy Resources Ltd.*[641] illustrates. In January 1979, Norcen first expressed an interest in investing in Hanna; after several years of informal discussion with various Hanna principals, Norcen began making open-market purchases of Hanna stock in August 1981. On September 9, 1981, the Executive Committee of Norcen's Board of Directors met and discussed the stock acquisition program. According to the minutes of that meeting, the company's president and chief executive officer reported that Norcen had initiated the market transactions "with the ultimate purpose of acquiring a 51% position at a later date."[642] The minutes also noted that the committee had "ratified the prior stock purchases and supported the proposed U.S. stock acquisition program."[643]

Despite this internal decision, Norcen's subsequent public statements—its press releases, annual report, Schedule 13D, and Form 10-K—all characterized the open-market transactions as being for investment purposes only and disclaimed any present intention to increase Norcen's holdings of Hanna shares. On

---

641. 574 F. Supp. 1172, 1198-1200 (N.D. Ohio 1982).

642. *Id.* at 1178.

643. *Id.*

April 5, 1982, however, Norcen announced its intention to commence a tender offer the next day for control of Hanna. The district court granted Hanna's motion for a preliminary injunction under sections 10(b), 13(d), and 14(e) and Rule 10b-5.

In defending against plaintiffs' section 14(e) claims, defendants argued that, even assuming that Norcen had decided as early as September 1981 to seek control of Hanna, the subsequent Schedule 13D, annual report, and Form 10-K all preceded, and thus were not filed "in connection with," the April 1982 announcement of a tender offer. The court deemed this construction of section 14(e) "overly restrictive" and concluded that injunctive relief should issue "as a remedy for misleading statements made by the defendants during the period preceding the announcement of Norcen's tender offer for Hanna because such an offer was contemplated long before it was actually announced and reliance on the statements in issue was probable under the circumstances."[644]

In reaching its decision, the *Hanna* court relied heavily on *Applied Digital Data Systems, Inc. v. Milgo Electronic Corp.*,[645] which held section 14(e) applicable to conduct that followed a corporation's public announcement of its intent to make an exchange offer in the future. Rejecting defendants' claim that the Williams Act did not apply until the bidder actually made the offer to the shareholders or at least filed it with the SEC, the court observed that Rule 10b-5, after which section 14(e) was "closely patterned," "requires that a complained of action take place 'in connection with the purchase or sale of a security,' yet it repeatedly has been held to create a cause of action to enjoin purchases or sales of securities that have been proposed but not yet effected."[646] Moreover, defendants' limitation of section 14(e)'s disclosure provisions to post-offer conduct would allow the promulgation, "with relative impunity," of "numerous misstatements, omissions and half-truths . . . until the offer was

644. *Id.* at 1200.

645. 425 F. Supp. 1145, 1151-55 (S.D.N.Y. 1977).

646. *Id.* at 1153 (footnote omitted).

actually filed with and approved by the SEC," thereby thwarting the remedial purposes of the statute.[647] Accordingly, the court held that the public announcement of the proposed offer triggered the applicability of the Williams Act.

Whether a plaintiff may maintain an action under section 14(e) to challenge conduct in connection with a tender offer that *never* became effective probably depends on the nature of the asserted claim. A target's shareholders cannot sue the target under section 14(e) in such a situation because they never had an opportunity to tender and thus probably cannot show any reliance on the alleged deceptions in making investment decisions.[648]

In *O'Connor & Associates v. Dean Witter Reynolds, Inc.*,[649] however, the court upheld a cause of action for insider trading that had occurred prior to the announcement of an anticipated tender offer that ultimately was abandoned before becoming effective. The court held that

> the announcement of a proposed tender offer has significant market ramifications in the securities markets, regardless of whether the offer ultimately becomes effective or not. Informed decisionmaking by the security holder of a takeover target (whether shareholder or options trader) is defeated when others in the market trade on information which he lacks that a tender offer proposal has been made. Since the insiders' sole purpose in effecting the trades alleged in the complaint would have been to capitalize on the pending tender offer proposal, the alleged fraud was "in connection with a tender offer" under § 14(e) regardless of whether the offer actually became effective.[650]

The court went on to distinguish *Lewis v. McGraw*[651] by noting that, "in the present case, O'Connor alleges specific conduct

---

647. *Id.* at 1154.

648. *Panter v. Marshall Field & Co.*, 646 F.2d 271, 284 (7th Cir.), *cert. denied*, 454 U.S. 1092 (1981); *Lewis v. McGraw*, 619 F.2d 192, 195 (2d Cir.), *cert. denied*, 449 U.S. 951 (1980).

649. 529 F. Supp. 1179, 1191-92 (S.D.N.Y. 1981).

650. *Id.* at 1192.

651. 619 F.2d 192 (2d Cir.), *cert. denied*, 449 U.S. 951 (1980).

that it took, selling call options on [the target's] stock, that it would not have taken had it known of the tender offer bid."[652] *Lewis*, therefore, is read strictly as a "reliance" case, and not as an "in connection with" case.

6. The Target's Duty to Disclose Negotiations with a Bidder

One area of particular controversy is the question whether and when a target must disclose negotiations that it has conducted with a bidder. While this issue might not, strictly speaking, be a "defensive consideration" in the context of a target's battle against an undesirable bidder, the target may have to defend itself against such nondisclosure claims asserted by shareholders or by the initial or a subsequent bidder. Many of the cases dealing with this disclosure issue arise under section 10(b) or section 14(a) (governing proxy solicitations), rather than under section 14(e).

The general rule, as articulated by the courts, appears to be that a company need not disclose the existence or substance of preliminary inquiries or negotiations that do not involve "hard facts" and have not yet ripened into a firm offer. *Reiss v. Pan American World Airways, Inc.*[653] illustrates such a situation.

Pan Am had been interested in acquiring National Airlines since May 1977; National, however, advised Pan Am in January 1978 that National was not interested in a deal. During the next few months, Pan Am made further overtures to National, but all proved fruitless. When two other airlines began campaigns to control National, however, Pan Am began purchasing National shares, acquiring 0.4 percent of the company by August 15. On that date, Pan Am authorized the call of $25 million of its convertible debentures and the acquisition of up to 10 percent of National's stock; the company also authorized further

652. 529 F. Supp. at 1192.
653. 711 F.2d 11 (2d Cir. 1983).

negotiations with National. The press release issued that day, however, announced only the redemption program and mentioned nothing about National. Between August 15 and 23, Pan Am negotiated with National and increased its National stock holdings. Finally, on August 23, National and Pan Am issued press releases reporting that a firm merger offer was under consideration. Plaintiffs, convertible debenture holders who had sold their debentures between August 15 and 22, sued Pan Am under section 10(b) and Rule 10b-5, claiming that the company should have disclosed its attempts to negotiate a merger with National. Had they known of the negotiations, they alleged, plaintiffs would have converted their debentures into capital stock instead of selling them.

The court rejected the claim that Pan Am should have disclosed the unsettled, evolving negotiations with National and held that disclosure would not have served the underlying purposes of the securities laws. "Such negotiations," the court observed,

> are inherently fluid and the eventual outcome is shrouded in uncertainty. Disclosure may in fact be more misleading than secrecy so far as investment decisions are concerned. We are not confronted here with a failure to disclose hard facts which definitely affect a company's financial prospects. Rather, we deal with complex bargaining between two (and often more) parties which may fail as well as succeed, or may succeed on terms which vary greatly from those under consideration at the suggested time of disclosure. We have no doubt that had Pan Am disclosed the existence of negotiations on August 15 and had those negotiations failed, we would have been asked to decide a section 10b-5 action challenging that disclosure.[654]

Reiss involved a situation in which the parties were negotiating but had not yet arrived at a firm offer, much less an agreement in principle. Where negotiations have progressed further, however, disclosure might be required. Some cases appear to hold that a

654. *Id.* at 14.

company must disclose a firm merger or acquisition offer, even if that offer has been rejected.[655]

Another court has focused on the existence of an agreement in principle as triggering the disclosure requirements—at least where the company previously disclosed that it was considering unspecified merger or acquisition alternatives.[656] The court observed that,

> so long as merger or acquisition discussions are preliminary, general disclosure of the fact that such alternatives are being considered will suffice to adequately inform shareholders; a duty to disclose the possible terms of any transaction and the parties thereto arises only after an agreement in principle, regarding such fundamental terms as price and structure, has been reached.[657]

This case, however, appears to leave open the question whether the target would have been liable had it not disclosed that it was considering other alternatives to the pending hostile tender offer.

The Court of Appeals for the Third Circuit, in *Greenfield v. Heublein, Inc.*,[658] attempted to isolate specific factors as a means of resolving uncertainty about the need to disclose. The case grew out of Heublein's effort to escape from the clutches of General Cinema Corporation and to throw itself into the arms of its white knight, R.J. Reynolds. General Cinema had been interested for some time in acquiring Heublein and, through

---

655. *See Texas Partners v. Conrock Co.*, 685 F.2d 1116, 1120-21 (9th Cir. 1982), *cert. dismissed*, 460 U.S. 1029 (1983) (past firm offer might have been a material fact that should have been disclosed); *South Coast Servs. Corp. v. Santa Ana Valley Irrigation Co.*, 669 F.2d 1265, 1273 (9th Cir. 1982) (proxy materials soliciting shareholder approval of proposed sale of assets must disclose firm offers from other potential purchasers if those offers are more favorable than the one being endorsed by management, but "[t]here is no duty to disclose inquiries or indications of interest that do not fall within the category of firm or definite offers").

656. *Starkman v. Marathon Oil Co.*, 772 F.2d 231, 243 (6th Cir. 1985), *cert. denied*, 106 S. Ct. 1195 (1986).

657. *Id.*

658. 742 F.2d 751 (3d Cir. 1984), *cert. denied*, 469 U.S. 1215 (1985).

open-market purchases, had bought 18.9 percent of Heublein's shares. Reynolds also had its eye on Heublein but refused either to engage in a bidding war or to seize the company through hostile means. In July 1982, Heublein's attempts to negotiate with General Cinema broke down, and the latter issued a series of "non-negotiable demands." Heublein considered these demands unacceptable and entered into "preliminary merger discussions" with Reynolds on July 9. "[N]o formal understanding or agreement was reached" as a result of these discussions.[659] On July 14, as General Cinema's efforts to acquire Heublein intensified, Heublein stock on the New York Stock Exchange experienced a dramatic increase in volume traded and a moderate rise in price. At the Exchange's request, Heublein issued a press release stating that the company " 'was aware of no reason that would explain the activity in its stock in trading on the NYSE today.' "[660] Heublein and Reynolds again met on July 15 and 26, with merger price being discussed for the first time at the latter meeting. At yet another meeting on July 27, the parties finally agreed on an acquisition price of $60 per share. The NYSE halted trading of Heublein's stock at 1:24 p.m. on July 28, and, on July 29, the Heublein and Reynolds boards approved the merger, which then was publicly announced.

Plaintiff, a Heublein shareholder, had been aware of the "no corporate development" statement issued on July 14. Relying on this statement, plaintiff set a sale price of $45.25 for his holdings and, on July 26, placed a "good till cancelled" order to sell his stock should it reach that price. Heublein stock reached $45.25 on July 27, and plaintiff's shares were sold pursuant to the order. Deprived of the benefit of the $60 merger price, plaintiff sued under sections 10(b) and 14(e), claiming that Heublein improperly had failed to disclose the substance of its discussions with Reynolds and General Cinema. The district court entered summary judgment for defendants, and the Court of Appeals affirmed.

---

659. *Id.* at 754.

660. *Id.*

The court held that, as a matter of law, Heublein and Reynolds had not reached an agreement in principle—and Heublein therefore had no duty to disclose—until some time after plaintiff sold his stock on July 27. This conclusion rested on the fact that Heublein and Reynolds had not agreed on price until late in the afternoon of July 27 (after the sale had occurred). The Court of Appeals held that, absent " 'fundamental agreement on the *price and structure* of a merger, the merger is simply too tentative to give rise to a duty of disclosure.' "[661] Rejecting plaintiff's urging of "a less rigid 'intent of the parties to merge' standard," the court observed:

> Such a standard would leave both courts and corporations with insufficient guidance to determine when disclosure of merger negotiations should be made. This uncertainty, coupled with the possibility of substantial liability for tardy disclosure, would likely result in corporations issuing early public statements announcing the details of all merger talks. Not only would this have a disruptive effect on the stock markets, but, considering the delicate nature of most merger discussions, might seriously inhibit such acquisitive ventures.
>
> Under the facts of the present case, it was more appropriate for the court below to determine that an agreement in principle to merge had been reached when the parties reached agreement on "price and structure." Although it is difficult to draw a bright line definition that will apply to all cases, these two factors are typically critical aspects of any merger. Agreement as to price and structure provides concrete evidence of a mature understanding between the negotiating corporations. They constitute a useable and definite measure for determining when disclosures need be made. Finally, with both price and structure agreed to, there is only a minimal chance that a public announcement would quash the deal or that the investing public would be misled as to likely corporate activity.[662]

Greenfield thus gave birth to the "price and structure" test for determining the need to disclose merger negotiations.

---

661. *Id.* at 756 (quoting district court opinion).

662. *Id.* at 757.

Greenfield, however, has not met with universal approval. The Court of Appeals for the Seventh Circuit rejected the "price and structure" rule in *Michaels v. Michaels*,[663] a case involving a family corporation with three shareholders, because "[t]he reasons for 'price and structure' standard of materiality disappear when there is no public market for the shareholder's stock."[664] In such a context, disclosure of preliminary negotiations could not cause speculative investment in the target's stock, thereby raising its price and perhaps ruining a possible deal. Nor could disclosure harm investors who bought at an inflated price and who would suffer a loss if the price were to fall upon collapse of the negotiations. The court therefore concluded that plaintiff "had a right as a shareholder to know about corporate developments, but there was no offsetting need to protect other shareholders and investors from potentially misleading disclosure."[665]

Greenfield has aroused controversy in another respect as well. In addition to ruling that Heublein had no obligation to disclose its negotiations with Reynolds, the court also held that Heublein's July 14 "no corporate developments" statement was not itself materially misleading even though the company had issued the statement while negotiating with Reynolds. Heublein, reasoned the court, legitimately believed that its dealings with Reynolds remained strictly confidential and that no one privy to this information had engaged in insider trading. Accordingly, the July 14 statement was accurate because Heublein "was understandably unable to explain what had caused the dramatic increase in activity in Heublein's stock that day."[666]

At least one court has emphatically rejected *Greenfield*'s approach to "no corporate developments" statements. On relatively similar facts, *Schlanger v. Four-Phase Systems, Inc.*[667] held

663. 767 F.2d 1185 (7th Cir. 1985), *cert. denied*, 106 S. Ct. 797 (1986).
664. *Id.* at 1196.
665. *Id.*
666. 742 F.2d at 759.
667. 582 F. Supp. 128, 132 (S.D.N.Y. 1984).

that *Greenfield* "is wrong, essentially because it fails to distinguish between cases involving false or misleading statements, and situations involving a decision merely to remain silent and not disclose pre-merger negotiations." The court agreed that a company has no duty to disclose "inchoate merger negotiations." But once a company voluntarily chooses to make a statement of fact—that there are no corporate developments responsible for a perceived change in trading patterns and price—it must disclose all material facts necessary to make its statement not misleading.[668]

The SEC also has adopted this position and has expressly rejected *Greenfield.* According to the SEC's ruling in *In the Matter of Carnation Co.*, "an issuer statement that there is no corporate development that would account for unusual market activity in its stock, made while the issuer is engaged in acquisition discussions, may be materially false and misleading."[669]

Carnation involved yet another acquisition in the making: this time, Nestle, S.A.'s friendly tender offer for all of Carnation's shares. In June and July 1984, Carnation and Nestle had discussed acquisition possibilities, both in telephone conversations and at meetings. The parties clearly intended to conclude a deal, but no specifics had been formulated. During this period and in early August, numerous news stories noted unusual activity in Carnation stock and reported rumors that Carnation was a takeover candidate. Finally, on August 7, Carnation's treasurer, Michael Malone, announced that there was " 'no news from the company and no corporate developments that would account for the stock action.' " Malone had not been informed of the Carnation-Nestle negotiations and had not discussed his statement with anyone prior to issuance. Meetings between Carnation and Nestle continued in August, and the parties discussed—but did not

---

668. *Id.* at 133-34.

669. Exchange Act Release No. 22214, [1984-1985 Transfer Binder] Fed. Sec. L. Rep. (CCH) ¶ 83,801, at 87,596 (July 8, 1985) (footnote omitted).

agree upon—per-share acquisition price. Two Carnation representatives traveled to Nestle headquarters in Switzerland to pursue the negotiations. While the Carnation officials were in Switzerland, Malone—who remained unaware of the talks—issued another statement, on August 20, saying that Carnation knew of " 'no corporate reason for the recent surge in its stock prices.' " Malone also was quoted as saying that he had heard rumors of a possible Nestle acquisition of Carnation but that, " 'to the best of my knowledge there is nothing to substantiate [the rumors]. We are not negotiating with anyone.' " Carnation and Nestle finally concluded and announced their deal in early September.

The SEC conducted a private investigation of Malone's statements and found them materially false and misleading. The Commission stated that,

> [w]henever an issuer makes a public statement or responds to an inquiry from a stock exchange official concerning rumors, unusual market activity, possible corporate developments or any other matter, the statement must be materially accurate and complete. If the issuer is aware of nonpublic information concerning acquisition discussions that are occurring at the time the statement is made, the issuer has an obligation to disclose sufficient information concerning the discussions to prevent the statements made from being materially misleading.[670]

The Commission recognized the issuer's countervailing interests: its desire to respond to market rumors and to prevent the sabotaging of secret and fragile negotiations. Nevertheless, the issuer must insure that its statements are not misleading. To balance these potentially conflicting desires and responsibilities,

> an issuer that wants to prevent premature disclosure of non-public preliminary merger negotiations can, in appropriate circumstances, give a "no comment" response to press inquiries concerning rumors or unusual market activity. A "no comment" response would not be appropriate where, *inter alia*, the issuer has

---

670. *Id.* at 87,595 (footnote omitted).

> made a statement that has been rendered materially false or misleading as a result of subsequent events or market rumors are attributable to leaks from the issuer.[671]

The SEC did not impose sanctions on Carnation but promised to "take appropriate enforcement action" against issuers that fail to comply with the above rules.[672] Thus, even though *Greenfield* might support an issuer that makes a "no corporate developments" statement while merger negotiations are pending, that issuer might find itself enmeshed in a potentially costly and time-consuming SEC investigation for such a statement.

The SEC also has taken the position that a target, in preparing its Schedule 14D-9 (which must be filed in response to a tender offer[673]), may withhold information concerning the possible terms of any ongoing negotiations if the target believes that disclosure of the terms would jeopardize continuation of those talks. However, the Schedule must disclose "the fact of negotiations." It is sufficient to note that " 'negotiations are being undertaken or are underway and are in the preliminary stages. . . .' "[674] Thus, the target may have a greater duty to disclose the existence of negotiations once a tender offer has been made and a Schedule 14D-9 must be prepared than would be the case in the period preceding an offer.

Without regard to the question whether a target must disclose the existence or substance of negotiations, a company that does make such disclosures must not misstate its intentions with respect to those negotiations, as *In re Anderson, Clayton Shareholders' Litigation*[675] illustrates. Anderson, Clayton was in the final stages of implementing a recapitalization plan (valued at

---

671. *Id.* at 87,596 n.6.

672. *Id.* at 87,597.

673. *See supra* § III.2.A(2) (discussing Schedule 14D-9).

674. *In the Matter of Revlon, Inc.*, Exchange Act Release No. 23320, [Current] Fed. Sec. L. Rep. (CCH) ¶ 84,006, at 88,146 (June 16, 1986) (quoting Instruction to Item 7(a) of Schedule 14D-9).

675. Nos. C.A. 8387, 8501 (Del. Ch. June 10, 1986).

$43-47 per share) and had scheduled a shareholders' meeting on June 3, 1986 for a vote on the proposal. On May 29, however, the investment banking firm of Bear, Stearns & Co., Inc., together with the firm of Gruss & Company (collectively, "B/S/G"), delivered to the company a letter expressing an interest in making a cash tender offer for all of Anderson, Clayton's stock at $54 per share.

Anderson, Clayton's board met later that same day and resolved to continue with the pending recapitalization proposal but also to "meet with representatives of the Bear, Stearns/Gruss group and to seek to resolve the numerous uncertainties posed by the Bear, Stearns/Gruss letter proposal. . . ." The board also resolved to provide B/S/G with "any information reasonably requested . . . subject to appropriate confidentiality protection."

Four days later, on June 2, Anderson, Clayton distributed, by mailgram, a proxy supplement relating to the B/S/G offer. The four-page statement included the full text of B/S/G's letter and informed shareholders that the board continued to recommend the recapitalization plan. However, the letter also stated:

> While deciding to convene the stockholders' meeting as scheduled [on June 3], the Board of Directors authorized management to meet with representatives of the Bear, Stearns/Gruss group and to seek to resolve the numerous uncertainties posed by the letter proposal. Representatives of the Company are continuing to discuss the Bear, Stearns/Gruss proposal with representatives of those firms. Prior to consummation of the proposed Recapitalization, the Board will consider any proposals then available to the Company; such consideration and decision may take place either before or after the stockholder vote on the Recapitalization.

The shareholders' meeting was held the next day, June 3; polls closed at 5:00 p.m. on June 5, to give shareholders additional time to consider the late-breaking news about the B/S/G offer. In addition, Anderson, Clayton established a toll-free telephone number that shareholders could call to send a mailgram revoking prior proxies and voting anew on the recapitalization proposal. The shareholders voted by an overwhelming majority to accept the recapitalization plan, although 68 percent of the small number of shareholders who used the telephone line voted against the plan.

Meanwhile, no substantive negotiations occurred between Anderson, Clayton and B/S/G. Moreover, the company declined to provide information to B/S/G because the latter refused to enter into a two-year standstill agreement as a precondition to receiving information. With no progress on the B/S/G front, Anderson, Clayton's board met on June 7 and voted to proceed with the recapitalization, which the shareholders already had ratified. Anderson, Clayton shareholders and B/S/G sued to enjoin consummation of the recapitalization, scheduled for June 10, and the court granted a preliminary injunction, finding that Anderson, Clayton's June 2 proxy supplement had been materially misleading.

The court did not fault the board for rejecting B/S/G's offer; indeed, the court observed that

> [a] reasonable director or a reasonable shareholder could, on strictly economic grounds, prefer the recapitalization to even a firm B/S/G offer at $54 per share. . . . Thus, had the board in the proxy statement said that even were the B/S/G proposal a firm offer, it would reject it because on its view the recapitalization presented better value to the shareholders, shareholder approval of the recapitalization, in those circumstances, would end this matter.

The shareholders, however, had not approved the recapitalization in the face of a firm B/S/G offer; rather, they had chosen only between the recapitalization and a contingent B/S/G offer, and they had been assured by the proxy statement that the board would negotiate with B/S/G and would attempt to resolve the proposal's contingencies even if and after the shareholders approved the recapitalization. Thus, held the court, the shareholder vote "may only be interpreted as a qualified approval of the recapitalization, that is approval contingent upon the board's pursuing in good faith the B/S/G proposal," as promised by the proxy statement.

The court found, however, that the Anderson, Clayton board had not attempted in good faith to resolve the uncertainties of the B/S/G offer and thus had acted contrary to the assertions contained in the proxy statement. This failure to negotiate constituted

> a species of inaccuracy on a material aspect of the matter that flaws the vote quite as much as the misrepresentation of a material fact would. Indeed, in the circumstances, I regard the statement that the Company was, as of June 2, "continuing to discuss the Bear, Stearns/Gruss proposal with members of those firms" as at least misleading when the limited contacts and restricted nature of those contacts is known.

The principle of *Anderson, Clayton* is simple: if the target states that it will negotiate with a bidder, it must insure that its statement is neither false nor materially misleading. A misstatement of an intention to negotiate may be actionable whether or not the target has a duty to disclose those negotiations in the first place.

CHAPTER

3

STATE LAW REGULATION OF TENDER OFFER RESPONSES: THE BUSINESS JUDGMENT RULE

As the Supreme Court's decision in *Schreiber v. Burlington Northern, Inc.*[676] made clear, a cause of action alleging a breach of fiduciary duty, rather than a misstatement or nondisclosure of material information, falls within the purview of state corporation law, and not within that of the federal securities acts. Consequently, a target seeking to challenge a bidder's tactics as alleged breaches of fiduciary duty, or a bidder seeking to enjoin a target's defensive tactics as allegedly causing improper entrenchment of target management and harm to target shareholders, must rely on state law principles of corporate governance: the duty of care, the duty of loyalty, and the business judgment rule.

A. The Role of Target Management

As an initial matter, it is necessary to consider what role management ought to be allowed to play in a takeover context. May management actively oppose a tender offer or merger proposal that it allegedly believes is not in the best interests of the target corporation, or must management refrain from any opposition and passively allow the shareholders to approve or reject any and all offers?

The issue has received much attention from commentators. Some writers believe that maximization of shareholder wealth can best be accomplished through "managerial passivity" in the face of a premium tender offer. This theory holds that defensive maneuvers may defeat a takeover attempt without any assurance that a higher bid will emerge either during the battle against the initial offeror or at a later time. Shareholders thus stand to lose the opportunity to sell their shares at a premium, and incumbent management—which, under this theory, is primarily interested in remaining in power—becomes even more deeply entrenched, without regard to its performance in handling the

676. 472 U.S. 1, 105 S. Ct. 2458 (1985).

affairs of the corporation.[677]

Other commentators reject this approach and maintain that management is justified in engaging in a wide variety of defensive tactics to defeat takeover attempts that management considers to be contrary to the best interests of the corporation. These writers believe that the main proponents of the free-market approach to takeovers are raiders, arbitrageurs, and professional investors whose interest in a quick, short-term profit is inconsistent with the long-term interests of shareholders, employees, and other corporate constituencies as well as with the corporate and national need for long-term business planning. This school of thought poses the (loaded) question as "[w]hether the long-term interests of the nation's corporate system and economy should be jeopardized in order to benefit speculators interested not in the vitality and continued existence of the business enterprise in which they have bought shares, but only in a quick profit on the sale of those shares?"[678]

The judiciary has noted the opposing schools of thought; indeed, the Court of Appeals for the Second Circuit recently wrote:

> The efforts of targeted management to resist acquisitive moves, and the means they employ, have been alternatively praised and damned. Proponents of corporate "free trade" argue that defensive techniques permit managers to entrench themselves and thus avoid accountability for their performance, at the expense of shareholders who are denied the opportunity to maximize their investment in sought-after corporations. Opponents contend that takeover struggles squander enormous capital resources which could better be spent to improve industrial productivity and to develop and commercialize new technologies.[679]

---

677. *See, e.g.*, Easterbrook & Fischel, "The Proper Role of a Target's Management in Responding to a Tender Offer," 94 Harv. L. Rev. 1161 (1981).

678. Lipton, "Takeover Bids in the Target's Boardroom," 35 Bus. Law. 101, 104 (1979) (emphasis omitted).

679. *Norlin Corp. v. Rooney, Pace Inc.*, 744 F.2d 255, 258 (2d Cir. 1984) (footnotes omitted); *accord Dynamics Corp. of Am. v. CTS Corp.*, 794 F.2d 250 (7th Cir.), *probable jurisdiction noted*, 107 S. Ct. 258 (1986).

But although cognizant of these divergent concerns, the courts uniformly have treated defensive tactics as business decisions lying within the discretion of target management, subject, of course, to management's fiduciary duties to shareholders.

B. Boundaries of Management's Discretion

The business judgment rule is the legal foundation of management's prerogatives in running the corporation and resisting undesirable takeover attempts. If the corporation's directors have exercised their informed business judgment and have acted in what they perceive to be the best interests of the company and its shareholders, the business judgment rule usually will shield management from liability for its decisions and actions. In order to rely on this rule, however, directors must have fulfilled their duties of care and loyalty: they must have made an effort to inform themselves before exercising their business judgment, and they must have considered the best interests of the corporation and its shareholders.

1. The Recent History of the Business Judgment Rule

The general willingness of courts to treat targets' defensive tactics as business decisions subject to the protection of the business judgment rule might itself seem somewhat ironic. After all, takeovers—or, at least, hostile takeovers—involve transfers of stock by shareholders to third parties, and these transactions do not by themselves affect the corporation's internal affairs, to which the business judgment rule traditionally has applied. Moreover, one might argue that the focus of the rule is inappropriate, insofar as it highlights the directors' motives and actions, rather than the impact of the chosen defensive measures on the corporation's shareholders, to whom the takeover bid is addressed. Finally, it is possible that permitting a target's directors to invoke the rule allows them to insulate from judicial scrutiny decisions that they may have made for their own protection and self-perpetuation.[680]

Nevertheless, the business judgment rule has remained, until fairly recently, a virtually impregnable "safe harbor" for incumbent directors faced with takeover attempts. Even now, the instances in which courts have refused to uphold board decisions under the business judgment rule might amount not to a reformulation of the rule but instead to a gradual evolution of judicial standards concerning the varieties of defensive conduct that will be tolerated in specific takeover settings. In an area of the law that is in such a state of flux, the burden of proof becomes an unusually important factor, both in litigation strategy and as an indicator of the skepticism that some courts bring to their review of specific defensive tactics.[681]

The Delaware Supreme Court recently restated the business judgment rule in its classic form by describing it as "a presumption that in making a business decision the directors of a corporation acted on an informed basis, in good faith and in the honest belief that the action taken was in the best interests of the company."[682] The court went on to restate its view of the two prongs of the rule—the duties of loyalty and care—that must be satisfied before directors can invoke the rule's protection.

Only disinterested, loyal directors can rely on the rule. This duty of loyalty demands that directors neither appear on both sides of a transaction nor reap an economic benefit different from that flowing to the corporation as a whole or to all of its shareholders.[683] Furthermore, the court held that only directorial acts of "gross negligence" (or worse) lie outside the protection of the business judgment rule.[684] This standard is

---

680. *See generally* Balotti, Finkelstein & Abrams, "Fiduciary Standards in Control Contests," *16th Annual Institute on Securities Regulation* 323, 359–61 (PLI No. 464, 1984) (summarizing views of commentators).

681. *See infra* § III.3.B(4) (discussing burdens of proof).

682. *Aronson v. Lewis*, 473 A.2d 805, 812 (Del. 1984).

683. *Id.*

684. *Id.*

more likely to apply to the manner in which directors make their decisions (the duty of care) than to the substantive decisions themselves.[685]

The primary purpose test has sometimes been presented as an alternative to the business judgment rule, especially in contexts involving changes in corporate control. This test focuses on whether the board took the challenged actions primarily to achieve a proper purpose—for example, did the board act primarily to benefit the corporation or to entrench and perpetuate itself in office?

Some commentators argue that, at least in takeover litigation, the standards of business judgment and primary purpose do not actually diverge.[686] In two relatively early cases involving struggles for corporate control, the Delaware courts employed the primary purpose test to approve a repurchase of stock from a notorious corporate raider[687] and the use of corporate funds to repurchase a block of stock held by another company whose president was well known as a proponent of aggressive tactics that threatened the target's normal operations.[688] More recently, in *Unocal Corp. v. Mesa Petroleum Co.*,[689] the Delaware Supreme Court evaluated a selective stock repurchase by incumbent management in light of the principle that "the directors may not have acted solely or primarily out of a desire to perpetuate themselves in office."[690] The court combined this primary purpose analysis with a business judgment rule inquiry, apparently without treating the two as separate tests. Because there probably is little actual difference in the standards, the main significance of the primary purpose focus may be the

---

685. *See Smith v. Van Gorkom*, 488 A.2d 858 (Del. 1985), discussed in § III.3.B(2), *infra*; *see also* 1 R.F. Balotti & J.A. Finkelstein, *The Delaware Law of Corporations and Business Organizations* §4.6, at 77 (1986).

686. *See, e.g.*, Lipton, "Takeover Bids in the Target's Boardroom," 35 Bus. Law. 101, 124 (1979).

687. *Cheff v. Mathes*, 41 Del. Ch. 494, 199 A.2d 548, 554 (Del. 1964).

688. *Kors v. Carey*, 39 Del. Ch. 47, 158 A.2d 136, 141 (1960).

689. 493 A.2d 946 (Del. 1985), discussed in § III.3.B(3), *infra*.

690. *Id.* at 955.

tendency of courts to impose the burden of proof on the directors in cases involving certain defensive tactics, thereby negating the normal presumption in favor of directors' conduct under the business judgment rule.

Through the early 1980s, it seemed that courts would continue to approach takeover litigation with a laissez-faire attitude that routinely resulted in grants of protection under the business judgment rule for directorial decisions to pursue even the most aggressive defensive strategies. Today, however, some courts are examining these defensive tactics more closely.

Courts probably are more likely to scrutinize the care with which the directors exercised their authority. After all, as *Smith v. Van Gorkom*[691] illustrates, it is relatively easy for courts to evaluate whether a board took sufficient pains to obtain enough information to meet this duty. Far more difficult is determining whether a board satisfied its fiduciary duty of loyalty, given the inherent conflict between a board's collective desire to maintain the status and position of its members and its duty to promote the welfare of the corporation and its shareholders.

Application of the business judgment rule to specific circumstances has produced a range of results. *Norlin Corp. v. Rooney, Pace Inc.*[692] was one of the first cases to suggest that courts might cut back on the protection available under the business judgment rule. In *Norlin*, the Court of Appeals for the Second Circuit held that target directors who issued stock to an employee stock option plan, in order to consolidate voting control of almost a majority of the corporation's shares in their "own hands by complex, convoluted, and deliberate maneuvers," would not be protected by the business judgment rule.[693]

The re-examination of the scope of the business judgment rule continues. In *Unocal Corp. v. Mesa Petroleum Co.*, the Delaware Supreme Court declared that a corporation "does not have unbridled discretion to defeat any perceived threat by any

---

691. 488 A.2d 858 (Del. 1985), discussed in § III.3.B(2), *infra*.

692. 744 F.2d 255 (2d Cir. 1984).

693. *Id.* at 265.

Draconian means available."[694] Instead, a form of proportionality test applies: "[i]f a defensive measure is to come within the ambit of the business judgment rule, it must be reasonable in relation to the threat posed. This entails an analysis by the directors of the nature of the takeover bid and its effect on the corporate enterprise."[695]

The cases that follow in this section and the rest of this book demonstrate how the application of the business judgment rule to an array of defensive tactics, executed in specific factual contexts, is resulting in a new, even if perhaps inconsistent, willingness of courts to find target directors liable for uninformed and/or disloyal defensive maneuvers. Directors faced with takeover challenges can no longer feel automatically protected from liability regardless of how aggressively they act to "protect" their companies from the snares set by hostile bidders.

2. The Duty of Care

The duty of care imposes on corporate directors the responsibility not simply to make decisions but to make *informed* decisions. In determining whether—and how—to fight a takeover attempt, the target's directors must carefully consider the offer and its alternatives before approving a responsive course of action. The directors generally should consider the opinions of attorneys, investment bankers, and other professionals concerning the offer and should formulate a strategy based on these opinions. Developing a record of meetings and reports, and consideration of various options, all are crucial to the defense of a possible suit for breach of fiduciary duty and to invocation of the business judgment rule.

Of recent cases concerning directors' duty of care, none has sent greater tremors through corporate boardrooms (and through issuers of directors' and officers' liability insurance) than

---

694. 493 A.2d 946, 955 (Del. 1985).

695. *Id.*

has *Smith v. Van Gorkom.*[696] The case evolved out of the 1981 cash-out merger of Trans Union Corporation into a wholly owned subsidiary of Marmon Group, Inc., which was owned by the well known entrepreneurs Jay and Robert Pritzker.

Trans Union was a company with a problem: although it had an annual cash flow of hundreds of millions of dollars, it could not generate sufficient taxable income to offset its increasingly large investment tax credits. In July 1980, the company prepared a five-year forecast that listed four alternative uses for the projected 1982 – 85 equity surplus: stock repurchases, dividend increases, a major acquisition program, and combinations of the preceding three alternatives. The report did not discuss the possibility of selling the company. During Senior Management meetings in August and September, however, the idea of a leveraged buy-out ("LBO") of the company arose. Trans Union's Chief Financial Officer, Donald Romans, stated that his department had cursorily considered this possibility and had determined that an LBO at $50 per share would be feasible but that $60 per share would be "very difficult." He cautioned, however, that his assessment did not purport to establish a fair price for the company or for all of its stock.

Despite this lack of a valuation of the company, Jerome Van Gorkom, Trans Union's Chairman and Chief Executive Officer, approached Jay Pritzker on September 13, 1980, with a financing structure that would enable Pritzker to buy Trans Union at $55 per share. Van Gorkom did not consult with any other directors or with Senior Management (except for the company's controller) before presenting his proposal to Pritzker.

Several days later, Pritzker advised Van Gorkom of his interest in the $55-per-share cash-out merger proposal, and several more meetings ensued. At none of these meetings, however, did the parties discuss the $55-per-share price. The deal proceeded at a very fast pace, and, on September 18, only five days after he was first approached, Pritzker insisted that Trans Union's board of directors act on the merger proposal within three days. He also

696. 488 A.2d 858 (Del. 1985).

demanded that Trans Union sell him one million shares at $38 per share (75 cents above market price).

Van Gorkom called meetings of Senior Management and of the board for September 20. No one except the controller and the President and Chief Operating Officer (Bruce Chelberg) was told the purpose of the meetings. The company's investment banker was not invited to attend.

At the meeting of Senior Management, Van Gorkom described the Pritzker offer but did not furnish copies of the proposed merger agreement. Romans discussed a new study showing that the price range for an LBO was between $55 and $65 per share. Van Gorkom neither saw the study nor asked that it be made available for the board meeting. Romans objected to the $55 price as too low and criticized other aspects of the proposal, as did most other members of Senior Management. Nevertheless, Van Gorkom proceeded directly to the board meeting as scheduled.

Trans Union's board consisted of five "inside" and five "outside" directors; none of the "outside" directors was an investment banker or a trained financial analyst. The board listened to a 20-minute oral presentation by Van Gorkom but never received copies of the proposed merger agreement. Van Gorkom outlined the terms of the proposal, which had to be acted on by the following evening, but he did not disclose either "the methodology by which he alone had arrived at the $55 figure, or the fact that he first proposed the $55 price in his negotiations with Pritzker."[697] Van Gorkom told the board that, because Trans Union would be allowed to receive (but not actively to solicit) competing offers for a period of 90 days, approval of the proposal would amount merely to putting the company "up for auction" and allowing the market and the shareholders to evaluate the fairness of the $55 price.

James Brennan, Trans Union's attorney, then advised the board that receipt of a fairness opinion as to price was not legally required and that the directors might be sued if they rejected the

697. *Id.* at 868.

offer. Finally, Romans spoke. He informed the board that he had known nothing about the proposal until that very morning; that he had performed no studies indicating a fair price for the stock or the value of the company; and that $55 was "in the range of a fair price," but "at the beginning of the range."[698]

After meeting for two hours, and based solely on Van Gorkom's presentation, Chelberg's supporting representations, Romans' comments, Brennan's legal advice, and their knowledge of the market, the directors approved the proposed merger agreement, with two conditions: that the company be allowed to accept, but not solicit, any better offer within the 90-day "market test period" and to disclose proprietary information to other potential bidders. Van Gorkom executed the merger agreement that same night, while hosting a formal social event for the opening of the Chicago Lyric Opera. "Neither he nor any other director read the agreement prior to its signing and delivery to Pritzker."[699]

On September 22, Trans Union issued a press release announcing that it had entered into a "definitive" merger agreement. Senior Management reacted very negatively, however, and, to curb dissension and defections, Pritzker agreed to modify the merger agreement in several respects. The Trans Union board approved these proposed amendments, sight unseen, on October 8, and authorized Salomon Brothers, the company's investment banker, to solicit other offers. On October 9, the company issued a press release stating that Pritzker had obtained the financing needed to consummate the merger, that Pritzker had purchased one million Trans Union shares at $38 per share, that Trans Union was not permitted actively to seek competing offers, and that Trans Union's shareholders would meet after February 1, 1981 to vote on the Pritzker offer unless a more favorable offer were received before that date.

---

698. *Id.* at 869.
699. *Id.*

The next day, Pritzker prepared the proposed amendments that Trans Union's board already had approved. The amendments, as actually drafted, varied considerably from those that Van Gorkom had represented to the board on October 8, and they placed "serious constraints on Trans Union's ability to negotiate a better deal and withdraw from the Pritzker agreement."[700] But Van Gorkom executed the amendments without conferring further with the board and perhaps without comprehending their implications. Salomon Brothers ultimately failed to produce another willing purchaser, and, on January 26 and February 10, 1981, respectively, the directors and the shareholders approved the Pritzker merger. Trans Union shareholders sued to rescind the merger or, alternatively, to recover damages. The trial court granted judgment for the defendant directors; the Delaware Supreme Court reversed.

The Supreme Court began its analysis with the principle that a board of directors has responsibility for managing corporate business and affairs and must exercise its managerial powers consistently with its fiduciary duty to the corporation and its shareholders. This fiduciary duty consists of a duty of care as well as a duty of loyalty. The duty of care demands that directors exercise their business judgment in an informed manner, after having apprised themselves of all material and reasonably available information. As the court observed:

> Since a director is vested with the responsibility for the management of the affairs of the corporation, he must execute that duty with the recognition that he acts on behalf of others. Such obligation does not tolerate faithlessness or self-dealing. But fulfillment of the fiduciary function requires more than the mere absence of bad faith or fraud. Representation of the financial interests of others imposes on a director an affirmative duty to protect those interests and to proceed with a critical eye in assessing information of the type and under the circumstances present here.[701]

---

700. *Id.* at 870.
701. *Id.* at 872.

The court also stressed that "[t]he issue of whether the directors reached an informed decision to 'sell' the Company on September 20, 1980 must be determined only upon the basis of the information *then* reasonably available to the directors and relevant to their decision to accept the Pritzker merger proposal."[702] The court thus rejected what it characterized as the "*post hoc* approach" advanced by the directors, who had argued that the court should consider not only what they knew and learned on September 20 but also what they learned and did during the following months that preceded shareholder approval of the proposal. Subsequent knowledge and actions, held the court, were relevant only to the extent that they could cure any infirmities in the initial September 20 decisions.

Plaintiff had neither made any allegations nor offered any proof of fraud, bad faith, or self-dealing on the part of Trans Union's directors; the sole issue was whether the directors had fulfilled their duty of care in approving the Pritzker proposal. Under Delaware law, the applicable standard of care is one of gross negligence, and the court applied this standard in determining whether the board's business judgment had been an informed one.[703]

The court found that the directors had acted in a grossly negligent manner because they

> (1) did not adequately inform themselves as to Van Gorkom's role in forcing the "sale" of the Company and in establishing the per share purchase price; (2) were uninformed as to the intrinsic value of the Company; and (3) given these circumstances, at a minimum, were grossly negligent in approving the "sale" of the Company upon two hours' consideration, without prior notice, and without the existence of a crisis or emergency.[704]

The court proceeded to detail the congeries of considerations that led it to find the board's conduct so egregious:

---

702. *Id.* at 874 (emphasis added).

703. *Id.* at 873.

704. *Id.* at 874.

> the Board based its September 20 decision to approve the cash-out merger primarily on Van Gorkom's representations. None of the directors, other than Van Gorkom and Chelberg, had any prior knowledge that the purpose of the meeting was to propose a cash-out merger of Trans Union. No members of Senior Management were present, other than Chelberg, Romans and Peterson; and the latter two had only learned of the proposed sale an hour earlier. Both general counsel Moore and former general counsel Browder attended the meeting, but were equally uninformed as to the purpose of the meeting and the documents to be acted upon.
>
> Without any documents before them concerning the proposed transaction, the members of the Board were required to rely entirely upon Van Gorkom's 20-minute oral presentation of the proposal. No written summary of the terms of the merger was presented; the directors were given no documentation to support the adequacy of $55 price per share for sale of the Company; and the Board had before it nothing more than Van Gorkom's statement of his understanding of the substance of an agreement which he admittedly had never read, nor which any member of the Board had ever seen.[705]

This presumably unusual concatenation of circumstances added up to gross negligence.

The directors offered four principal reasons in support of the trial court's finding that the board had reached an informed decision: (*a*) the magnitude of the premium, or spread, between the $55 offering price and the $38 current market price, (*b*) the board's freedom to accept a better offer during the so-called "market test" period, (*c*) the collective experience and expertise of the "inside" and "outside" directors, and (*d*) the board's reliance on Brennan's "advice" that the directors might be sued if they rejected the Pritzker offer. The Delaware Supreme Court rejected each of these defenses.

First, with respect to the premium price, the court observed that, while a substantial premium may be one reason for directors to recommend a merger or acquisition proposal, the

---

705. *Id.*

mere existence of such a premium "does not provide an adequate basis upon which to assess the fairness of an offering price" "in the absence of other sound valuation information."[706] Exclusive reliance on market price as the sole basis for determining the sufficiency of the premium here constituted gross negligence because Van Gorkom and other directors knew that the market consistently had undervalued Trans Union's stock. Despite this knowledge, the board never commissioned a study designed to value the company as a going concern or even to assess its major asset: its cash flow.

The court disclaimed its intention to transform Delaware's corporate law into a full employment act for investment bankers:

> We do not imply that an outside valuation study is essential to support an informed business judgment; nor do we state that fairness opinions by independent investment bankers are required as a matter of law. Often insiders familiar with the business of a going concern are in a better position than are outsiders to gather relevant information; and under appropriate circumstances, such directors may be fully protected in relying in good faith upon the valuation reports of their management.[707]

In this case, however, reliance on background knowledge and vague representations of fairness was unjustified.

> [T]he record establishes that the Board did not request its Chief Financial Officer, Romans, to make any valuation study or review of the proposal to determine the adequacy of $55 per share for sale of the Company. On the record before us: The Board rested on Romans' elicited response that the $55 figure was within a "fair price range" within the context of a leveraged buy-out. No director sought any further information from Romans. No director asked him why he put $55 at the bottom of his range. No director asked Romans for any details as to his study, the reason why it had been undertaken or its depth. No director asked to see

---

706. *Id.* at 875.
707. *Id.* at 876.

> the study; and no director asked Romans whether Trans Union's finance department could do a fairness study within the remaining 36-hour period available under the Pritzker offer.[708]

Second, the court rejected defendants' "market test" defense, holding that the directors had "no rational basis" for expecting a market test to work and that the merger agreement probably did not allow the board freely to put the company up for auction sale to the highest bidder.[709] Trans Union had issued an initial press release, stating that the company had entered into "definitive agreements" with the Pritzkers, and a subsequent press release, announcing the grant to the Pritzkers of an option to purchase, at any time, one million shares at 75 cents above the then-current market price. The initial press release, however, did not disclose Trans Union's limited right to receive and accept higher offers, and the mention in the various press releases of the execution of "definitive agreements" and of the stock option undoubtedly helped to deter potential bidders. The board thus acted with gross negligence in relying on a market test to validate the fairness of the Pritzker proposal.

Third, the court found that "[t]he directors' unfounded reliance on both the premium and the market test as the basis for accepting the Pritzker proposal undermines the defendants' remaining contention that the Board's collective experience and sophistication was a sufficient basis for finding that it reached its September 20 decision with informed, reasonable deliberation."[710] Nor did the court accept the defense of reliance on legal advice. The fact that attorney Brennan had correctly advised the board that Delaware law did not require the directors to obtain either a fairness opinion or an outside valuation of the company did not excuse the board's failure to obtain "adequate information regarding the intrinsic value of the Company, upon which a proper exercise of business

---

708. *Id.* at 877 (footnote omitted).

709. *Id.* at 878.

710. *Id.* at 880 (footnote omitted).

judgment could be made. . . ."[711] And Brennan's "mere acknowledgement" that the directors might be sued if they rejected the Pritzker offer could not "be rationally translated into a justification for a board permitting itself to be stampeded into a patently unadvised act."[712]

The court therefore held the directors of Trans Union liable to the shareholders for the fair value of Trans Union's shares, to the extent that such value exceeded the $55-per-share Pritzker offer, and remanded the case for a determination of damages. The suit ultimately was settled.

Van Gorkom undoubtedly is an unusual case: it is relatively rare for a court to discover the total abdication of directorial responsibility that the Delaware Supreme Court found in the instant case. Yet *Van Gorkom* vividly illustrates, by negative example, how a court might expect an informed board to act, and it thus helps define the contours of the duty of care.

In contrast to *Van Gorkom* is the Delaware Supreme Court's decision in *Moran v. Household International, Inc.*,[713] upholding Household's adoption of a Rights Plan, or "poison pill." The Plan entitled each holder of Household common stock to receive one Right per common share upon either the announcement of a tender offer for 30 percent of Household's shares or the acquisition of 20 percent of Household's shares by any single entity or group. Once issued, the Rights would be immediately exercisable to purchase 1/100 share of new preferred stock for $100. (In the case of a 30-percent tender offer, the Rights would be redeemable by the board for 50 cents each; in the case of a 20-percent acquisition, the Rights would not be redeemable.) If a Rights holder did not exercise his Rights for preferred stock, and if a merger or consolidation thereafter occurred, the holder could exercise each Right to purchase $200 worth of shares of the acquiring company's common stock for $100.

---

711. *Id.* at 881.

712. *Id.*

713. 500 A.2d 1346 (Del. 1985).

Household had not adopted the Plan in the heat of battle with a corporate raider; instead, the Plan was intended to serve as a preventive measure to ward off unwanted future offers. Household had been concerned about the climate of hostile takeovers and also about the possibility of an LBO of the company by Dyson-Kissner-Moran Corporation ("D-K-M"), Household's largest shareholder. (This proposal, however, never progressed beyond the discussion stage.)

Household therefore retained Goldman, Sachs & Co. and prominent takeover counsel to formulate a policy for presentation to the board of directors at its August 14, 1984 meeting. Materials were distributed to the directors in advance of the meeting.

Household's attorneys and investment banker attended the board meeting and discussed the proposed Rights Plan. Counsel explained to the directors

> that his recommendation of the Plan was based on his understanding that the Board was concerned about the increasing frequency of "bust-up" takeovers, the increasing takeover activity in the financial service industry, . . . and the possible adverse effect this type of activity could have on employees and others concerned with and vital to the continuing successful operation of Household even in the absence of any actual bust-up takeover attempt.[714]

The board approved the Plan, and John Moran, D-K-M chairman and a Household director, filed suit to set it aside. The trial court upheld the Plan, and the Delaware Supreme Court affirmed.

The court noted that there were no allegations of bad faith on the part of directors and specifically held that the board had made an informed—or at least not grossly negligent—business decision in adopting the Plan. Unlike the situation in *Van Gorkom*, where the directors hastily had approved a merger agreement that they never had seen, at a price the fairness of

---

714. *Id.* at 1349 (footnote omitted).

which had not been evaluated, the Household board had acted with due deliberation.

> The information supplied to the Board on August 14 provided the essentials of the Plan. The Directors were given beforehand a notebook which included a three-page summary of the Plan along with articles on the current takeover environment. The extended discussion between the Board and representatives of Wachtell, Lipton [Household's counsel] and Goldman, Sachs before approval of the Plan reflected a full and candid evaluation of the Plan. Moran's expression of his views at the meeting served to place before the Board a knowledgeable critique of the Plan. The factual happenings here are clearly distinguishable from the actions of the directors of Trans Union Corporation who displayed gross negligence in approving a cash-out merger.[715]

The directors therefore had fulfilled their duty of care and thus were entitled to the protection of the business judgment rule.

The lesson learned from *Van Gorkom*, *Moran*, and other cases to be discussed in the remainder of this book is that directors of target companies must be meticulous in preparing defenses (if, indeed, defenses be justified) to unwanted tender offers. In deciding on defensive strategies, the board should consider the following factors:

- *Homework.* The company's management (or an investment banker) should analyze the adequacy of the bidder's offer. Discounted cash flow analysis is helpful, having been stressed by the Delaware Supreme Court in *Smith v. Van Gorkom*[716] and *Weinberger v. UOP, Inc.*[717] So, too, is information about book value, replacement cost, liquidation values, market prices for the company's shares, and sales of comparable companies.

---

715. *Id.* at 1356.
716. 488 A.2d 858, 876 (Del. 1985).
717. 457 A.2d 701, 712–13 (Del. 1983).

- *Documentation.* The directors should be informed of the nature of the proposed transaction before the meeting at which they are asked to consider it. The absence of such advance information proved to be a devastating factor against defendants in both *Van Gorkom*[718] and *Gimbel v. Signal Companies, Inc.*[719] It is desirable, if possible, to send to directors, in advance of the meeting, drafts of major documents such as the merger agreement, materials about the buyer, and information bearing on the buyer's ability to obtain financing, if financing is a condition of the offer. If important materials are not sent in advance, management (or an investment banker or attorney) should take time at the meeting to summarize the key terms of the documents. In *Van Gorkom*, neither the chief executive officer nor any other director had read the merger agreement before it was signed, and this neglect clearly troubled the court.
- *Absence of unnecessary rush.* Courts recognize that some business decisions—especially those made during a hostile tender offer—may have to be made expeditiously.[720] If there is no business reason for haste, however, the record should show the absence of precipitate action.
- *Investment banker.* As the Delaware Supreme Court noted in *Van Gorkom*, an investment banker's advice is not legally required, particularly in the absence of a conflict of interest such as exists in a management leveraged buy-out.[721] Such advice, however, is nonetheless helpful, especially if the company's officers are not capable of preparing a skilled valuation study.

---

718. 488 A.2d at 874.

719. 316 A.2d 599, 614 (Del. Ch.), *aff'd per curiam*, 316 A.2d 619 (Del. 1974) (preliminary injunction issued against major asset sale because, in part, management had failed to give directors notice of subject matter of meeting at which sale was considered).

720. *See, e.g., Moran v. Household Int'l, Inc.*, 490 A.2d 1059, 1075 (Del. Ch.), *aff'd*, 500 A.2d 1346 (Del. 1985) ("[t]he time constraints and rush of events which occur when a company is 'in play' dictate a quick response by the board of a target company").

721. 488 A.2d at 876.

- *Background of the transaction; alternatives.* The directors should be informed of the context of the proposed transaction and of major offensive and defensive alternatives that were considered. In *Van Gorkom*, the court emphasized that the board had not been told that the chief executive officer had fixed the price of the transaction; nor had Trans Union's directors been informed of the criteria on which Van Gorkom had based his asking price for the company.
- *Legal issues.* Advice of counsel is useful concerning legal issues such as the meaning of contractual provisions, fiduciary duties, antitrust or tax matters, etc.[722]
- *Minimization of conflict of interest.* If a director has an interest on the other side of a corporate transaction, he or she promptly should disclose that interest to the other directors. In a management leveraged buy-out, the interests of the company should be represented by a committee of disinterested directors, who should consider retaining their own outside experts (investment bankers and attorneys) to advise them on the fairness of the proposed transaction.

3. The Duty of Loyalty

In addition to a duty of care, corporate directors owe a duty of loyalty to the corporation's shareholders, for whom they serve as fiduciaries. This duty requires the directors to act in the best interests of the corporation and its shareholders. Fulfillment of this obligation usually will insulate directors from liability for defensive measures adopted in a takeover context as long as the directors can articulate a valid and not insignificant business purpose underlying their actions and decisions. This business purpose can even be to defeat a hostile tender offer, provided that the directors seek to defeat the offer in order to protect the

722. *See Van Gorkom*, 488 A.2d at 881 n.22 ("in an appropriate factual context a proper exercise of business judgment may include, as one of its aspects, reasonable reliance upon the advice of counsel").

corporation and its shareholders, rather than to secure their own jobs or to perpetuate their own control of the company.

The issue arose in *Unocal Corp. v. Mesa Petroleum Co.*,[723] when Unocal, during the pendency of a hostile tender offer by Mesa, sought to make a selective exchange offer for its own shares and to exclude Mesa from participating in that offer. Mesa, already the owner of approximately three percent of Unocal's stock, had commenced a two-tier, "front-end-loaded" cash tender offer for 37 percent of Unocal's outstanding shares at $54 per share. The second tier, "back end" of the offer was intended to eliminate remaining publicly held shares through an exchange of "junk bond" securities purportedly worth $54 per share, but highly subordinated.

Unocal's board met twice, for a total of 11-1/2 hours, to consider Mesa's offer and determine how to respond to it. The first meeting, held five days after Mesa had launched its bid, lasted 9-1/2 hours and featured detailed presentations by counsel concerning the board's state and federal law obligations and by an outside investment banker concerning the inadequacy of the offer. Using slides to outline the valuation techniques employed to analyze recent business combinations in the oil and gas industry, the investment banker opined that Unocal shareholders could expect to receive more than $60 per share as the minimum cash value from a sale or orderly liquidation of all of Unocal's stock. He also presented various defensive strategies—including a self-tender at $70 to $75 per share—that the directors could adopt if they deemed Mesa's offer inadequate and decided to oppose it. The board's outside directors then met separately with the attorneys and financial advisers and determined to advise the board to fight the Mesa bid with a self-tender. Two days later, in a two-hour meeting, the board approved a self-tender at $72 per share.

The board resolved, however, to exclude Mesa from the offer and thus to deny Mesa the opportunity to tender to Unocal, at

723. 493 A.2d 946 (Del. 1985).

$72 per share, Mesa's holdings of Unocal stock. As the court explained:

> Legal counsel advised that under Delaware law Mesa could only be excluded for what the directors reasonably believed to be a valid corporate purpose. The directors' discussion centered on the objective of adequately compensating shareholders at the "back-end" of Mesa's proposal, which the latter would finance with "junk bonds". To include Mesa would defeat that goal, because under the proration aspect of the exchange offer (49%) every Mesa share accepted by Unocal would displace one held by another stockholder. Further, if Mesa were permitted to tender to Unocal, the latter would in effect be financing Mesa's own inadequate proposal.[724]

Mesa sued to enjoin the selective exchange offer and obtained a preliminary injunction. The Delaware Supreme Court reversed.

The court held that Unocal's directors had authority under Delaware law to deal selectively with the corporation's shareholders, "provided the directors have not acted out of a sole or primary purpose to entrench themselves in office."[725] Moreover, the board had a "fundamental duty and obligation to protect the corporate enterprise, which includes stockholders, from harm reasonably perceived, irrespective of its source."[726] The court then proceeded to examine whether the directors had acted in good faith to fulfill their duty of loyalty to Unocal and its shareholders or whether they primarily had sought to perpetuate their own tenure.

The court concluded that the board had acted with a valid purpose: the directors' intent was either to defeat what they reasonably believed to be an inadequate offer or, in the alternative, to provide $72 worth of senior debt to the 49 percent of Unocal's shareholders who, in the second tier of Mesa's offer, otherwise would be forced to accept "junk bonds" worth far less

---

724. *Id.* at 951.

725. *Id.* at 954.

726. *Id.*

than $54. The court also recognized that Mesa's two-tier, "front-loaded" offer was

> a classic coercive measure designed to stampede shareholders into tendering at the first tier, even if the price is inadequate, out of fear of what they will receive at the back end of the transaction. Wholly beyond the coercive aspect of an inadequate two-tier tender offer, the threat was posed by a corporate raider with a national reputation as a "greenmailer."[727]

The fact that Mesa would be excluded from participating in the offer did not render the directors' actions improper, for inclusion of Mesa would have negated the very purposes behind the self-tender: it would have compelled Unocal effectively to subsidize Mesa's continuing effort to buy Unocal at $54 per share and would have allowed Mesa to reap the same benefits allotted to the other shareholders, who were being protected from Mesa's own coercive and inadequate offer. "The board," observed the court, "continues to owe Mesa the duties of due care and loyalty. But in the face of the destructive threat Mesa's tender offer was perceived to pose, the board had a supervening duty to protect the corporate enterprise, which includes the other shareholders, from threatened harm."[728] The board thus had fulfilled its duties to Unocal and its shareholders.

In *Revlon, Inc. v. MacAndrews & Forbes Holdings, Inc.*,[729] by contrast, the Delaware Supreme Court held that Revlon's board had breached its duty of loyalty to Revlon's shareholders, even though the directors had not acted to entrench themselves. The case arose out of Pantry Pride, Inc.'s dogged effort to acquire Revlon—an effort that had begun well before Pantry Pride announced, on August 14, 1985, that it would make a hostile tender offer for Revlon at $45 per share. The Revlon board met five days later and, based on the advice of the company's investment bankers, concluded that the Pantry Pride proposal

---

727. *Id.* at 956 (footnotes omitted).

728. *Id.* at 958.

729. 506 A.2d 173 (Del. 1986).

was inadequate. The investment bankers also explained that Pantry Pride intended to finance the tender offer with "junk bonds," followed by a break-up of Revlon and disposition of its assets (a "bust-up" tender offer). At the recommendation of its attorneys, Revlon adopted two defensive measures: a "poison pill" and a stock repurchase plan.

On August 23, Pantry Pride finally commenced its cash tender offer for any and all shares of Revlon at $47.50 per common share and $26.67 per preferred share. Revlon's board advised shareholders to reject the offer and commenced the stock repurchase program, exchanging for each tendered share of common stock one Senior Subordinated Note (the "Notes") and one-tenth of a share of Cumulative Convertible Exchangeable Preferred Stock. In response to these maneuvers, Pantry Pride announced a new tender offer and ultimately raised its bid to $53 per share.

Meanwhile, Revlon hunted around for an appropriate "white knight" and finally found one: Forstmann Little & Co. The Revlon board, on October 3, agreed to an LBO of the company by Forstmann at $56 per share. The plan also involved selling off various Revlon divisions to facilitate the acquisition. To effectuate this scheme, the Revlon board agreed to waive certain covenants contained in the Notes, which limited Revlon's ability to sell assets. When the company announced the waiver of the covenants, the market value of the Notes fell sharply, and noteholders complained and threatened litigation.

Pantry Pride still had not lost interest in Revlon and raised its $53 offer to $56.25. Pantry Pride also announced its intention to engage in fractional bidding and to top any Forstmann offer by a slightly higher one. Forstmann then raised its own offer to $57.25 per share, conditioned on (*a*) a lock-up option to purchase two Revlon divisions at $100 – $175 million below fair value if another acquiror were to purchase 40 percent of Revlon's shares, (*b*) a no-shop provision, (*c*) the removal of the poison pill and the Notes covenants, and (*d*) a $25 million cancellation fee. In return, Forstmann agreed to support the faltering market value of the Notes by an exchange of new notes. The Revlon board approved the offer (which was contingent on immediate acceptance) because (*i*) the offer was higher than Pantry Pride's, (*ii*) it protected the noteholders, and (*iii*) Forstmann's financing was in place. Pantry Pride challenged the Revlon agreement and defensive measures; it also raised its own bid to $58 per share. The trial court granted a preliminary injunction, and the Delaware Supreme Court affirmed.

The court held that the Revlon board had acted reasonably, and in accordance with its fiduciary obligations, in adopting the poison pill and the exchange offer. These measures were taken at the beginning of the battle, in the face of an inadequate offer of $45 or $47.50 per share. The pill and the exchange offer undoubtedly were major factors in causing Pantry Pride to raise its bid to an eventual high of $58 per share and, at least initially, in protecting Revlon from a "bust-up," "junk bond" takeover by a small, highly leveraged company.

In time, however, the corporation's situation—and thus the directors' responsibilities—changed. Instead of keeping the company intact and protecting its shareholders from being stampeded into tendering at an inadequate price, the focus shifted to selling and dismantling the company on the most favorable terms. As the court explained:

> when Pantry Pride increased its offer to $50 per share, and then to $53, it became apparent to all that the break-up of the company was inevitable. The Revlon board's authorization permitting management to negotiate a merger or buyout with a third party was a recognition that the company was for sale. The duty of the board had thus changed from the preservation of Revlon as a corporate entity to the maximization of the company's value at a sale for the stockholders' benefit. This significantly altered the board's responsibilities under the *Unocal* standards. It no longer faced threats to corporate policy and effectiveness, or to the stockholders' interests, from a grossly inadequate bid. The whole question of defensive measures became moot. The directors' role changed from defenders of the corporate bastion to auctioneers charged with getting the best price for the stockholders at a sale of the company.[730]

---

730. *Id.* at 182.

In light of the directors' new role as "auctioneers," the court found that the board had breached its "primary duty of loyalty" to Revlon's shareholders by acceding to the lock-up option and the other conditions (the no-shop clause and the cancellation fee) that Forstmann had demanded in exchange for its bid of \$57.25 per share. Once they decided to sell the company, the directors had a duty to obtain "the highest price for the benefit of the stockholders."[731] Forstmann's offer of \$57.25 (contingent on the lock-up) admittedly exceeded Pantry Pride's then-current offer of \$56.25 but only marginally, when adjusted for the time value of money. The Forstmann bid, however, did have one unique feature: Forstmann had promised to shore up the sagging value of the Notes, whose holders were threatening litigation.

But it was precisely this advantage that, according to the court, the board had no right to consider. In exchange for an offer of only marginal superiority, Revlon had granted a lock-up option that effectively ended bidding for the company (despite Pantry Pride's stated intention to top any Forstmann offer), that protected the noteholders, and that saved the directors from litigation—all at the expense of the shareholders, who might have received at least \$58 per share had the lock-up (and the poison pill) been rescinded. In preferring the interests of the noteholders (whose rights already were fixed by contract and who required no further protection) to those of the shareholders, the board had breached its duty of loyalty. Moreover, the board had sacrificed the shareholders' interests to protect their own. "In reality," held the court,

> the Revlon board ended the auction in return for very little actual improvement in the final bid. The principal benefit went to the directors, who avoided personal liability to a class of creditors to whom the board owed no further duty under the circumstances. Thus, when a board ends an intense bidding contest on an insubstantial basis, and where a significant by-product of that action is to protect the directors against a perceived threat of

731. *Id.*

> personal liability for consequences stemming from the adoption of previous defensive measures, the action cannot withstand the enhanced scrutiny which *Unocal* requires of director conduct.[732]

The no-shop provision was similarly improper: it ended, rather than enhanced, the bidding contest at a time when the board's primary duty became "that of an auctioneer responsible for selling the company to the highest bidder."[733]

The *Revlon* court also observed that "the directors must analyze the nature of the takeover and its effect on the corporation in order to ensure balance—that the responsive action taken is reasonable in relation to the threat posed."[734] The poison pill and the exchange offer met this proportionality test,[735] but the lock-up and the ancillary agreements did not: they obtained for the shareholders an almost insignificant improvement in the final bid and served only to end the auction for the company.[736]

The duty of loyalty, therefore, demands that directors act in the best interests of the corporation and its shareholders. Directors breach that duty when they subordinate corporate and shareholder interests to those of other parties, including themselves.

4. Burdens of Proof

When corporate directors have acted on an informed basis and in the best interests of the corporation and its shareholders, thereby fulfilling the duties of care and loyalty, the business judgment rule generally will insulate the directors from liability for their conduct. There is some difference of opinion, however,

---

732. *Id.* at 184.
733. *Id.*
734. *Id.* at 180.
735. *Id.* at 181.
736. *Id.* at 184.

as to who must show fulfillment or nonfulfillment of those two duties in a takeover context.

Under Delaware law, which is so influential in takeover jurisprudence, the *directors* bear the initial burden of showing their entitlement to the "safe harbor" of the business judgment rule. If the directors can show that they satisfied their duties of care and loyalty, the burden will shift to the plaintiff to rebut that showing.

The Delaware Supreme Court articulated this allocation of burdens in *Unocal Corp. v. Mesa Petroleum Co.*[737] in evaluating the propriety of Unocal's selective exchange offer that prevented Mesa from tendering its holdings of Unocal shares. The court declared that

> [w]hen a board addresses a pending takeover bid it has an obligation to determine whether the offer is in the best interests of the corporation and its shareholders. In that respect a board's duty is no different from any other responsibility it shoulders, and its decisions should be no less entitled to the respect they otherwise would be accorded in the realm of business judgment. . . . There are, however, certain caveats to a proper exercise of this function. Because of the omnipresent specter that a board may be acting primarily in its own interests, rather than those of the shareholders, there is an enhanced duty which calls for judicial examination at the threshold before the protections of the business judgment rule may be conferred.
>
> . . . In the face of this inherent conflict directors must show that they had reasonable grounds for believing that a danger to corporate policy and effectiveness existed because of another person's stock ownership. . . . However, they satisfy that burden "by showing good faith and reasonable investigation. . . ."[738]

Finding that Unocal's board had acted on an informed basis and had reasonably believed in the necessity of eliminating the Mesa

737. 493 A.2d 946 (Del. 1985).

738. *Id.* at 954 – 55 (citations and footnote omitted) (quoting *Cheff v. Mathes*, 41 Del. Ch. 494, 199 A.2d 548, 555 (Del. 1964)).

threat, the court held that the selective exchange offer constituted a reasonable exercise of business judgment.

The Delaware Supreme Court returned to the burden of proof issue in *Moran v. Household International, Inc.*,[739] which involved the validity of a "poison pill" Preferred Share Purchase Rights Plan. The court declared:

> in *Unocal* we held that when the business judgment rule applies to adoption of a defensive mechanism, the initial burden will lie with the directors. The "directors must show that they had reasonable grounds for believing that a danger to corporate policy and effectiveness existed. . . . [T]hey satisfy that burden 'by showing good faith and reasonable investigation. . . .' " In addition, the directors must show that the defensive mechanism was "reasonable in relation to the threat posed." . . . Moreover, that proof is materially enhanced, as we noted in *Unocal*, where, as here, a majority of the board favoring the proposal consisted of outside independent directors who have acted in accordance with the foregoing standards. Then, the burden shifts back to the plaintiffs who have the ultimate burden of persuasion to show a breach of the directors' fiduciary duties.[740]

The court restated the same principles in *Revlon, Inc. v. MacAndrews & Forbes Holdings, Inc.*[741]

Under Delaware law, then, the defendant directors bear the initial burden of making a *prima facie* showing of care, loyalty, and reasonableness. Having made such a showing, they may invoke the business judgment rule—unless the plaintiff can demonstrate, for example, that the directors' decisions "were primarily based on perpetuating [the directors] in office, or some other breach of fiduciary duty such as fraud, overreaching, lack of good faith, or being uninformed. . . ."[742]

Delaware's allocation of the burden of proof in a takeover context has influenced the law of other jurisdictions as well. In

---

739. 500 A.2d 1346 (Del. 1985).

740. *Id.* at 1356 (citations omitted) (quoting *Unocal*, 493 A.2d at 955).

741. 506 A.2d 173, 180 (Del. 1986).

742. *Unocal Corp. v. Mesa Petroleum Co.*, 493 A.2d 946, 958 (1985).

Dynamics Corp. of America v. CTS Corp.,[743] the Court of Appeals for the Seventh Circuit recently relied on Delaware law in invalidating, under Indiana law, a "flip-in poison pill."[744] The court noted the virtues of the business judgment rule and its

> sensible policy of judicial noninterference with business decisions made in circumstances free from serious conflicts of interest between management, which makes the decisions, and the corporation's shareholders. Not only do businessmen know more about business than judges do, but competition in the product and labor markets and in the market for corporate control provides sufficient punishment for businessmen who commit more than their share of business mistakes. When however there is a serious conflict of interest, and in particular when management is making decisions that may thwart the operation of the market in corporate control, the judicial role (under Delaware law, and we assume Indiana law as well) is less deferential. When managers are busy erecting obstacles to the taking over of the corporation by an investor who is likely to fire them if the takeover attempt succeeds, they have a clear conflict of interest, and it is not cured by vesting the power of decision in a board of directors in which insiders are a minority (five of CTS's eight directors are outsiders). No one likes to be fired, whether he is just a director or also an officer. The so-called outsiders moreover are often friends of the insiders. And since they spend only part of their time on the affairs of the corporation, their knowledge of those affairs is much less than that of the insiders, to whom they are likely therefore to defer.[745]

"These problems," continued the court, "have seemed serious enough to warrant a more searching judicial review of corporate decisions concerning defensive measures to takeovers than of decisions concerning ordinary business decisions."[746] The court therefore followed Delaware case law and placed the initial burden on the directors.

---

743. 794 F.2d 250 (7th Cir.), *probable jurisdiction noted*, 107 S. Ct. 258 (1986).
744. *See infra* § III.4.B. (discussing poison pills).
745. 794 F.2d at 256.
746. *Id.*

New York, however, has adopted a contrary approach: under New York law, the *plaintiff* bears the initial burden of proving that the directors breached their fiduciary duty. The Court of Appeals for the Second Circuit recently discussed this aspect of New York law in *Hanson Trust PLC v. ML SCM Acquisition, Inc.*[747]

Hanson Trust arose out of a struggle for control of SCM. The war's opening salvo consisted of Hanson's $60-per-share cash tender offer for any and all shares of SCM. SCM and its "white knight," Merrill Lynch Capital Markets ("Merrill"), responded with a counter-tender offer of $70 per share (part cash, part debentures) for a leveraged buy-out. Not to be outdone, Hanson raised its bid to $72 cash, conditioned on SCM's not locking up corporate assets. SCM-Merrill then raised its offer to $74 cash and debentures. In an attempt to get rid of Hanson, SCM also granted Merrill an irrevocable "crown jewel" lock-up option, which would enable Merrill to buy SCM's two most profitable divisions (at $350 and $80 million) if any other party were to acquire more than one-third of SCM's outstanding shares. Hanson eventually raised its bid to $75 cash, contingent on the withdrawal or judicial invalidation of the lock-up option. The district court denied Hanson's motion for a preliminary injunction, ruling that the grant of the option constituted a valid exercise of the SCM board's business judgment. The Court of Appeals reversed and remanded for prompt issuance of a preliminary injunction.

The court began its analysis with a discussion of the duty of care that SCM's directors owed to the corporation and its shareholders.

> Under the duty of care, a director, as a corporate fiduciary, in the discharge of his responsibilities must use at least that degree of diligence that an "ordinarily prudent" person under similar circumstances would use. See N.Y. Bus. Corp. L. § 717. In evaluating this duty, New York courts adhere to the business

---

747. 781 F.2d 264 (2d Cir. 1986), discussed in § III.4.M(1), *infra*.

> judgment rule, which "bars judicial inquiry into actions of corporate directors taken in good faith and in the exercise of honest judgment in the lawful and legitimate furtherance of corporate purposes." . . .
>
> Thus, in duty of care analysis, a presumption of propriety inures to the benefit of directors; absent a prima facie showing to the contrary, directors enjoy "wide latitude in devising strategies to resist unfriendly [takeover] advances" under the business judgment rule. . . .
>
> Although in other jurisdictions, directors may not enjoy the same presumptions per the business judgment rule, at least in a takeover context, *see e.g.*, *Unocal Corp. v. Mesa Petroleum Co.*, 493 A.2d 946, 954 – 55 (Del. Sup. 1985) (initial burden on directors in takeover context to show reasonable grounds for believing that takeover would endanger corporate policy; satisfied by directors' showing good faith and reasonable investigation), under New York law, the initial burden of proving directors' breach of fiduciary duty rests with the plaintiff.[748]

The court found that plaintiffs had made a *prima facie* showing of a breach of the duty of care. The evidence showed that, in the course of a three-hour, late-night meeting, the board had rushed to grant the lock-up option despite the lack of a determination as to the fairness of the option prices and despite the lack of need for a hasty decision. "In short, the SCM directors' paucity of information and their swiftness of decisionmaking strongly suggest a breach of the duty of due care."[749] Plaintiffs' *prima facie* case therefore "shifted the burden of justification to SCM,"[750] which failed to meet that burden.

Under New York law, therefore, the plaintiff must make an initial showing of improper conduct on the part of defendant directors. The plaintiff can make that showing by presenting evidence of hasty, uninformed decisionmaking, as in *Hanson Trust*, or of improper motives or self-interest, as in *Norlin Corp. v.*

---

748. *Id.* at 273 (citations omitted).

749. *Id.* at 275.

750. *Id.* at 277.

Rooney, Pace Inc.,[751] in which the court enjoined the voting of shares issued to a newly created employee stock option plan ("ESOP") because "the ESOP was created solely as a tool of management self-perpetuation."[752] "Once a prima facie showing is made that directors have a self-interest in a particular transaction, the burden shifts to them to demonstrate that the transaction is fair and serves the best interests of the corporation and its shareholders."[753]

5. The Interplay of the Duties of Care and Loyalty

Although a court may rely more heavily on either the duty of care or the duty of loyalty in evaluating defensive measures adopted in a specific takeover setting, corporate directors must satisfy both duties in order to enjoy the protection afforded by the business judgment rule. Courts often are imprecise in separating these strands of their analyses, however, and the two duties sometimes tend to merge in the course of discussions of the conduct at issue.

For example, courts have held that a board evaluating a proposed tender offer price must gather information sufficient to permit an intelligent assessment of the adequacy of that price. If the board obtains this information and conducts a thorough evaluation, it probably will have satisfied its duty of care. This information gathering and processing function, however, is intimately related to the substantive decision that the directors must make about whether the offer best serves the interests of the company's shareholders—a decision that involves the duty of loyalty. An initial failure to fulfill the duty of care (by failing to obtain the requisite information) necessarily implies an inability to act in the best interests of the shareholders and thus to fulfill the duty of loyalty; satisfaction of the duty of care, however, does

---

751. 744 F.2d 255 (2d Cir. 1984), discussed in § III.4.H., *infra*.

752. *Id.* at 266 (footnote omitted).

753. *Id.* at 264.

not itself mean that the directors also have satisfied the duty of loyalty.

The recent decision of the Court of Appeals for the Seventh Circuit in *Dynamics Corp. of America v. CTS Corp.*[754] illustrates both the inevitable intertwining of judicial analyses of the duties of care and loyalty in takeover settings and the influential role that Delaware cases play in takeover jurisprudence throughout the country. Dynamics ("DCA") had first become a major CTS shareholder in 1980, one year before the incumbent managers took over that company. During the period from 1981 through 1986, CTS's rate of return had declined markedly, in part because of a series of unfortunate acquisitions to which DCA had objected. Finally, on March 10, 1986, DCA had had enough. It announced a partial tender offer and declared that it would field a slate of candidates for the board of directors election originally scheduled for April 24.

The same day (March 10), without consulting the company's outside directors and without studying the financial implications of the proposed deal, CTS management announced its opposition to DCA's aggressive tactics. The following day, CTS retained Smith Barney Harris Upham & Co., Inc., as its investment adviser under a contract providing for a $75,000 bonus if DCA lost the proxy fight. On March 12, the CTS board met to consider DCA's actions, and on March 13, without consulting his board, CTS's chairman wrote a letter to the shareholders asking them not to vote for the candidates proposed by DCA.

On March 22, Smith Barney presented a poison pill plan to the board. Under the terms of the plan, one shareholder's acquisition of 15 percent or more of CTS's stock would trigger the right of all other shareholders to purchase a securities package, consisting of CTS stock and a CTS debenture, for 25 percent of its pre-trigger market price. If all DCA stockholders exercised their rights, DCA would wind up after its tender offer

754. 794 F.2d 250 (7th Cir.), *probable jurisdiction noted*, 107 S. Ct. 258 (1986), discussed in § III.3.B(4), *supra*, and §§ III.4.B(2)(b) and III.5.B(2), *infra*.

with a total of 20.7 percent, instead of 27.5 percent, of the outstanding CTS stock. (Prior to the tender offer, DCA already had owned 9.6 percent of CTS's common stock.) In the process, DCA would suffer a loss of roughly $24 million in completing the acquisition. In its "fairness opinion" accompanying the proposed plan, Smith Barney advised the CTS board that DCA's tender offer was unfair but did not opine on the fairness or unfairness of DCA's $43 offering price. Without discussing the offering price, the CTS directors unanimously adopted the poison pill plan.

The Court of Appeals, without being very explicit, meshed its analyses of the duties of care and loyalty. After expressing general skepticism about the use of poison pills, the court grudgingly admitted that pills cannot all be condemned under state law (in this case, Indiana law, construed in accordance with Delaware precedents) as breaches of fiduciary duty, given the "present incomplete evidence of the actual effects of these measures."[755]

The CTS board, however, probably had not been diligent enough to have met its duty of care, although the court did not expressly so hold. Despite its hesitancy to prescribe precisely what steps a board must take in assessing and reacting to hostile tender offers, the court declared that "it is apparent that the insiders on the board, in particular the chairman, decided from the start to block the tender offer, before its ramifications for shareholder welfare were considered; judgment first, trial later, as the Queen of Hearts said in *Alice in Wonderland*."[756] The court implicitly criticized CTS's reliance on Smith Barney, which, by accepting the bonus provision in the contract, had every incentive to block the offer, no matter what were its terms.

The court was unwilling to find that the presence of outsiders on the CTS board corrected the bias of the inside directors; in fact, it presented (in dictum) an extraordinary critique of the role

---

755. 794 F.2d at 256.

756. *Id.* at 257.

that outside directors generally play in corporate governance.[757] Moreover, the court found it hard to believe that the board conscientiously could have judged the adequacy of the offer without assessing the fairness of the offering price. The court also discounted CTS's argument that only some CTS shareholders could receive the tender offer price: at least a fifth of the shareholders could have availed themselves of the opportunity, while the remainder would have benefited from the general rise in the market price resulting from the new interest in CTS stock.

CTS argued that the hostility of its ongoing relationship with DCA, its stockholder, entitled it summarily to reject DCA's offer without conducting a thorough investigation. The court rejected this contention both because DCA had been correct in advising against some of CTS's ill-fated acquisitions (which advice had led to the current climate of animosity) and because personal feelings should not be "allowed to interfere with the board's fiduciary obligations."[758]

Despite the board's apparent lack of due care, the court might have upheld a hastily adopted pill plan had that plan been "a plausible measure for maximizing shareholder wealth. . . ."[759] Analyzing the plan in terms that implied that the board had not met its fiduciary duty of loyalty, however, the court found that such was not the case.

The court declared that the value of CTS as a company would not increase simply through implementation of the pill and that the additional debt that CTS would assume under the plan would reduce net earnings, create a danger of default if CTS's creditors were to call their loans because of the company's assumption of additional debt, and increase the volatility of CTS's net earnings by increasing the company's fixed costs. All of these factors would tend to depress the price of CTS stock. The court did admit that the immediate effect of executing the

---

757. *Id.* at 256; *see supra* § III.3.B(4).

758. *Id.* at 258.

759. *Id.*

plan would be to raise CTS's debt-to-equity ratio, a development that would benefit CTS shareholders if the ratio previously had been too low. However, the court had no information suggesting that the ratio had in fact been too low, and it noted that too high a debt-to-equity ratio could increase the risk of bankruptcy.

The court focused most directly on the board's duty of loyalty (without specifically mentioning it) in rejecting CTS's contention that the pill plan was needed to protect minority shareholders from an unfair "back-end" transaction. Because DCA had announced its intention only to acquire enough shares to bring its total holdings to 27.5 percent of CTS's stock, the poison pill was

> to be administered prematurely. If the rationale is to protect minority shareholders, it [the pill] should be triggered by a transaction that creates a majority shareholder or that attempts to squeeze out the minority shareholders, and it should give the minority the same price per share as the majority—not a higher price calculated to kill off the tender, indeed to kill off any tender.[760]

Finding this result unacceptable, the court invalidated CTS's poison pill because "[i]t effectively precludes a hostile takeover, and thus allows management to take the shareholders hostage. To buy CTS, you must buy out its management."[761] To CTS's argument that, once DCA gained control of the CTS board and proxy machinery, it would be able to coerce the remaining shareholders into selling their shares for too low a price, the court replied that the contention, if correct, simply "underscores the importance of not impeding tender offers too much, since the premise of the argument is that management cannot be trusted to protect the interests of the shareholders."[762]

Thus, without using specific labels, the court applied both tests of fiduciary duty and found that the CTS board had not

---

760. *Id.* at 259.

761. *Id.*

762. *Id.*

acted with sufficient care or loyalty in adopting the pill. The court's analysis suggests a willingness to accord the board greater latitude with respect to its duty of care if the plan at issue truly serves shareholder interests. Because the CTS plan failed to do so, the court upheld the grant of a preliminary injunction barring the plan's implementation.

After the rejection of its first pill, CTS went back to the drawing board and came up with an alternative plan, under which each CTS shareholder would receive, as a dividend, a right to exchange shares of CTS for one-year notes that had principal amounts of $50 and that bore interest at ten percent per year. These rights would become exercisable and would trade separately from the stock only if a person or group acquired 28 percent or more of CTS's common stock. The rights would be distributed five days after the occurrence of such a triggering event. Distribution of the rights, however, would be postponed for 120 days if the acquisition of 28 percent or more of the stock were coupled with an announced intention to buy all remaining outstanding CTS shares for $50 or more in cash. Furthermore, the rights would be extinguished if the sale were completed within the announced time frame. Finally, the company retained the authority to redeem the rights for $.05 per share at any time prior to the triggering event or a fully negotiated sale.

When DCA challenged the new plan, the district court that had enjoined the first poison pill refused to grant a preliminary injunction against implementation of the second one.[763] The court first found that the CTS board had worked much harder to satisfy its fiduciary duty of care and had made an informed decision. Relying on *Unocal Corp. v. Mesa Petroleum Co.*,[764] the court then required the directors to show that the plan bore a reasonable relation to the threat posed.

The court found that the new rights plan had been recommended to the full CTS board by a special committee of

---

763. *Dynamics Corp. of Am. v. CTS Corp.*, 635 F. Supp. 1174 (N.D. Ill.), *aff'd in part, vacated in part, and remanded*, No. 86-1888 (7th Cir. Nov. 3, 1986).
764. 493 A.2d 946 (Del. 1985).

CTS's outside directors. Acting with the assistance of its own counsel, this committee had determined that, in light of the expected aftermarket price for the remaining shares, DCA's partial tender offer at $43 a share was financially inadequate. Once this group decided that a sale of CTS was the proper course, it acted reasonably and in good faith in adopting a "back-end" rights plan—that is, a plan giving shareholders a right to put their shares to the issuer at a specified price, if a bidder acquires more than a specified percentage of the target's stock—modeled after the one upheld in *Revlon, Inc. v. MacAndrews & Forbes Holdings, Inc.*[765] The $50 exercise price had been set only after consultation with Smith Barney and receipt of second opinions from two other investment bankers suggesting that $50 represented the high end of realizable value for CTS over a one-year period.

The court therefore held that, although the board's fears of what steps DCA might take once it executed its tender offer were conjectural, these doubts limited only the scope of what response was reasonable, not the validity of the decision that a present sale of the company as a whole would benefit CTS's shareholders. (The court based this finding, in part, on DCA's never having disclaimed the possibility of initiating a second-step merger after executing the partial tender offer.) Although the court agreed that the CTS strategy of seeking a white knight to buy the company and structuring a pill plan to preserve the company's ability to conduct an auction was not the *most* reasonable one that CTS could have adopted in light of its concerns over future unfairness to shareholders, the court found the plan a reasonable response, as required by *Moran v. Household International, Inc.*[766]

In so doing, the court expressly followed *Revlon*'s reasoning that a "back-end" plan merely would start an orderly bidding process for the company and would not deter all hostile offers. By definition, the plan expired upon the launching of a tender

---

765. 506 A.2d 173 (Del. 1986), discussed in §§ III.3.B(3), *supra*, and III.4.B(2)(b), *infra*.

766. 500 A.2d 1346 (Del. 1985).

offer of $50 or more and thus did not insulate CTS from all hostile takeovers. The court also refused to restrict *Revlon* to cases involving offerors determined to execute bust-up takeovers financed by junk bonds. Instead, the court held that, "[o]nce a board of directors decides to sell the company, they have a duty to insure that shareholders receive maximum value. Any rights plan which aims to insure an orderly auction of the company is therefore a reasonable response."[767]

Once the directors had shown the reasonableness of their actions, the burden shifted back to plaintiff to prove, under the primary purpose test, that the directors nevertheless had breached their fiduciary duty. The court rejected the argument that the new plan was designed primarily as a vehicle to allow CTS's management to win the proxy contest: the court did not view the white knight strategy as a "ploy," and there was no direct evidence of golden parachutes or other tactics designed to promote entrenchment. Moreover, the court did not find that the directors had acted with the primary desire to insulate themselves from personal liability for earlier defensive tactics.

Finally, the court examined the balance of hardships and the threat of irreparable harm and found that denial of a preliminary injunction would cause little injury to DCA because, if DCA gained control of the board, it could redeem the rights. Instead, "[t]he chief effect of the plan is to change the terms on which the upcoming proxy fight will be waged."[768] The shareholders would decide whether they wished to see CTS sold in the coming year, not who would manage it better. Because the rights plan would insure a fair fight on this issue, the court refused to enjoin enforcement of the new CTS poison pill. The Court of Appeals for the Seventh Circuit, however, recently remanded the case for further consideration of the second pill.[768a]

---

767. *Dynamics Corp. of Am. v. CTS Corp.*, 635 F. Supp. 1174, 1180 (N.D. Ill) (citations omitted), *aff'd in part, vacated in part, and remanded*, No. 86-1888 (7th Cir. Nov. 3, 1986).

768. 635 F. Supp. at 1182.

768a. *Dynamics Corp. of Am. v. CTS Corp.*, No. 86-1888 (7th Cir. Nov. 3, 1986) (discussed in § III.4.B(2)(b)).

6. State Legislative Responses

As the cases discussed above have illustrated, corporate management no longer enjoys the automatic protection of the business judgment rule, especially in the context of hostile takeovers. This new judicial climate, coupled with the general rise in litigation and the increasingly frequent imposition of personal liability on directors and officers, has produced a crisis in the availability of director and officer liability insurance. In response to this situation, state legislatures have begun to enact new statutes that limit directors' personal exposure to damages for performance of their duties. These statutes are being crafted against the background of the business judgment rule: they expressly carve out from the scope of that rule certain conduct that the legislatures wish to protect, while leaving other forms of conduct subject to analysis under standard business judgment principles.

- *Delaware.* Effective July 1, 1986, Delaware modified section 102 of the Delaware General Corporation Law to permit Delaware corporations to limit or eliminate personal monetary liability of directors in derivative or stockholder suits seeking damages for directors' breaches of their duty of care. Any Delaware corporation wishing to avail itself of this option must amend its certificate of incorporation (with the approval of the shareholders) to include such a limitation.

  The legislation, however, places some restrictions on the scope of the protection that a corporation can grant to its directors: the certificate of incorporation may not limit or eliminate a director's liability for (*a*) breaches of loyalty to the corporation or its shareholders, (*b*) acts or omissions not in good faith or involving intentional misconduct or a knowing violation of law, (*c*) negligent or unlawful payment of dividends or purchases of the corporation's stock, or (*d*) deriving an improper personal benefit from any transaction. Moreover, the protection available under the new statute applies only to those directors who have breached their duty of care while acting as directors, rather than as officers, employees, or stockholders. In essence, then, the statute covers certain negligent acts or omissions by directors who, despite their negligence, were proceeding in good faith. Had Trans Union's charter contained such a limitation on liability, it probably would have insulated the directors in *Smith v. Van Gorkom*[769] from personal liability.

The Delaware legislation applies only to monetary damages; it does not affect the availability of injunctive and equitable relief even for conduct covered by the statute. Moreover, as a state law, the measure presumably does not limit the liability of directors to third parties whom those directors injure by violating federal securities laws or RICO. Because its coverage is limited to derivative and shareholder actions, the law also would probably not insulate directors from personal liability based on state law causes of action brought by non-stockholders. It is an open question whether the new statute would allow a Delaware corporation to indemnify a board member for a monetary settlement or judgment in a derivative action based on conduct not immunized by the statute.

- *New York.* The New York Business Corporation Law ("BCL") recently was revised to broaden the permissible scope of indemnity protection for directors and officers. The new law generally makes available to directors and officers of New York corporations indemnity provisions comparable to those allowed under Delaware law; however, the New York statute does not provide for equivalent limitations on liability. The revised section 721 of the BCL now provides that the indemnification of, and advancement of litigation expenses to, an officer or director, as permitted by the BCL, are not exclusive of other rights to which a director or officer may be entitled pursuant to a corporation's certificate of incorporation, its bylaws, or, when authorized by the certificate of incorporation or bylaws, (*a*) a resolution of shareholders, (*b*) a resolution of directors, or (*c*) an

769. 488 A.2d 858 (Del. 1985).

agreement providing for indemnification. However, a company may not indemnify a director or officer if a judgment or other final adjudication adverse to that director of officer establishes (*i*) that his or her acts were committed in bad faith or resulted from active and deliberate dishonesty and that those acts were material to the cause of action adjudicated, or (*ii*) that he or she personally gained an actual financial profit or other advantage to which he or she was not legally entitled.

Prior to these new amendments, indemnification in New York had been strictly limited by statute. Even under the "non-exclusivity" provision now in place, it remains unclear how far a corporation may go in providing substantive (as compared to procedural) protection exceeding the statutory standard. It is more likely, for example, that bylaws adopted under the new section 721 could permit a less stringent standard of conduct to be applied to indemnification of directors for third-party claims than for claims in derivative suits.

New York also has amended section 722(c) of the BCL to allow indemnification of officers and directors for amounts paid as settlements in derivative suits, provided that (*a*) the officer or director acted "in good faith, for a purpose which he reasonably believed to be in . . . the best interests of the corporation" and (*b*) a court determines that the officer or director is entitled to the payments. (These provisos conform the standards used in derivative suits to those already used in New York in settlements of third-party actions.)

□ *Other States.* Although Delaware was the first state to act to limit liability for directors' breaches of the duty of care, other state legislatures are considering similar proposals. At least two states have already surpassed Delaware by explicitly allowing indemnification of directors for judgments and settlements in derivative actions. This practice has normally been considered illogical: in a derivative suit, the corporation is the party ultimately injured, and reimbursing the agent who inflicted the injury therefore would leave the corporation uncompensated.

Missouri and Indiana, however, have chosen to disregard this traditional wisdom. Both states now allow indemnity payments to officers and directors in derivative actions for negligence, including gross negligence. The Missouri law requires shareholder approval of such indemnification. The Indiana statute is broader because it does not require shareholder approval and makes indemnification mandatory after August 1987; it also extends indemnity coverage to liability for securities law violations if the directors believed that they were acting in good faith and serving the corporation's best interests.

Many of the new laws undoubtedly will be challenged in court on assorted grounds. The initial struggles will concern the validity of the statutes themselves. If the statutes are upheld, the next round of skirmishes will focus on establishing the types of behavior that fit within the particular categories of conduct protected by the statutes. As noted above,[770] the conceptual distance between the duty of care and the duty of loyalty is not necessarily as broad as it might at first seem. Regardless of the ultimate resolution of the fights over the validity and applicability of new statutes limiting officer and director liability, however, their passage seems inevitable in light of the ever-widening chinks in the business judgment rule's armor and the increasing difficulty of convincing qualified, experienced individuals to serve as corporate directors.

770. *See supra* § III.3.B(5).

CHAPTER

4

SPECIFIC DEFENSIVE DEVICES AND STRATEGIES

As corporate raiders and other bidders have become more aggressive and creative in developing new takeover techniques, corporations and their attorneys have searched for new and better defensive strategies either to rebuff the bidder or, at least, to increase the target board's leverage in negotiating a favorable deal. Targets recently have used a wide array of defensive devices, both singly and in combination, albeit with varying degrees of success.

The legal validity of these defensive devices under the corporate law of the target's state of incorporation often turns on the applicability of the business judgment rule.[771] An inherent problem with almost all defensive tactics (which will be discussed in turn) is that they often have the effect of perpetuating incumbent management and therefore are subject to attack as having been adopted for an improper purpose—entrenchment—rather than for the proper purpose—enhancement of shareholders' interests. Nonetheless, courts do recognize that a corporation may legitimately attempt to defeat certain takeover attempts, and they frequently approve the use of these defensive devices.

A. Shark Repellents

Shark repellents are charter and bylaw provisions that are designed to discourage unwanted takeovers. Corporations often adopt these provisions as part of their long-term anti-takeover planning. The provisions may provide for supermajority votes, "fair price" guarantees, or a variety of other limitations on the corporation's ability to engage in business combinations with other entities. In addition, shark repellents often make a change in control more difficult to achieve by, for example, staggering the terms of members of the board of directors, repealing cumulative voting provisions, or restricting the ability of

---

771. *See supra* § III.3.

shareholders to call a special meeting or to act by written consent without a meeting.

Of course, amendments to the certificate of incorporation require approval of the company's shareholders, and, before proposing any shark repellents, the company should carefully review the likelihood that the shareholders will adopt them. A proxy solicitation firm can assist in assessing shareholders' likely reactions to particular proposals. Shareholder rejection of proposed shark repellents could suggest to a potential acquiror that the shareholders might be receptive to an acquisition proposal. The target also should be aware that some standard amendments, while discouraging unsolicited tender offers, may reduce the board's flexibility to respond to a tender offer. In addition, there is considerable debate about shark repellents' effectiveness in deterring takeovers, both desirable and undesirable, and about the amendments' impact on the value of the company's stock.[772]

1. Supermajority and Fair Price Provisions[773]

If the holders of a simple majority of a target's shares can approve a merger or a sale of assets, a bidder acquiring 51-percent of the target's stock could force a freeze-out merger at a price lower than the one at which it acquired its 51-percent interest, leaving the target's minority shareholders with only appraisal rights and, perhaps, other limited legal remedies. A potential target thus might consider amending its certificate of incorporation to

---

772. *See* Office of the Chief Economist of the Securities and Exchange Commission, *Shark Repellents: The Role and Impact of Antitakeover Charter Amendments*, [1984 – 1985 Transfer Binder] Fed. Sec. L. Rep. (CCH) ¶ 83,714 (Sept. 7, 1984); J. Pound, *The Impact of Antitakeover Charter Amendments on Contests for Corporate Control* (Investor Responsibility Research Center, Inc., Jan. 1985).

773. For a general discussion of supermajority and fair price provisions, see Investor Responsibility Research Center, Inc., *Supermajority and Fair Price Requirements Background Report B* (Feb. 1985).

require a greater vote than a simple majority of shareholders to approve a merger and/or a sale of assets.

There are various alternatives to a straight supermajority provision. For example, the charter could require a supermajority vote only if the acquiror owned a specified percentage of the target's stock (say, ten percent) before the merger; alternatively, it could require a "majority of minority" vote, meaning that a merger or a sale of assets must be approved by a majority of shares not including those owned by a holder of a specified percentage (say, five percent) of stock if that holder is proposing the merger or sale. A supermajority requirement, however, not only deters undesirable takeovers; it also might limit the company's chances of receiving a favorable takeover proposal and thus entrench inept management.

Another type of shark repellent, commonly known as a fair price provision, requires supermajority approval for a merger with a significant shareholder unless the price (or percentage premium over market price) that that shareholder pays to minority shareholders in the merger equals or exceeds the highest price (or percentage premium) paid by the acquiror in acquiring the target's shares before the merger. In addition, fair price provisions typically require a supermajority vote for a merger in certain circumstances—for example, (*i*) if dividends have been cut since the significant shareholder acquired his position in the target's stock, (*ii*) if the significant shareholder has purchased more stock since becoming a significant shareholder, (*iii*) if a full proxy statement does not accompany the merger proposal, and (*iv*) if the directors not associated with the large shareholder have not been permitted to select an investment banker to opine on the merger's fairness to the public shareholders.

Supermajority and fair price provisions discourage hostile and coercive partial and front-end-loaded tender offers but have little effect on other types of offers; consequently, they may deter financially weak acquirors. Unless state law provides otherwise, the target should protect its supermajority shark repellents by adopting a supermajority requirement governing the repeal or amendment of those provisions.

Courts generally have sustained shark repellents against challenges by shareholders or bidders. In *Morrissey v. County Tower Corp.*,[774] for example, the court held that certain charter and bylaw changes approved by shareholder vote were lawful and had been adopted for a proper corporate purpose. The charter amendments reduced the number of seats on the company's board, required supermajority voting for any mergers with an entity holding ten percent or more of the company's shares, restricted such mergers in various ways, and classified the board to stagger the directors' terms. The amendments had been proposed and adopted after plaintiff had accumulated a large block of stock but before he had announced any takeover plans.

The court held that, under Missouri law, "once a proposal which calls for the business judgment of the board of directors is ratified by the stockholders, a court will only interfere if the matter complained of is ultra vires, illegal, fraudulent, unfair or dishonest."[775] The court observed that the charter amendments had been adopted to discourage attempts to gain control of the company in a way that would be unfair to its shareholders and noted that management had disclosed the possible entrenching effect of the proposal before the shareholders approved the amendments.

In *Martin Marietta Corp. v. Bendix Corp.*,[776] the court declined preliminarily to enjoin Bendix from holding a hastily called shareholders' meeting, during the pendency of a tender offer by Martin Marietta, to adopt provisions requiring supermajority approval of any hostile merger with a 20-percent shareholder and preventing shareholder action by consent (without a meeting). Bendix itself had made a tender offer for Marietta, which, in a so-called "Pac-Man defense," had turned around and launched its own tender offer for Bendix. Sufficient shares had been tendered in response to each offer, and each corporation thus had the voting power to obtain control of the other. The battle

---

774. 559 F. Supp. 1115 (E.D. Mo.), *aff'd*, 717 F.2d 1227 (8th Cir. 1983).

775. *Id.* at 1123.

776. No. 6942 (Del. Ch. Sept. 19, 1982).

in the Delaware Court of Chancery raised the question whether Bendix or Marietta management would run the combined corporation.

Because of certain differences between Delaware law (under which Bendix was incorporated) and Maryland law (under which Marietta was incorporated), Marietta could assume control of the Bendix board before Bendix could assume control of Marietta's board, even though Bendix was the first of the corporations to become the majority shareholder of the other. The proposed Bendix charter amendment would have precluded Marietta's ability immediately to oust the Bendix board by written consent of the holders of a majority of the company's shares and thus would have allowed Bendix to take control of Marietta's board first.

Marietta argued that the charter amendments were invalid because Bendix management allegedly had proposed them on short notice solely for the purpose of perpetuating its control of Bendix. Bendix naturally denied the charge and insisted that the charter changes were necessary to enable the company to consummate its plan to acquire Martin Marietta, which plan had been adopted with a legitimate corporate purpose. The ten-day notice given to the Bendix shareholders complied with Delaware law and was the earliest notice practicable in light of Marietta's actions. Bendix also contended that the proposed amendments were designed to protect non-tendering Bendix shareholders from the coercive second step of Marietta's two-tier tender offer.

Although it recognized that the charter amendments, if approved, would have the likely effect of perpetuating Bendix management's control of the company, the court found it unlikely that the Bendix board had acted with the primary purpose of entrenchment, in view of the sequence and timing of events spawned by Bendix's tender offer and Marietta's Pac-Man defense. The court noted that the Bendix board's actions in proposing the charter amendments did not completely remove the company's destiny from the control of the marketplace and the shareholders, for the holders of a majority of Bendix shares still had to approve the proposed amendments.

Similarly, *FMC Corp. v. R.P. Scherer Corp.*[777] declined to enjoin a shareholders' meeting at which the shareholders would consider a provision requiring supermajority approval of hostile mergers with entities holding ten percent or more of the company's shares. (A simple majority vote was required for mergers approved by the board.) The court found that plaintiff and the intervening target shareholders had not established irreparable harm and thus were not entitled to an injunction. Although plaintiff had made a tender offer for the target's shares, the bidder could avoid imminent irreparable harm by withdrawing its offer, which was conditioned on disapproval of the charter amendment. The court also noted that the intervenors' damages would be readily calculable if the bidder were to withdraw the tender offer and cause the price of the securities to fall.

Seibert v. Gulton Industries, Inc.[778] dismissed a claim alleging that the adoption of a supermajority voting provision violated Delaware law. This provision required a vote of 80 percent of the corporation's shares to approve hostile mergers but only of a simple majority to ratify mergers approved by the board.

The plaintiff shareholder argued that Delaware law did not permit a company to adopt a shifting percentage, based upon a decision by the board, for shareholder approval of mergers. By empowering the board to determine the vote required to approve a merger, plaintiff contended, the proposed amendment impermissibly disenfranchised the shareholders. The court noted that plaintiff had failed to present any public policy argument against the shifting supermajority voting provision and dismissed the complaint for failing to state a claim upon which relief could be granted.

In *Seibert v. Milton Bradley Co.*,[779] applying Massachusetts law and relying in part upon *Seibert v. Gulton Industries, Inc.*,[780] the

---

777. No. 6889 (Del. Ch. Aug. 6, 1982).

778. No. 5631 (Del. Ch. June 21, 1979), *aff'd*, No. 219 (Del. Jan. 4, 1980).

779. 380 Mass. 656, 405 N.E.2d 131 (1980).

780. No. 5631 (Del. Ch. June 21, 1979), *aff'd*, No. 219 (Del. Jan. 4, 1980).

court upheld the validity of a bylaw requiring supermajority (75 percent) shareholder approval of mergers and consolidations and of any amendment, modification, or repeal of the bylaw itself, but empowering the board of directors to amend, modify, or repeal the bylaw by a two-thirds vote. The court rejected the arguments that the bylaw violated Massachusetts statutes giving shareholders the power to determine bylaws and requiring a single standard for shareholder votes on mergers and consolidations. The court noted that shareholder approval of the bylaw undercut any argument that the bylaw violated the public policy of protecting shareholders' right to vote.

But in *American Pacific Corp. v. Super Food Services, Inc.*,[781] the court granted a preliminary injunction staying a shareholders' meeting called to consider four charter and bylaw amendments and to elect directors. The four amendments provided for: (*i*) a classified (staggered) board of directors, with one third of the board to be elected annually; (*ii*) a vote of a supermajority (80 percent) *and* a "majority of the minority" (a majority of the shares not owned by a shareholder who owns five percent or more of the company's shares and who has proposed a merger or a sale of assets) for approval of mergers or sales of assets; (*iii*) a vote of a supermajority (80 percent) *and* a "majority of the minority" (a majority of the shares not owned by a five-percent-or-more shareholder without regard to whether that shareholder has proposed a merger or a sale of assets) for the repeal of the voting requirements mentioned above; and (*iv*) a requirement that special shareholder meetings could be called only by the company's chief executive officer or by a majority of its board of directors. The board also had adopted, without shareholder approval, new provisions requiring a majority vote of the directors or a supermajority vote of the shareholders for most bylaw amendments.

Plaintiff shareholder filed suit to postpone the shareholders' meeting so that plaintiff could wage a proxy contest challenging the shark repellent amendments and the slate of directors. In

781. No. 7020 (Del. Ch. Dec. 6, 1982).

finding that plaintiff had established a probability of success on the merits, the court focused on the proposed amendment requiring supermajority *and* majority of the minority votes for repeal of the special voting requirements for mergers and sales of assets. The court stated that the company had acted unjustly in attempting to exclude holders of five percent or more of the company's shares from the vote; the court also held that the exclusion "technically violate[s] [Delaware General Corporation Law] Section 242(c)(4) by allowing a numerically smaller number of stockholders, because of the blanket disqualifications therein, to alter a provision regarding a supermajority vote."[782] Moreover, as defendant admitted, the board's unilateral adoption of new procedures for amending the bylaws was invalid because the stockholders had not approved those procedures.

In finding irreparable injury, the court noted the confusion and misinformation that the company had created by stating that the proposed amendments were legal, by misinforming the shareholders about the vote necessary to approve a classified board, and by belatedly trying to correct this misinformation. The court declared that plaintiff's "right to that battle cannot be diminished by an uninformed or misguided electorate"[783] and concluded that post-meeting nullification of amendments would create an "insurmountable obstacle of confusion and antipathy"[784] that would affect plaintiff's ability to wage a second proxy contest.

---

782. *Id.*, letter op. at 8. Del. Gen. Corp. L. § 242(b)(4) states that "the provision of the certificate of incorporation requiring such greater vote [*i.e.*, a supermajority vote] shall not be altered, amended or repealed except by such greater vote."

783. Letter op. at 9.

784. *Id.* at 12.

2. Elimination of Consent or Requiring Unanimity for Consent

Unless a corporation's certificate of incorporation provides otherwise, Delaware law allows the holders of a majority of a company's stock to act by written consent, without needing to call a meeting of shareholders.[785] This provision permits an acquiror to assert control immediately upon acquiring 51 percent of the target's shares and to amend the target's certificate of incorporation to eliminate a classified board of directors or other shark repellents. If the board is not classified, the majority shareholder, without calling a shareholders' meeting, could remove the entire board without cause and appoint a new slate of directors.

A potential target thus should consider amending its certificate of incorporation to prohibit the taking of action without a meeting except, perhaps, upon written consent of all of the company's shareholders. Such an amendment effectively would prevent an acquiror from acting other than through a shareholders' meeting; it also would limit shareholder participation in corporate management.

In *Edelman v. Phillips Petroleum Co.*,[786] the court refused to issue a preliminary injunction to block a shareholder vote on a recapitalization plan accompanied by charter and bylaw

---

785. Del. Gen. Corp. Law § 228 provides:

> (a) Unless otherwise provided in the certificate of incorporation, any action required by this chapter to be taken at any annual or special meeting of stockholders of a corporation, or any action which may be taken at any annual or special meeting of such stockholders, may be taken without a meeting, without prior notice and without a vote, if a consent in writing, setting forth the action so taken, shall be signed by the holders of outstanding stock having not less than the minimum number of votes that would be necessary to authorize or take such action at a meeting at which all shares entitled to vote thereon were present and voted.

786. No. 7899 (Del. Ch. Feb. 12, 1985), discussed in detail in § III.4.G(1), *infra*.

amendments. The proposed amendments, which were part of an anti-takeover package proposed by Phillips management to thwart Mesa Partners' efforts to take over Phillips, provided for a "classified board of directors, elimination of the shareholders' ability to act by written consent, and other anti-takeover measures."[787] As part of a settlement agreement eliminating the takeover threat, Pickens agreed to vote in favor of the Phillips board's proposals.

Despite plaintiff's claims that the Phillips board had acted for entrenchment purposes, the court declined to prevent Phillips and Mesa from consummating the plan. The court noted that the anti-takeover package "decreases the risk that Phillips will be subject to future takeover efforts which might be destructive of shareholder value."[788] Moreover, the plan would not insure the entrenchment of present management, and Phillips' shareholders would be free to reject the proposed bylaw amendments.

3. Consent Procedure and Record Date

Even if elimination of a consent procedure is impossible or undesirable, a potential target might be able to amend its bylaws or certificate of incorporation to provide that any shareholder who wants the corporation to act by consent must notify the company's board of directors and request that it set a record date to determine those shareholders eligible to sign a consent. The amendment could require the board to set a record date that would give management a reasonable opportunity to react to the proposed transaction and, if appropriate, to solicit proxies in opposition, so that shareholders would hear both sides of the story. The amendment also could fix a date (for example, 30 days after the mailing of proxy materials) for determining whether the

---

787. *Id.*, slip op. at 4.

788. *Id.* at 16.

proposed action has been approved by a majority of the company's shareholders.

There are limits, however, to a board's authority to adopt bylaws delaying action by consent. In *Datapoint Corp. v. Plaza Securities Co.*,[789] for example, the Delaware Supreme Court invalidated a bylaw amendment that would have postponed the effectiveness of shareholder action by written consent until the later of either 45 days after the record date for a vote by consent or the final determination of the legal sufficiency of the consents. Datapoint's directors had adopted the bylaw in response to a takeover threat by one of the company's shareholders, Asher Edelman, who controlled more than ten percent of the company's outstanding stock and who had announced his intention to solicit shareholder consents to remove the board and to elect his own nominees. Edelman sued to invalidate the new bylaw, and the Delaware Court of Chancery granted a preliminary injunction; the Delaware Supreme Court affirmed.

Addressing the question whether the bylaw conflicted with section 228 of the Delaware Corporation Law, which allows shareholder action by written consent unless the corporation's charter provides otherwise, the court observed that, under Delaware law, written consents are considered to be effective upon signing. The bylaw amendment would greatly delay the effectiveness of any action by consent and thus was inconsistent with the statute. The court specifically declined to hold that "section 228 must be construed as barring a board of directors from adopting a bylaw which would impose minimal essential provisions for ministerial review of the validity of the action taken by shareholder consent";[790] however, the court held, it was arbitrary and unreasonable to impose a 45-day delay designed to give management time to distribute an opposing solicitation.

---

789. 496 A.2d 1031 (Del. 1985).

790. *Id.* at 1036.

In a later case, *Empire of Carolina, Inc. v. Deltona Corp.*,[791] the Delaware Court of Chancery held that, notwithstanding *Datapoint*, a board of directors may set a record date for stockholder action by written consent, in accordance with the terms of the Delaware statute. On October 7, 1985, Empire, a 29-percent shareholder of Deltona, disclosed, in a Schedule 13D and in a letter to Deltona, its intention to solicit written consents to replace all of Deltona's directors and demanded to inspect the stockholder list. On the same day, Empire executed a written consent but neither delivered the consent nor even notified Deltona of its execution. Deltona previously had entered into an agreement to issue four million shares of voting preferred stock to a white knight, a move that would sufficiently dilute Empire's holdings to make it unable to obtain written consents from a majority of Deltona's shareholders.

Upon receiving Empire's October 7 letter, Deltona set November 18, 1985—a date after the scheduled issuance of Deltona preferred stock to the white knight—as the record date for determining those shareholders entitled to express written consent to the Empire proposal. To establish October 7 (rather than November 18) as the record date, Empire brought suit in the Delaware Chancery Court.

In support of its claim, Empire relied on section 213(b)(2) of the Delaware Corporation Law, which provides that "[t]he record date for determining stockholders entitled to express consent to corporate action in writing without a meeting, when no prior action by the board of directors is necessary, shall be the day on which the first written consent is expressed." Empire contended that it had expressed its consent on October 7 and that Deltona thus had acted illegally in setting November 18 as the record date.

The court held, however, that Empire's mere execution of the consent, together with its Schedule 13D and its letter to Deltona, did not constitute an "expression" of that consent within the meaning of the statute. The court noted that "[t]he

---

791. 501 A.2d 1252 (Del. Ch.), *aff'd mem.*, 505 A.2d 452 (Del. 1985).

use of the words 'is expressed' in the statute . . . requires that the executor of a written consent who seeks to impose a stockholder record date on a corporation must clearly, explicitly, directly and unmistakeably make known that fact to the corporation."[792] Empire, however, had not informed Deltona of the executed consent. Thus, when Deltona's board, having no knowledge of Empire's October 7 consent, established November 18 as the record date, it had acted in accordance with section 213(a) of the statute, which empowers the board to fix a record date of not more than 60 days prior to action by consent.

The court then addressed Empire's argument that, even if the board did not violate section 213, its adoption of the November 18 record date violated section 228, which permits shareholder action by written consent and which had been discussed in *Datapoint*. Holding that neither section 228 nor *Datapoint* precluded the board from fixing November 18 as the record date, the court explained the difference between *Datapoint* and the instant case:

> In that case, the board of the corporation attempted to restrict the shareholder consent process through by-laws, although 8 Del. C. § 228 does not provide for the imposition of any restrictions except by a charter amendment. The Court therefore held that a board could not impose any restrictions on the written consent process except as to reasonable requirements necessary to assure the sufficiency of the written consents. In the present case, however, the Board acted in conformity with express authority set forth in 8 Del. C. § 213(a). Neither the holding in *Datapoint* nor any provision in the Delaware Code imposes on the Board of Directors of a corporation a mandate to set a record date which would give any stockholder an advantage with respect to taking action by written consent. To the contrary, 8 Del. C. § 213(a) gives the directors discretion in fixing a record date as long as the date selected is within the parameters established by the statute.[793]

---

792. 501 A.2d at 1255.

793. *Id.* at 1256.

4. Authority to Consider Non-Economic Factors

Some companies have found it desirable to amend their certificates of incorporation to authorize the board of directors expressly to consider the impact of an acquisition proposal not only on shareholders but also on the company's employees, customers, and suppliers as well as on the communities in which its facilities are located. Even in the absence of such a provision, however, a target's board might sometimes be justified in weighing those issues. As shareholder rejection of such an amendment could cast doubt on the propriety of the board's considering such factors, it is questionable whether a target should attempt to insert this type of provision in its charter.

The Delaware Supreme Court alluded to consideration of non-economic matters in *Unocal Corp. v. Mesa Petroleum Co.*[794] Discussing the requirement that defensive measures be "reasonable in relation to the threat posed," the court observed that the target's directors could consider, among other things, a hostile tender offer's "impact on 'constituencies' other than shareholders (*i.e.*, creditors, customers, employees, and perhaps even the community generally). . . ."[795] In *Revlon, Inc. v. MacAndrews & Forbes Holdings, Inc.*,[796] however, the Delaware Supreme Court clarified its statement in *Unocal*:

> *Unocal* permits consideration of other corporate constituencies. Although such considerations may be permissible, there are fundamental limitations upon that prerogative. A board may have regard for various constituencies in discharging its responsibilities, provided there are rationally related benefits accruing to the stockholders. . . . However, such concern for non-stockholder interests is inappropriate when an auction among active bidders is in progress, and the object no longer is to protect or maintain the corporate enterprise but to sell it to the highest bidder.[797]

---

794. 493 A.2d 946 (Del. 1985).
795. *Id.* at 955.
796. 506 A.2d 173 (Del. 1986).
797. *Id.* at 182.

Thus, as a practical matter, consideration of non-economic factors may be permissible only when the target defends against a partial bid or seeks to remain independent. In the context of a bidding war for total control of the company, however, the board probably may not consider such factors.

5. Cumulative Voting

A potential target might consider amending its certificate of incorporation to provide for cumulative voting in elections of directors. Cumulative voting might permit management to compete more effectively with an acquiror if the acquiror has a large (but minority) position in the target's common stock; however, such a provision would be to an acquiror's advantage if the acquiror held only a relatively small percentage of the target's common stock, and it would have little effect if the acquiror owned a majority of the target's stock. State law may restrict a company's ability to repeal cumulative voting rights.

6. Anti-Greenmail Amendment

In the past few years, some companies have proposed charter amendments that would require shareholder approval of any repurchase of shares from a limited number of shareholders at a premium price. While such amendments might discourage a greenmailer from acquiring a position in the company's stock with the hope of being bought out at a profit, the provisions also would reduce the company's flexibility to deal with an acquiror.

7. Increase in Authorized Shares

A potential target might create "blank check" preferred stock or increase the number of authorized shares of common stock (so that the company has authorized but unissued common stock). This reserve of stock will enable the company to grant stock lock-ups and to issue stock with disparate voting rights (subject to stock exchange requirements for shareholder approval of large stock issuances), if the need arises, without having to obtain shareholder approval.[798]

It might be necessary, however, to amend the company's charter to create the "blank check preferred" and to increase the number of authorized shares of common stock. If such amendments are needed, they should be adopted prior to the inception of a hostile takeover effort. The company might not have the time and/or the ability to secure shareholder approval for the authorization of such shares once a hostile tender offer has commenced, and the target's defensive options thus would be somewhat restricted.

8. Staggered Board

If a company has a staggered or classified board of directors, shareholders elect candidates for less than a majority of director slots in any single election. Existence of a staggered board prevents an acquiror from quickly gaining control of a company's management (absent an amendment to the corporate charter or the creation of vacancies on the board) and thus may help to deter hostile—although perhaps desirable—offers. Most companies with staggered boards elect one-third of the board each year. State law may restrict a company's ability to stagger its board.

The target should recognize, however, that many hostile takeovers have been launched against companies with staggered boards. Acquirors apparently believe that their acquisition of a majority of the target's shares will place the target's directors in an untenable position and will enable the acquiror to gain control, as a practical matter, in much less than the two years needed to elect a majority of a three-class board.

---

798. *See infra* § III.4.C.

9. Limitation on Director Eligibility, Size of Board, or Power to Remove Directors

Other limitations on the composition of the board of directors also can deter takeovers. A bylaw limiting eligibility for service on the board of directors could prohibit particular categories of shareholders from serving, thereby precluding an acquiror from electing its own nominees. Similarly, provisions limiting the size of the board and restricting shareholders' right to remove directors, with or without cause, can prevent an acquiror from creating vacancies on the board and filling them with its own candidates.

In *Financial Federation, Inc. v. Ashkenazy*,[799] however, the court held that a board had breached its fiduciary duty to a minority shareholder when it amended the corporation's bylaws to render a person or his representative ineligible to serve as a director if (*i*) he had acquired ten percent or more of the company's outstanding stock since 1979 and either was under investigation, was being sued, or was considered by the corporation's counsel to be in violation of the law, or (*ii*) he had acquired, since 1979, five percent or more of the voting stock in a savings and loan association that competed with the corporation. The court invalidated the amendment, finding that it had been adopted solely to exclude the minority shareholder from serving on the board.

10. Calling of Special Meetings

If a potential target's certificate of incorporation or bylaws provide that only the president or a majority of the company's directors may call special meetings, an acquiror would find it more difficult either to force a proxy fight against incumbent management other than at an annual meeting or to take control

799. [1984 Transfer Binder] Fed. Sec. L. Rep. (CCH) ¶ 91,489 (C.D. Cal. May 9, 1983).

of the company with less than a majority of shares. (The target should note, however, that some state statutes guarantee the right of a specified percentage of shares to call a shareholders' meeting.) Coupling such a provision with one requiring unanimity of shareholders for action by written consent would further increase the difficulty of changing the board of directors and taking effective control of the company (except at an annual meeting) even with ownership of 51 percent of the target's stock.

In *GAF Corp. v. Union Carbide Corp.*,[800] the court approved Union Carbide's actions in increasing the quorum requirement at shareholders' meetings from 40 percent to a majority of those shares entitled to vote and in allowing only the board, the chairman, and the president to call a special meeting of shareholders. The court found these actions to be "so self-evidently routine and within the wide latitude of business judgment afforded to a Board of Directors under New York corporate law, that no further notice thereof is required here."[801]

Under state law, however, an acquiror still may be able to amend the target's bylaws at an annual meeting, and these amendments could require shareholder approval of many corporate actions, including indemnification and selection of officers. For example, in its battle for control of Chicago Pneumatic Tool Company ("CP"), Danaher Corporation (a 67-percent shareholder) intended to vote its shares in favor of bylaw amendments that would transfer effective control of CP to holders of two-thirds of the company's shares. When CP postponed the annual meeting indefinitely, Danaher attempted to act by written consent. In *Danaher Corp. v. Chicago Pneumatic Tool Co.*,[802] a federal district court declared the bylaw amendments effective and ordered CP to hold its annual meeting.

---

800. 624 F. Supp. 1016 (S.D.N.Y. 1985), discussed in detail in § III.4.G., *infra.*

801. *Id.* at 1022.

802. Nos. 86 Civ. 3499, 3638 (S.D.N.Y. June 19, 1986).

11. Notice of Shareholders' Business

A potential target could amend its bylaws or certificate of incorporation to provide that any shareholder who wishes to bring any business before a meeting must give written notice of that business to the company within a reasonable amount of time before the meeting (for example, 60 to 90 days). Such a provision could help target management in dealing with an aggressive large shareholder. The charter or bylaws could contain a similar provision governing shareholder nominees for election as directors.

B. Poison Pills

The first shareholder rights agreement, more commonly known as a "poison pill," appeared in the defensive arsenal of a target company in June 1983, when Lenox, Inc. adopted a pill during its battle with Brown-Forman Distillers Corp.[803] A poison pill can substantially increase the cost of a hostile merger, often making such a transaction economically unsound. But pills do not necessarily deter friendly mergers, because the target's board typically may redeem a pill at a nominal price. Thus, a poison pill ultimately may serve to bring a would-be hostile bidder to the bargaining table.

The two principal types of rights plans are (a) a "call" plan, under which a holder of a right can buy securities at a discount under certain circumstances, and (b) a "put" or "back-end" plan, under which the holder of a right can require the rights issuer or the acquiring company to purchase securities under certain circumstances. Since November 19, 1985, when the Delaware Supreme Court upheld Household International's adoption of a poison pill,[804] many corporations have adopted pills of both

803. *See Wall St. J.*, June 16, 1983, at 2, col. 2.

804. *Moran v. Household Int'l, Inc.*, 500 A.2d 1346 (Del. 1985), discussed in § III.4.B(1)(e), *infra*.

varieties. More recent judicial decisions in other states, however, have raised questions about the circumstances under which companies may adopt pills and about the kinds of pills that courts will swallow.[805]

1. The Call Plan

a. How a Call Plan Works

Call plans are much more common than are put plans. A call plan is intended to encourage a potential acquiror to negotiate with the target, rather than launch a hostile bid, by making it extremely costly for a hostile bidder to accomplish a post-tender offer merger or to engage in certain self-dealing transactions with the target.

The typical call right, such as that issued by Household, essentially entitles the holder (once the right becomes exercisable) to buy stock at half price in certain situations. In the case of a merger between the rights issuer and an acquiror, the rights holders can buy, at half price, the stock of the company surviving the merger (whether the survivor be the issuer or the acquiror). Alternatively, if an acquiror of the issuer's shares engages in certain kinds of self-dealing transactions, the rights holders can purchase shares of the issuer at half price. The call right thus allows the issuer's stockholders to share in any benefit reaped by the acquiror through a squeeze-out merger or through self-dealing.

To implement a call plan, a company issues to its stockholders one right for each share of common stock. The issuance is in the nature of a dividend authorized by the directors and need not be approved by the shareholders.

---

805. *See e.g., Dynamics Corp. of Am. v. CTS Corp.*, 794 F.2d 250 (7th Cir.), *probable jurisdiction noted*, 107 S. Ct. 258 (1986); *Amalgamated Sugar Co. v. NL Indus.*, 644 F. Supp. 1229 (S.D.N.Y. 1986), both discussed in § III.4.B(1)(e), *infra*.

b. *Terms of a Typical Call Right*

A typical call right has the following terms:

- *Trading and exercisability.* The right is initially "stapled" to the common stock—that is, it trades together with the common stock—and is not exercisable until ten days after a third party acquires 20 percent or more of the company's stock or has started a tender offer for 20 percent or more of those shares. As soon as practicable thereafter, the company issues separate rights certificates, and the rights become exercisable and transferable separately in the market from the common stock.
- *Exercise price.* The right permits a holder to buy a share of the common stock of the issuer or acquiror (depending on the circumstances) at a price based on an estimate of the long-term value of the company's stock over the life of the right. The exercise price is typically a multiple of the market price (for example, three times) of the common stock on the date of issuance of the right.
- *Term and redeemability.* The right has a stated term of ten years, but it is redeemable by the target's directors at a nominal price (for example, ten cents) at any time before, or for a limited time after, the occurrence of a triggering event, such as the announcement that a third party has acquired 20 percent of the company's stock. The redemption feature allows the board to negotiate an acquisition of the company on terms favorable to all shareholders. Once the rights become nonredeemable, they affect white knight transactions as well as hostile bids.
- *Right to buy stock at half price under certain circumstances.* The call right permits its holder, under certain circumstances, to buy stock having a market value of twice the exercise price of the right. For example, if a merger occurs after the rights have become exercisable, the holder of each right is entitled to purchase that number of the surviving company's shares whose market value is twice the exercise price of the right. This feature is sometimes referred to as a "flip-over"

provision because the target shareholder's right "flips over" into a right to buy stock in the surviving company, even if that company is not the same as the original issuer of the right.

Similarly, if a third party acquires 20 percent or more of the target's stock and then engages in certain self-dealing transactions, the holder of each right (other than the 20-percent holder, whose rights become null and void) may receive that number of the issuer's shares whose market value is twice the exercise price of the right. Self-dealing transactions typically are defined to include any transaction in which the 20-percent holder or one of its affiliates merges into the target, transfers assets to the target in exchange for target stock, buys any target assets whose aggregate fair market value exceeds a specified amount, receives any compensation from the target other than for full-time employment, or receives disproportionate benefits as a result of any loan, advance, financial assistance, or tax advantage provided by the target. This feature is sometimes referred to as a "flip-in," because the right can be "flipped" into a position in the stock of the target company.

- *Voting.* The rights have no voting power.
- *Amendment.* The target may amend the rights agreement from time to time in any manner that does not adversely affect the interests of the rights holders. Amendments may extend either the term of the rights or, in the absence of a 20-percent shareholder, the period of time during which the rights may be redeemed.

c. *Variants from Typical Call Plans*

- *Automatic flip-in.* Some recent call plans have contained "flip-in" provisions under which the rights become exercisable to buy stock of the issuer or an acquiror at a fraction of market value whenever the acquiror buys more than a threshold amount of the issuer's stock, even if the acquiror does not engage in any coercive or self-dealing transactions. In *Dynamics Corp. of America v. CTS Corp.*,[806] the Court of Appeals for the Seventh Circuit upheld a preliminary injunction against the use of such an automatic "flip-in" provision, noting that the pill "effectively precludes a hostile takeover, and thus allows management to take the shareholders hostage."[807]

- *Window period for redemption.* A number of companies have adopted call plans that allow redemption of rights for a limited period of time following a bidder's acquisition of a threshold amount of shares. Such a "window period" may give the target's directors more time to react to the supposed acquisition attempt and may prevent premature triggering of the rights, especially if the acquiror reached the threshold amount by mistake (for example, through the inadvertent formation of a "group" under the securities laws). This redemption provision, however, may significantly reduce the call plan's deterrent effect because it lessens the risks to the bidder of exceeding the threshold and may pressure the target into finding a white knight once the company has been put in play during the "window period."
- *Redemption with shareholder approval.* Some call plans grant the stockholders the power to redeem the rights, by either a supermajority vote or a vote of a majority of the stockholders other than the 20-percent stockholder, even after an acquiror crosses the 20-percent line.
- *No flip-over for approved transactions.* In another variant of the plan, the "flip-over" provision applies only to transactions involving persons who acquire more than 20 percent of the target's stock without prior approval of the target's board of directors, whether or not the right already has become exercisable by reason of an unapproved 20-percent stock acquisition. The right thus is "poisonous" only to unsolicited acquirors, and the board may enter into a

806. 794 F.2d 250 (7th Cir.), *probable jurisdiction noted*, 107 S. Ct. 258 (1986), discussed in detail in § III.4.B(2)(b), *infra*.
807. 794 F.2d at 259.

white-knight transaction, without regard to the pill, even after the flip-over provision has taken effect against a hostile bidder. This variation, however, might tend to undercut the deterrent effect of the rights because, it might encourage a bidder who is not interested in acquiring 100 percent of the company to cross the 20-percent threshold in the hope of forcing the target to make a deal with a white knight.

d. *Tax and Accounting Aspects*

Neither the distribution of the rights, nor the subsequent "unstapling" of the rights from the common stock and the distribution of rights certificates, constitutes a taxable event for the company or its shareholders; rather, the rights are treated for tax purposes as capital assets in the hands of most shareholders. Each right probably would have a basis of zero, and its holding period would relate back to the holding period of the common stock from which the right was separated. If the rights become exercisable to purchase the target's stock at half price, the rights holder may recognize taxable income. If the rights become exercisable to purchase the acquiror's stock at half price, the holders would probably have to recognize taxable income even if they do not exercise the rights. The rights may also have some impact on the issuer's ability to engage in a tax-free reorganization.

Because the rights would be "out of the money" (*i.e.*, too expensive for anyone to want to exercise) when issued, they would not dilute earnings per share. Moreover, because the redemption date is neither fixed nor determinable, accounting guidelines would not require recognition of the redemption amount as a long-term obligation of the issuer. Under certain circumstances, however, the rights could impair the issuer's ability to consummate a business combination that qualifies for pooling of interests treatment.

The rights issuer need not register with the SEC the common stock issuable upon exercise of the rights because the rights will not be exercised—and the stock will not be issued—until some future triggering event has occurred. The SEC staff, however, has taken the position that such stock must be registered once the rights have been exercised and the stock actually has been issued.

e. *Call Plan Cases*

In *Moran v. Household International, Inc.*,[808] the Delaware Supreme Court upheld, under the business judgment rule, the issuance of rights with a flip-over provision. The case arose out of Household's approval of a poison pill plan as an anticipatory defensive measure against unwanted tender offers. Although Household was not the target of a tender offer at the time its board approved the plan, some overtures had been made, and board members were concerned about the general increase in hostile takeover activity.

Household's plan provided that each shareholder would receive, for each share of common stock, a right to buy 1/100 of a share of nonredeemable preferred stock at an exercise price of $100 per 1/100 of a share. The rights were to be issued as a dividend, without shareholder approval, and initially would trade together with the common stock. Two events could trigger the "unstapling" of the rights from the common stock: (*i*) the acquisition by any person (including a group) of 20 percent of Household's stock, or (*ii*) the announcement of a tender offer for 30 percent or more of Household's shares. Household could redeem the rights, at a price of $ .50 per right, until the close of the day on which any person announced a 20-percent acquisition or until any person announced a 30-percent tender offer. If the rights were neither redeemed nor exercised and a merger or consolidation occurred after a triggering event, the surviving company would be obliged to allow the rights holders to exercise each right to purchase $200 of the surviving company's common stock for $100.[809]

---

808. 500 A.2d 1346 (Del. 1985).

809. *Id.* at 1349.

John A. Moran, a Household director who also was chairman of Household's largest shareholder, challenged the plan, claiming that it violated Delaware's General Corporation Law, that is usurped stockholders' right to receive tender offers, and that it fundamentally restricted shareholders' right to conduct a proxy contest. The court rejected all three arguments.

First, the court held that section 157 of the Delaware General Corporation Law authorizes the issuance of rights, even for non-financing purposes, and that the rights issued under Household's plan had real economic value and thus were not sham securities. Moreover, the plan's flip-over provision was valid because it was the equivalent of certain securities' "anti-dilution clauses," which insure that, in the event of a merger, the holders of those securities will be able to convert their securities into those that replace the issuer's stock. The court also upheld the rights plan against a Commerce Clause challenge because the action of the Household board could not be considered state action.

Second, the court rejected the argument that the plan usurped shareholders' right to receive hostile tender offers and noted that Sir James Goldsmith's acquisition of a controlling interest in Crown Zellerbach Corporation, despite the latter's poison pill, demonstrated the fallacy of such a contention.[810] A bidder still could attempt to acquire the company in a variety of ways,

> ranging from tendering with a condition that the Board redeem the Rights, tendering with a high minimum condition of shares and Rights, tendering and soliciting consents to remove the Board and redeem the Rights, to acquiring 50% of the shares and causing Household to self-tender for the Rights. One could also form a group of up to 19.9% and solicit proxies for consents to remove the Board and redeem the Rights.[811]

Moreover, the court viewed the plan as less destructive than other defensive mechanisms (such as recapitalizations and issuer

810. *See* discussion in § III.4.B(1)(f), *infra*.

811. 500 A.2d at 1354.

exchange offers) that other target companies successfully had used to thwart unwanted takeovers. The rights plan did not give Household's board unfettered discretion to determine whether to redeem the poison pills and did not change the company's structure of governance; the board's discretion continued to be tempered by the directors' fiduciary duties to the corporation and its shareholders.

Third, the court held that the plan did not impermissibly infringe on shareholders' right to conduct a proxy contest; rather, sufficient evidence supported the Chancery Court's conclusion that the plan's effect on proxy contests would be minimal. The Supreme Court noted that, although the plan could preclude an insurgent's acquisition of more than 20 percent of the company before waging a proxy battle, " 'it does not limit the voting power of individual shares.' "[812]

Having determined that the Household board had authority, under Delaware's General Corporation Law, to adopt its poison pill plan, the court next considered whether the board's action passed muster under the business judgment rule.[813] The court expressly observed that the business judgment rule applies to "actions by which target companies have sought to forestall takeover activity they considered undesirable"; because Household's plan was a "pre-planned," anticipatory defense mechanism, the court held application of the business judgment rule to be "even more appropriate."[814] This position is consistent with that taken by other courts concerning anticipatory defensive measures.

The directors, however, bore the initial burden of establishing that " 'they had reasonable grounds for believing that a danger to corporate policy and effectiveness existed. . . . [T]hey satisfy this burden "by showing good faith and reasonable investigation. . . ." ' "[815] In short, the board was obliged to show

812. *Id.* at 1355 (quoting Chancery Court's opinion).

813. *See supra* § III.3.B(2) (discussing *Moran* and business judgment rule).

814. 500 A.2d at 1350.

815. *Id.* at 1356 (quoting *Unocal Corp. v. Mesa Petroleum Co.*, 493 A.2d 946, 955 (Del. 1985)).

that it had fulfilled its duties of care and loyalty to the shareholders. In addition, the court required the board to establish that "the defensive mechanism was 'reasonable in relation to the threat posed.' "[816] Only after the board met these burdens would plaintiffs have to show that the board had breached its fiduciary duties.

The court found that the board had met its burdens under the business judgment rule. Applying the gross negligence standard articulated in *Smith v. Van Gorkom*,[817] the court held that the board had satisfied its duty of care and had acted on an informed basis in adopting the plan. Before voting, the directors had received a summary of the plan and had heard from outside counsel and investment bankers as well as from a director (Moran) who disapproved of the plan. Plaintiffs argued that the board was not fully informed because it had not been told that the plan could inhibit a proxy contest or could preclude all hostile acquisitions. Having found no such inhibition or preclusion, the court rejected the contention.

The court also held that the board had fulfilled its duty of loyalty. A majority of Household's board consisted of "outside" independent directors, and the board had reacted to a perceived threat of coercive two-tier tender offers. Moreover, the poison pill plan was "reasonable in relation to the threat posed" because the board reasonably had believed that the company was "vulnerable to coercive acquisition techniques and adopted a reasonable defensive mechanism to protect itself."[818]

However, continued the court,

> [w]hile we conclude for present purposes that the Household Directors are protected by the business judgment rule, that does not end the matter. The ultimate response to an actual takeover bid must be judged by the Directors' actions at that time, and

---

816. *Id.* (quoting *Unocal*, 493 A.2d at 955).
817. 488 A.2d 858, 873 (Del. 1985), discussed in § III.3.B(2), *supra*.
818. 500 A.2d at 1357.

> nothing we say here relieves them of their basic fundamental duties to the corporation and its stockholders. . . . Their use of the Plan will be evaluated when and if the issue arises.[819]

Thus, the board's decision whether or not to redeem the rights at some future time would itself be evaluated under the business judgment rule.

In *Horwitz v. Southwest Forest Industries, Inc.*,[820] the United States District Court for the District of Nevada refused to issue a preliminary injunction enjoining implementation of a poison pill plan similar to the one upheld in *Moran v. Household International*. Southwest Forest's plan involved the issuance of one warrant for each share of outstanding common stock; the warrants were exercisable only upon a stockholder's acquisition of 20 percent of the company's shares or upon the commencement of a tender offer for 30 percent of the stock, at which time the warrant holders could purchase shares of the company's common stock at $50 per share. (At the time of the warrants' issuance, the stock was selling at $17 per share.) Upon the consummation of a merger, however, each warrant holder would be entitled to buy $100 worth of stock in the new company for $50. The plan further provided that the company could redeem the warrants at 25 cents each before the occurrence of a triggering event; in the event of a merger, however, the acquiror could buy back unexercised warrants only "at an exorbitant cash premium."[821]

Applying Nevada law, the district court ruled that directors' actions in averting takeovers will be upheld if reasonable and taken in good faith; defensive tactics are illegitimate only if their primary purpose is to entrench present management. The court found that Southwest Forest's board had obtained both legal and financial advice in formulating the poison pill and had adopted the plan in order to further the company's five-year development and expansion goals.

---

819. *Id.*

820. 604 F. Supp. 1130 (D. Nev. 1985).

821. *Id.* at 1132.

In analyzing the balance of hardships, the court pointed out the "serious confusion" both within the company and among investors that would result from a preliminary injunction, the speculative nature of plaintiff's alleged harm, and the warrants' potential benefit even to plaintiff. Citing *Moran v. Household International*, the court also noted the trend of decisions in other jurisdictions and determined that plaintiff had not shown a likelihood of prevailing on the merits.

Similarly, the United States District Court for the Eastern District of New York, in *APL Corp. v. Johnson Controls, Inc.*,[822] denied a motion for a preliminary injunction against implementation of a poison pill rights dividend declared by Johnson Controls. Relying on *Moran v. Household International* and *Horwitz v. Southwest Forest Industries*, the court ruled that adoption of poison pill plans "may be acceptable where the tactic is not borne [*sic*] out of improper motives or intentions."[823] In light of the murky state of the law in the area, the court found that APL had not established a likelihood of success on the merits.

The recent decision of the Court of Appeals for the Seventh Circuit in *Dynamics Corp. of America v. CTS Corp.*,[824] however, casts some doubt on the validity of poison pill call plans with "flip-in" features dependent on events other than coercive or self-dealing transactions. The story began when Dynamics Corporation of America ("DCA") announced a partial tender offer for shares of CTS stock and declared that it would solicit proxies to elect its own slate of directors to CTS's board. Twelve days later, CTS's directors adopted a shareholder rights call plan with a flip-in provision providing that, if any person acquired more than 15 percent of CTS's stock, all shareholders (other than the acquiror, whose rights would become null and void) would be entitled to purchase a package (consisting of CTS

---

822. No. 85–C–990 (E.D.N.Y. March 25, 1985).

823. Slip op. at 7.

824. 794 F.2d 250 (7th Cir.), *probable jurisdiction noted*, 107 S. Ct. 258 (1986), discussed in detail in § III.3.B(5), *supra*.

common stock and debentures) at 25 percent of its pre-trigger market value. The object of the flip-in feature was to inflict an immediate economic loss on any bidder that refused to negotiate with management. The rights plan also contained a flip-over provision of the sort sustained by the Delaware Supreme Court in *Moran v. Household International*: this provision enabled a rights holder, in the event of a merger between an acquiror and CTS, to purchase common stock in the acquiring company having a market value of twice the exercise price of the right.

The sole issue before the Court of Appeals was the legality of the flip-in feature. The district court had issued a preliminary injunction against enforcement of this feature; the Court of Appeals affirmed.

The court began with the observation that the CTS directors had not evaluated the supposedly threatening DCA offer "in a cool, dispassionate, and thorough fashion"; rather, the directors had determined to block the offer at any cost.[825] After pointing out that the price of CTS shares had dropped substantially the day after the poison pill had been announced and had risen again upon release of the district court's order invalidating the pill, the court analyzed the dilutive effect that the plan would have on the company's equity and the substantial debt burden that it would create. Finally, the court took issue with the pill's 15-percent trigger and the exorbitant value that the plan bestowed on existing minority shareholders:

> If the rationale is to protect minority shareholders, [the pill] should be triggered by a transaction that creates a majority shareholder or that attempts to squeeze out the minority shareholders, and it should give the minority the same price per share as the majority—not a higher price calculated to kill off the tender, indeed to kill off any tender. CTS's shareholder rights agreement is triggered much earlier, and at a higher price. It effectively precludes a hostile takeover, and thus allows management to take the stockholders hostage. To buy CTS, you must buy out its management.[826]

825. 794 F.2d at 257.

826. *Id.* at 259.

Ultimately, the CTS board adopted, and the district court upheld, a "put" pill keyed to the board's assessment of the fair value of the company's shares. The Court of Appeals, however, recently remanded the case for further consideration of the second pill.[827]

Amalgamated Sugar Co. v. NL Industries[828] also invalidated a poison pill plan, which NL Industries had adopted after rejecting an acquisition proposal and buying back the shares of the would-be acquiror. The rights plan was only one of several steps expressly intended to prevent a takeover in which NL shareholders would not receive full value for their stock.

Under the plan, NL declared a dividend of one right per share of common stock, to be distributed to all holders of record as of May 30, 1986. The rights could be traded only with the common shares, could not be exercised, and were redeemable by the NL board for five cents each until there was either (*A*) an announcement that a shareholder had acquired 20 percent or more of NL's common stock or (*B*) a tender offer for 30 percent or more of NL's common shares. Upon the occurrence of either event, the rights certificates would be distributed and would trade separately from NL common stock, with each right certificate being exercisable (except by the 20-percent shareholder or the 30-percent tender offeror) to purchase 1/100 of a share of newly issued NL junior preferred stock for $50.

After the occurrence of any of several events constituting a second trigger—such as a merger or any of several other defined transactions with a 20-percent shareholder—the plan's flip-in and flip-over provisions would be activated. Under the flip-in provision, if NL were the surviving company in a merger with a 20-percent shareholder and if one of several defined events occurred, all rights holders except the acquiring person would be entitled to purchase $100 worth of NL common stock per right for $50, thus diluting the equity and voting power of the acquiring person but also of other NL shareholders who had

827. For a detailed discussion of the CTS "put" pill, see § III.4.B(2)(b), *infra*.

828. 644 F. Supp. 1229 (S.D.N.Y. 1986).

sold their rights. Under the plan's flip-over provision, if an acquiring person merged or otherwise combined with NL and if the acquiring person were the surviving entity, all other shareholders holding rights would be entitled to buy $100 worth of the acquiror's stock per right for $50.

After NL had adopted its rights plan, Amalgamated Sugar offered to buy all NL shares and asked NL's board to redeem the rights. When NL rejected Amalgamated's proposal and declined to redeem the rights, Amalgamated sued to enjoin the operation of the rights plan, announced that it had acquired more than 20 percent of NL's common stock, and commenced a cash tender offer for any and all NL shares, conditioned on judicial invalidation of the pill.

Amalgamated moved for a preliminary injunction, which the court granted. Applying the law of New Jersey (where NL was incorporated), the court held that the adoption of the rights plan was *ultra vires* because the plan unlawfully discriminated among shareholders of the same class or series by disadvantaging the acquiring person vis-a-vis other common stockholders.[829] After distinguishing *Moran v. Household International Corp.*—a case decided under Delaware law—on a number of grounds, the court turned to what it viewed as the key distinction: in *Moran*, the Delaware Supreme Court had concluded that the rights plan at issue was not "much of an impediment on the tender offer process." In *NL*, however, the district court determined that "the rights plan does prevent stockholders from receiving tender offers and the change of NLI's structure, which at least theoretically would be effected by this rights plan, is more extreme than any that have been analyzed in other cases."[830] The court proceeded to analyze, in detail, why it viewed the Household plan as a significantly less effective deterrent to hostile tender offers than was the NL plan. The *NL* case was ultimately settled without an appeal.

829. *Id.* at 1234.
830. *Id.* at 1238.

Although not a poison pill case *per se*, the decision upholding springing warrants in *Gearhart Industries, Inc. v. Smith International, Inc.*,[831] is applicable to a poison pill analysis. Gearhart had issued $98,700,000 of subordinated debentures, accompanied by springing warrants, as a defensive maneuver in response to Smith International's purchase of over one-third of Gearhart's stock and its announced intention to continue its acquisition program. The warrants authorized the purchase of 2,961,000 shares of Gearhart common stock at a price of $33.00 per share, but the occurrence of a triggering event (such as a tender offer) would drop the exercise price of the warrants to $24.60 per share.

Smith contended that Gearhart's directors had issued the warrants primarily for entrenchment purposes and thus had violated their fiduciary duties to the company and its shareholders. In affirming the district court's refusal to enjoin the warrants plan, the Court of Appeals for the Fifth Circuit stated that, under Texas law, courts should not interfere with the business judgment of corporate directors unless the transaction at issue is fraudulent or *ultra vires*. The court found no evidence of an entrenchment motive; moreover, even assuming, for the sake of argument, that the directors had breached their duty of loyalty, the court went on to find that the directors had met their burden of showing that the transaction was fair to the corporation.

The court's determination of fairness rested on several facts: the board had received expert financial and legal advice; the type of transaction was "commonplace"; the warrants were "an integral and necessary part" of the transaction; the exercise price (after the occurrence of the triggering event) was consistent with the market price of Gearhart stock prior to the Smith acquisitions; and there were credible business reasons for the transaction.[832] Issuance of the warrants was not impermissible merely because one of the reasons for the action was the desire to block an anticipated tender offer.

---

831. 741 F.2d 707 (5th Cir. 1984).

832. *Id.* at 722–23.

f. *Affirmative Use of Call Plans*

The case of *Crown Zellerbach Corp. v. Goldsmith*[833] illustrates an interesting potential use of a poison pill as an affirmative measure in tender offer litigation. Crown Zellerbach had been the target of a series of open-market purchases by a buying group led by Sir James Goldsmith. After accumulating approximately 9.3 percent of Crown Zellerbach's common stock, defendants announced a tender offer but withdrew it on April 26, 1985, following Crown's announcement of a proposed spin-off of certain divisions. In early May, however, defendants bought additional Crown shares in privately negotiated purchases and increased their aggregate holdings to 19.88 percent of the company.

Several months before defendants had purchased their initial position in the company, Crown had announced the distribution of common stock rights that entitled holders to purchase shares of stock in an acquiring company at a bargain price. Crown's board retained the authority to redeem the rights for 50 cents each, unless an acquiror purchased 20 percent of Crown's shares or made a tender offer for 30 percent of the stock. Defendants now threatened to trigger the rights by crossing the 20-percent threshold; however, in what the court called a "high stakes game of 'chicken,' " they declared a one-day moratorium on additional purchases to give the company a final chance to redeem the rights, which, once triggered and rendered unredeemable, would effectively preclude Crown from merging with a white knight and engaging in certain other transactions.[834]

Crown sued to enjoin further acquisitions, claiming that defendants' buying program constituted a creeping tender offer and violated the Williams Act. The court denied the injunction, finding, in part, that defendants' additional purchases would not irreparably harm Crown because they could be rescinded if made illegally.

833. 609 F. Supp. 187 (S.D.N.Y. 1985).

834. *Id.* at 188.

Crown's board ignored Goldsmith's threat and did not redeem the rights; nevertheless, Goldsmith bought more than 20 percent of Crown's common stock and eventually acquired control of the board. However, neither Goldsmith nor anyone else could merge with the company without suffering the dilutive effect of the pill. Ultimately, James River Corporation (Goldsmith's company) exchanged shares with Crown in a transaction designed not to constitute a second trigger under the rights plan. Goldsmith ended up with a significant portion of Crown's assets, and the second trigger was never pulled.

Crown had adopted an interesting litigation position: by arguing that its poison pill, if triggered, would cause it irreparable harm, the company essentially contended that its rights plan was a "suicide pill." One can question whether such a claim should be effective, because a target making that argument would be seeking an injunction against a harm that it had inflicted on itself by implementing the poison pill and, specifically, by refusing to redeem the rights. However, in the recent *NL* decision, the district court granted relief against a poison pill even though the harm alleged by the plaintiff bidder resulted from the bidder's voluntarily crossing the ownership threshold and triggering the pill.*

Crown Zellerbach also raises the issue, left unresolved in *Moran v. Household International*, whether the Crown board, in not redeeming the rights, breached its fiduciary duty to Crown's shareholders by making the company unacquirable. The *Crown Zellerbach* litigation was settled, and the court never reached this question.

**Amalgamated Sugar Co. v. NL Indus.*, 644 F. Supp. 1229 (S.D.N.Y. 1986).

2. The Put Plan

a. *How a Put Plan Works*

While historically less common than "call" rights plans, "put" rights plans have been adopted by a number of companies, including Phillips, Revlon, Great Lakes International, and CTS. Put plans are used most often when target companies need a defense against specific bidders under specific circumstances.

Under a put plan, as under a call plan, a company's board issues rights to shareholders as a dividend, without shareholder approval. A put right typically enables its holder (other than a holder of more than a specified percentage of the company's stock) to "put" to the issuer a share of common stock for a specified amount of cash, debt securities, preferred stock, or a combination of the above, in the event that a third party acquires more than a specified percentage of the company's stock and does not offer to buy the rest of the stock at a specified price (which is usually equal to the value of the cash or securities receivable if the rights are exercised). The price can be a fixed amount, as under the Revlon plan, which gave shareholders (other than a 20-percent holder) the right to exchange a Revlon share for $65 in notes if a third party acquired 20 percent of Revlon's stock and did not offer to buy the remaining shares for $65 each. Alternatively, the price can be set by a formula to equal the highest price per share paid by a bidder in acquiring the issuer's stock.

Until recently, the legality of put plans seemed less certain than did that of call plans, the latter having been established by the Delaware Supreme Court in *Moran v. Household International*. However, some courts recently have invalidated call plans,[835] while others have upheld put plans. The Delaware Supreme Court, in *Revlon, Inc. v. MacAndrews & Forbes Holdings, Inc.*, commented favorably on the adoption of a put plan as a means of protecting shareholders "from a hostile takeover at a price

---

835. *See supra* § III.4.B(1)(e).

below the company's intrinsic value, while retaining sufficient flexibility to address any proposal deemed to be in the shareholders' best interests."[836] And a federal district court recently upheld, under Indiana law, the use of a put plan as a defense against a hostile takeover, although the Court of Appeals for the Seventh Circuit remanded the case for further consideration of the plan.[837]

The issuer should be aware that a put plan may raise certain legal questions not raised by a call plan, including the need to comply with restrictions under loan agreements and state corporation statutes concerning the redemption of stock. A put plan also might raise fraudulent conveyance issues, on the theory that the company has given rights holders the right to put shares to the company for excessive consideration.[838] In addition, if the put right is not available to the bidder (or to other shareholders owning in excess of a specified threshold percentage of the target's stock), there is at least a question whether the put plan constitutes an exclusionary tender offer and thus is inconsistent with the "all holders" rule that the SEC adopted in 1986.

b. Cases

In *Revlon, Inc. v. MacAndrews & Forbes Holdings, Inc.*,[839] the Delaware Supreme Court, in dictum, approved Revlon's use of a put poison pill. Revlon's board had adopted a "Note Purchase Rights Plan" in response to Pantry Pride's announcement of its intention to commence a hostile tender offer for Revlon at $45 per share. Under the plan, each Revlon shareholder received a dividend of one right per share of common stock, each right entitling its holder to exchange a share of stock for a $65

---

836. 506 A.2d 173, 181 (Del. 1986) (dictum). For a detailed discussion of *Revlon*, see § III.3.B(3), *supra*, and § III.4.B(2)(b), *infra*.

837. *Dynamics Corp. of Am. v. CTS Corp.*, 635 F. Supp. 1174 (N.D. Ill.), *aff'd in part, vacated in part, and remanded*, No. 86-1888 (7th Cir. Nov. 3, 1986). For a detailed discussion, see § III.3.B(5), *supra*.

838. *See supra* § II.8. (discussing fraudulent conveyances).

839. 506 A.2d 173 (Del. 1986), discussed in detail in § III.3.B(3), *supra*.

principal Revlon note at 12 percent interest with a one-year maturity. The rights were to become exercisable when anyone acquired beneficial ownership of 20 percent or more of Revlon shares, unless the purchaser acquired all of Revlon's stock for cash at $65 or more per share. The plan further provided that the rights would not be exercisable by the 20-percent holder and that Revlon's board could redeem each right for ten cents before the occurrence of a triggering event.

The court concluded that, in adopting the rights plan, Revlon's board had "acted reasonably and in good faith and upon reasonable investigation. Under the circumstances it cannot be said that the Rights Plan as employed was unreasonable, considering the threat posed."[840] The court noted that Revlon's investment bankers had advised the directors that Pantry Pride's offer of $45 per share was grossly inadequate and that Pantry Pride (being small and highly leveraged) was likely to finance the Revlon acquisition through "junk bonds" and to sell off the acquired assets to satisfy the acquisition debt. Moreover, the court observed, the rights plan, "[f]ar from being a 'show-stopper,' " had in fact spurred bidding for the company to new heights.[841] The validity of the rights plan, however, was not really at issue in *Revlon* because Revlon's board had redeemed the rights in connection with any cash proposal of $57.25 per share or higher. All pertinent offers exceeded that price.

Another put plan recently was at issue in *Dynamics Corp. of America v. CTS Corp.*[842] and was upheld by the same district court that had preliminarily enjoined a flip-in call plan adopted by the same target company in the face of a perceived threat from the same bidder.[843] Under the flip-in call plan, CTS shareholders would have received rights entitling them to buy CTS securities at a fraction of market value. In striking down

840. *Id.* at 181.

841. *Id.*

842. 635 F. Supp. 1174 (N.D. Ill.), *aff'd in part, vacated in part, and remanded,* No. 86-1888 (7th Cir. Nov. 3, 1986).

843. *See supra* § III.4.B(1)(e).

this plan, which CTS's board had adopted soon after Dynamics Corporation of America ("DCA") began a partial tender offer and announced a proxy contest to replace the CTS board, the court noted that the plan would deter all hostile takeovers, regardless of the offering price. The Court of Appeals for the Seventh Circuit affirmed the ruling.

Following the district court's decision, CTS's outside directors formed a committee, selected special counsel, and, after consulting with CTS's investment banker, concluded that DCA's partial tender offer at $43 per share was financially inadequate, in light of the expected aftermarket price for the remaining shares. The investment banker also informed the committee that, if DCA were to succeed in its tender offer and to acquire close to 28 percent of CTS, the other CTS shareholders might not be able to receive a premium over the market price of their shares through the sale of CTS to another company.

The committee therefore recommended, and the full CTS board approved, the adoption of a put plan, under which each CTS shareholder would receive, as a dividend, a right to exchange his shares for one-year notes with a principal amount of $50, bearing interest at 10 percent per year. The rights would become exercisable, and would trade separately from the common stock, only if a person or group acquired beneficial ownership of 28 percent or more of CTS's stock. The rights would be distributed to all CTS shareholders other than the acquiror five days after the date of the triggering event. Distribution of the rights would be postponed for 120 days, however, if a bidder purchased 28 percent of CTS's stock and announced his intention to buy all outstanding CTS shares for $50 or more in cash; the rights would be completely extinguished if the transaction were completed within the time frame set forth in the plan. CTS could redeem the rights for five cents per share at any time prior to the distribution event or a fully negotiated sale.

The court ruled that the directors had sustained their initial burden of showing both that they had acted with good faith and after reasonable investigation and that the put plan was reasonable in relation to the threat posed. The court noted with approval the board's appointment of a special committee of outside directors, the committee's retention of separate counsel, the board's seeking of advice from an investment banker, and the board's careful consideration of alternatives. The court also found that the directors had some basis for believing that DCA's acquisition of a 28-percent block would reduce the board's ability to sell CTS to another buyer.

In addition, the court observed that the put plan had been modeled on the one approved in dictum in *Revlon*; moreover, CTS's board had fixed the $50 put price based on the advice of the company's investment banker as to the high end of realizable value over the one-year life of the plan. Other investment bankers had concurred in this opinion. In addition, the rights issued under the plan would expire in the event of a completed tender offer for $50 or more in cash, so the plan could not be said to insulate management from all hostile offers. The plan thus served to promote an orderly auction of the company, consistent with the board's duty (once the board decided to sell the company) to seek maximum value for the shareholders.

The court rejected DCA's contention that the rights plan was invalid because the directors had adopted it primarily to entrench themselves. The board was committed to selling the company, and there was no direct evidence that golden parachutes had motivated that decision.

On appeal, however, the Court of Appeals for the Seventh Circuit remanded the case for further consideration of the put plan. With respect to the procedural adequacy of the pill's adoption, the court noted that it was unclear whether the CTS investment banker's compensation might have involved a bonus of some sort if the company were sold to a white knight—a factor that would have given the investment banker (Smith Barney) an improper incentive to formulate a plan designed to defeat DCA's offer. The court also observed that DCA's outside directors were not really disinterested because they probably stood to lose their directorships (and directors' fees) in the event of a takeover. However, the court did not believe that these questions, by themselves, warranted a reversal—or even a remand—of the district court's ruling.

Far more serious was the question why the poison pill was to be activated at a 28-percent, rather than a 50-percent, ownership level. The record contained no evidence showing that DCA (or any other bidder) could use 28-percent ownership "or any other fractional ownership short of 50 percent" to take a "blocking position" either to thwart corporate attempts to promote the welfare of other shareholders or to squeeze out those shareholders. The court declined to hold that 28-percent ownership could *not* create a blocking position; however, it did insist that the defendants present evidence to justify setting the triggering percentage below the level that would give a minority shareholder an actual legal right to block decisions taken by the majority.

The court also ruled that, because the entire premise of the second pill was to facilitate the sale of CTS, the pill could not be upheld if its trigger price were unreasonably high. The court was troubled by the method used to fix the $50 valuation and believed that the issue warranted further consideration by the district court. The Court of Appeals noted that Smith Barney had determined the price primarily by multiplying CTS's expected earnings for the coming year by a price-earnings multiple of 15.5, which seemed high, and that the projected earnings represented "a wildly extravagant forecast," being more than three times higher than an earlier estimate of earnings for the year.

Moreover, the court reiterated its general skepticism concerning the propriety of poison pills, noting that CTS's pill essentially prevented shareholders from deciding to sell the company at less than $50 per share unless the directors approved the acquisition. The court recognized that Delaware courts have "emphatically refused to outlaw the poison pill" and acknowledged that CTS's plan "is said to be modeled on the one upheld in *Revlon, Inc. v. MacAndrews & Forbes Holdings, Inc.* . . . and indeed bears a family resemblance to it." Revlon, however, had adopted its pill *before* the directors decided to sell the company, and Revlon's directors had not yet assumed the role of auctioneers. CTS, by contrast, had adopted the second pill *after* the board had decided to sell CTS, and the directors therefore had a duty to obtain the highest possible price. The CTS pill thus needed to be "a reasonable element of a plan for a corporate auction." The court declared that

> [i]t would be premature to decide in this case that, as a matter of Indiana law, a board of directors intent on selling the corporation for the highest possible price cannot set a reservation price [here, $50] and cannot use a poison pill as the means of doing so. But even if it can, the reservation price must be reasonably related to the value of the corporation, and the decision to establish such a price and do so by means of a poison pill must be made in good faith after proper consideration.

The court instructed the district court to consider these issues on remand.

In attacking CTS's pill, DCA also argued that the plan violated provisions of the Indiana corporation statute providing that all shares of the same class must have the same rights and preferences. The court rejected this contention, noting Delaware case law permitting discrimination among *shareholders* (rather than among *shares*). Moreover, the court rejected as frivolous the claim that the Indiana statute violates the Commerce Clause if it permits poison pills. The Commerce Clause, held the court, "does not require states to outlaw private transactions that may impede interstate commerce."

Revlon and *CTS* thus suggest that a put plan with a put price that approximates the fair value of the company's shares may be defensible, especially if the issuer's board adopts the plan on an informed basis. If the put price is unreasonably high, however, or if the ownership threshold that triggers the rights issuance is unjustifiably low, the put plan could be invalidated for the reasons articulated by the Court of Appeals in *CTS*.

3. Other Types of Poison Pills

a. Value Assurance Plans

Related in concept to a put plan is a "value assurance plan" such as that adopted by Mayflower Group, Inc., in May 1986, in response to an unsolicited tender offer at $29.25 per share by Laidlaw Transportation. Under the plan, Mayflower's directors declared a dividend in the form of an unsecured, contingent, two-year Mayflower note.

To oversimplify the terms of the plan: if Laidlaw (or anyone else) acquired 30 percent of Mayflower, the principal amount of the note would become equal to the difference between $33 and the average price per share paid by the 30-percent holder. If the 30-percent holder did not effect a merger with Mayflower within six months, the market price of the public shares would be averaged with the price of the shares acquired by the 30-percent holder, to determine a recalculated principal amount of the note. If the Laidlaw offer were terminated (as, in fact, it was) without at least 30 percent of Mayflower's common stock's having been acquired, the principal amount of the note would equal the difference, if any, between $30 per share (plus interest but less dividends since the issuance of the note) and the greater of $25.75 or the highest 30-day average price of the Mayflower shares during the two years following the termination of the Laidlaw offer. The notes could be redeemed for five cents each until Laidlaw terminated its offer or until someone acquired 30 percent of Mayflower's stock in a merger at a price of $30 or more per share. A 30-percent holder could not become a registered noteholder.

Unlike a put plan, a value assurance plan like Mayflower's does not require a stockholder to surrender his shares. Moreover, a bidder cannot tailor its offer to fit the plan, because, the lower the bidder's adjusted price, the higher becomes the "value assurance" payment.

But a value assurance plan resembles a put plan insofar as both require the board to set a fixed value on the company's stock in response to a specific unsolicited bid, and both obligate the company to pay amounts related to that fixed value. These amounts, however, are likely to be limited by restrictions in loan agreements.

Because a value assurance plan does not require the company to pay the full fixed value of shareholders' stock, but only a specified shortfall from that value, payments made under a value assurance plan should have a less dramatic effect on the company's capitalization—and hence raise less significant questions of fraudulent conveyance or improper payment to stockholders—than might payments made under a put plan. At present, the validity of value assurance plans has not been judicially determined, although, in economic effect, such plans are similar to put plans. The tax consequences of payments under value assurance plans also are unclear, although there is a real likelihood that they would be taxed as ordinary income. Moreover, one might question whether there actually is economic reality to the portion of the plan that requires the company to pay money to its shareholders if a hostile bidder withdraws its offer, because shareholders' equity will be reduced by the amount of the payment. However, the existence of that debt obligation may put pressure on the directors to come up with an attractive economic alternative (white knight or otherwise) before the contingent value assurance note becomes due.

b. *Voting Plans*

A voting plan attempts to dilute the voting power of a bidder through the distribution to shareholders of preferred stock carrying special voting rights. Upon the occurrence of a triggering event, the voting strength of the poison pill stock may increase sharply in the hands of non-bidders or decrease sharply in the bidder's hands.

The plan adopted by Asarco Incorporated, for example, provided for the distribution of a new series of preferred stock that initially carried no voting power. Upon the occurrence of a triggering event (one person or group's acquiring 20 percent of any class of stock), the stock would gain significant voting power in the hands of all shareholders except the 20-percent shareholder who made the acquisition. A federal district court enjoined the implementation of the voting plan under New Jersey law, holding that Asarco lacked authority to issue preferred stock that would create different voting rights within the same class.[844] A federal court in New York, applying Delaware law, enjoined implementation of a similar plan adopted by Richardson-Vicks, Inc.[845]

CityFed Financial Corporation also instituted a voting plan under which it issued, as a dividend on common stock, new preferred stock carrying significant voting power. The occurrence of triggering events, including the accumulation by one person (or group) of five percent of the new preferred or 15 percent of the outstanding voting securities, automatically would dilute the voting power of the new preferred in the hands of the five- or 15-percent holder to 1/100 of its former strength. A federal district court in New Jersey refused to enjoin implementation of CityFed's plan.[846]

c. *Debt Plans*

A different type of poison pill, essentially a recapitalization designed to take effect only on the occurrence of a triggering event, was adopted by AMF Incorporated as a defense against a takeover by corporate "raider" Irwin Jacobs. A federal court enjoined the use of this plan in *Minstar Acquiring Corp. v. AMF Inc.*[847]

Minstar, controlled by Jacobs, made a tender offer for AMF in April 1985, after getting a "running start" by purchasing 7.5 percent of AMF's shares. If successful, the tender offer would

---

844. *Asarco Inc. v. Holmes A Court*, 611 F. Supp. 468 (D.N.J. 1985), discussed in detail in § III.4.C(2), *infra*.

845. *Unilever Acquisition Corp. v. Richardson-Vicks, Inc.*, 618 F. Supp. 407 (S.D.N.Y. 1985).

846. *City Federal Savings and Loan Ass'n v. Mann*, No. 84 – 4010 (D.N.J. Aug. 5, 1985).

847. 621 F. Supp. 1252 (S.D.N.Y. 1985).

have given Minstar 50.5 percent of AMF's stock. The AMF board, taking particular note of the potential for a back-end merger at a lower price, unanimously rejected Minstar's offer as inadequate and not in the shareholders' best interests. The board also adopted both an employee benefit plan[848] and a rights plan designed to thwart Minstar's hostile bid.

Under the rights plan, AMF would issue, as a dividend to all stockholders of record as of May 20, 1985, one right for each share of common stock. The non-transferable rights would entitle the holders to exchange one share of common stock for a package consisting of a $5.75 principal share of 14.5 percent subordinated debentures, due in 1995, and one-tenth of a share of new preferred stock. The rights would become exercisable only after a person acquired 30 percent of AMF's common stock, and then only for forty days; they would become unredeemable upon a change of control. The debentures carried restrictions on AMF's ability to incur additional debt or to sell or transfer assets; the new preferred stock carried substantial dividend rights (set at an annual rate of 15.5 percent, calculated on the liquidation price of $172.50 per share). The new preferred had no voting rights unless accrued dividends were unpaid, in which case the new preferred shareholders would be able to elect two board members. The plan also required that any merger be approved by the new preferred stockholders voting as a class.

In preliminarily enjoining the rights plan, the court found the "non-transferability of the Rights in the instant case [to be] the fatal flaw."[849] This non-transferability provision would divide common stockholders into two classes: pre-May 20 shareholders (who received the rights dividend) and post-May 20 shareholders (who did not). Relying on *Asarco Inc. v. Holmes A Court*,[850] the court reasoned that defendants had violated the corporation law of New Jersey (where AMF was incorporated) by according significantly different rights to shareholders of the same class,

848. *See infra* § III.4.G(2).

849. 621 F. Supp. at 1258.

850. 611 F. Supp. 468 (D.N.J. 1985), discussed in detail in § III.4.C(2), *infra*.

based upon when they purchased their shares. The court also held that the non-transferability provision unreasonably restrained the alienability of the common stock and that the plan had the "impermissible effect of vesting veto power over any merger in the hands of the non-tendering May 20th stockholders."[851] Such major structural and voting changes, the court declared, must be approved by the shareholders.

The court also enjoined issuance of the debentures because they constituted an "integral part" of the rights plan. In dictum, the court noted its "grave doubt that the restrictions on incurring new debt and the restraint on the transfer of more than 1% of AMF's assets may be validly accomplished by the unilateral action of the Board. . . ."[852]

4. Possible Antidotes

Rights plans of any variety do not render a target company invulnerable to attack and do not relieve the board of directors of its duty to consider an acquisition offer if one is made, particularly because the directors typically reserve the power to redeem the rights. As the Delaware Supreme Court stated in *Moran v. Household International, Inc.*, "[t]he ultimate response to an actual takeover bid must be judged by the Directors' actions at that time, and nothing we say here relieves them of their basic fundamental duties to the corporation and its stockholders."[853]

The following sections discuss a number of ways to deal with rights plans. More methods are likely to be devised.

a. High Minimum

A bidder can attempt to evade the deleterious effects of a poison pill by conditioning its tender offer on the tender of a high

851. 621 F. Supp. at 1259.

852. *Id.*

853. 500 A.2d 1346, 1357 (Del. 1985).

percentage—say 95 percent—of the rights. Even this strategy, however, might not neutralize the pill because, in the case of a call plan, the remaining five percent of the rights still would have a substantial dilutive effect. Rights issued under a put plan would pose less of a problem.

b. No Back-End Merger

If a company has only a typical call plan (without an automatic "flip-in" provision triggered by an acquiror's exceeding a specified ownership level), a bidder could content itself with buying enough stock to take control of the company but could refrain from effecting a merger (to gain 100 percent of the shares) or from engaging in any of the self-dealing transactions that would trigger the rights. Sir James Goldsmith adopted precisely this technique in his bid for Crown Zellerbach, which had a *Household*-type call plan. Sir James notified Crown of his intention to buy more than 20 percent of the company's stock and thus to make the rights unredeemable. Crown's directors did not redeem the rights; Sir James bought more than 20 percent, and he eventually acquired control of the board. As a result, neither Sir James' acquisition vehicle nor any other bidder could merge with Crown without triggering the rights' dilutive effect. As noted above, James River Corporation exchanged shares with Crown Zellerbach in a transaction designed to sidestep the rights plan.

Adopting both a put plan and a call plan, however, would tend to deter even a bidder like Goldsmith from exceeding the threshold ownership level, even if he did not plan to effect a merger. Thus, a company with a plan could, if threatened by such a bidder, adopt a put plan once the hostile bid is announced, with the put price set to take account of existing circumstances. Alternatively, the company could adopt an automatic "flip-in" provision in the initial call plan. This strategy, however, may not be advisable.

In any event, not all bidders will be willing to buy control of a target without being able to effect a merger or to engage in self-dealing transactions. If, for example, the bidder needs access to the target's assets to repay debts incurred to finance the acquisition, the bidder's lenders might well insist that the bidder be able to acquire 100 percent of the target's outstanding share. Some bidders also will want to acquire 100 percent of the company to avoid having to face charges of conflicts of interest that minority shareholders might raise.

c. *Redemption of the Rights*

A bidder could ask the board to redeem the rights. This "request" might be made in one of several ways.

Unless the rights immediately become unredeemable as soon as an acquiror crosses whatever line the company has drawn, a bidder who acquires more than 50 percent of the company's shares could act by consent, under the Delaware statute, to remove the incumbent directors and to vote in a new slate that would redeem the rights before they became unredeemable. This option, however, might not be available if the company's charter (which can be amended only by a vote of the shareholders) curtails action by consent or if its bylaws (which, within limits, can be amended by director action) provide for the lapse of a period of time before the taking of action by consent.

Alternatively, before acquiring whatever percentage of the target's stock would make the rights unredeemable, the bidder could wage a proxy fight to elect a new slate of directors committed to redeeming the rights in the event of a tender offer for at least a minimum price per share. The bidder could couple its proxy fight with a tender offer at an attractive price, conditioned on redemption of the rights. If the company has a classified board of directors, however, and if the classification cannot be repealed without a supermajority vote requiring more shares than the bidder owns, the bidder will not be able to elect a majority of the directors at any one meeting of shareholders.

A third, and weaker, approach would be for the bidder to wage a proxy fight in support of a non-binding, precatory shareholder proposal requesting the directors to redeem the rights. Cooper Laboratories tried this method in 1985, as a shareholder of the Rorer Group. But although the majority of Rorer shares voted to ask Rorer's directors to redeem the company's poison pill, the directors nevertheless declined to do so.

d. *Conditional Offer*

A bidder might condition its tender offer on the redemption of the rights by the target's directors. If a vast majority of the shares are tendered pursuant to the offer, and if the board has not been able to find a more favorable alternative for the shareholders, the target's directors might find themselves under considerable pressure to redeem the rights. Directors may well realize that, if they do not redeem the rights and if the offeror terminates its offer, the price of the company's stock could sink well below the tender offer price, and the directors themselves could face potentially troublesome litigation for failing to remove a barrier to an offer that the shareholders found attractive. A bidder might put additional pressure on the target's board by making a two-fold tender offer at a generous per-share price if the rights are redeemed but at a lesser per-share price (although still at a premium over market) if the rights are not redeemed.

5. Advantages and Disadvantages of Rights Plans

a. *Advantages*

The principal advantage of the various kinds of rights plans is that they encourage a bidder to deal directly with the target's board before trying to acquire the company. Directors presumably know more about the company's value and prospects than do the shareholders, and they are not susceptible to the "prisoner's dilemma" that may induce shareholders to accept a tender offer at almost any premium over market price. Thus, the board may be able to negotiate a better transaction than the shareholders would receive if the bidder went to them directly with an unsolicited tender offer. A put or back-end right in particular helps to insure that all shareholders will receive fair value for their shares.

Rights plans (either put or call) also may give a target's directors more time to consider and respond to an acquisition proposal than they otherwise would have in the event of a hostile tender offer, which must remain open for only 20 business days. If a company has adopted a rights plan, a bidder might be encouraged first to approach the target's board to negotiate a transaction. If negotiations prove fruitless, some of the alternatives available to the bidder (for example, a proxy fight or consent solicitation) may take longer to complete than would a hostile tender offer. Meanwhile, the target has gained extra time, which the directors can use to consider more advantageous alternatives to the bidder's proposal—for example, a merger or other transaction with an alternative suitor (a "white knight"), or a recapitalization.

In addition, a rights plan could reduce the chance of an outsider's winning control of a company through a proxy fight: the plan might deter the outsider (individually or as part of a group of dissident shareholders) from buying an amount of stock exceeding the plan's threshold level, and, without a sizable position in the target's stock, an outsider might have difficulty prevailing in a proxy fight. Nevertheless, the outsider might succeed by presenting an attractive economic proposal to the shareholders (such as, "vote for my slate, and we will redeem the rights to allow any tender offer at a price of $X or higher").

Finally, a rights plan may induce a bidder to make as attractive an offer as possible (such as an "any and all" cash offer) in order to maximize the pressure on the board to redeem the rights. This result would directly benefit all shareholders.

b. Disadvantages

By deterring unsolicited tender offers made directly to shareholders, a rights plan may discourage bidders from proposing acquisitions that the stockholders might find attractive. As noted above, however, a poison pill does not deter bidders from proposing acquisitions to the directors, and it may help the directors to obtain the best deal possible.

Rights plans tend not to be popular with institutional shareholders. Indeed, it is possible that institutional investors might try to require corporations adopting poison pills to include in their proxy statements a shareholder proposal requesting the board to allow shareholders to vote on the question whether the rights should be redeemed.

Another disadvantage may arise from the use of a call plan: as the Goldsmith-Crown Zellerbach story[854] illustrates, a call plan that does not include an automatic "flip-in" provision may encourage a bidder to acquire a majority of a target's stock without effecting a merger. Once the call rights become unredeemable, the target might have trouble merging with a white knight, because the white knight would suffer dilution in the event of a merger. The Crown Zellerbach situation, however, may be unique because, unlike Goldsmith, many bidders would be reluctant to obtain control of a company without being able to acquire 100 percent of its equity through a follow-up merger; they also would be concerned that the self-dealing provisions of a call plan might prohibit them from engaging in certain kinds of transactions with their newly acquired company. Moreover, directors who wish to consummate a white knight transaction usually can redeem the rights before the bidder crosses the magic line and the rights become unredeemable; alternatively, the directors can adopt a put plan to deter the bidder from buying more shares.

Because a rights plan usually gives the board significant leverage in negotiating with a bidder, it is conceivable that a court considering the directors' response to an acquisition offer might hold the directors of a company with a rights plan to a higher fiduciary standard (or might impose on the directors a heavier burden of proof) than would be the case in the absence of the plan. However, the Delaware Supreme Court has stated that directors deciding whether to redeem rights in the face of a

---

854. *See supra* § III.4.B(1)(f).

tender offer "will be held to the same fiduciary standards any other board of directors would be held to in deciding to adopt a defensive mechanism, the same standards as they were held to in originally approving the Rights Plan."[855]

A call rights plan involves the dedication of a substantial number of authorized but unissued shares. The company cannot issue the rights without shareholder approval unless it already has sufficient authorized but unissued shares in reserve, in case the rights should in fact be exercised.

By adopting a put plan, the board creates the possibility of a major recapitalization that could saddle the company with sizable debt or substantial dividend requirements. Although the dividends or interest on the senior securities will benefit all shareholders (other than the one who triggers the exercisability of the puts), the resulting recapitalization may adversely affect the company's relations with lenders, who may be concerned about, among other things, the decrease in the company's equity, the possibility of fraudulent conveyances, and the difficulty of obtaining waivers or consents from the public holders of the senior securities to be issued on exercise of the puts. For the same reasons, the possible recapitalization may adversely affect an issuer's credit rating.

A put plan also may require the issuer's board to determine in advance a fair price for the company's stock. Fairness, of course, depends on various circumstances, which may change rapidly. Thus, a company might wish to defer implementing a put plan pending the appearance of a bidder who is not deterred by a call plan. The board then could set the put price in light of the existing circumstances.

A company adopting any form of rights plan would have to disclose that plan in any proxy statement seeking shareholder approval of a shark repellent charter amendment, and the existence of the plan might make shareholders less willing to vote for the shark repellent. The rights plan, however, might be as much of a shark repellent as the company needs. In any event, it

---

855. *Moran v. Household Int'l, Inc.*, 500 A.2d 1346, 1354 (Del. 1985).

is questionable whether the existence of a pill would have any effect on shareholders' willingness to approve, for example, a proposal to classify the board or to require supermajority voting.

Some critics have suggested that a rights plan may adversely affect the market price of a company's shares. The evidence on this point, however, is inconclusive. In fact, a March 5, 1986 study by the SEC's Office of the Chief Economist concerning the short-term effect of such plans on market prices concluded that an announcement of a rights plan in the midst of takeover speculation results in an average decline of 2.4 percent in the price of the issuer's shares, while an announcement in the absence of takeover speculation does not have any statistically significant impact on market price. Other, more complete, studies by investment bankers have concluded that the mere announcement of the adoption of a rights plan, absent pending takeover speculation about the target, does not have a significant impact on the market price of the rights issuer's shares.

A more recent study by the SEC's Office of the Chief Economist, however, concludes that poison pills can decrease shareholder wealth. The study of 245 companies focused on "long-term changes in stock prices for 30 companies involved in change of control contests and on changes in stock prices for all 245 companies over a two day period during which adoption of poison pills were [*sic*] announced."* The SEC economists found that adoption of pills caused "price declines for firms with imminent takeover threats" and "negative price effects for certain types of pills when no threat is imminent."** The data were statistically significant.

What the future holds for poison pills is unclear. It *is* clear, however, that rights plans have generated a considerable amount of controversy. Supporters claim that the plans enable target management to negotiate more effectively on behalf of shareholders and to protect them from inadequate, partial, or

---

*SEC, " 'Poison Pills' Decrease Shareholder Wealth, Study Finds," News Release 86–65, at 1 (Oct. 28, 1986).

***Id.* at 2.

two-tier offers, as well as from other allegedly abusive practices. Critics contend that pills deter takeovers and proxy contests, entrench possibly inept management, and constitute recapitalizations effected without shareholder approval.

The SEC recently issued a Concept Release[856] discussing the debate on pills and seeking information about their use, costs, and benefits. The Release also solicited comment concerning the desirability of a governmental response, on the state or federal level, to the issues raised by these plans.

C. Restructured Voting Rights

Another defense that has been used by a number of companies is the restructuring of shareholders' voting rights to concentrate voting power in friendly hands.[857] This tactic generally takes one of two forms: the company either creates two classes of common stock with disparate voting rights or issues a new class of supervoting preferred stock. The first approach, dual-class common stock, requires shareholder approval of a charter amendment and thus is useful only as part of the company's advance planning. Once a hostile acquiror has appeared and the target must react quickly, use of blank check preferred to create a new issue of supervoting preferred stock (a method not requiring shareholder approval) usually is preferable.

1. Dual-Class Common Stock

In order to create dual-class common stock, the company must obtain shareholder approval to amend the certificate of incorporation. If the company does not have authorized but

856. Exchange Act Release No. 23486, [Current] Fed. Sec. L. Rep. (CCH) ¶ 84,018 (July 31, 1986).

857. For a general discussion of unequal voting rights plans, see J. Seligman, *The One Share, One Vote Controversy*, Investor Responsibility Research Center, Inc. (January 1986).

unissued shares in its treasury, it also will need shareholder approval to authorize additional shares of common stock. A number of companies, including Coastal, Hechinger, People Express, and Wang Laboratories, have implemented dual-class common stock plans. The validity of dual-class common stock, however, has not been extensively litigated—probably because the companies' shareholders approved the plans.

The American Stock Exchange and the National Association of Securities Dealers permit dual-class common stock, within certain limits. In the fall of 1986, the New York Stock Exchange proposed a rule permitting the listing of dual-class common stock with disparate voting rights, provided that certain conditions are satisfied. The rule cannot take effect without the SEC's approval. The American Stock Exchange recently approved a proposal eliminating all restrictions on the issuance of dual-class common.

a. Terms

i. Voting and Dividend Rights

Dual-class common stock generally is structured so that one class has low-voting shares (one vote per share) and the other has high-voting shares (for example, ten votes per share). The high-voting shares often carry lesser rights with regard to dividends, liquidation, and transferability. These high-voting, low-dividend shares consequently will be attractive only to those shareholders whose primary interest is in control of the company, while the low-voting, high-dividend shares will be attractive to most other investors.

The classes typically vote separately for the election of directors, with the class holding the low-dividend shares electing the majority of the board, but the two classes usually vote together on other matters. The low-voting shareholders generally retain the power to elect at least 25 percent of the company's directors, in compliance with American Stock Exchange requirements.[858]

---

858. *See infra* § III.4.C(1)(c)(ii).

ii. Convertibility

All common shareholders are given the opportunity to own shares in either of the common stock classes, through either an exchange offer[859] or a convertibility feature of the high-voting stock. Most companies implementing a dual-class common stock plan anticipate that management and other inside shareholders will elect to retain the high-voting securities, while other shareholders will prefer the high-dividend securities. Although most plans allow shareholders to convert from high-voting to low-voting stock at any time, some plans grant this right for only a limited period of time, in order to induce shareholders to convert immediately and thus to reduce the size of the high-voting class and to concentrate voting power in fewer hands.

iii. Transferability

Under most plans, shareholders cannot transfer the high-voting class of securities and must convert their holdings into low-voting shares before selling them. Some companies provide for the automatic conversion of high-voting stock into low-voting stock upon transfer. This feature encourages shareholders to convert their stock, thereby increasing management's voting control.

b. Distribution

The issuer can distribute high-voting common stock to shareholders as a dividend on either common or preferred stock or through an exchange offer. Exchange offer distribution avoids the need for a convertibility mechanism and for conversion incentives. Management shareholders immediately can exercise their exchange rights and acquire their enhanced voting power, while investment-oriented shareholders can refrain from exercising their rights.

---

859. *See infra* §§ III.4.E and G.

c. *Exchange Rules*

i. New York Stock Exchange

Until 1986, the New York Stock Exchange ("NYSE") prohibited the listing of companies having classes of common stock with disparate voting rights. This rule was often referred to as a "one share/one vote" rule. The NYSE recently asked the SEC to approve a revision of this policy to allow dual-class common stock under certain circumstances.

Under the proposed rule, the NYSE will permit a listed company to have dual-class common stock with disparate voting rights if a majority of shares of the company's publicly held common stock *and* a majority of the company's independent directors affirmatively approve the disparate voting rights. The new rule also will grant currently listed companies that are in violation of the rule a period of two years within which to come into compliance.

ii. American Stock Exchange

The American Stock Exchange ("AMEX") permits listing of dual-class common stock with disparate voting rights. However, the AMEX has issued the following guidelines:

1. the low-voting class of common stock must be able to elect at least 25 percent of the board of directors;
2. the ratio of disparity of the voting power between the classes must not exceed ten to one;
3. the company may not create additional common or preferred stock that can diminish the voting power of the low-voting class;
4. if the high-voting class accounts for less than a certain percentage of the company's total capitalization, the high-voting shares must lose certain of their attributes; *and*
5. while not required, dividend preferences should accompany the low-voting common stock.

In November 1986, however, the AMEX's Board of Governors approved a proposal to amend the AMEX's rules to end any restrictions on dual-class issuances by listed companies.*

iii. NASD

The National Association of Securities Dealers ("NASD") currently has no voting restrictions on listed dual-class common stock. In the past year, however, the NASD has considered two proposals governing the voting rights of classes of common stock issued by NASDAQ/National Market System companies. The first proposal would mandate one share/one vote for all classes of common stock of such companies. The second proposal would permit classes of common stock with disparate voting rights if the creation of such classes were approved by the holders of at least two-thirds of the outstanding shares entitled to vote and were reapproved every ten years thereafter by a similar vote. In addition, the difference in voting rights between such classes could not exceed ten to one. Both proposals would exempt existing classes of common stock with disparate voting rights from the new rules under a "grandfather" provision.[860]

d. Proposed Legislation

In 1985, Senator Alfonse D'Amato and Representative John Dingell introduced bills[861] designed to implement the one share/one vote rule as a matter of federal law. The proposed legislation would amend the Exchange Act to prohibit registration with any stock exchange or with the NASD of securities having disparate voting rights within a class. The bills would permit currently listed companies having dual-class common stock with unequal voting rights to remain listed on an exchange or NASDAQ if the

---

**See* 51 Fed. Reg. 41, 717 n. 23 (Nov. 18, 1986) (citing Letter from Arthur Levitt, Jr., to John S.R. Shad, dated Nov. 10, 1986).

860. *Cf.* Sec. Reg. & L. Rep. vol. 18, no. 12 (March 21, 1986) at 389 (discussing study for NASD by Daniel Fischel, who found no benefit from prohibiting trading of common stock with dual classes of voting rights).

861. H.R. 2783 and S. 1314, 99th Cong., 1st Sess. (1985).

issuers were admitted to listed trading prior to June 17, 1985, and remained continuously listed. Companies failing to meet these requirements would have two years within which to conform their securities' voting rights before being subject to delisting.

2. Supervoting Preferred Stock

Unlike dual-class common stock, supervoting preferred stock has been the subject of a number of recent judicial opinions. Because companies usually issue supervoting preferred stock by using existing blank check preferred, and thus need not obtain shareholder approval of the plans, courts have been troubled by changes in common shareholders' voting rights or by restrictions on the alienability of common stock.

Supervoting preferred stock generally accords supervoting rights to all shareholders except those who hold large numbers of shares. Another variation, used in at least one plan, is to grant favorable voting rights to long-term investors. Some plans specify a trigger giving rise to enhanced voting rights; others do not. Unlike the usual type of poison pill, which attempts to make a hostile takeover financially infeasible or undesirable, supervoting preferred does not erect financial obstacles to an acquisition of shares; instead, it thwarts a hostile acquiror's ability to elect its own slate of directors to amend the issuer's charter or bylaws, or, perhaps, to block a white knight deal.

In *Unilever Acquisition Corp. v. Richardson-Vicks, Inc.*,[862] a federal district court granted a preliminary injunction against Richardson-Vicks' issuance of preferred stock that would carry different voting rights if transferred. Richardson-Vicks had announced the plan as a defensive move in response to a takeover attempt by Unilever.

Unilever initially had approached Richardson-Vicks with a "friendly" any and all offer of $54 per share. When Richardson-

862. 618 F. Supp. 407 (S.D.N.Y. 1985).

Vicks rejected the proposal, Unilever brought suit and announced a cash tender offer for all shares at $56 per share, if the Richardson-Vicks board would approve the offer, or at $48 per share, if the board would not. The next day, without shareholder approval, Richardson-Vicks' board responded by announcing the issuance of a dividend of preferred stock: one share of preferred for each five shares of common. The new preferred stock allowed the holder to cast 25 votes per share unless the share were transferred, in which case the new holder would be able to cast only five votes per share for 36 months following the transfer. Because the Richardson family held approximately one-third of the company's outstanding common shares, issuance of the new preferred stock would prevent Unilever from gaining voting control for 36 months even if it purchased all shares held outside the Richardson family.

The court held that the preferred stock issuance violated both Delaware law and the company's certificate of incorporation. The court deemed the shift in the preferred stock's voting power to be a restriction on transferability inconsistent with section 202(b) of Delaware's General Corporation Law; it also concluded that the plan discriminated among holders of the same issue of stock, in violation of Richardson-Vicks' certificate of incorporation, which allows the board to set terms for the issuance of preferred stock only if all shares have identical voting rights. "Under Delaware law," the court concluded, "a change in corporate structure of this magnitude, reducing the transferability of a shareholder's ability to vote and the value of his or her asset to this degree, requires stockholder approval which has not been obtained."[863]

Similarly, in *Asarco Inc. v. Holmes A Court*,[864] another federal court preliminarily enjoined the issuance of preferred stock that would carry significantly less voting power in the hands of a 20-percent stockholder than in the hands of an owner of less than 20 percent. The court held that the New Jersey Business

863. *Id.* at 410.

864. 611 F. Supp. 468 (D.N.J. 1985).

Corporation Act did not permit the corporation or its directors to issue or modify classes of stock to create different voting rights within the same class.

Corporate raider M.R.H. Holmes A Court, through open-market purchases, had acquired a substantial interest in Asarco. Believing that Holmes A Court's takeover tactics might not be beneficial to the company's shareholders, Asarco's board unanimously approved the issuance of preferred stock dividends to all common stockholders, who would receive one-tenth of a share of preferred for each share of common. The preferred stock initially would carry no voting rights; however, if any person or group acquired 20 percent of the common or 20 percent of the new preferred, each one-tenth of a share of new preferred owned by shareholders other than the 20-percent holder would carry five votes. These voting rights could be extinguished by an any and all cash offer conforming to certain specified fair price criteria.

Declining to rule that the directors had breached their duties of care and loyalty by issuing the new preferred stock, the court held that the board's decision was protected under New Jersey law by the business judgment rule. "The fact that the independent Asarco directors own shares of stock which may be affected by the [new preferred stock issuance] and that their likelihood of reelection is enhanced, is not sufficient to deprive their decision of the benefit of the business judgment rule."[865] Because the plan altered the structure of the corporation, "removing decisions in takeover matters from individual stockholders and reposing them in the Board," the court placed on the directors "the burden of articulating the reasonableness of their plan"; plaintiffs, however, still bore the "burden of persuasion."[866] The court held that plaintiffs had not sustained their burden.

However, the court concluded that the issuance of the new preferred stock was invalid under New Jersey's corporation

865. *Id.* at 473.
866. *Id.* at 474.

statute. Although it rejected plaintiffs' argument that New Jersey law permits the issuance of blank check stock only for corporate financing purposes, the court held that New Jersey law does not authorize the issuance of stock having different voting rights within each class. The new Series C Preferred Stock, explained the court, "would have different voting rights within the series, depending upon whether or not a Series C share were held by a 20 percent holder. In light of the piggyback aspect of the issuance of the Preferred Stock the common stock would have different voting rights depending on presence or absence of 20 percent ownership."[867] The court therefore enjoined the issuance of the new preferred stock.

Yet another preliminary injunction issued in *Packer v. Yampol*,[868] in which the court enjoined the voting of two newly issued series of supervoting preferred stock. The suit was filed by the Lafer, Amster group, which sought to wage a proxy contest for control of Graphic Scanning Corporation.

On February 14, 1986, the Lafer, Amster group filed an amended Schedule 13D, disclosing that the group owned 10.6 percent of Graphic's common stock and that it might wage a proxy contest. On February 20, 1986, the day that Graphic's directors first learned of the amended 13D, three directors met with Graphic's attorneys to discuss and respond to the Schedule. Four days later, the Graphic board approved the issuance of 52,500 shares of Series A preferred stock to Barry Yampol, Graphic's chairman and chief executive officer, for $5,250,000. Each share of Series A stock carried 140 votes.

Graphic's board also issued 100,000 shares of Series B preferred stock to Monar Company, N.V., and Battery, N.V., two friendly Netherlands Antilles corporations controlled by Dibo Attar (an Italian investor), for $10,000,000. In addition, Monar and Battery received two-year warrants for one million shares of Graphic common stock at $8.75 per share. The holders of Series B stock were entitled to vote on certain matters, and the

867. *Id.* at 477–78.

868. No. 8432 (Del. Ch. April 18, 1986).

affirmative votes of 80 percent of Series B shares were required to approve certain mergers, asset sales, and other transactions if (i) any entity acquired voting securities representing 50 percent or more of the votes entitled to be cast to elect directors, (ii) a majority of Graphic's directors were replaced, or (iii) Yampol's ownership of the Series A preferred stock were reduced to 80 percent or less.

The Series A and B preferred stock together represented 33 percent of Graphic's total voting power. When added to Yampol's common stock holdings, the new preferred stock put 44 percent of the voting power in the hands of Monar, Battery, and Yampol.

The Delaware Chancery Court concluded that the issuance of preferred stock constituted a manipulation of corporate machinery primarily for the purpose of entrenching management. The court noted that "[t]he protections of the business judgment rule are available only to directors who are independent and disinterested with respect to the transaction under challenge"[869] and that Graphic's directors "had professional, financial and personal relationships with Yampol, and received financial benefits from the company of which he was Chairman, which suggests a motivation for such directors' loyalty to Yampol and dependence upon his continued goodwill."[870] The court did not decide whether Graphic could issue supervoting preferred stock either under Delaware law or under its own charter.

In rejecting defendants' position that the stock had been issued primarily to raise capital, the court noted that Attar (who controlled Monar and Battery) had known of the proxy contest with plaintiffs; that Graphic had never before used supervoting preferred stock to solve its cash flow problems; that, one year earlier, Graphic had considered supervoting preferred stock as an anti-takeover measure; that the timing of the stock issuance and the related negotiations indicated an entrenchment purpose;

869. Slip op. at 35.

870. *Id.*

that defendants had failed to explain why the issuance could not have been made conditional upon the preferred stock's not being voted in the upcoming election; and that defendants had failed to take a number of logical capital raising moves, such as enlisting the services of an investment banker. The court observed that the new preferred stock carried the right to exercise one-third of the total voting power as well as to veto mergers and significant asset sales; moreover, preferred shareholders received warrants to purchase one million shares for $15,250,000 (plus $100 for the warrants). "To purchase the equivalent voting power a purchaser of common stock would have had to pay $155,000,000 at the current market prices."[871]

Somewhat akin to supervoting preferred is preferred stock carrying class veto power. In *Telvest, Inc. v. Olson*,[872] the Delaware Chancery Court enjoined the issuance, during a takeover battle, of dividends of such stock. Under a supermajority class voting provision, holders of 20 percent of the new stock would have been able to block certain extraordinary transactions, including any hostile merger with a party owning 20 percent or more of the target's outstanding shares. The court held that the provision requiring a supermajority class vote impermissibly altered the voting rights of the target's shareholders without their approval.

In *National Education Corp. v. Bell & Howell Co.*,[873] however, the author of the *Telvest* opinion declined to enjoin an issuance of preferred stock as a dividend paid to Bell & Howell's common shareholders even though the terms of the stock provided that preferred shareholders must approve certain mergers and other transactions by an 80 percent class vote. The court distinguished *Telvest* by pointing out that Bell & Howell's preferred stock, unlike that in *Telvest*, had real economic value as preferred stock and had not been issued to entrench incumbent management in the heat of a takeover battle:

---

871. *Id.* at 46.

872. No. 5798 (Del. Ch. March 8, 1979).

873. C.A. No. 7278 (Del. Ch. Aug. 25, 1983).

> I must confess at this point that I am not totally convinced that the rationale in *Telvest* controls here. I remain of the opinion that the decision was a proper one on its facts. The piggyback preferred stock that was to be issued there as a stock dividend to the common shareholders was clearly a sham insofar as it purported to be preferred stock. It carried no real preferences whatever other than a grant of increased voting power. So viewed, it was nothing more than an attempt by a board of directors, by resolution, to change the existing voting rights of the common shareholders without their consent so as to make hostile acquisition of the corporation more difficult to achieve. Moreover, it was action taken in direct response to an ongoing hostile take-over attempt.
>
> That factual situation is not present here. In this case the new preferred stock does have rights in addition to those relating to voting power. It is said that the new preferred will have independent trading value. . . . It is not clear on the present record that plaintiff will be able to show that the action constitutes an improper manipulation of the corporate machinery for the purpose of entrenching incumbent management, even though that may constitute an inevitable by-product to a degree.[874]

Plaintiff argued that Bell & Howell's board lacked the authority to issue the new preferred stock without shareholder approval. Bell & Howell responded—and the court agreed—that the Delaware legislature had amended the Delaware Corporation Law expressly to undo part of the effect of *Telvest*, and this amendment allowed a corporation's certificate of incorporation to authorize the board to fix preferred stock preferences and voting rights by resolution. Bell & Howell's certificate of incorporation included such a provision.

874. Slip op. at 10.

3. Other Voting Restructuring Plans

Other companies, with shareholder approval, have adopted variations on the dual-class stock and supervoting preferred stock plans. J.M. Smucker and American Family, among others, did not create dual-class stock but adopted charter amendments under which common stockholders who have held their shares for at least four years are entitled to ten votes per share, while stockholders who have held their shares for fewer than four years receive only one vote per share. Stock held in "street" name is presumed to have been held for fewer than four years.

Other plans, like Asarco's,[875] have limited the voting power of large shareholders without creating new preferred stock or a second class of common stock. MCI and Figgie International Holdings have adopted such plans by charter amendment. The Delaware Supreme Court has upheld the legality of a charter amendment providing that holders of more than a specified amount of stock may vote only a fraction of their total holdings.[876]

The key distinction between these variations and the supervoting stock issuances that the courts have struck down[877] is that the variations were implemented with shareholder approval. Before adopting a charter amendment creating disparate voting rights, companies also should check the current rules of the pertinent self-regulatory organization(s): the NYSE, the AMEX, or the NASD.[878]

---

875. *See supra* § III.4.C(2).

876. *Providence & Worcester Co. v. Baker*, 378 A.2d 121 (Del. 1977).

877. *See supra* § III.4.C(2).

878. *See supra* § III.4.C(1)(c).

D. Antitrust Challenges

Corporate raiders often seek to acquire a target because the target's business would complement or support their own. Sometimes a target will sue a raider on antitrust grounds, alleging that the combination of the two businesses would be anticompetitive. Moreover, a target occasionally will acquire assets during or in anticipation of a tender offer to create or support an antitrust claim.

1. Acquisitions by Target

In *Panter v. Marshall Field & Co.*,[879] the Court of Appeals for the Seventh Circuit held that the presumptions of Delaware's business judgment rule applied to defensive acquisitions and other decisions made by a target's directors in the face of a hostile tender offer. Carter Hawley Hale ("CHH"), a national retail chain, had announced its intention to acquire Marshall Field, another operator of retail department stores. After determining that the company should expand internally and that an acquisition by CHH would pose serious antitrust problems in light of the existing and potential competition between the two retailers, Field's board refused to negotiate with CHH, filed an antitrust suit against the bidder, and pursued acquisition and expansion plans that exacerbated the antitrust problems of a Field-CHH combination. Field shareholders sued to enjoin the board's defensive tactics, contending that "the defendants breached their fiduciary duty as directors to the corporation and its shareholders by adopting a secret policy to resist acquisition regardless of benefit to the shareholders or the corporation; by failing to disclose the existence of such a policy; by making defensive acquisitions; and by filing an antitrust suit against CHH."[880]

---

879. 646 F.2d 271 (7th Cir.), *cert. denied*, 454 U.S. 1092 (1981).

880. *Id.* at 293.

The district court and the Court of Appeals ruled that plaintiffs had not adduced sufficient evidence of bad faith, overreaching, self-dealing, or other fraud to overcome the presumptions of the business judgment rule. The court noted that a majority of the directors were independent and that the board had relied on expert advice. Moreover, defendants had adduced "uncontrovertible evidence" that the acquisitions were a "reasonable and natural" expansion of Field's business. Thus, declared the court,

> even if the desire to fend off CHH was among the motives of the board in entering the transaction, because the plaintiffs had failed to establish that such a motive was the sole or primary purpose, as has been required by Delaware law since the leading case of *Cheff v. Mathes*, . . . the mere allegation, or even some proof, that a given transaction was made on "unfavorable" terms does not meet the fairly stringent burden the business judgment rules imposes [*sic*] on plaintiffs.[881]

Royal Industries, Inc. v. Monogram Industries, Inc.,[882] however, reached a somewhat different conclusion. A federal district court there held that a target's directors, by deciding to acquire a competitor of the company that had launched a tender offer for the target, had breached their fiduciary duty because the proposed acquisition was intended solely to thwart the tender offer. Applying California law, the court concluded that the acquisition served no business purpose, was a waste of corporate assets, and catered only to the interests of the target's management, to the shareholders' detriment. The court therefore enjoined the acquisition.

---

881. *Id.* at 297 (footnote and citation omitted).

882. [1976–1977 Transfer Binder] Fed. Sec. L. Rep. (CCH) ¶ 95,863, at 91,136 (C.D. Cal. Nov. 29, 1976).

2. Standing of Target Under the Clayton Act

Instead of (or in addition to) making its own defensive acquisitions in an effort to block a pending or threatened takeover attempt, a target might sue to enjoin the proposed hostile takeover on the ground that consummation of the transaction would violate section 7 of the Clayton Act.[883] Section 7 prohibits mergers, acquisitions, and other combinations "where in any line of commerce or in any activity affecting commerce in any section of the country, the effect of such acquisition may be substantially to lessen competition, or to tend to create a monopoly."[884] If the offeror engages in a line of commerce that is similar to (or that overlaps) that of the offeree, the target might claim that a combination of the two companies might substantially lessen competition or tend to create a monopoly in the market(s) in which the two companies currently compete.

Faced with a Clayton Act allegation, defendant bidders frequently assert that target companies lack standing under section 7 and that only the Federal Trade Commission and the Department of Justice may challenge the acquisition on antitrust grounds. Questions of antitrust standing, especially in the context of section 7, inevitably revolve around the Supreme Court's ruling in *Brunswick Corp. v. Pueblo Bowl-O-Mat, Inc.*[885] and the concept of "antitrust injury."

The *Brunswick* case was filed by several bowling centers, which alleged that defendant had violated section 7 by acquiring and operating other bowling centers that were on the verge of going out of business. Plaintiffs asserted that, had defendant not acquired the failing centers, those bowling alleys would have ceased operation, thereby decreasing competition in the relevant

---

883. 15 U.S.C. § 18; *see Panter v. Marshall Field & Co.*, 646 F.2d 271 (7th Cir.), *cert. denied*, 454 U.S. 1092 (1981) (holding that target's directors had right to challenge tender offer on antitrust grounds if they believed it to be illegal).

884. 15 U.S.C. § 18.

885. 429 U.S. 477 (1977).

market and increasing plaintiffs' profits. The Supreme Court granted certiorari to consider "whether antitrust damages are available where the sole injury alleged is that competitors were continued in business, thereby denying respondents an anticipated increase in market shares."[886]

The Court held that plaintiffs were not entitled to recover damages under the Clayton Act. Recognizing that "[e]very merger of two existing entities into one, whether lawful or unlawful, has the potential for producing economic readjustments that adversely affect some persons," the Court cautioned that "Congress has not condemned mergers on that account; it has condemned them only when they may produce anticompetitive effects."[887] The anticompetitive effect (if any) in this case resulted from the entry of "a 'deep pocket' parent into a market of 'pygmies,' " but the injury sustained by plaintiffs was unrelated to that anticompetitive effect: plaintiffs "would have suffered the identical 'loss'—but not compensable injury—had the acquired centers instead obtained refinancing or been purchased by 'shallow-pocket' parents. . . ."[888] Thus, observed the Court, "it is quite clear that if [plaintiffs] were injured, it was not 'by reason of anything forbidden in the antitrust laws': while [plaintiffs'] loss occurred 'by reason of' the unlawful acquisitions, it did not occur 'by reason of' that which made the acquisitions unlawful."[889]

From this discussion emerged the rule of "antitrust injury": to recover treble damages based on violations of section 7, "[p]laintiffs must prove *antitrust* injury, which is to say injury of the type the antitrust laws were intended to prevent and that flows from that which makes defendants' acts unlawful. The injury should reflect the anticompetitive effect either of the violation or of anticompetitive acts made possible by the violation."[890]

---

886. *Id.* at 484 (footnote omitted).

887. *Id.* at 487.

888. *Id.*

889. *Id.* at 488.

890. *Id.* at 489 (emphasis in original).

When confronted with antitrust challenges in lawsuits brought by target companies, tender offerors frequently have moved to dismiss the antitrust claims on the ground that the targets have suffered no "antitrust injury" and therefore lack standing to sue under section 7. Several courts have accepted this standing argument.[891]

In *Carter Hawley Hale*, for example, plaintiff ("CHH") sought to enjoin a tender offer by The Limited on the ground that the proposed acquisition might substantially lessen competition in the "moderate-price women's fashion apparel" and the "special-sized women's apparel" markets, in which the bidder and the target competed. CHH complained that the tender offer would result in the termination of competition between the two companies, the disruption of CHH's business affairs, the disclosure of trade secrets that gave CHH a "competitive advantage," and the loss of CHH's independent existence.

The court dismissed the section 7 claim and held that CHH had not alleged "antitrust injury": CHH's injuries, if any, would result not from the possibility of substantially lessened competition but simply from the combination of two companies into one. "Put another way, each of these 'injuries' to CHH would occur in the event of a merger, whether or not the merger would substantially lessen competition."[892]

Moreover, the court held, CHH lacked standing to raise a section 7 claim alleging anticompetitive effects flowing from the elimination of competition:

> If the proposed merger is completed, CHH will be a part of the very entity it claims will have a supercompetitive advantage, *i.e.*, it suffers no antitrust harm. As pointed out by Professors Areeda and Turner, it is inconsistent for CHH to complain of this outcome on *antitrust* grounds. Those who will be injured by any

891. *See Central Nat'l Bank v. Rainbolt*, 720 F.2d 1183, 1186–87 (10th Cir. 1983); *Carter Hawley Hale Stores, Inc. v. The Limited, Inc.*, 587 F. Supp. 246 (C.D. Cal. 1984).

892. 587 F. Supp. at 250.

> anticompetitive effect of the proposed merger and thus have standing to complain under § 7 are consumers and competitors of the surviving corporation.[893]

The court's observations echo dictum in *Missouri Portland Cement Co. v. Cargill, Inc.*,[894] in which the Court of Appeals for the Second Circuit remarked that "the uninitiated would find it somewhat difficult to discern what 'loss or damage' Cargill's tender offer could inflict on MP [the target] as a corporation, as distinguished from its management. A cornerstone of MP's antitrust argument is that acquisition of control by Cargill would make MP not too weak but too strong."[895]

The majority of courts that have addressed the issue, however, have concluded that a takeover target does have standing to obtain *injunctive* relief, under section 16 of the Clayton Act,[896] to restrain an acquisition that would violate section 7.[897] These decisions emphasize that actions for injunctive relief under section 16 do not involve the problems of multiple recovery and assessment of damages that mandate narrower standing rules in

893. *Id.* (footnotes omitted).

894. 498 F.2d 851 (2d Cir.), *cert. denied*, 419 U.S. 883 (1974).

895. *Id.* at 867.

896. 15 U.S.C. § 26.

897. *See e.g.*, *Marathon Oil Co. v. Mobil Corp.*, 669 F.2d 378 (6th Cir. 1981), *cert. denied*, 455 U.S. 982 (1982); *Grumman Corp. v. LTV Corp.*, 665 F.2d 10, 16 & n.4 (2d Cir. 1981); *Kennecott Copper Corp. v. Curtiss-Wright Corp.*, 584 F.2d 1195, 1203 (2d Cir. 1978); *Laidlaw Acquisition Corp. v. Mayflower Group, Inc.*, 636 F. Supp. 1513 (S.D. Ind. 1986); *Gearhart Indus., Inc. v. Smith Int'l, Inc.*, 592 F. Supp. 203, 211 & n.1 (N.D. Tex.), *modified on other grounds*, 741 F.2d 707 (5th Cir. 1984); *Arnett v. Gerber Scientific, Inc.*, 566 F. Supp. 1270, 1274 (S.D.N.Y. 1983); *MLC, Inc. v. North Am. Philips Corp.*, 1983 – 1 Trade Cas. (CCH) ¶ 65,351 (S.D.N.Y. May 3, 1983); *Whittaker Corp. v. Edgar*, 535 F. Supp. 933 (N.D. Ill. 1982); *Frank B. Hall & Co., Inc. v. Ryder Sys., Inc.*, No. 82 C 0092 (N.D. Ill. July 12, 1982); *Chemetron Corp. v. Crane Co.*, 1977 – 2 Trade Cas. (CCH) ¶ 61,717, at 72,932 (N.D. Ill. Sept. 8, 1977); *Babcock & Wilcox Co. v. United Technologies Corp.*, 435 F. Supp. 1249, 1255 – 56 (N.D. Ohio 1977); *Copperweld Corp. v. Imetal*, 403 F. Supp. 579, 588 (W.D. Pa. 1975).

treble damages actions under section 4 (15 U.S.C. § 15).[898]

Courts upholding the standing of target companies have recognized a target's interest in preserving its competitive position in the market and in preventing disruption of its business or disclosure of its trade secrets. They also have acknowledged that the advantages of diminished competition accrue not to the target but only to the surviving entity and that "[t]he target company is entitled under § 16 to preserve its separate existence as a competitor."[899] Moreover, the target may well find itself

> in the unenviable role of an unwilling participant in an incipient Section 7 violation. Is it to sit back and permit itself to be acquired only to find itself a defendant in an action brought either by the Government or a private person who is injured by the lessening of competition? We think not. As the Court has observed, Section 7 is a prophylactic measure, intended "primarily to arrest apprehended consequences of intercorporate relationships before those relationships could work their evil. . . ."[900]

Thus, the target company usually may sue for injunctive relief under sections 7 and 16 of the Clayton Act. The definitive answer to the standing question, however, is not yet available. During its 1986–87 Term, the Supreme Court will hear argument in the appeal from the decision in *Monfort of Colorado, Inc. v. Cargill, Inc.*,[901] in which the Court of Appeals for the Tenth Circuit held that a private plaintiff has standing under

---

898. *Cf. A.D.M. Corp. v. Sigma Instruments, Inc.*, 628 F.2d 753, 754 (1st Cir. 1980) (affirming dismissal of action for damages but noting that plaintiff's section 7 allegation "could in the proper circumstances state a claim for injunctive relief" under section 16).

899. *Grumman Corp. v. LTV Corp.*, 665 F.2d 10, 16 (2d Cir. 1981) (footnote omitted).

900. *Chemetron Corp. v. Crane Co.*, 1977–2 Trade Cas. (CCH) ¶ 61,717, at 72,932 (N.D. Ill. Sept. 8, 1977) (*quoting United States v. E.I. duPont de Nemours & Co.*, 353 U.S. 586, 597 (1957)).

901. 761 F.2d 570, 573–78 (10th Cir. 1985), *cert. granted*, 106 S. Ct. 784 (1986).

sections 7 and 16 to seek to enjoin its competitor's acquisition of another competitor. Should the Court ultimately deny standing to a competitor, the decision might well have severe ramifications on the jurisprudence of target standing.

3. Standing of Target Under the Hart-Scott-Rodino Act

The Hart-Scott-Rodino Antitrust Improvements Act of 1976 (the "H-S-R Act"), which added section 7A[902] to the Clayton Act, establishes a "premerger notification and waiting period" that must precede the consummation of any merger, acquisition, or other combination falling within certain jurisdictional limits. The purpose of the premerger notification and waiting requirements is to afford the FTC or the Antitrust Division (depending on which body assumes responsibility for reviewing the particular transaction) an opportunity to determine whether the proposed merger or acquisition might have anticompetitive effects in the markets (if any) in which the companies compete. The Act confers on the Government the authority to seek injunctive relief should any antitrust problems appear imminent.[903]

Not surprisingly, target companies occasionally have sought to add claims under the H-S-R Act to their arsenal of defensive weapons against hostile takeovers and have attempted to enjoin those offers based on the bidders' alleged violation of the Act. The few courts that have addressed such claims, however, have concluded that no private right of action exists under the Act and that target companies lack standing to seek injunctive (or

---

902. 15 U.S.C. § 18a.

903. 15 U.S.C. § 18a(a). The H-S-R Act is discussed more fully in § II.5., *supra*.

other) relief to remedy alleged noncompliance with the Act's requirements.[904]

Relying on the Act's legislative history, these courts have determined that the Act was intended to benefit only the FTC and the Antitrust Division

> "by giving the government antitrust agencies a fair and reasonable opportunity to detect and investigate large mergers of questionable legality before they are consummated. The government will thus have a meaningful chance to win a premerger injunction—which is often the only effective and realistic remedy against large, illegal mergers—before the assets, technology, and management of the merging firms are hopelessly and irreversibly scrambled together, and before competition is substantially and perhaps irremediably lessened, in violations [sic] of the Clayton Act."[905]

The legislative history contains no indication that Congress intended to extend the new cause of action to private plaintiffs, who already had the right to sue (under section 16) to enjoin violations of section 7 of the Clayton Act. Thus, while there have been few rulings on the issue, and none by an appellate court, it would appear that a target may not rely on the H-S-R Act in attempting to enjoin a hostile takeover bid.

E. Purchase by the Target of Its Own Shares from Persons Other than the Bidder

In some circumstances, a target may wish to defend against an unwanted takeover attempt by buying its own shares from its

---

904. *Hanna Mining Co. v. Norcen Energy Resources Ltd.*, [1982 Transfer Binder] Fed. Sec. L. Rep. (CCH) ¶ 98,742, at 93,739 – 40 (N.D. Ohio June 11, 1982); *Hammermill Paper Co. v. Icahn*, No. 80 – 47 – B (W.D. Pa. April 24, 1980).

905. *Hanna Mining Co. v. Norcen Energy Resources Ltd.*, [1982 Transfer Binder] Fed. Sec. L. Rep. (CCH) ¶ 98,742, at 93,739 (N.D. Ohio June 11, 1982) (quoting H.R. Rep. No. 1373, 94th Cong., 2d Sess. 5).

shareholders through a tender offer, in privately negotiated transactions, or on the open market. For reasons quite apart from legal considerations, such repurchases sometimes may be counterproductive—such as when the bidder has made a cash offer, at a fair price, for all of the target's shares, while the target is able to buy only a portion of its own stock, or when the bidder is already the target's principal shareholder and the repurchases simply will increase the bidder's share of the company's outstanding voting stock. In other cases, however, a repurchase may afford greater value to the target's shareholders and may absorb some shares that might otherwise be tendered to a hostile bidder. If the repurchase takes the form of an exchange offer, in which the target issues debt or other securities for outstanding common stock, the new securities may also contain covenants making a leveraged acquisition by a bidder more difficult.[906]

A company's periodic market purchases of its own stock may be desirable. Such a program may have the practical effect of enabling the company to buy out its most restless stockholders, thereby increasing a potential hostile acquiror's difficulty or expense in establishing a toehold position in the company's stock. If a corporation purchases its own stock on the open market, the repurchase program also may serve generally to maintain or increase the stock price, thereby discouraging potential acquirors from making a run on the company at a premium price.

But a periodic or one-time repurchase program also has disadvantages. The cost of the repurchases might deplete the company's cash reserves and thus reduce its flexibility in the event of a hostile tender offer. Moreover, the repurchases could impair a friendly acquiror's ability to account for an acquisition during the following two years as a pooling of interests (unless the acquiree has successfully negotiated the pitfalls of APB 16 and SEC Accounting Series Releases 146 and 147A and can demonstrate by "persuasive evidence" that the repurchases were

906. Such exchange offers are discussed in the section on recapitalizations, *see infra* § III.4.G.

not made in contemplation of the pooling transaction). Reduction in the number of outstanding shares also means that a hostile tender offeror would need fewer shares to obtain control.

In addition to weighing these strategic considerations carefully, a company considering a repurchase program must bear in mind SEC rules, state securities laws, common law considerations of due care and loyalty, restrictions under state corporation law limiting repurchases of stock in certain circumstances (for example, Delaware's statutory prohibition against repurchases when or as a result of which the company's capital is or would be impaired), restrictions in the company's debt instruments, financing issues, and federal statutes such as the Williams Act provisions relating to self-tender offers.

1. State Law Duties of Care and Loyalty

Challenges to defensive self-tenders and other forms of issuer repurchases usually require courts to analyze the validity of the defensive maneuvers under state law principles of business judgment. Courts generally will decline to enjoin self-tenders if the issuer's directors fulfilled their duties of care and loyalty and acted reasonably in relation to any perceived threat to the company; however, courts usually will enjoin self-tenders if the issuer's directors breached their fiduciary duties or if their actions bore no rational relation to the purported danger that the board allegedly sought to avert.

In *GAF Corp. v. Union Carbide Corp.*,[907] a federal district court declined to issue a preliminary injunction against Union Carbide's defensive self-tender offer. GAF, a 10-percent shareholder of Carbide, had made an unsolicited, all-cash tender offer for approximately 71 percent of Carbide's outstanding shares, an offer that GAF planned to finance by liquidating large segments of Carbide. In response to this bid, Carbide's board

---

907. 624 F. Supp. 1016 (S.D.N.Y. 1985).

authorized the issuance of high-interest debentures and notes containing covenants restricting sales of the company's assets, and Carbide offered to exchange the newly issued notes and debentures, together with $20 in cash per share of Carbide stock tendered, for 70 percent of the outstanding shares of Carbide common stock. The new notes and debentures, which were not callable for several years, also included covenants limiting the company's ability to incur additional debt. GAF sued to enjoin Carbide's exchange offer.

Applying New York law, the court held that Carbide's defensive measures fell within the ambit of the business judgment rule. Although Carbide's board of directors bore the burden of coming forward with evidence of their lack of self-interest and of the reasonableness and fairness of the exchange offer, the directors met that burden. The board consisted of a majority of independent, outside directors, and, the court held, "no inference of self-interest is to be drawn from the mere facts that an outside Director acts to defeat a hostile offer and that his action allows him to remain on the Board."[908] The court concluded that the "action of the [GAF] Board to foster the future and intact existence of Carbide, except for such sales of assets as would reasonably be needed to prune aspects of the Company and leave it substantially alive as it presently is, represents a reasonable view on the part of the Board of what is best for shareholders."[909]

The Delaware Supreme Court also upheld a self-tender in *Unocal Corp. v. Mesa Petroleum Co.*,[910] vacating a preliminary injunction entered by the Chancery Court. Unocal Corporation's defensive self-tender was an attempt to ward off the advances of Mesa Petroleum, a 13-percent Unocal stockholder controlled by T. Boone Pickens, Jr.

Mesa had commenced an unsolicited "front-end-loaded" cash tender offer for approximately 37 percent of Unocal's

---

908. *Id.* at 1022.

909. *Id.* at 1019.

910. 493 A.2d 946 (Del. 1985).

outstanding stock and had disclosed that, if successful in its tender offer, it would effect a back-end merger in which each remaining share of Unocal would be converted into highly subordinated Mesa debentures—"junk bonds." Unocal's board determined Mesa's offer to be grossly inadequate and resolved to commence an exchange offer in which 49 percent of Unocal's shares would be exchanged for securities valued at $72 per share. The offer, however, specifically excluded Mesa from tendering, and Mesa sued to enjoin it. The Chancery Court granted a preliminary injunction, holding that Unocal's discriminatory exchange offer was impermissible under Delaware law. The Delaware Supreme Court reversed.

The court stated that the business judgment rule "is applicable in the context of a takeover . . . [but,] [b]ecause of the omnipresent specter that the board may be acting primarily in its own interests, rather than those of the corporation and its shareholders, there is an enhanced duty which calls for judicial examination at the threshold before the protections of the business judgment rule may be conferred."[911] As the court explained, the target's directors must establish that they did not act "solely or primarily out of a desire to perpetuate themselves in office" but, rather, that they were "motivated by a good faith concern for the welfare of the corporation and its stockholders, which in all circumstances must be free of any fraud or other misconduct."[912] The board must also show that it "had reasonable grounds for believing that a danger to corporate policy and effectiveness existed because of another person's stock ownership" and that its action was "reasonable in relation to the threat posed."[913] The Unocal board could satisfy its burden of showing reasonable grounds for believing that Mesa's stock ownership endangered corporate policy and effectiveness by demonstrating the directors' own good faith and reasonable investigation. Proof of good faith and reasonable investigation,

911. *Id.* at 954.

912. *Id.* at 955.

913. *Id.*

held the court, "is materially enhanced, as here, by the approval of a board comprised of a majority of outside independent directors who have acted in accordance with the foregoing standards."[914]

Unocal's board, composed of eight outside and six inside directors, had unanimously approved the company's self-tender. Moreover, the eight outside directors had met separately, before the vote was taken, to discuss Mesa's tender offer and Unocal's response, and they then advised the entire board to approve the proposed transaction.

The court concluded that Unocal's board reasonably perceived the Mesa tender offer to pose a threat of a grossly inadequate, two-tier coercive takeover coupled with a threat of greenmail. The court also found that the selective self-tender was "reasonably related to the threats posed."[915] "[W]hile the exchange offer is a form of selective treatment, given the nature of the threat posed here the response is neither unlawful nor unreasonable."[916] (The SEC's later-adopted "all holders rule,"[917] however, represents an attempt, under federal law, to prohibit discriminatory tender offers such as the one upheld in *Unocal*.)

In *Southeastern Public Service Co. v. Graniteville Co.*,[918] a federal district court declined preliminarily to enjoin Graniteville from funding a leveraged employee stock option plan and from making a self-tender offer in the face of substantial stock accumulations by corporate raider Victor Posner. Finding that the board reasonably had perceived Posner's activities as posing a threat to Graniteville, the court applied the business judgment rule and upheld the board's attempts to keep Posner from obtaining control of the company. The board had based its actions on Posner's reputation in the business community and on the advice of outside experts.

---

914. *Id.*

915. *Id.* at 956.

916. *Id.* at 957.

917. For a detailed discussion of the "all holders rule," see § II.4.B(7), *supra*.

918. No. 83 – 1028 – 8 (D.S.C. May 25, 1983).

Another federal court, in *Pogo Producing Co. v. Northwest Industries, Inc.*,[919] declined to enjoin a defensive self-tender offer that had been commenced either to deter an unsolicited tender offer or, if the hostile offer were successful, to provide a greater number of shareholders with an opportunity to sell their shares. Northwest Industries and Sedco had jointly commenced a cash partial tender offer for Pogo stock; Pogo's board recommended that the shareholders reject the Northwest/Sedco bid and authorized the company to commence a cash self-tender for Pogo shares at the same price and for the same number of shares specified in the Northwest/Sedco offer. Northwest and Sedco sued, arguing that the self-tender lacked any legitimate purpose and was nothing more than an attempt by the directors to maintain control of Pogo.

Applying Delaware law, the court concluded that the self-tender was "made in good faith" and was "not primarily motivated by a desire to entrench [the Pogo directors] or incumbent management."[920] The court found that the directors reasonably had concluded both that the hostile bidders lacked the experience to manage Pogo and that they would probably effect a second-step merger, which would provide inadequate consideration for the remaining Pogo shares, if they succeeded in acquiring a majority of Pogo's stock through their partial tender offer.

Lowenschuss v. The Option Clearing Corp.[921] also declined to enjoin a self-tender offer, this one by Phillips Petroleum Company. Plaintiff was a dealer in options who had gambled on the outcomes of both a recapitalization vote by Phillips shareholders and a tender offer for Phillips by Carl Icahn. When the Phillips shareholders failed to approve the defensive recapitalization plan by the necessary margin, Phillips announced a self-tender offer, which would increase the long-

919. No. H–83–2667 (S.D. Tex. May 24, 1983).

920. Slip op. at 10.

921. No. 7972 (Del. Ch. March 27, 1985).

term debt of the corporation by $4.5 billion while reducing shareholder equity by about 76 percent.

Plaintiff argued that the self-tender was, in essence, a recapitalization scheme that could be instituted only with shareholder approval. Relying primarily on section 160 of the Delaware Code, which empowers a corporation to repurchase its shares, the court held that plaintiff had not demonstrated a probability of success on the merits.

The Delaware Court of Chancery, however, recently enjoined a defensive self-tender in *AC Acquisitions Corp. v. Anderson, Clayton & Co.*,[922] preventing Anderson, Clayton from proceeding with a self-tender for approximately 65 percent of its stock. The court concluded that the self-tender, if allowed to proceed, would have a coercive effect on Anderson, Clayton's shareholders and, as a practical matter, would preclude them from tendering into a competing, unsolicited tender offer.

Anderson, Clayton had announced a proposed recapitalization that coincided with the termination of certain trusts established for the benefit of the four daughters of the company's founder. The trusts, in the aggregate, held 30 percent of the company's stock. Under the proposed recapitalization, each outstanding share of stock would be converted into a right to receive $37 in cash and .5334 of a share of new common stock of the recapitalized company. The Anderson, Clayton board concluded that the present value of the recapitalization to the Anderson, Clayton shareholders was between $43 and $47 per share.

To finance this recapitalization proposal, Anderson, Clayton contemplated borrowing substantial amounts of cash and terminating overfunded pension plans. The company also planned to establish an ESOP, which would acquire a 25-percent equity interest in the recapitalized company. The resulting

---

922. [Current] Fed. Sec. L. Rep. (CCH) ¶ 92,942 (Del. Ch. Sept. 18, 1986). *But cf. Gelco Corp. v. Coniston Partners*, Civil No. 3-86-847 (D. Minn. Nov. 10, 1986) (refusing to enjoin target's exchange offer and distinguishing *AC Acquisitions Corp.).*

corporation, of course, would be a smaller, more highly leveraged entity.

Shortly before the shareholders were scheduled to vote on the recapitalization proposal, a group consisting of Bear, Stearns & Co., Inc., Gruss Petroleum Corp., and Gruss Partners (collectively, "BS/G") announced an interest in acquiring all of Anderson, Clayton's stock for $54 per share. After some unfruitful negotiations with Anderson, Clayton, BS/G sued to enjoin the proposed recapitalization, and the court issued such an injunction.

After further unproductive negotiations in which BS/G continued to express an interest in acquiring Anderson, Clayton for cash, BS/G commenced an all-cash tender offer for all outstanding shares of Anderson, Clayton common stock at $56 per share. BS/G also announced its intention, if the tender offer succeeded, to effect a second-stage cash merger at $56 per share. BS/G conditioned its obligation to buy any tendered shares on, among other things, its acquisition of a majority of the outstanding Anderson, Clayton shares.

The following day, Anderson, Clayton's board resolved both to recommend that the shareholders reject the BS/G tender offer and to commence a self-tender for up to 8 million shares (or approximately 65 percent) of the company's outstanding stock at $60 per share. BS/G moved for a preliminary injunction against consummation of Anderson, Clayton's self-tender.

The court found that, "[i]n electing to reject the BS/G $56 proposal and to recommend that shareholders reject the BS/G tender offer, and in electing to pursue their alternative transaction, the Board proceeded without seeking the opinion of its investment banker as to whether the Company Transaction [*i.e.*, the self-tender] represented greater current value to the Company's shareholders than did the BS/G proposal."[923] Citing *Unocal Corp. v. Mesa Petroleum Co.*, the court held that,

923. *Id.* at 94,599.

> where a board takes action designed to defeat a threatened change in control of the company, a more flexible, intermediate form of judicial review [than the business judgment rule in its full strength] is appropriate. . . . First, there must be shown some basis for the Board to have concluded that a proper corporate purpose was served by implementation of the defensive measure and, second, that measure must be found reasonable in relation to the threat posed by the change in control that instigates the action.[924]

As to the first element, the court concluded that the Anderson, Clayton board had carried its burden.

> The first inquiry concerns the likelihood that defendants will be able to demonstrate "a reasonable ground for believing that a danger to corporate policy or effectiveness" exists by reason of the BS/G offer. . . . Stated in these precise terms, the Company Transaction may seem not to satisfy this aspect of the *Unocal* test. There is no evidence that the BS/G offer—which is non-coercive and at a concededly fair price—threatens injury to the shareholders or to the enterprise. However, I take this aspect of the test to be simply a particularization of the more general requirement that a corporate purpose, not one personal to the directors, must be served by the stock repurchase. As so understood, it seems clear that a self-tender in these circumstances meets this element of the appropriate test.[925]

The court observed that the Anderson, Clayton board

> does not seek to justify the Company Transaction as necessary to fend off an offer that is inherently unfair. Rather, Defendants account for their creation of the Company Transaction as the creation of an option to shareholders to permit them to have the benefits of a large, tax-advantaged cash distribution together with a continuing participation in a newly-structured, highly-leveraged Anderson, Clayton.[926]

---

924. *Id.* at 94,600.
925. *Id.* at 94,600 – 01. (quoting *Unocal*, 493 A.2d at 955) (citation omitted).
926. *Id.* at 94,601.

The court concluded that "[t]he creation of such an alternative, with no other justification, serves a valid corporate purpose (certainly so where, as here, that option is made available to all shareholders on the same terms). . . . That valid corporate purpose satisfies the first leg of the *Unocal* test."[927]

However, the court continued, "[t]he fatal defect with the Company Transaction . . . becomes apparent when one attempts to apply the second leg of the *Unocal* test and asks whether the defensive step is 'reasonable in relation to the threat posed.' "[928] On this point, the court accepted plaintiffs' argument that the Anderson, Clayton self-tender effectively coerced shareholders to tender into the Anderson, Clayton offer rather than into the BS/G offer even if those shareholders might otherwise have found the BS/G bid more attractive. The court explained the coercive effect as follows:

> (1) Stockholders tendering into the BS/G offer have no assurance that BS/G will take down their stock at $56 a share since that offer is subject to conditions including a minimum number of shares tendered and abandonment of the Company Transaction; and (2) Tendering shareholders would thereby preclude themselves from participating in the "fat" front-end of the Company Transaction and risk having the value of all their shares fall very dramatically. In such circumstances, plaintiffs say, to characterize the Board's action as an attempt to preserve the ability of a shareholder to choose is a charade, They claim that the Company Transaction is coercive in fact and in the circumstances presented, improperly so in law.
>
> . . . .
>
> I conclude as a factual matter for purposes of this motion that no rational shareholder could afford not to tender into the Company's self-tender offer at least if that transaction is viewed in isolation. The record is uncontradicted that the value of the Company's stock following the effectuation of the Company

927. *Id.*
928. *Id.*

> Transaction will be materially less than $60 per share. The various experts differ on how much less. . . . What is clear under either view, however, is that a current shareholder who elects not to tender into the self-tender is very likely, upon consummation of the Company Transaction, to experience a substantial loss in the market value of his holdings. The only way, within the confines of the Company Transaction, that a shareholder can preclude himself from such an immediate financial loss is to tender into the self-tender so that he receives his *pro rata* share of the cash distribution that will, in part, cause the expected fall in the market price of the Company's stock.
>
> I conclude that an Anderson, Clayton stockholder, acting with economic rationality, has no effective choice as between the contending offers as presently constituted. Even if a shareholder would prefer to sell all of his or her holdings at $56 per share in the BS/G offer, he or she may not risk tendering into that proposal [sic] and thereby risk being frozen out of the front end of the Company Transaction, should the BS/G offer not close.[929]

The court concluded that "a defensive step that includes a coercive self-tender timed to effectively preclude a rational shareholder from accepting the any-and-all offer cannot, in my opinion, be deemed to be reasonable in relation to any minimal threat posed to stockholders by such offer."[930]

Although the court did not issue a detailed injunction, it directed the parties to submit proposed orders crafted to eliminate the coercive nature of Anderon, Clayton's self-tender and to give the shareholders a meaningful choice between that offer and the BS/G offer. The court suggested that

> [t]his may perhaps be done by the issuance of an injunction against effectuation of any aspect of the Company Transaction (including the taking down of loans to finance the purchase of stock, or the sale of stock to the ESOP trustee or others) for a short period (e.g., thirty days) and by conditioning the effectiveness of such order upon plaintiffs' committing to furnish

929. *Id.* at 94,601 – 02. (footnotes omitted).

930. *Id.* at 94,602.

> to shareholders before it [sic] closes its tender offer notice of the terms of the order entered and an undertaking to either purchase shares tendered or to return them within such period. This would enable any person who may wish to tender to BS/G to do so and still be free to participate in the Company Transaction if the BS/G tender offer is not closed. In this way, if a majority of Anderson, Clayton's shareholders would prefer to cash out their interest in the Company at the price BS/G offers, they may elect to do so without fear of thereby risking consigning themselves to participate fully in the less advantageous "back-end" of the Company Transaction. If, on the other hand, a majority of such shares prefer the Company Transaction, and thus the § 11 condition of the BS/G offer [that BS/G obtain a majority of the outstanding shares] is not satisfied, the majority will have the Company Transaction available promptly.[931] The Quaker Oats Company ultimately purchased Anderson, Clayton.

In *Crane Co. v. Harsco Corp.*,[932] a federal district court also determined that a hostile bidder had established a likelihood of being able to show that the directors of a tender offer target had breached their fiduciary duties in approving a stock repurchase program. The court's ruling on this issue is dictum, however, because the court declined to issue a preliminary injunction against the repurchases on the ground that plaintiff had failed to demonstrate that denial of relief would cause irreparable injury.

In analyzing the merits of plaintiff's claim, the court placed on the target, Harsco, the burden of showing that the repurchase program was primarily in the corporation's interest. Harsco could carry its burden by

> show[ing] that some consideration other than the perceived threat to control was the primary reason for the stock purchase; or [by] admit[ting] that the stock purchase was intended primarily as a defensive maneuver, and show[ing] that the directors reasonably determined that a change in control would constitute

931. *Id.* at 94,603.

932. 511 F. Supp. 294 (D. Del. 1981).

> "a clear threat to the future business or existing, successful business policy" of the corporation.[933]

Harsco, which had undertaken the repurchase program as a defensive maneuver, failed to demonstrate the threat posed by Crane's tender offer. The court rejected Harsco's contention that Crane would harm a Harsco subsidiary by misusing proprietary information; moreover, Harsco produced no evidence that Crane "would be likely to impose business methods that are fundamentally incompatible with Harsco's."[934]

2. Financing Issues

- *State law limits on funds available.* Most states have statutes limiting the sources and amounts of capital that a company may use to purchase its own stock. In Delaware, for example, a corporation may not purchase its own shares if the purchase would impair the corporation's capital or if the company's capital already is impaired.[935] Directors of a company that makes purchases of its own stock in violation of this restriction are jointly and severally liable to the company and its creditors for any amounts unlawfully paid.[936]
- *Loan agreements.* A company's loan agreements typically will contain financial covenants restricting the company's ability to pay dividends or to repurchase its own shares. A corporation should review these covenants before undertaking a repurchase program or self-tender.
- *Fraudulent conveyance issues.* If stock repurchases leave the target with unreasonably small capital or render the

---

933. *Id.* at 305 (quoting *Kaplan v. Goldsamt*, 380 A.2d 556, 569 (Del. Ch. 1977)).

934. *Id.* at 306.

935. Del. Gen. Corp. L. § 160(a)(1).

936. *Id.* § 174.

company insolvent, the company's creditors may be able to recover the amounts paid by the company to its shareholders on the theory that the transaction was made without adequate consideration and thus constituted a fraudulent conveyance.[937]

3. Federal Law Questions

a. *Rule 13e–1*

Section 13(e)(1) of the Exchange Act[938] and Rule 13e – 1 promulgated thereunder[939] provide that, once an entity other than the issuer (i) makes a tender offer for any class of equity securities either of any issuer that has a class of equity securities registered under section 12 of the Exchange Act or of any issuer that is an investment company registered under the Investment Company Act of 1940 and (ii) has filed its Schedule 14D – 1 with the SEC and the issuer has received notice of that filing, the issuer may not, during the pendency of the tender offer, purchase any of its own equity securities unless it has (A) filed with the SEC a statement containing certain specified information, including the amount of the securities to be purchased, the purpose of the purchase, and the source and amount of funds to be used, (B) paid a specified filing fee, and (C) provided its security holders with the same information at any time within the preceding six months.

ORBANCO, Inc. v. Security Bank of Oregon[940] illustrates the operation of this rule. After the commencement of an unsolicited tender offer, two officers and directors of the target corporation purchased its stock, although the target had not

937. For a discussion of fraudulent conveyances, see § II.8., *supra*, and § III.4.G., *infra*.

938. 15 U.S.C. § 78m(e)(1).

939. 17 C.F.R. § 240.13e – 1 (1986).

940. 371 F. Supp. 125 (D. Or. 1974).

filed with the FDIC the equivalent of the disclosure statement required to be filed with the SEC under Rule 13e – 1 in the case of non-banking corporations. The court required the two officers to tender their unlawfully purchased shares to the hostile tender offeror, which was obliged to pay the officers only the price for which they had purchased those shares. The court ordered the tender offeror to pay the difference between that purchase price and the tender offer price to the shareholders from whom the insiders unlawfully had purchased their stock.

In *Crane Co. v. Harsco Corp.*,[941] the court held that a tender offeror had standing to bring an action for injunctive relief under section 13(e)(1) based on a target's allegedly improper purchase of its own shares. However, the court found that the offeror had failed to establish either a reasonable probability of success on the merits or a likelihood of imminent irreparable injury and therefore denied plaintiff's motion for a preliminary injunction.

b. *Rule 13e–4*

The SEC's Rule 13e – 4[942] deals with issuer tender offers, a term that is defined to refer to any tender offer made by an issuer or by an affiliate of an issuer for any class of the issuer's own equity securities. The Rule contains general proscriptions on fraud in terms that parallel the language of Rule 10b – 5, but it also includes detailed regulations concerning issuer tender offers.

Before commencing an issuer tender offer, or as soon as practicable on the date of commencement, the issuer must file with the SEC a completed Schedule 13E – 4[943] disclosing certain information requested in the instructions contained on that form. The issuer also must report any material change in the disclosed information by promptly filing with the SEC ten copies of an amendment to the Schedule. In addition, the issuer

941. 511 F. Supp. 294 (D. Del. 1981).
942. 17 C.F.R. § 240.13e – 4 (1986).
943. 17 C.F.R. § 240.13e – 101 (1986).

must report the results of its tender offer by filing with the SEC, no later than ten days after termination of the offer, ten copies of a final amendment to the Schedule 13E – 4.

Rule 13e – 4(e)(1) also requires the issuer to publish, send, or give to its shareholders a statement containing information about the scheduled termination date of the issuer tender offer, whether the offer may be extended, the applicable withdrawal dates, the proration date (if the issuer tender offer is for fewer than all securities of a class), and the facts and data reported in Items 1 through 8 of the Schedule 13E – 4. If the issuer tender offer involves the registration of securities under the Securities Act, any prospectus relating to those securities must include all information that the issuer must provide to shareholders under Rule 13e – 4. The issuer must disclose, in the manner prescribed in Rule 13e – 4(e)(2), any material change in the facts previously reported to security holders.

In August 1986, the SEC amended Rule 13e – 4 to conform the timetable for issuer tender offers to the schedule applicable to other tender offers. The issuer must leave its tender offer open (unless the offer is withdrawn) until at least the later of (i) 20 business days from the date of the offer's commencement or (ii) ten business days from the date when the issuer first publishes or otherwise provides to shareholders a notice of an increase or decrease in the percentage of the class of securities sought, in the consideration offered, or in the dealer's soliciting fee. However, the issuer's (or its affiliate's) acceptance for payment of an additional amount of securities that does not exceed two percent of the class of securities sought will not be deemed to constitute such an increase.

The issuer (or affiliate) making the tender offer must permit shareholders to withdraw tendered securities at any time during the pendency of the tender offer or, if the shares have not yet been accepted for payment, after the expiration of 40 business days from the commencement of the offer. The issuer must accept tendered securities on a *pro rata* basis if the tender offer is for fewer than all of the outstanding equity securities of a class and if the shareholders have tendered a greater number of securities than the issuer is bound or willing to accept for payment. If the issuer increases the offer's consideration after commencing the tender offer, it must pay the increased consideration to all security holders whose tendered shares are accepted for payment.

Until the expiration of at least ten business days after termination of the issuer tender offer, the issuer and its affiliates are prohibited, except pursuant to the tender offer, from purchasing any security that is the subject of the offer, any security of the same class and series or any right to purchase any such security, and, in the case of an exchange offer, any security offered under the exchange offer and any security of the same class or series or any right to purchase any such security.

As with non-issuer tender offers, the issuer-offeror must open its tender offer to all holders of the relevant class of securities. Moreover, the offeror must pay to each shareholder the highest consideration paid to any security holder during the tender offer.

The foregoing discussion outlines the general requirements of Rule 13e – 4. Of course, in planning an issuer tender offer, counsel should consult Rule 13e – 4 for its detailed requirements and exceptions.

Rule 13e – 4 does not define what constitutes an issuer tender offer. As with non-issuer tender offers, most courts that have considered the question have looked to a wide variety of factors, and there seems to be an increasing reluctance to hold that open-market purchase programs constitute tender offers.[944]

c. *Rule 10b–6*

This Rule generally prohibits persons (including the issuer) who are interested in a "distribution" of securities from bidding for or purchasing either the security that is being distributed or its equivalent. This proscription can limit a target's defensive

944. *See e.g., SEC v. Carter Hawley Hale Stores, Inc.*, 760 F.2d 945 (9th Cir. 1985), discussed in detail in § II.2.D., *supra.*

maneuvers by precluding open-market purchases or a self-tender offer if the target is engaged in a distribution of securities.

The Rule applies to most distributions, whether or not they are subject to registration under the Securities Act. However, the Rule specifically excludes from its scope any distribution of securities under employee or shareholder benefit plans sponsored by the issuer; nor does it apply to "technical" distributions by issuers that have outstanding securities convertible into or exchangeable for another class of securities. The SEC has the power to grant exemptions from the Rule.

F. Greenmail

Greenmail is a payment by a target to repurchase, at a premium price, shares held by an acquiror. A target will make this payment to buy out a troublesome shareholder and to avoid a takeover or other shift of control.

Some commentators consider greenmail both to be unfair to other shareholders who do not receive a greenmail premium and also to be a management entrenchment device.[945] Moreover, greenmail has been criticized as being an ineffective defense to a hostile takeover effort. After all, once a company has paid greenmail to one raider, there is nothing to stop another raider from demanding the same tribute.

This problem is the phenomenon known as "double dipping." If a target pays greenmail to one raider, whose market activities and takeover threats have run up the price of the company's stock, the price of the target's stock usually will fall following the pay-off. This decline in price, coupled with the target's having displayed its willingness to pay greenmail, may encourage a

---

945. Office of the Chief Economist of the Securities and Exchange Commission, *The Impact of Targeted Share Repurchases (Greenmail) on Stock Prices*, [1984 – 1985 Transfer Binder] Fed. Sec. L. Rep. (CCH) ¶ 83,713 (Sept. 11, 1984).

second greenmailer to try its luck at extorting a premium from the target. If the target pays off the second greenmailer, the stock price again will decline, and the cycle theoretically will repeat itself *ad infinitum*. Indeed, St. Regis recently had to seek a white knight after it had paid off two greenmailers, only to find itself confronted by a third.

Nonetheless, a company may find it advantageous to pay greenmail either to avoid a costly takeover battle or to prevent working control (but less than 100 percent) of the company from falling into the hands of a raider who is ill-motivated or ill-equipped to run the company effectively. When a target pays consideration other than cash for a raider's stock, the amount of the premium may be more difficult to assess, and the repurchase thus may be more difficult to challenge.

1. Judicial Treatment

In *Cheff v. Mathes*,[946] a case of both historical and analytical importance, the Delaware Supreme Court reversed a Chancery Court award of damages in a derivative action alleging an improper use of corporate funds for payment of greenmail. Plaintiffs alleged that the corporation's directors had breached their fiduciary duties by paying greenmail in order to perpetuate their own control of the company.

The Supreme Court held that the board would not be liable for buying out the dissident shareholder if the greenmail decision was made for a proper business purpose; if, however, the board acted primarily to retain control, the payment would be improper.[947] The court placed on the directors the burden of establishing the reasonableness of the board's alleged belief that the dissident shareholder's ownership of stock posed a threat to corporate policy and effectiveness. The directors could satisfy this burden by showing that they had acted with good faith and

946. 41 Del. Ch. 494, 199 A.2d 548 (Del. 1964).
947. 199 A.2d at 554.

upon reasonable investigation; they would not be penalized for an honest mistake of judgment.[948]

The court concluded that the directors justifiably believed that the dissident shareholder's growing stock holdings endangered the existence or policies of the company. The shareholder's poor reputation, the employee unrest caused by the shareholder's increasing stock ownership, and professional advice all supported the board's conclusion.

Subsequent decisions have granted directors a fair amount of leeway to pay greenmail. In *Edelman v. Phillips Petroleum Co.*,[949] for example, the court declined preliminarily to enjoin a special shareholders' meeting called to approve a recapitalization plan that was incidental to an agreement to pay off corporate raider T. Boone Pickens and his company, Mesa Petroleum. The settlement agreement with Mesa provided for a greenmail buy-out of Mesa's shares in exchange both for Mesa's vote in favor of recapitalization and for a standstill agreement.

The court declared Phillips' resistance to Mesa's takeover attempt to be the "most defensible aspect" of Phillips' overall anti-takeover strategy.[950] Both the nature of Mesa's two-tier, bust-up tender offer and Pickens' reputation as a corporate raider justified Phillips' efforts. The court concluded that "[t]he approval by Phillips Board of the terms for Mesa's exit, standing alone, would appear defensible under the business judgment rule as a repurchase at a premium of the shares of a dissident."[951]

Good v. Texaco, Inc.[952] approved a settlement and dismissal of a class action and a derivative action in connection with the payment of greenmail by Texaco to an investment group known as the Bass Brothers group. In early 1984, while Texaco was acquiring Getty Oil Company at a cost of over $10 billion, the

948. *Id.* at 555.

949. No. 7899 (Del. Ch. Feb. 12, 1985), discussed in detail in § III.4.G., *infra.*

950. Slip op. at 11.

951. *Id.* at 15.

952. No. 7501 (Del. Ch. May 14, 1984), *aff'd sub nom. Polk v. Good*, 507 A.2d 531 (Del. 1986).

Bass group, which already was a significant Texaco shareholder, increased its holdings in Texaco and hinted that it might buy up to 20 percent of Texaco's outstanding stock. When the Bass group proposed what Texaco's directors considered to be an unfavorable joint venture, the Texaco board concluded that rejection of the venture could result in a hostile takeover move by the Bass group.

After consulting with its investment banker and outside corporate counsel, Texaco decided to repurchase the Bass group's stock. For $650 million in cash and 12.6 million shares of Texaco voting preferred stock (carrying five percent of Texaco's total voting power), the Bass group entered into standstill and voting agreements with Texaco.

Plaintiff shareholders filed several suits attacking the repurchase, claiming that Texaco's directors had paid an excessive price for the shares, had wasted corporate assets, had acted primarily for entrenchment purposes, had breached their fiduciary duties to Texaco shareholders, and had impermissibly engaged in vote-buying by means of the voting agreement. Texaco and the Bass group proceeded to amend their voting agreement to provide that the group's stock would be voted in proportion to the votes cast by other Texaco shareholders. After extensive discovery, the parties agreed to settle the suit by entering into an agreement endorsing the mirror voting provision and requiring disclosure of discovery information to shareholders and payment of plaintiffs' attorneys' fees.

The court found ample precedent for applying the business judgment rule to the board's decision to repurchase shares from dissident shareholders who appeared to threaten the best interests of the corporation. But because a threat of this sort also could challenge the board's continuing control of the company, the court required the directors to show that they had acted primarily in the corporation's interests in repurchasing the shares. The board could satisfy this burden by showing reasonable justification for believing that the dissidents' ownership of shares presented a "reasonable threat" to the continued existence of the corporation or its policies.[953] Based on this standard, the court concluded that the Texaco directors would stand a "better than even chance" of prevailing on the merits.[954]

The Delaware Supreme Court affirmed the Chancery Court's approval of the settlement and wrote:

> Here, the presence of the 10 outside directors on the Texaco board, coupled with the advice rendered by the investment banker and legal counsel, constitute a *prima facie* showing of good faith and reasonable investigation. . . . With 10 of the 13 directors being independent, the plaintiffs thus bore a heavy burden of overcoming the presumptions thus attaching to the board's decisions. . . .
>
> The events occurring from the outset of the Bass group's acquisition of Texaco stock, up to the repurchase, created reasonable grounds for a justifiable belief by the directors that there was a threat to Texaco. The payment of a premium of approximately 3% over market seems reasonable in relation to the immediate disruptive effect and the potential long-term threat which the Bass group posed. Clearly, that was a benefit to the Company and most of its stockholders.[955]

In *Abella v. Universal Leaf Tobacco Co.*,[956] a federal district court granted summary judgment to defendants in a shareholder derivative action asserting that the corporation's directors had breached their fiduciary duties in approving a greenmail payment. The court found little doubt that the directors had determined to pay the greenmail in order to induce a raider to withdraw its tender offer for the corporation. However, the directors presented unrebutted affidavits and exhibits demonstrating their good faith in approving the payment and showing reasonable grounds for their decision. Based on the

---

953. Slip op. at 31.

954. *Id.* at 36.

955. *Polk v. Good*, 507 A.2d 531, 537 (Del. 1986) (citations omitted).

956. 546 F. Supp. 795 (E.D. Va. 1982).

unrefuted evidence of good faith, the court ruled that defendants were entitled to summary judgment as a matter of law.

Similarly, *Heine v. The Signal Companies, Inc.*[957] held that the directors of Signal had not breached their fiduciary duty to the company by authorizing a purchase of the company's stock from a dissident shareholder at a premium. Signal also had offered the same price to other shareholders for a limited number of shares in a self-tender offer. The court noted that Delaware law permits such purchases, provided that the directors, in approving the transaction, did not act primarily out of a desire to perpetuate themselves in office. The court required the directors to establish that the transaction was primarily in the corporation's interest, and it held that they had no difficulty meeting this burden.[958]

By contrast, *Heckmann v. Ahmanson*[959] affirmed a preliminary injunction prohibiting a greenmailer from spending the greenmail payment pending trial on the validity of the transaction. The case arose out of a March 1984 attempt by the Steinberg Group to take over Disney, which had defended against the Steinberg Group's purchases of Disney stock by acquiring Arvida Corporation for $200 million worth of newly issued Disney stock and by assuming Arvida's $190 million debt.

The Steinberg Group brought a shareholder's derivative action challenging the Arvida purchase; it also continued to purchase Disney stock and announced its decision to make a tender offer. Disney's directors quickly responded with an offer to repurchase the Steinberg Group's stock at $60 million above the Group's purchase cost. To consummate the repurchase, Disney borrowed the entire amount to be paid to the Steinberg Group. Disney stockholders challenged the greenmail payment in a suit brought against the Steinberg Group and the Disney directors.

---

957. [1976–1977 Transfer Binder] Fed. Sec. L. Rep. (CCH) ¶ 95,898 (S.D.N.Y. March 4, 1977).

958. *Id.* at 91,322–23.

959. 168 Cal. App. 3d 119, 214 Cal. Rptr. 177 (2d Dist. 1985) (the "Disney" case).

Applying California law, the court found a reasonable probability that plaintiffs would succeed in proving that the Steinberg Group had aided and abetted the Disney directors' breach of their fiduciary duties to Disney's shareholders. The court noted that

> [t]he Steinberg Group knew it was reselling its stock at a price considerably above market value to enable the Disney directors to retain control of the corporation. It knew or should have known Disney was borrowing the $325 million purchase price. From its previous dealings with Disney, including the Arvida transaction, it knew the increased debt load would adversely affect Disney's credit rating and the price of its stock. If it were an active participant in the breach of duty and reaped the benefit, it cannot disclaim the burden.[960]

Because Disney's directors appeared to have personally benefited from the greenmail payment by insuring their continued tenure in office, the court required them to prove that the transaction was fair to the corporation and was entered into in good faith. The court found insufficient the conclusory statement of the directors' attorney that the company had repurchased the shares to avoid the damage to the corporation and its shareholders that would have resulted from a Steinberg tender offer.[961]

Moreover, the court ruled that the Steinberg Group had "assumed a fiduciary duty to the other shareholders"[962] when it filed a derivative suit against Disney to challenge the Arvida purchase. The Group thus was not free to use its "position as class representative for its own financial advantage"[963] and simply to abandon its litigation against the Disney directors as part of a greenmail deal. Such conduct, the court held, constituted a breach of the Steinberg Group's own fiduciary duties to the Disney shareholders.

960. 214 Cal. Rptr. at 182–83.

961. *Id.* at 183.

962. *Id.*

963. *Id.* at 184.

Unocal Corp. v. Mesa Petroleum Co.,[964] although not a greenmail case, illustrates one way that a company might deal with a would-be greenmailer. To avoid the coercive effect of Mesa's two-tier tender offer, Unocal offered to repurchase, at a premium, the shares held by all of its stockholders *except* the corporate raider. The court noted that Delaware law authorized selective stock repurchases and that the only difference between greenmail and the selective self-tender was which shareholders would receive the payment. The court found it ironic that the raider, which had a reputation as a greenmailer, would complain about Unocal's selective stock repurchase.[965]

2. Proposed Legislation

The SEC does not like greenmail and has proposed legislation to limit it. In March 1984, the Commission announced its agreement with a recommendation of the Tender Offer Advisory Committee, which had proposed that "[r]epurchase of a company's shares at a premium to market from a particular holder or group that has held such shares for less than two years would require shareholder approval. This rule would not apply to offers made to all holders of a class of securities."[966]

Two months later, the SEC sent proposed tender offer legislation to Capitol Hill. One provision would have limited greenmail payments by specifying that a company may buy back its securities for more than the market price from a person who has held more than three percent of the outstanding shares for a period of less than two years only if (i) a majority of the aggregate

964. 493 A.2d 946 (Del. 1985), discussed in detail in § III.3.B(2), *supra*.

965. *Id.* at 957.

966. Statement of John S.R. Shad, Chairman of SEC, Before House Subcomm. on Telecommunications, Consumer Protection, and Finance Concerning Recommendations of the SEC Advisory Committee on Tender Offers, [1983 – 1984 Transfer Binder] Fed. Sec. L. Rep. (CCH) ¶ 83,511 (March 28, 1984).

voting shares gives prior approval or (ii) a similar offer is made to other holders of the same class of securities.

Congress adjourned in October 1984 without adopting the SEC's recommended Williams Act amendments. Although anti-greenmail legislation has been reintroduced in Congress, there remains doubt about whether it will be adopted. The White House has opposed changes to the Williams Act that would curb tender offer tactics, stating that such legislation "would intrude unnecessarily into state law and constitute an unwarranted step toward imposition of a substantive federal corporation law."[967]

A bill introduced in Congress in 1985 reproposed the limits on greenmail recommended by the SEC in 1984.[968] Other bills attempted to limit greenmail by creating income tax disincentives for the receipt of such payments.[969]

3. Federal Issues

Any company considering a greenmail defense or making a greenmail payment should pay attention to the federal securities law issues that such a payment might raise.[970] Federal disclosure requirements may make a greenmail transaction less appealing to all involved parties because publicity about the arrangement might invite other potential acquirors to consider the target company, stimulate other shareholders to challenge the payment, or affect the market for the company's shares.

Recent SEC proceedings against B.F. Goodrich for nondisclosure of a greenmail premium[971] highlight the

967. Letter from Treasury Secretary Donald Regan to Chairman John Dingell of the House Energy and Commerce Committee (Sept. 25, 1984).

968. S. 860, 99th Cong., 1st Sess. (1985).

969. H.R. 1003, H.R. 1100, S. 476, S. 414, S. 632, H.R. 2476, 99th Cong., 1st Sess. (1985).

970. *See generally* § 3(a)(9) of the Exchange Act, 15 U.S.C. § 78c(a)(9), and Rules 10b–6, 10b–18, 13e–1, and 13e–4, 17 C.F.R. §§ 240.10b–6, 240.10b–18, 240.13e–1, and 240.13e–4 (1986).

971. *In re B.F. Goodrich Co.* (SEC, Jan. 15, 1986).

importance of complying with federal disclosure requirements.[972] After Goodrich had repurchased its shares from corporate raider Carl Icahn at a price of $41 million, which represented a 25-percent premium over the market price, the company issued a press release concerning the transaction. The press release, however, did not reveal that the company had paid a premium, that the payment constituted a takeover defense, or that the seller was Carl Icahn. The SEC instituted proceedings against Goodrich for failing to disclose the details of the greenmail transaction in its subsequently filed Form 10-K and its 1985 proxy materials containing an anti-greenmail proposal. The proceedings were settled simultaneously with the institution of public proceedings.

In early December 1986, Smith Barney Inc. sued Goodyear Tire & Rubber Co. and Sir James Goldsmith to recover losses that it allegedly suffered when Sir James ended his bid to acquire Goodyear. The firm had taken a substantial position in Goodyear stock, whose value had plunged when Sir James dropped his bid for Goodyear in return for Goodyear's repurchase of his stock at a substantial premium over market price. Smith Barney sued for at least $17 million in damages, based on the difference between the premium that Goodyear had paid Sir James and the stock's closing market price that same day. Smith Barney did not contend that greenmail is *per se* illegal; rather, it alleged that, by acting contrary to their public assertion that no such payment would be made or received, Goodyear and Sir James committed "frauds or deceits" that violated the federal securities laws.

4. The Future of Greenmail

Greenmail payments appeared to be especially prevalent in 1983 and 1984; the problem then seemed to subside. Double dipping

---

972. *See* "B.F. Goodrich Settles S.E.C. Disclosure Charges Over Icahn Stock Repurchasing," 18 Sec. Reg. & L. Rep. 104 (Jan. 24, 1986).

clearly made some targets think twice about paying off raiders who sought a quick profit. Moreover, courts began to react adversely to greenmailers and to sanction some rather radical defensive devices designed to shield companies from such pirates and their demands. Indeed, T. Boone Pickens' reputation as a greenmailer had quite a lot to do with the Delaware Supreme Court's willingness to uphold the discriminatory self-tender offer in *Unocal Corp. v. Mesa Petroleum Co.*[973] This judicial backlash has led some greenmailers to take pains to avoid being seen as such, and many raiders now announce their unwillingness to accept greenmail.

But greenmail has not disappeared; it simply has become more sophisticated. For example, a company might repurchase its securities from a bidder by paying a combination of cash and warrants whose value equals the repurchased stock's prevailing market value. The warrants, however, are designed to provide substantial tax benefits to the bidder, which thus is able to turn the trick at a profit to itself (although without a loss to the repurchaser).

Alternatively, the target may repurchase its shares for an equivalent amount of cash—but may also agree to buy an unwanted division or subsidiary of the bidder at an inflated price. When Chesebrough-Ponds repurchased, at market price, Carl Icahn's five-percent interest in the company, Chesebrough also purchased the Polymor division of Icahn-controlled ACF Industries at a price considered to be in excess of the entity's true value.[974] Greenmail still lives, but in disguise.

---

973. 493 A.2d 946, 957 – 59 (Del. 1985).

974. *See* "Chesebrough Buys Icahn Stake," *New York Times*, April 10, 1984, at D3, col. 6.

G. Recapitalizations

In the last few years, several target companies have responded to hostile takeovers by implementing major recapitalizations (also known as financial restructurings). A recapitalization often can provide shareholders with a superior financial alternative to a hostile bid and can create a management-controlled block of stock, thereby making the target less attractive to present and future bidders. The typical recapitalization plan changes the corporation's debt-to-equity ratio through market purchases of and exchange offers for a large percentage of the target's outstanding common stock or achieves the same result through a reclassification or merger. The consideration for stock purchases and exchanges often consists of a combination of cash, debt securities, and new equity securities.[975] A shareholder typically receives cash and/or securities and remains a stockholder in a much more highly leveraged company.

A recapitalization may defeat a hostile bid because it may enable the target's management to deliver value to shareholders for their shares in an amount that constitutes a substantial premium over historical market prices and that exceeds the consideration offered by the hostile bidder. Enhancing the value of the company's shares also may make the company less attractive to hostile bidders. Moreover, a recapitalization leaves the target public and independent, and it may concentrate a controlling block of shares in the hands of officers and employees. A recapitalization also may increase the target's earnings per share because the company will end up with fewer shares of outstanding stock and may be better able to take advantage of the cash flows of its businesses.

Recapitalizations often involve the creation of debt instruments with covenants and preferred stock with certain designated rights, and these covenants and rights may impede a bidder's ability to finance a takeover, particularly when the

---

975. The objectives and effects of a recapitalization resemble those of a "put plan," discussed in the section on poison pills, *see supra* § III.4.B(2).

bidder is highly leveraged and intends to rely on the target's assets and income to repay its own financing obligations. (Indeed, even a bidder that is not highly leveraged may find a debt-loaded target less attractive.) Restrictive covenants or provisions could limit the target's ability to sell its assets and incur additional debt; they also could limit transactions with affiliates or payments of cash dividends. In some instances, the covenants and provisions do not apply to actions approved by a majority of the target's directors who are not affiliated with the bidder. The target should note, however, that a bidder nevertheless may be able to proceed with a leveraged acquisition of a recapitalized company if the bidder is willing to refinance the target's existing debt.

Finally, a recapitalization may keep the target independent and publicly held, while creating a management-related block of stock that reduces the threat of any future takeover. The management-related block of shares may arise in various ways. For instance, the company could issue a multiple of common shares for each common share to an employee stock option plan ("ESOP"), stock incentive plan, or equity partnership plan, while other shareholders would receive, for each share of common, only one share of common stock plus cash and debt securities. Alternatively, the company could create new stock option, pension, or other plans. The company must insure that public shareholders receive value substantially equivalent (as determined by investment bankers) to that received by management and the plans under its control.

The issuance of shares to an ESOP or other large shareholder has served an important purpose not related to retaining control of the corporation: it has helped to insure the taxation of shareholders' receipt of cash and debt securities at capital gains rates rather than as a dividend (which, for individuals, is usually taxed at a significantly higher rate). Under section 302 of the Internal Revenue Code,[976] if a shareholder's stock interest in a corporation is partially redeemed, the redemption is treated as a

---

976. 26 U.S.C. § 302.

sale or exchange (taxable as a capital gain) if the distribution of cash and debt securities is "substantially disproportionate" with respect to the shareholder—that is (to oversimplify), if the shareholder's share of the corporation's voting stock after the transaction is less than 80 percent of his share of the company's voting interest before the transaction. To achieve this result, a large increase in the percentage of voting stock held by one acquiror (such as an ESOP) is essential. The importance of achieving substantial disproportionality in connection with a distribution, however, may recede under the 1986 Tax Reform Act as tax treatment of capital gains and of dividends becomes more equal.

Many recapitalizations require shareholder approval, either to authorize the issuance of securities needed to effect the plan or to approve a merger or reclassification. If a shareholder vote is required, the company may wish to seek concurrent shareholder approval of certain other defensive mechanisms as part of the recapitalization plan. Such defensive mechanisms may include "shark repellent" charter amendments prohibiting shareholder action by written consent, classifying the board of directors, and implementing fair price and supermajority voting requirements. A single proxy statement could describe the entire package, and, when shareholders vote to receive the enhanced value for their shares, they also could vote for the charter amendments.

Although a recapitalization may provide a useful defense to hostile takeovers, there are severe limitations to its use. A recapitalization, by its very nature, involves a fundamental restructuring of the corporation, a substantial increase in the company's debt-to-equity ratio, and a drastic reduction (in some cases, to negative amounts, on a book basis) in stockholder equity. Such changes compel a redirection of corporate strategy, requiring the company to focus on cash generation, maximization of cash flow, and reduction of overall operating costs. To accomplish these goals and to pay off the newly incurred debt burden, the company typically is forced to sell some of its assets, to eliminate certain businesses that do not yield a substantial short-term return on investment, and to reduce research and development. The change in the debt-to-equity ratio also is likely both to cause credit agencies to lower the company's credit ratings and to affect adversely the company's relations with current lenders.

The target's existing debt instruments may forbid certain types of recapitalization financing. For example, covenants limiting the target's ability to incur additional debt may prevent the target from borrowing money to finance the proposed recapitalization. If the debt instruments contain covenants relating to a "restricted payments" test, the target may be barred from making open-market purchases or exchange offers that involve cash. If such covenants exist, the target may attempt to convince lenders to amend or waive restrictive covenants or otherwise consent to the incurrence of additional debt, or it may be forced to prepay and refinance the debt in question.

During the short time (approximately four weeks) available to a company that wishes to recapitalize as a defense to a hostile takeover bid, a target may find it impossible to obtain necessary consents from public debt holders; private debt holders, however, might grant such amendments, waivers, or consents in exchange for the tightening of other covenants or for a boost in the basis points of their debt instruments. Because of these constraints, a corporation should attempt, when negotiating its debt instruments, to obtain certain exemptions in order to leave room for a defensive recapitalization.

The target's certificate of incorporation also may prove to be an obstacle to certain types of recapitalizations if it does not authorize a sufficient number of unissued shares to enable the company to effect its plan. Similarly, the charter's failure to authorize blank check preferred may prevent the company from issuing preferred stock, absent stockholder approval of an amendment to the certificate of incorporation to authorize the required preferred stock. A company contemplating a recapitalization that will require shareholder approval of such a charter amendment will have to consider the possibility that its shareholders will not approve the proposal. Phillips Petroleum, for example, had to abandon a recapitalization plan and implement an alternative one because its shareholders refused to vote for the initial proposal.[977]

Recapitalizations also raise various questions under state and federal law. For example, the company must determine the necessity of registering new securities being offered in an exchange offer: under certain circumstances, such securities need not be registered under the Securities Act of 1933. Section 3(a)(9) of the Act reads:

> (a) Except as hereinafter expressly provided, the provisions of this [Title] shall not apply to any of the following classes of securities.
>
> . . . .
>
> (9) Except with respect to a security exchanged in a case under Title 11 [of the United States Code], any security exchanged by the issuer with its existing security holders exclusively where no commission or other remuneration is paid or given directly or indirectly for soliciting such exchange. . . .[978]

In a recapitalization that involved the exchange of common stock for cash and securities, Union Carbide relied on section 3(a)(9) as its justification for not registering the new securities. Often, however, a registration statement is required, especially when the recapitalization plan involves the creation of new employee pension plans.

State laws may pose other problems, particularly if the relevant statutes permit corporations to make distributions only out of surplus. For instance, section 174 of the Delaware General Corporation Law provides that a corporation may not purchase or redeem any of its shares for cash or other property when the corporation's capital is impaired or when such a purchase or redemption would cause the impairment of the corporation's capital. As a result of this law, recapitalizations in Delaware often are structured as statutory mergers (in which a newly created

---

977. The Phillips plan is discussed in § III.4.G(1), *infra*.

978. 15 U.S.C. § 77c(a)(9).

subsidiary merges into the company upon consummation of the recapitalization), rather than as stock redemptions or repurchases. But even if it structures its plan as a statutory merger, the company should appraise its assets and take all other reasonable steps to insure that its recapitalization complies with section 174 and to avoid raising fraudulent conveyance issues.

Of course, any reevaluation of assets to achieve the surplus may also create substantial legal issues. For instance, in an action brought by a bidder to enjoin target Warnaco, Inc.'s recapitalization, the court stated:

> Since the statutes do not provide for a specific method of calculating value for public disclosure, the question is whether . . . [the bidder] has proven that what [the target] has done is so far removed from the range of permissible methods of calculating value as to be deemed unlawful. No method of evaluation is guaranteed.
>
> . . . .
>
> [The bidder] has raised a number of questions about the justification and efficacy of the evaluation, the timing of it, the accuracy of the underlying data, the propriety of the processing and the soundness of the judgment. Undoubtedly, there are a great many other questions which could be posed to the appraiser, to management, to the Directors, and to the financial advisors. Ultimately, it might well be found as a fact that the value of particular assets and, in turn, the total is not as the appraiser opines. Indeed, it might yet be shown that the appraiser's opinion is so contradicted by the answers to the questions as yet unasked, by different facts and by contrast to standards of proper accounting, including GAAP, that it is found improper to state the finances of the corporation in reliance upon it. Thus, the recapitalization would itself be unlawful as premised upon an unlawfully stated surplus.
>
> . . . .
>
> These questions clearly demonstrate the existence of a justiciable issue, the merits of which warrant litigation. However, [the bidder] has not gone so far as to establish that the hardships

> tip so decidedly in its favor as to warrant the grant of its motion under the test specified by the Court of Appeals. [The bidder] has not demonstrated that it is likely to prevail on the issue because the raising of questions merely makes the proposed recapitalization suspect. . . . In a different respect, the same lack of proof suggests that it cannot be found that the balance of the hardships tips decidedly in [the bidder's] favor. The denial of an injunction now will not prevent the shareholders from asking all pertinent questions and assessing the risk that the proposal is held invalid when its merits are fully explored. [The bidder] will have a full opportunity to challenge the recapitalization and make a full presentation on the issues, as opposed to this preliminary presentation. Damages awarded then with possible injunctive relief have not been shown to be inadequate. A finding that the bidder has not met its burden does not reflect a predisposition on the merits. Neither will this denial preclude nor disadvantage the presentation of other claims that might be made. It constitutes neither an endorsement nor a vindication of the actions of either management or the directors, nor anyone else.
>
> As both parties have agreed, essentially this is a decision to be made in the market place, by the shareholders.[979]

Fraudulent conveyance issues may arise under state statutes, such as the Uniform Fraudulent Conveyance Act and the Uniform Fraudulent Transfer Act, and under federal statutes, specifically the Bankruptcy Code. A fraudulent conveyance may occur whenever a company makes any transfer or incurs any obligation without receiving fair consideration. A creditor of the company may sue to invalidate any such transfer or obligation if the company, at the relevant time (and depending on applicable law), (a) was insolvent, (b) was rendered insolvent by the particular distribution, (c) was engaged in a business or transaction for which its assets constituted unreasonably small capital, or (d) intended to incur, or believed that it would incur, debts beyond its ability to pay as such debts matured.

---

979. *Warnaco Inc. v. Galef*, No. B – 86 – 146, slip op. at 12, 13, 15 – 16 (D. Conn. April 25, 1986).

Under these fraudulent conveyance statutes, any payment of cash or issuance of subordinated debt by a financially impaired company to its stockholders may be deemed to have been made without fair consideration, because the recapitalization does not provide any additional value to the company from the perspective of its existing creditors. If the recapitalization sufficiently weakens the company so that it meets the test of financial impairment under the relevant statutes, the cash payment or debt issuance could be invalidated and recaptured from stockholders by the company's creditors under state law or, in the event of subsequent bankruptcy proceedings, by the debtor or bankruptcy trustee under state or federal law. Moreover, under certain circumstances, third-party lenders who partially financed the cash payments to stockholders could be defendants in a fraudulent conveyance action, and their debt claims could be subject to subordination.[980]

Because of the possibility that their creditors might raise fraudulent conveyance claims as a result of a proposed or consummated recapitalization, corporations typically disclose these issues in their SEC filings pertaining to the recapitalization. For instance, in the February 5, 1986 tender offer by Amsted Industries Inc. and its employee stock ownership plan for shares of Amsted, the bidders made the following disclosures:

> a. If, because of the indebtedness to be incurred to finance the Acquisition, the Acquisition were deemed, among other things, to render the Company insolvent, leave it with an unreasonably small amount of capital or render it unable to pay its contemplated debts as they become due, a creditor of the Company (or Trustee in bankruptcy) might, under Federal and/or state insolvency law, be entitled to recover from the Company's stockholders all amounts received in respect of the Shares, the Offer or the Merger.

980. Fraudulent conveyances are discussed in greater detail in § II.8., *supra*.

b. If a court in a lawsuit by an unpaid creditor or representative of creditors of the Company, such as a trustee in bankruptcy or the Company as debtor in possession, were to find that, at the time the Company distributed the Offer Price or the Merger Price to the holders of Shares, the Company (*i*) was insolvent, (*ii*) was rendered insolvent by reason of such distributions, (*iii*) was engaged in a business or transaction for which the assets remaining with the Company constituted unreasonably small capital, or (*iv*) intended to incur, or believed that it would incur, debts beyond its ability to pay such debts as they matured, such could void the distributions to holders of Shares and require that such holders return the same (or equivalent amounts) to the Company or to a fund for the benefit of its creditors (including, under certain circumstances, the Banks). In addition, if a court were to find that the Company in fact came within any of the foregoing clauses (i) through (iv), a creditor, a trustee in bankruptcy or the Company as a debtor in possession could also seek to avoid the grant of security interests by the Company to the Banks. This could result in an event of default with respect to such indebtedness which, under the terms of such indebtedness (subject to applicable law), would allow the holders thereof to accelerate their debt. In addition, based upon general bankruptcy law principles, holders of Debentures may become equitably subordinated to general creditors of the Company. The measure of insolvency for purposes of the foregoing will vary depending upon the law of the jurisdiction which is being applied. Generally, however, the Company would be considered insolvent if the sum of the Company's debts is greater than all of the Company's property at a fair valuation, or if the present fair saleable value of the Company's assets is less than the amount that will be required to pay its probable liability on its existing debts as they become absolute and matured. Based on management's estimates described below, the Company believes that the fair market value of its assets exceeds the sum of the Company's debts and that the Company is not and will not be considered insolvent under the first test set forth in the preceding sentence. However, such estimates were based on the assumption that the Company continues as a going concern, as opposed to being based upon the sale value of such assets in a liquidation separately from each other. There can be no assurance that a court would value the Company's assets on a going concern basis in order to determine whether the Company was "insolvent" or that, regardless of the method of valuation, a court would not determine that the Company was insolvent at the time of

> consummation of the Offer or the Merger. However, management of the Company believes that following the Merger, the Company will be able to repay its debts as they mature, as shown in the projections set forth in "SPECIAL FACTORS—Certain Projections," and that following the Merger, the Company will have sufficient capital for the businesses in which the Company will be engaged.

One way for the target to protect itself against fraudulent conveyance risks is to obtain an appraisal that would provide the basis for reevaluation of the assets on its balance sheet and for creation of a reevaluation surplus.

1. Examples of Recapitalizations in General

The purposes and effects of recapitalizations, as well as judicial responses to them, can best be understood by analyzing a few recent recapitalizations and the litigation that they engendered. The CBS recapitalization illustrates how a company may seek to recapitalize itself to fend off an unwanted tender offer.

In 1985, Turner Broadcasting System, Inc. announced a hostile, highly leveraged exchange offer for CBS. The offer involved junk bonds and no cash; the junk bonds had a face value of $175 but were appraised at an actual value of somewhere between $120 and $150. CBS responded with its own offer to repurchase 21 percent of its common stock by exchanging each common share for $40 in cash and a ten-year senior note with a principal amount of $110.

CBS intended to finance this offer by selling some of its assets and by reducing expenses; it also privately placed a significant amount of preferred stock and entered into two revolving credit agreements. The preferred stock, credit agreements, and senior notes contained covenants and conditions limiting liens, sales and leasebacks, sales of assets, and incurrence of additional debt. Moreover, these covenants and conditions were designed so that a breach would occur upon consummation of the Turner offer and a second-step merger. CBS also disclosed its expectation that the recapitalization, with the terms and conditions in the debt and preferred stock, would likewise deter other hostile bids in the future. All of this added up to a formidable defense against the Turner bid, but it had a price: the recapitalization tripled CBS's corporate debt and increased the company's debt-to-equity ratio from approximately 20 percent to 66 percent.

Turner challenged the recapitalization, but a federal district court, in *Turner Broadcasting System, Inc. v. CBS, Inc.*,[981] declined to enjoin the CBS exchange offer. The court emphasized that the CBS board had discussed and nearly implemented a similar recapitalization plan in 1984 and had determined, after adequately examining the Turner offer, that its own recapitalization plan would be better both for the company and for its shareholders. The court declared that, "although it is highly probable that the [Turner] tender offer had the effect of forcing CBS to act more quickly on its recapitalization plan, the . . . tender offer was not the catalyst that made CBS decide to consider the recapitalization program."[982]

Furthermore, the court found that CBS's directors had not acted with the primary purpose of entrenching themselves and had appropriately exercised their business judgment in concluding that the Turner offer was not in the best interests of CBS's shareholders. Even though application of the primary purpose test was required under New York law because of the inherent conflict of interest in the stock repurchases, the court ruled that the board had "made a sufficient showing of fairness by demonstrating through the evidence presented that the transactions entered into were for a proper corporate purpose."[983]

Similarly, in *Edelman v. Phillips Petroleum Co.*,[984] the court declined to enjoin the submission of Phillips' recapitalization plan to the company's shareholders. The Phillips proposal, which had arisen in response to a takeover effort by T. Boone

---

981. 627 F. Supp. 901 (N.D. Ga. 1985).

982. *Id.* at 905.

983. *Id.* at 906.

984. No. 7899 (Del. Ch. Feb. 12, 1985).

Pickens' Mesa Partners through open-market purchases and an announced tender offer, was part of a settlement agreement between Phillips and Mesa. The settlement, which was subject to the approval of Phillips' shareholders, was designed to end the war between the two companies and also to terminate Mesa's ability to obtain control of Phillips.

The story of the Phillips recapitalization proposal and the settlement agreement is a complicated one. The events began with a series of claims and counterclaims between Mesa and Phillips following the commencement of Mesa's takeover attempt. On December 20, 1984, the Delaware Chancery Court granted Mesa a preliminary injunction prohibiting Phillips from enforcing a standstill agreement between Mesa and General American Oil Company of Texas, which agreement was designed to protect Phillips from a hostile bid.

Prior to that court order, the Phillips board had developed and approved an alternative anti-takeover strategy that included an exchange offer resembling the recapitalization plan at issue in the 1985 proceedings. After the court's December 20, 1984 ruling, however, Phillips and Mesa worked out a settlement agreement under which Phillips would repurchase Mesa's block of stock. In addition to specifying the terms of the repurchase, the agreement included a recapitalization plan in which each Phillips shareholder would exchange common stock for a combination of debt and equity securities. The recapitalization would increase the corporation's debt-to-equity ratio and would result in Phillips' employees' owning 40 percent of the company's outstanding common stock.

The plan provided for the exchange of each share of common stock for .62 of a share of common stock and .38 of a share of preferred stock; each share of preferred stock would then be exchanged for a debt security package valued at $60. In addition, Phillips would sell up to 32 million shares of its common stock to an ESOP and would purchase $1 billion worth of its own stock on the open market. These open-market purchases were intended to boost the price of the common stock after the recapitalization.

The recapitalization plan was subject to shareholder approval, and the settlement agreement provided that, if such approval were not obtained, Phillips would repurchase Mesa's shares at $53 per share. The agreement also included charter and bylaw amendments consisting of basic anti-takeover provisions classifying the board of directors and prohibiting shareholder action by written consent. In addition, Phillips' board adopted a put plan.

The Phillips board, 11 of whose 16 members were outside directors, approved the recapitalization plan on December 23, only three days after the Chancery Court's decision, at a meeting attended by five outside lawyers and seven representatives of two investment banks. The plan was a modified, less drastic version of the exchange offer that the board had discussed and approved prior to the court's decision.

Plaintiff Albert Edelman then brought a shareholder derivative suit to enjoin Mesa and Phillips from implementing the settlement agreement and distributing proxies for a shareholder vote. The court denied the injunction.

The court treated the recapitalization plan as a cross between a preplanned general defensive strategy, which courts typically are more inclined to uphold, and a more legally precarious reactive defensive strategy effectively forestalling the Mesa takeover effort. While recognizing that plaintiff had raised "serious questions" regarding the legality and fairness of the settlement agreement, the court applied a presumption of good faith and upheld the Phillips board's actions under the business judgment rule. The court particularly emphasized that the settlement was subject to shareholder approval:

> [S]ince much, but not all, of the conduct here under review will be subject to shareholder approval, it would be precipitous for this Court to preclude shareholder ratification if (a) the proposed recapitalization is not void under the Delaware General Corporation Law . . . or (b) the proxy materials present director action and the background of the proposal fairly and completely.[985]

985. Slip op. at 9.

The court also recognized a number of positive aspects of the plan:

> [T]he recapitalization plan . . . constitutes a means whereby [shareholders other than Mesa] may share in whatever benefits may be perceived to have occurred in the takeover bargaining. It has other important results. It provides a strong employee incentive towards productivity by creation of the ESOP and, importantly, decreases the risk that Phillips [would] be subject to future takeover efforts which might be destructive of shareholder value. But there is nothing in the plan which directly ensures continuation of present management and to the extent that the proposed by-law amendments including reclassification of directors' terms have such effect the shareholders are free to reject them.[986]

Moreover, although the recapitalization plan "significantly reduce[d] the number of publicly-held shares [it did] not render Phillips acquisition proof."[987] The court thus declined to view the recapitalization plan as an entrenchment device and held that the draconian nature of Mesa's two-tier, bust-up offer and the reputation of T. Boone Pickens as a corporate raider justified the board's decision to fend off Mesa's takeover efforts.

Following the ruling permitting Phillips to submit its recapitalization plan to its shareholders, Carl Icahn, another hostile raider, commenced a tender offer for the company. The shareholders proceeded to reject the recapitalization plan, whereupon Phillips changed its proposal to an exchange offer having better terms and not requiring shareholder approval. Phillips issued debt securities in exchange for about 50 percent of its common stock and sold some of its assets to reduce the debt that it had incurred as a result of the exchange offer.

Had Phillips' shareholders approved the recapitalization plan, and had the company then implemented it, Phillips' long-term debt would have doubled, and its equity would have been reduced by a third. Moreover, the recapitalization would have

---

986. *Id.* at 16.
987. *Id.* at 8.

created a substantial block of stock controlled by employees through an ESOP. The existence of such a block, combined with defensive amendments to Phillips' certificate of incorporation, would have constituted substantial obstacles to a bidder seeking control of Phillips.

The validity of another recent recapitalization was at issue in *GAF Corp. v. Union Carbide Corp.*,[988] in which a federal district court upheld a recapitalization plan that Union Carbide had developed to provide shareholders with an alternative to a hostile bid by GAF. GAF had made a cash tender offer, at $68 per share, for 48 million shares of Union Carbide; the offer was conditioned upon the valid tender of a minimum of 46 percent (31,000,000) of Carbide's outstanding shares of capital stock and upon GAF's obtaining sufficient financing to pay for the tendered shares.

The Carbide board reacted by announcing a "Comprehensive Restructuring Program," under which the company anticipated selling at least $500 million worth of its assets, withdrawing $500 million in surplus funds from its Retirement Program Plan, and exchanging between 35 and 70 percent of its outstanding voting common stock for $20 per share plus certain notes and debentures containing restrictive covenants limiting the company's ability to sell assets and to incur additional debt in the future. The debt instruments would be noncallable for periods of four, five, and seven years.

GAF sued for a preliminary injunction to prevent Carbide from consummating the proposed exchange offer. Applying the business judgment rule, the court upheld the exchange offer, despite the restrictive covenants in the notes and debentures, and stated:

> Courts . . . should be very circumspect in entering this area at the behest of a tender offeror and declaring some of these methods of raising capital proper, some improper, unless there is no reasonable business justification, evaluated according to that

---

988. 624 F. Supp. 1016 (S.D.N.Y. 1985).

> particular company's situation, for restrictions placed in the debt instruments. Whether the covenants have an ancillary effect on the tender offeror's plans for the target company is irrelevant, even if that effect was intended.[989]

The court noted that the recapitalization plan would not become effective unless Carbide's shareholders accepted the exchange offer and refused to tender to GAF. GAF thus had to present its case to the shareholders, rather than to the court:

> Self-appointed potential acquirers of control are not a protected species in corporate law. The hostile offeror is not entitled to have Boards of Directors smooth his path to control. That has to be earned with fairness and proof in the competition for the voting stock that satisfies the shareholders that they should sell and are being offered a fair price.[990]

Other recent defensive recapitalizations include Revlon's exchange offer, which was upheld in *Revlon, Inc. v. MacAndrews & Forbes Holdings, Inc.*,[991] and Anderson, Clayton's proposed restructuring, which was preliminarily enjoined in *AC Acquisitions Corp. v. Anderson, Clayton & Co.*[992] Both cases are discussed elsewhere in this book.

2. Recapitalizations and ESOPs

Companies that recapitalize in response to hostile bids often use existing ESOPs or create new employee benefit plans as a means of placing substantial blocks of stock in the control of management. Such blocks have various purposes: (*i*) they may help dilute the holdings of the bidder; (*ii*) they may permit a cash

---

989. *Id.* at 1020 (emphasis added).

990. *Id.*

991. 506 A.2d 173 (Del. 1986), discussed in detail in § III.3.B(3) and III.4.B(2)(b), *supra*.

992. [Current] Fed. Sec. L. Rep. (CCH) ¶ 92,942 (Del. Ch. Sept. 18, 1986), discussed in detail in § III.3.B(3), *supra*.

distribution in the recapitalization to be taxed on a capital gains basis; (*iii*) they may constitute an attractive means, from a tax point of view, of compensating officers and employees; (*iv*) they may help the company to finance the recapitalization; and (*v*) when used in conjunction with various charter provisions such as a supermajority voting provision, they may render the company relatively immune to future takeover attempts.

a. Financing a Recapitalization Through a Leveraged ESOP

Depending upon its particular circumstances, a company may be able to finance a significant amount of its recapitalization through a leveraged ESOP—that is, an ESOP that incurs a significant amount of debt to acquire the company's stock. (An ESOP, unlike most pension plans, may be leveraged.) A leveraged ESOP thus borrows cash to purchase "qualifying employer securities" on the open market or from the issuer. "Qualifying employer securities" consist of common stock and certain convertible preferred stock. The ESOP later repays its loan by using periodic cash contributions that the employer makes to the ESOP, and the shares held by the ESOP are allocated to employees as the loan is repaid. Employees thus become the beneficial owners of the allocated shares as those shares vest in accordance with the plan's vesting schedule. The amount of principal repayments may not exceed 25 percent of the payroll of plan participants in any fiscal year.

Under current law, reliance on leveraged ESOPs offers two major tax advantages over the use of a simple exchange offer or self-tender. First, all of the amounts contributed by the company to the ESOP (both the principal as well as the interest due on the ESOP's loan) are tax deductible, while, in the case of a self-tender, the company can deduct only interest payments. Second, under current law,[993] qualifying lenders (such as banks

---

993. As of October 1, 1986. The tax legislation contemplated to be effective in 1987 may affect the use of an ESOP. At this time, however, it is difficult to determine the precise nature of that effect.

and certain finance companies) are permitted to exclude from their taxable income one-half of the interest received from loans to leveraged ESOPs; the ESOP therefore may (depending on the tax rate of the lender) be in a position to bargain for a reduction in the interest rate that would otherwise apply to its loan.

Employees may place up to 25 percent of the payroll into an ESOP trust in order to make loan payments or trust loans; 25 percent of payroll contributed over ten or 15 years could create a large ESOP loan. (If, however, substantial divestitures are planned in the future as part of the recapitalization, projected payroll contributions would be correspondingly reduced.) The tax benefit of being able to deduct such a loan, together with a reduced rate of interest on this portion of the debt financing, could permit significantly greater borrowing.

An ESOP also can be useful in a recapitalization because it may acquire stock directly from an unrelated party, even for a premium above current market value, subject to certain fiduciary constraints.[994] Hence, the ESOP may be able to pay a premium price to repurchase shares held by a hostile bidder.

A possible drawback to using an ESOP in a recapitalization is that the stock held in the ESOP, unlike treasury stock repurchased by the company itself, remains outstanding and thus may dilute any public shareholdings that survive the recapitalization. This dilution could be substantial and might offset the benefits accruing to stockholders from the company's increased borrowing capacity.

However, an ESOP funded at the maximum rate probably would replace or be combined with existing pension plans and their funding requirements. For instance, existing benefit arrangements may be converted into a "floor plan" to reduce duplications of benefits. A "floor plan" is a pension plan that provides a benefit equal to the difference between the target's existing plan and the value of the benefit provided by the ESOP; if the value of the ESOP stock increases, future contributions to

---

994. *See infra* § III.4.G(2)(b) (discussing fiduciary duties).

the floor plan decrease. If the stock does not perform well, the floor plan assures employees of a minimum benefit.

When planning a transaction involving a leveraged ESOP, the company's board must consider the numerous restrictions arising from ESOPs' status as qualified employee benefit plans. For example, fiduciary responsibilities inherent in such a plan may dictate retention of independent trustees and advisers for the ESOP. Moreover, party in interest rules may bar the payment by (or on behalf of) the ESOP of a "tender premium" in excess of fair market value to any seller who is a "disqualified person," such as an employee or director of the target. Finally, there are restrictions on the voting of shares held by an ESOP: plan participants receive the right to vote allocated ESOP shares, while voting rights on unallocated shares may be passed through to participants or voted by the ESOP trustees.

From a strategic point of view, a company therefore must weigh the benefits of a leveraged ESOP in delivering immediate value to shareholders against the disadvantages of such an approach—the additional complexity, the potential loss of control over ESOP shares, and the risk of litigation instigated by a hostile bidder (or by the Secretary of Labor). Various courts and the Department of Labor have analyzed these issues in a number of contexts, including tender offers involving Hi-Shear Corporation, Calumet Industries, Norlin Corporation, Continental Air Lines, Graniteville Corporation, Chicago Pneumatic Tool Company, and Phillips Petroleum.[995] The cases suggest that courts tend to increase their scrutiny when companies institute the ESOPs during hostile tender offers.

b. *Fiduciary Duties and ESOPs*

In using ESOPs as part of a recapitalization plan or other defense against a hostile bid, a company must realize that trustees of any employee benefit plan under the Employee Retirement Income

---

995. These transactions are discussed in §§ III.4.E(1), *supra*, and III.4.H., *infra*.

Security Act ("ERISA") are fiduciaries who must act "solely in the interest of the participants and beneficiaries" of the plan, for the "exclusive purpose" of providing benefits to participants, and "with the care, skill, prudence, and diligence" of the traditional "prudent man."[996] When these trustees also are the directors of a target that is attempting to fight off a hostile tender offer, conflicts of interest may arise. If, in response to the tender offer, the trustees purchase stock on behalf of the ESOP, the trustees' motives for acquiring the securities could be questioned: did the trustees intend to benefit the plan, or did they intend merely to defend the target against the hostile bidder?

In *Donovan v. Bierwirth*,[997] the Court of Appeals for the Second Circuit addressed the fiduciary obligations of a plan's trustees in the context of a hostile tender offer by LTV for Grumman. Although the case was decided on the narrow issue whether the trustees of Grumman's Pension Plan (the "Plan") acted with due care in deciding to purchase shares of Grumman stock, the court discussed the role of directors and officers who also act as pension plan trustees in tender offer situations.

The Grumman Plan had three trustees, all of whom were Grumman officers, and two of whom were deeply involved in Grumman's attempts to thwart LTV's hostile bid. The trustees determined that it was not in the best interests of the Plan's beneficiaries for the Plan to tender its 3.8 percent interest in Grumman to LTV. Furthermore, the trustees decided to increase the Plan's holdings of Grumman securities to eight percent, claiming that a further investment in the company was desirable and that the increased market activity caused by the LTV offer would support large-scale purchases by the Plan.

The Secretary of Labor brought an action alleging that the Plan's trustees had breached their fiduciary duties. The Court of Appeals held that the trustees had not exercised due care in formulating the Plan's investment strategy: they had failed to seek advice from independent counsel and had not adequately

---

996. ERISA § 404(a), 29 U.S.C. § 1104(a).

997. 680 F.2d 263 (2d Cir.), *cert. denied*, 459 U.S. 1069 (1982).

investigated LTV's intentions regarding the Plan in the event that LTV acquired control of Grumman.

The court rejected defendants' contention that the trustees had increased the Plan's holdings because they believed Grumman securities to be a good investment for the Plan. The court noted that the trustees had believed that the LTV tender offer would fail, and yet they had decided to increase the Plan's holdings at prices inflated by the pending tender offer; had the trustees purchased the securities after the LTV offer's expected failure, the securities would have been less expensive. Moreover, such purchases would have been unwise even had the tender offer succeeded, because the trustees had decided not to tender the Plan's shares to LTV and thus could not have taken advantage of the tender offer premium.

The trustees also argued that, "once they had reasonably decided not to tender the shares already in the fund since success of the offer would run counter to the interests of the beneficiaries, it followed that they should do everything else they lawfully could do to thwart the offer."[998] The court ruled, however, that the trustees remained responsible for assessing the risks and benefits of their actions and that they had not made an appropriate assessment.

Implicit in this decision is the principle that trustees, when acting on behalf of a Plan, may consider the interests only of Plan participants and beneficiaries. The court did not deny that Plan trustees, in a hostile tender offer situation, may undertake a course of action "which benefits the corporation as well as the beneficiaries";[999] the benefit to the corporation, however, may not be more than incidental to "action which, after careful and impartial investigation, [the trustees] reasonably conclude best to promote the interests of participants and beneficiaries. . . ."[1000] The court also observed that the activities of the two trustees who had participated in Grumman's tender offer defense

---

998. 680 F.2d at 274.

999. *Id.* at 271.

1000. *Id.*

"precluded their exercising the detached judgment required of them as trustees of the Plan"[1001] and that these persons, who had been outspoken in their opposition to the tender offer, should have resigned as trustees.

Bierwirth demonstrates that trustees of ERISA plans must display a degree of care and loyalty comparable to that required of directors considering a tender offer. More importantly, trustees of ERISA plans should not play an active role in determining the target's position on a tender offer if they also wish to act on behalf of the plan in considering that offer.

H. Issuance of Stock

If a target company wishes to fend off a hostile offer in order to remain independent (rather than to merge with a white knight), the company might consider issuing stock to a "white squire," which will not enter the bidding contest but will become a continuing (and, presumably, friendly) presence in the target's shareholder constituency. Issuance of stock to a white squire assures friendly voting especially when accompanied by a voting or a standstill agreement or, if the white squire is an ESOP, by management's serving as the ESOP trustee.

Whenever a company increases the number of outstanding shares of stock, it dilutes the equity of all present stockholders, including that of any holder seeking to wrest control of the issuer. Moreover, the issuance of a block of shares to a single person or entity that supports the company's management may make a potential acquiror less inclined to commence a tender offer or proxy fight. If that block consists of preferred stock entitled to vote as a separate class on certain extraordinary transactions, such as a merger or a sale of assets, a would-be acquiror's ability to gain control of the issuer is further impaired.

1001. *Id.*

The New York Stock Exchange requires shareholder approval as a prerequisite for listing a new issue of common stock (or securities convertible into common stock) representing more than 18.5 percent of the company's outstanding shares. The NASD does not have a similar requirement for companies whose securities are traded over the counter.

Instead of seeking white squires, companies sometimes set up ESOPs and issue a large number of shares to the ESOP trustee for the benefit of the employees. The ESOP may borrow money to pay for the stock, and the company may guarantee the ESOP's indebtedness. The company could then make tax deductible annual contributions to the ESOP, and the ESOP trustee could use those contributions to repay the loan.

Issuances of stock primarily involve questions of state law: whether the issuer received adequate consideration for the shares, whether the company issued the shares for a proper purpose, and whether the company's directors fulfilled their duties of care and loyalty in approving the arrangements. Stock issuances also might raise questions under stock exchange rules. It is unlikely, however, that federal law questions will arise—provided that the issuer has met its disclosure obligations.

Courts have not always looked favorably upon issuances of stock either to ESOPs or to white squires. *Frantz Manufacturing Co. v. EAC Industries*,[1002] for example, enjoined management's attempt to issue treasury stock to an ESOP in order to dilute the holdings of a bidder that had acquired 51 percent of the company's stock. Plaintiff, which had purchased its 51-percent interest in the target from three shareholders in privately negotiated transactions, executed a consent to elect its nominee to fill a vacancy on the target's board and to amend the target's bylaws to require that all board actions be unanimous. In response, the target's chief executive officer arranged for the company's ESOP to purchase a large block of stock pursuant to a general board resolution authorizing the company's officers to fund the ESOP. This maneuver diluted the bidder's holdings to

---

1002. 501 A.2d 401 (Del. 1985).

44 percent. Claiming that management's action was an unauthorized attempt at entrenchment, plaintiff sued to nullify the stock issuance.

The Delaware Supreme Court held that, "[a]lthough the directors generally act under the protection of the business judgment rule both in prospective measures and in reactive measures seeking to ward off a threatened hostile takeover, corporate action which seeks to undo a takeover bid *after* control has already passed to another group is not protected by the business judgment rule."[1003] The court also noted the Chancery Court's finding that management had funded the ESOP with treasury stock for the primary purpose of perpetuating the board's control of the company; the court declared that, "when a board acts for the sole or primary purpose of perpetuating its own control, this improper motive overrides the ordinary protection of the business-judgment rule."[1004] In addition, the court held that the issuance violated the bylaw amendment requiring that any board action be taken by unanimous vote.

In *Norlin Corp. v. Rooney, Pace Inc.*,[1005] the Court of Appeals for the Second Circuit also declined to apply the business judgment rule to a target's decision to place stock in friendly hands because the board had acted with no purpose other than "to oppose, at all costs, the [takeover] threat. . . ."[1006] In response to a hostile takeover attempt, Norlin's directors had issued new voting stock to a wholly owned subsidiary and a newly created ESOP, thereby assuring that the directors could maintain voting control over the company.

The Court of Appeals affirmed the district court's preliminary injunction against the voting of the newly issued securities and rejected Norlin's claim that the defensive measure was an appropriate way to give the target more time to determine what to do about the takeover attempt:

1003. *Id.* at 408 (emphasis in original).

1004. *Id.*

1005. 744 F.2d 255 (2d Cir. 1984).

1006. *Id.* at 265.

> The company asserts that the shareholders will benefit if the directors are insulated from challenges to their control, for an interim period of unspecified duration, so that all . . . future operations can be considered with professional guidance. This argument stands our prior cases on their heads. It is true that in conformity with the duty of care, we have required corporate managers to examine carefully the merits of a proposed change in control. We have also urged consultation with investment specialists in undertaking such analysis. . . . The purpose of this exercise, however, is to insure a reasoned examination of the situation *before* action is taken, not afterwards.[1007]

The court observed that, under New York law,

> the business judgment rule governs only where the directors are not shown to have a self-interest in the transaction at issue. . . . Once self-dealing or bad faith is demonstrated, the duty of loyalty supersedes the duty of care, and the burden shifts to the directors to "prove that the transaction was fair and reasonable to the corporation."[1008]

Applying these precepts, the court found "more than adequate" evidence of the directors' self-interest and desire to entrench themselves: the transferred stock was to be voted by the directors; the stock had been issued immediately after a takeover threat was made; the ESOP had been created on the very day on which the shares were issued to it; and the board had offered no rationale for the stock transfers other than its determination to oppose the takeover threat. Based on these facts, the court concluded that, "[w]here, as here, directors amass voting control of close to a majority of a corporation's shares in their own hands by complex, convoluted and deliberate maneuvers, it strains credulity to suggest that the retention of control over corporate affairs played no part in their plans."[1009] Thus, the directors had breached their duty of loyalty to the company and

---

1007. *Id.* at 267 (citation omitted) (emphasis in original).
1009. *Id.* at 265.
1009. *Id.*

its shareholders and could not take shelter under the business judgment rule's umbrella. Nor could the directors prove the fairness and reasonableness of the stock issuances, for an examination of the relevant facts showed that "the ESOP was created solely as a tool of management self-perpetuation."[1010]

Klaus v. Hi-Shear Corp.[1011] also held that a target improperly had issued stock to an employee stock option trust ("ESOT") primarily as an entrenchment device to dilute the vote of a 45-percent shareholder. The transaction thus did not constitute a valid exercise of business judgment by the corporation's directors. The court noted that the purported business purpose for the issuance of stock to the ESOT was disproportionately minor in comparison with the advantage that incumbent management gained from the issuance.

Because plaintiff had overcome the presumptions of the business judgment rule by showing that the transaction was part of an entrenchment scheme, the Court of Appeals for the Ninth Circuit concluded that plaintiff had established a probability of success on the merits. However, the court overturned the district court's grant of an injunction because plaintiff had not made a sufficient showing of irreparable harm.

Podesta v. Calumet Industries, Inc.[1012] enjoined the voting both of shares issued to a newly created ESOP and of shares purchased pursuant to warrants issued to a white squire. The court held that Calumet's board had approved the two transactions for "the primary, if not the sole, purpose of retaining control of Calumet."[1013]

The court found that the company had first considered creating an ESOP only three weeks before adopting the plan, which had been "negotiated in a great rush, coinciding with the setting of a date for the annual meeting and a record date for the

---

1010. *Id.* at 266.

1011. 528 F.2d 225 (9th Cir. 1975).

1012. [1978 Transfer Binder] Fed. Sec. L. Rep. (CCH) ¶ 96,433 (N.D. Ill. May 9, 1978).

1013. *Id.* at 93,556.

election" of directors.[1014] Because the board had neglected to arrange financing for the ESOP, the corporation effectively loaned the money for the ESOP's original purchase of shares. Moreover, management would not have accepted an ESOP that would not permit all of its shares to be voted in the upcoming elections. With respect to the warrants transaction with the white squire, the court found that the deal was the product of a rushed meeting culminating in an oral agreement and that management had decided upon this arrangement because the executives considered it to be less vulnerable to attack than would a direct issuance of stock.

In another white squire case, *Consolidated Amusement Co. v. Rugoff*,[1015] the court enjoined a corporation from diluting a major shareholder's voting rights by issuing stock to friendly parties at below-market prices. Emphasizing the inadequacy of the price charged for the stock, the court found that the sales had been engineered to keep the president in control of the company.

> [T]his so-called sale was not a good faith placement of stock with an investor for the purpose of providing funds and sharing risks. Rather, it was an indirect purchase, or a "parking" of shares in which Rugoff [the president of the target company] in effect was the true principal, guarantying the ostensible purchaser . . . against loss, who in turn was holding the stock "for [Rugoff], and [Rugoff] alone."[1016]

But stock issuances to ESOPs and white squires are not necessarily doomed. In *Danaher Corp. v. Chicago Pneumatic Tool Co.*,[1017] for example, a federal district court denied a motion to rescind Chicago Pneumatic's ("CP's") funding of its ESOP with

---

1014. *Id.*

1015. [1978 Transfer Binder] Fed. Sec. L. Rep. (CCH) ¶ 96,584 (S.D.N.Y. Oct. 6, 1978).

1016. *Id.* at 94,480.

1017. 633 F. Supp. 1066 (S.D.N.Y. 1986). *See also Gelco Corp. v. Coniston Partners*, Civil No. 3-86-847 (D. Minn. Nov. 10, 1986) (refusing to enjoin target's issuance of a block of shares to Merrill Lynch).

one million shares of common stock even though that corporate action helped to frustrate plaintiff Danaher's tender offer for CP.

Because the transaction had "the capacity to secure management," the court shifted to CP the burden of showing the appropriateness of the ESOP funding.[1018] However, the court found that defendants had "succeed[ed] in proving that these transactions were entered into in good faith for the corporate benefit and did not have as a primary or dominant motivation the preservation of control in management."[1019] CP's board had authorized the million-share funding four months before Danaher began acquiring CP shares; moreover, CP had transferred the first 300,000 shares to the ESOP before the company ever could have suspected Danaher's designs. "There is every indication," the court concluded, "that [the establishment and funding of the ESOP were] undertaken because the Board and management of CP believed [they] would be a good thing for their corporation and there is virtually nothing to support plaintiffs' contention that [the transaction] was done to barricade management."[1020]

I. The Pac-Man Defense

Another defense to a hostile tender offer is the Pac-Man ("I'll eat you before you eat me") defense,[1021] in which the target responds to an actual or anticipated tender offer by making a tender offer for the bidder's stock. The Pac-Man strategy raises some interesting questions concerning (a) whether the defensive tender offer can be completed before the initial bidder succeeds

---

1018. *Id.* at 1070.

1019. *Id.* at 1070–71.

1020. *Id.* at 1071.

1021. The Pac-Man defense takes its name from the popular video game. The player of the game controls the Pac-Man, which is chased and (if caught) eaten by ghosts. However, when the Pac-Man is "energized" by a "power dot," the Pac-Man itself can pursue the ghosts and score points by eating them.

in its own takeover attempt and (b) which corporation will first be able to elect new management of the other company.[1022] A target contemplating a Pac-Man offer will need to consider the same issues that arise in connection with any other tender offer.

In one of several cases spawned by Bendix Corporation's bid for control of Martin Marietta Corporation and Marietta's defensive tender offer for Bendix, a federal court, applying the business judgment rule, deferred to the Marietta board's decision to continue its Pac-Man defense even after Bendix had become Marietta's majority shareholder.[1023] Bendix had commenced a tender offer for Marietta on August 25, 1982. Five days later, Marietta countered with a tender offer for Bendix. On September 7, United Technologies joined the fray by making a tender offer for Bendix stock on the same terms as Marietta's offer; eight days later, United raised its offering price by $10 per share. By the time the court issued its opinion on September 22, Bendix owned over 58 percent of Marietta's common stock, and the "series of offers, referred to in the media as a three-ring circus, had expanded to seven rings with ongoing performances in two federal courts in New York, two state courts in Delaware, and a state and federal court in Michigan."[1024]

Bendix argued that Marietta had violated its fiduciary duties under Maryland law by proceeding with its Pac-Man tender offer despite the known wishes of its majority shareholder, Bendix. The court assumed, for the sake of analysis, the validity of "the doubtful proposition" that a corporation must accede to the wishes of its majority shareholder; even given that assumption, however, Marietta's board ultimately owed its fiduciary duties to the shareholders, not the management, of Bendix, "for the simple reason that it is Bendix' shareholders, not Bendix' management, who beneficially own a majority of Marietta."[1025]

1022. *See* discussions of the Martin Marietta/Bendix battle in §§ III.2.B(1) and III.4.A., *supra*.

1023. *Martin Marietta Corp. v. Bendix Corp.*, 549 F. Supp. 623 (D. Md. 1982).

1024. *Id.* at 626.

1025. *Id.* at 633.

The court held that Marietta's board had acted in a manner that it reasonably believed would be in the best interests of Bendix' shareholders, because the board "reasonably believe[d] that a combination of the corporations would be best achieved pursuant to the terms of Marietta's offer rather than Bendix' offer."[1026]

The court found "substantial evidence" that Marietta's board viewed Bendix' management as having "little managerial competence or experience in Marietta's business; the court also noted that only two of Marietta's 14 directors were inside directors. Marietta's refusal to halt its tender offer allowed Bendix' shareholders to decide for themselves whether the tender offer was in their own best interests.

The Bendix/Marietta battle eventually ended when Allied Corporation acquired Bendix. Allied caused Bendix to exchange some of Bendix' Marietta stock for all of the Bendix stock owned by Marietta and then merged Bendix into Allied. Bendix shareholders received $85 in Allied stock and fixed income securities. Marietta remained independent, with Allied as a 39 percent shareholder (subject to a ten-year standstill agreement).

J. Employee Compensation

Companies that consider themselves potential takeover targets often compensate senior executives with a package that includes "golden parachutes." Golden parachutes are severance contracts between a corporation and its top management providing benefits upon the termination of executives' employment. The benefits usually are payable in the event of a change in control or of a termination of the executives' employment in other specified circumstances.

To the extent that golden parachutes increase the cost of acquiring a company, their adoption may be a defensive measure

1026. *Id.*

for a target. The extra cost to an acquiror, however, usually is insubstantial in relation to the total acquisition cost. Moreover, it can be argued that golden parachutes are not defensive devices at all; rather, they help assure that corporate management will consider takeover bids without giving undue consideration to their own continuing employment. In addition, proponents of golden parachutes often contend that such contracts are necessary to attract and retain top executives in an era of proliferating takeover activity. Critics, however, argue that parachutes are nothing more than a wasteful product of management self-interest.[1027]

Golden parachutes triggered by a change in corporate control may be designed to take effect only in hostile takeover situations or in all takeover contexts. Some contracts require not only a change in control but also a second trigger, such as a dismissal of the executive without cause, a material adverse change in the executive's responsibilities or compensation, or a demand that the executive relocate. Parachute agreements also vary in their inclusion or exclusion of mitigation clauses, under which parachute benefits are offset by the executive's compensation from new employment.

Golden parachute payments may be subject to significant tax penalties if the payments' present value exceeds an amount representing three times the "base amount," defined as the employee's average yearly compensation in the preceding five years.[1028] If the parachute payments exceed three times that base amount by even $1, the company cannot deduct any portion of the payment in excess of the base amount. Moreover, the recipient must pay a nondeductible 20-percent excise tax on the excess amount. The penalties do not apply, however, to the extent that the employer or employee can prove, by clear and

---

1027. For general discussions of golden parachutes, see Note, "Golden Parachutes and the Business Judgment Rule: Toward a Proper Standard of Review," 94 Yale L.J. 909 (1985); Comment, "Golden Parachutes: A Perk that Boards Should Scrutinize Carefully," 67 Marquette L. Rev. 293 (1984).

1028. *See* 26 U.S.C. § 280G.

convincing evidence, the reasonableness of the excess payment as compensation for personal services actually rendered.

A related device is the pension parachute, which does not benefit top executives but compensates the beneficiaries of a company's pension plan. A pension parachute typically provides for the vesting of increased pension benefits to be paid out of the pension fund's surplus assets (the value of the fund in excess of the value of its accrued liabilities). The triggering event for the vesting may be an unfriendly change in control, the termination of the pension plan within a specified period following a change of control, or the reduction of payments to the pension fund following a change of control.

Companies have adopted pension parachutes as defensive mechanisms on the theory that surplus assets in a pension fund might themselves attract raiders hoping to use the surplus to finance an acquisition. The pension parachute thus may insure that any such surplus will redound to the benefit of the employees rather than to that of a corporate raider.

Both golden and pension parachutes are far more likely to withstand judicial scrutiny if they bear a reasonable relation to such factors as the nature of services rendered by the particular employees and those employees' length of service with the company.

1. Golden Parachute Cases

In *Koenings v. Joseph Schlitz Brewing Co.*,[1029] the Wisconsin Supreme Court reinstated a jury verdict awarding damages to plaintiff, a former assistant secretary and corporate counsel of Schlitz, under the terms of a golden parachute agreement. Plaintiff had resigned from his job after Schlitz merged with Stroh Brewing, claiming that his responsibilities had been

1029. 126 Wis. 2d 349, 377 N.W.2d 593 (1985), *reversing* 123 Wis. 2d 490, 368 N.W.2d 690 (Ct. App. 1985).

reduced following the merger and that his golden parachute therefore had been triggered.

Noting the taint of conflict of interest inherent in golden parachute arrangements, the Wisconsin Court of Appeals declined to analyze the agreement under the business judgment rule:

> We believe that, in this context, the business judgment rule is archaic and unresponsive to the fair treatment of stockholders. We agree with the academicians that tactics such as golden parachutes generally are in derogation of the fiduciary duties officers and directors owe to their stockholders. The effects of such tactics must be minimized. We agree with the scholars that management faced with merger suitors should maintain passivity and refrain from these types of activities.[1030]

The Court of Appeals held that, under Wisconsin law, golden parachutes are unreasonable and thus unenforceable on public policy grounds as a penalty, unless they have a mitigation clause for salaries earned by executives after separation from the company.

The Wisconsin Supreme Court reversed, referring to the Court of Appeals' ruling as "premature and wholly unwarranted."[1031] The court found no need to address the effect of the business judgment rule on the legality of golden parachutes; instead, it confined its analysis to the validity of the stipulated damages clause under Wisconsin contract law, stating:

> In this case, we review only the trial court's determination of the validity of the stipulated damages clause. We certainly do not pass judgment on the legality of golden parachutes as a corporate tool to provide job security to key employees, or, as they are sometimes used, as a defensive measure to a corporate takeover.[1032]

1030. 368 N.W.2d at 698.

1031. 377 N.W.2d at 599.

1032. *Id.*

In upholding the stipulated damages clause, the court credited, among other things, Schlitz's "valid economic purpose to attempt to lower employee attrition during a period of company uncertainty. . . ."[1033] Schlitz had adopted its golden parachute agreements during friendly merger negotiations with G. Heileman Brewing Company. Although that merger was not consummated, the agreement was still intact when Stroh took over Schlitz.

In *Weinberger v. Shumway*,[1034] however, a California court temporarily restrained the payment of $8 million under golden parachute contracts with former Signal executives then employed by Allied-Signal Inc. Plaintiffs' attorneys stressed that the facts of the case were extreme, because the executives were to receive their parachute payments even though the Allied-Signal merger had been a friendly one and none of the executives was to lose his job. Plaintiffs did not bring a companion suit in Delaware against Allied Corp., despite the fact that Allied executives stood to gain $22.8 million from their golden parachutes. Failure to sue in Delaware might have resulted from plaintiffs' recognition that Delaware would be likely to adopt a more permissive approach to severance agreements.

Parachutes also played a role in *Graphic Sciences, Inc. v. International Mogul Mines Ltd.*,[1035] in which the court considered a target corporation's claim that a corporate raider had violated the beneficial reporting provisions of the Williams Act. As a defense, the raider asserted that the target had "unclean hands" because it had entered into especially lucrative employment contracts with its executives during the takeover battle. Such conduct, the raider claimed, constituted bad faith on the target's part. The court rejected the defense, stating:

1033. *Id.* at 604.

1034. No. 547586 (Sup. Ct., San Diego, Cal. Sept. 19, 1985) (as reported in *Legal Times*, Sept. 30, 1985, at 1, col. 2).

1035. 397 F. Supp. 112 (D.D.C. 1974).

> The Court regards these measures as no more than reasonable and usual efforts by management to protect itself from, and defend against, a suspected takeover bid. The same is true of any attempt by [the target] to obtain a friendly merger. The Court does not think that these matters constitute "unclean hands."[1036]

A federal law challenge to golden parachutes arose in *Federal Savings and Loan Insurance Corp. v. Bass*,[1037] in which the FSLIC attacked the validity of parachutes benefiting the Basses, who were officers and directors of the federally insured Unity Savings Association, a wholly owned subsidiary of the Bass-controlled Bass Financial Corporation. The FSLIC alleged that the agreements were invalid because they had been adopted in violation of fiduciary duties imposed by common law and state statute on officers and directors of a savings and loan association and because they violated federal laws prohibiting savings institutions from entering into employment agreements that would constitute "unsafe and unsound practices."[1038]

The parachute agreements had been made when the company was in a "precarious and deteriorating financial condition."[1039] The agreements, whose ostensible purpose was to respond to a series of resignations that had shaken the company, were to be triggered by, among other events, the company's merger, consolidation, reorganization, liquidation, or dissolution.

The court did not need to reach the issue whether the directors properly had exercised their business judgment in approving the agreements because federal savings institution regulations provided the standard of review. The court deferred to the FSLIC's "reasonable" interpretation of the applicable regulation. Nevertheless, despite the fact that the "unsafe or unsound practice"[1040] regulation "supplants the directors' business judgment on the narrow point of officers' employment

---

1036. *Id.* at 127.

1037. 576 F. Supp. 848 (N.D. Ill. 1983).

1038. *Id.* at 850.

1039. *Id.*

1040. 12 C.F.R. § 563.39.

agreements,"[1041] the court did apply the business judgment rule to the facts before it. Characterizing the payment as a " 'bonus' that was to be received whether Unity prospered or failed,"[1042] the court concluded that the agreements could not satisfy the rule's rational basis test. Instead, the contracts constituted "a blatant attempt to secure the Basses' position at Unity's expense."[1043] The court noted that their financial investment in Unity provided ample incentive for the Basses to remain committed to the company, making further incentives entirely unnecessary.

2. Pension Parachute Cases

The issue of pension parachutes' validity arose in *GAF Corp. v. Union Carbide Corp.*[1044] Union Carbide, the target of a hostile tender offer by GAF, adopted a number of aggressive defensive measures, one of which consisted of amending the company's Retirement Plan to allow Carbide's board to vest, for the benefit of participating and retired employees, excess amounts of corporate funds (sometimes created by revaluation of fund investments) in the event of an " 'unfriendly change of control.' "[1045] When GAF attacked this measure, Carbide argued that the amendment merely allowed the board to increase pension benefits, as the company had done three times in the past when no tender offer had loomed on the horizon.

The court upheld Carbide's actions, declaring:

> The amendment does nothing more than allow the board to treat the pensioners equitably and fairly in the manner and in the measure in which past negotiated transactions enabled the Board to do. Under friendly terms, the interests of employees can be

1041. 576 F. Supp. at 852.
1042. *Id.* at 853.
1043. *Id.* at 852.
1044. 624 F. Supp. 1016 (S.D.N.Y. 1985).
1045. *Id.* at 1022.

> ironed out on the bargaining table with equity to all sides. It was the Board's judgment, which appears entirely reasonable, that it was prudent to reserve to itself this power in the event of an unfriendly assault on control to prevent a takeover bidder from jeopardizing future appropriate and necessary increases of pension benefits by his use of the funds to finance a takeover. Labor, at whatever level, should not be victimized or go unrequited by control contests. It is entirely reasonable for a Board to take such steps as will assure workers against such a possibility arising from the necessity for financing the obligations incurred in a control contest.[1046]

Moreover, the court observed, GAF itself conceded that the amendment gave Carbide's board no greater authority than the board already possessed. The "so-called 'Pension Parachute' issue is, in reality, a non-issue."[1047]

A pension parachute did not fare as well, however, in *Edelman v. Fruehauf Corp.*,[1048] in which the Court of Appeals for the Sixth Circuit affirmed a preliminary injunction enjoining Fruehauf from effectuating a management leveraged buy-out and taking other related measures to defeat a hostile tender offer by plaintiffs. As part of its defensive strategy, Fruehauf's board had amended the company's pension plan to provide that the $70 to $100 million of overfunding, which had been available for corporate use, would become irrevocably committed to the fund if anyone obtained a 40-percent interest in Fruehauf without board approval. Later, the board further amended the plan to give advance board approval to any 40-percent acquiror paying at least $48.50 per share. (Plaintiffs were offering $44 per share but gave signs of willingness to raise their bid; management's LBO was priced at $48.50 per share.)

The court found that the initial amendment "had the effect of making Fruehauf a less attractive takeover target, and thereby, of dampening the bidding process"; the second amendment

1046. *Id.*

1047. *Id.*

1048. 798 F.2d 882 (6th Cir. 1986).

showed that "the Board simply [had] decided to make a deal with management no matter what other bidders might offer."[1049] The board thus had breached its fiduciary duties by "rubber-stamp[ing]" management's proposed LBO and by ending the auction process. Accordingly, the court allowed defendants to act with respect to the pension plan only "in accord with defendants' fiduciary duty, so long as the impact of such actions is equal on all bidders."[1050]

Similarly, in *Minstar Acquiring Corp. v. AMF Inc.*,[1051] the court refused to apply the business judgment rule to a target company's deferred compensation plan, which, the court found, constituted an unlawful entrenchment device because it was triggered by a change of control.

K. Defensive Mergers

The preceding sections have discussed defensive measures taken by targets that intend to remain independent. Statistically, however, only a minority of targets maintains its independence following the commencement of takeover bids. Many target companies, if not taken over by the original hostile bidder, are acquired by an alternate suitor—a "white knight"—in a defensive merger. The target may prefer to deal with the white knight for a number of reasons: the white knight might make a higher offer than the initial bidder; it might intend to keep the target intact, while the initial bidder might intend to liquidate all or part of the company; it might be better able than the initial bidder to run the target's business. At times, a target might use a white knight to start an auction in which the company will be sold for the highest price. Regardless of the board's original strategic

1049. *Id.* at 886.

1050. *Id.* at 890.

1051. 621 F. Supp. 1252, 1260–61 (S.D.N.Y. 1985).

purpose, the entry of a white knight often results in a series of ascending bids, and there is no guarantee that the white knight will emerge triumphant.

As a result, white knights often will refuse to commence, or to continue, a bidding contest with a raider unless given an edge. Thus, targets frequently have granted stock and crown jewel lock-up options to induce white knights to enter into defensive mergers.

Some earlier defensive mergers involved devices that were precursors of the lock-up option in that they facilitated the white knight transactions in the face of hostile bids for control of the target. In *Crouse-Hinds Co. v. InterNorth, Inc.*,[1052] for example, Crouse-Hinds had entered into an agreement under which Belden Corporation would be merged into a Crouse-Hinds subsidiary. While the merger was pending, InterNorth commenced an unsolicited tender offer for 54 percent of Crouse-Hinds' outstanding common stock, to be followed by a second-step merger in which the remaining Crouse-Hinds common shares would be converted into InterNorth preferred stock.

After determining that the InterNorth offer was not in the best interests of the Crouse-Hinds shareholders, Crouse-Hinds entered into a modification of the Belden merger agreement whereby Crouse-Hinds agreed to commence an exchange offer for 49 percent of Belden's outstanding stock, which Crouse-Hinds agreed to vote in favor of the Belden merger. Tendering Belden shareholders would receive Crouse-Hinds common stock that would not be entitled to vote on the merger. After the exchange, Crouse-Hinds and Belden would consummate their merger on the same terms as the exchange offer.

InterNorth filed a suit challenging the exchange offer, which the district court enjoined. The Court of Appeals for the Second Circuit, however, reversed the injunction, finding insufficient evidence for the trial court's conclusion that the Crouse-Hinds directors had acted for the purpose of retaining their offices after the Belden merger.

1052. 634 F.2d 690 (2d Cir. 1980).

The Court of Appeals noted that Crouse-Hinds' board had agreed to the merger with Belden before learning of InterNorth's hostile intentions; the mere fact that the Belden merger would perpetuate the Crouse-Hinds directors in office did not demonstrate that entrenchment reasons had motivated the Crouse-Hinds directors to take additional steps to consummate the Belden merger in the face of InterNorth's hostile bid. Given the virtual lack of evidence of directorial self-interest, the court held that the exchange offer was protected under the business judgment rule.

As *Crouse-Hinds* illustrates, a white knight merger's incidental effect of perpetuating incumbent management's tenure does not itself suffice to overcome the protection of the business judgment rule. Some courts, however, now carefully scrutinize any white knight transaction in which the white knight receives preferential treatment and members of incumbent management receive an equity interest. Perhaps the most common example of such a situation is a white knight leveraged buy-out.

In *Edelman v. Fruehauf Corp.*,[1053] a group led by Asher Edelman made a series of proposals to acquire Fruehauf. After Fruehauf's board rebuffed its overtures, the Edelman group launched a cash tender offer for all Fruehauf shares at $44 per share. Fruehauf's management responded by negotiating with Merrill Lynch to arrange a two-tiered leveraged buy-out ("LBO") sponsored jointly by members of management and by Merrill Lynch.

Under the LBO proposal, a newly formed corporation would make a cash tender offer for approximately 77 percent of Fruehauf's stock at $48.50 per share. The tender offer would be funded with $375 million borrowed from Merrill Lynch, $375 million borrowed from Manufacturers Hanover Trust Company, and $100 million contributed by Fruehauf. Next, Fruehauf would be merged with the acquiring company, and all remaining shares would be converted into securities of the new corporation valued at $48.50.

1053. 798 F.2d 882 (6th Cir. 1986).

The plan provided for a total equity contribution to the new company of $25 million—$10 to $15 million from management, and the rest from Merrill Lynch. In return for their equity contribution, management would receive between 40- and 60-percent control of the new company. Fruehauf also would pay approximately $30 million to Merrill Lynch for loan commitment fees, advisory fees, and a "break-up" fee that Merrill Lynch would keep if the deal were not consummated. In addition, the LBO agreement contained a "no-shop" clause restricting Fruehauf's ability to negotiate with other bidders. A special committee of Fruehauf's outside directors approved the proposed LBO, which was then authorized by Fruehauf's board.

The Edelman group challenged the plan, and a federal district court concluded that Fruehauf's board had unreasonably preferred incumbent management in the bidding process. The court therefore enjoined the consummation of the LBO.

On appeal, the Court of Appeals for the Sixth Circuit affirmed the district court's order, with slight modifications of the terms of the injunction. The court concluded that the directors had not made

> a good faith effort to negotiate the best deal for the shareholders. They acted as interested parties and did not treat the Fruehauf managers and the Edelman Group in an even handed way but rather gave their colleagues on the Board, the inside managers, the inside track and accepted their proposal without furthering the process.[1054]

The court pointed to evidence showing that the board had accepted the LBO proposal without giving the Edelman group an opportunity to engage in further bidding or to top the LBO price offered to the shareholders. The court also focused on the corporate funds—including the break-up fee—to be paid to Merrill Lynch to facilitate the LBO and on the $100 million that Fruehauf made available for use in the tender offer. In addition, the court noted that Fruehauf's committee of outside directors

---

1054. *Id.* at 885.

had employed as its adviser the same investment banker that was in the process of negotiating management's LBO proposal; moreover, the board had amended Fruehauf's stock option, incentive compensation, and pension plans to provide that, if anyone obtained a 40-percent interest in Fruehauf without board approval, all company-issued stock options would become immediately exercisable, all incentive payments normally due in the future would become immediately due, and the $70 to $100 million of overfunding in the pension plan would become irrevocably committed to the pension fund.

In light of these circumstances, the court concluded that "the Board has failed to carry its burden of establishing that the management buyout was fair and reasonable"[1055] and ruled that the plan was not protected by the business judgment rule even though Fruehauf's disinterested directors had authorized the transaction after complete disclosure. "The evidence compels the conclusion that the directors simply 'rubber stamped' the management buyout proposal. In doing so, they breached their fiduciary duty."[1056]

Finally, the court held that,

> [o]nce it becomes apparent that a takeover target will be acquired by new owners, whether by a "raider" or by a team consisting of management and a "white knight," it becomes the duty of the target's directors to see that the shareholders obtain the best price possible for their stock. . . . When, in violation of this duty, directors take measures that are intended to put an end to the bidding, those measures may be enjoined. . . .
>
> In light of the clear failure of the Board to provide for a fair auction, the District Court was correct to devise injunctive relief setting a framework for an open bidding process.[1057]

1055. *Id.* at 886.
1056. *Id.*
1057. *Id.* at 886–87.

The injunction, as modified by the Court of Appeals, required the Fruehauf board, among other things, to refrain from using any Fruehauf assets in support of the LBO "unless the same accommodation is made to all other bidders, as determined by the Board of Directors acting in accordance with their fiduciary obligations."[1058] The order also directed defendants

> to refrain from taking any corporate actions which are intended to or have the effect of favoring or advantaging [sic] any particular bidder over any other bidder . . . [,] to make available upon reasonable notice to any potential bidder for Fruehauf all information concerning Fruehauf's business and properties . . . and to meet on mutually agreeable and reasonable terms with any potential bidder in good faith.[1059]

L. Stock Lock-Ups

Stock lock-up options give a white knight the right to purchase authorized but unissued stock of the target company under certain circumstances. These options serve two functions. First, the options give the white knight a "leg up" in consummating the transaction because, under certain circumstances, the white knight can exercise the options and vote the purchased shares in favor of the merger. Second, the options give the white knight a way to realize a profit if it is outbid: it can exercise the options and then tender the purchased shares to the higher bidder.

Use of a stock lock-up may require advance planning because the target's shareholders must approve any increase in authorized shares. However, many corporations secure "blank check" authorization from their shareholders to issue and fix the terms of new preferred stock. Such authorization gives the board more flexibility both in raising capital and in responding to unsolicited takeover bids.

1058. *Id.* at 890.

1059. *Id.*

Courts generally will invalidate lock-ups issued after control of the corporation has already shifted; they also will carefully scrutinize lock-ups that alter the voting power of the disinterested shareholders, as well as those issued for questionable consideration. A corporation whose shares trade on the New York Stock Exchange should be aware that it may not increase its amount of outstanding common stock by more than 18.5 percent without shareholder approval.[1060] Courts have construed NYSE delisting resulting from a lock-up transaction as an indication that the directors could not have been acting in the corporation's best interest.

Despite the judicial invalidation of crown jewel lock-ups in *Revlon* and *Hanson Trust*,[1061] recent cases have upheld stock lock-up options in some circumstances. In *Hecco Ventures v. Sea-Land Corp.*,[1062] for example, the Delaware Court of Chancery refused to issue a temporary restraining order preventing white knight CSX Corporation from completing its tender offer for Sea-Land Corporation despite the stock lock-up option that Sea-Land had granted to CSX.

During 1985, Sea-Land stockholder Harold Simmons acquired 26.2 percent of Sea-Land's outstanding shares and proposed a merger in which Sea-Land shareholders would receive $25 per share. The Sea-Land board, on the advice of its investment banker, rejected Simmons' offer as inadequate and directed its investment banker and its management to explore alternatives to obtain higher offers. Although 23 potential acquirors were contacted, only two expressed any interest, and, as of January 1986, Simmons remained the only active bidder. Negotiations continued with Simmons, who had increased his holdings to 39.5 percent; in April 1986, Simmons made a cash offer at $26 per share.

Immediately thereafter, CSX, one of the two companies that had expressed interest in Sea-Land in December 1985, proposed

1060. *NYSE Listed Company Manual* § 312.00.

1061. *See infra* § III.4.M. (discussing crown jewel lock-ups).

1062. No. 8486 (Del. Ch. May 19, 1986).

an acquisition at $28 per share, provided that Sea-Land granted CSX an option to purchase 6.5 million Sea-Land shares at $28 per share. Sea-Land informed Simmons of the CSX offer and invited him to top it; the company also provided Simmons with the same confidential data that it had shared with CSX. Simmons declined to make a higher offer. Instead, without Sea-Land's knowledge, Simmons negotiated to sell a call option to CSX, and CSX paid $5 per share for the option to purchase all of Simmons' shares for $28 per share.

After learning of the CSX-Simmons deal, Sea-Land's board tried but failed both to obtain a higher price from CSX and to dissuade CSX from demanding the stock lock-up option from Sea-Land. Then, on the advice of its investment bankers, the board approved the CSX proposal.

Plaintiff stockholders, in a class and derivative action, challenged the CSX deal and lock-up option, claiming that the transaction price was neither fair nor the highest available and that the option was part of an illegal conspiracy to halt bidding. The court held that plaintiffs had failed to show either a likelihood of success on the merits or irreparable harm.

The court expressly distinguished the facts before it from those of *Revlon, Inc. v. MacAndrews & Forbes Holdings, Inc.*[1063] Unlike the lock-up at issue in *Revlon*, the CSX deal did not put a halt to an active auction process for the target; nor did Sea-Land's board favor one bidder over another. Instead, the board had attempted to *start* an auction for the company: "[t]he Company Option challenged by plaintiffs was granted at the conclusion (and not, as in *Revlon*, in the midst) of the auction process."[1064]

The court also held that plaintiffs had failed to show that the denial of an injunction would cause irreparable harm:

> In *Revlon* and in *Hanson Trust PLC v. ML SCM Acquisition, Inc.*, . . . injunctive relief was required to "free up" an auction process involving actual bidders that were firmly committed to

---

1063. 506 A.2d 173 (Del. 1986).

1064. *Hecco Ventures v. Sea-Land Corp.*, No. 8486, slip op. at 11 (Del. Ch. May 19, 1986).

> offer higher prices than the bids that target management was supporting. Here, in contrast, there is no bidder other than CSX, there is no bid other than $28 per share, and there is no showing that an injunction would cause a different bidder or a higher bid to materialize.[1065]

The court therefore allowed the transaction to proceed.

In earlier cases, stock lock-up options had met with mixed success. In *Data Probe, Inc. v. CRC Information Systems*,[1066] for example, the court invalidated the exercise of a stock option that would have given its holder ownership of 66-2/3 percent of Data Probe's stock. The court found that the target's board had granted the lock-up option to a white knight to freeze the bidding for the company at an artificially low level, rather than to maximize shareholder value. Moreover, the size of the option, the granting of employment contracts to the directors, the indemnification of the directors by the white knight for any liability resulting from the issuance of the lock-up option, and the board's failure to demonstrate that it had acted in the best interests of the shareholders all suggested that the directors' actions were "self directed and marked by zealous devotion to their private interests."[1067]

Similarly, *Condec Corp. v. Lunkenheimer Co.*[1068] cancelled the issuance of a block of stock to a white knight. The target had agreed to exchange authorized but previously unissued common stock for preferred stock of the white knight. The court concluded that, in light of the haste with which the directors had approved the issuance of a block that would have amounted to about 20 percent of the target's outstanding stock, the primary purpose of the transaction appeared to be to prefer the white knight to the hostile raider so that incumbent management would not be displaced.

1065. *Id.* at 14 (citation omitted).

1066. As reported in N.Y.L.J. at 7, col. 2 (N.Y. App. Div. Dec. 28, 1984).

1067. *Id.*

1068. 43 Del. Ch. 353, 230 A.2d 769 (1967).

In *Buffalo Forge Co. v. Ogden Corp.*,[1069] however, the court upheld the sale of shares and the granting of a stock option to a white knight in conjunction with an attempt to defeat a hostile tender offer. Despite the white knight's participation in the bidding, the hostile tender offeror had succeeded in acquiring the target. After winning the bidding war and taking control of the target, however, the hostile offeror refused to pay dividends on the shares issued to the white knight, to honor the white knight's stock option, or to accept for purchase the shares tendered by the white knight. Instead, the hostile offeror sued to rescind the sale of the stock and the option granted to the white knight, claiming that the board's approval of the transactions was not protected by the business judgment rule because the directors had acted in their own self-interest.

The court held that plaintiff had failed to establish that the directors had been motivated by self-interest in fighting the hostile offer. The business judgment rule therefore protected the sale of the stock and the grant of the option, and the court upheld the contract.

In *Treadway Companies v. Care Corp.*,[1070] the Court of Appeals for the Second Circuit, reversing the district court, held that Treadway's directors had properly fulfilled their fiduciary duties when they approved an issuance of stock during a battle for corporate control. The court analyzed the transaction under the business judgment rule, noting that the possibility of a takeover was of great interest to Treadway and its shareholders and that "[i]t was only reasonable that Treadway's board . . .should examine the situation to make a judgment as to where the best interests of Treadway lay."[1071] Under New Jersey law, the court continued, plaintiff bore the initial burden of proving that the directors either had had an interest in the transaction or had acted in bad faith or with an improper purpose. The court concluded that plaintiff-bidder had not sustained this burden.

1069. 555 F. Supp. 892 (W.D.N.Y.), *aff'd*, 717 F.2d 757 (2d Cir.), *cert. denied*, 464 U.S. 1018 (1983).

1070. 638 F.2d 357 (2d Cir. 1980).

1071. *Id.* at 381.

The court found that the directors reasonably had decided to oppose the takeover once they determined it to be detrimental to the corporation.[1072] The board had authorized the stock issuance in conjunction with merger negotiations that the directors had undertaken in good faith. Moreover the Treadway directors expected to lose their positions as a result of the merger and thus were unlikely to have been motivated by self-interest.[1073] Because plaintiff could not overcome the presumption of the business judgment rule, the rule shielded the Treadway board's decision to issue stock to a white knight.

M. Crown Jewel Lock-Ups

Another form of lock-up is the "crown jewel" or asset lock-up. A crown jewel can be any asset of the target and is often a key division or subsidiary of the company. A crown jewel lock-up usually is an option granted to a white knight to purchase the particular asset for what might be considered an advantageous price outside a takeover context. The option often is conditioned upon the occurrence of a triggering event, such as a raider's obtaining a particular percentage of the target's stock. A crown jewel lock-up can succeed in fending off raiders who either are primarily interested in one division, subsidiary, or other asset or are unwilling to pursue the target if the latter were to lose its crown jewel.

Courts generally have been skeptical of crown jewel lock-ups that have been granted for inadequate consideration and have had the effect of disrupting competitive bidding for a target. The adequacy of the option's exercise price often is debatable, because the value of the particular asset (unlike the value of shares of a public company) is not established by a public trading

---

1072. *Id.*

1073. *Id.* at 383.

market. Valuation questions thus can degenerate into swearing matches between opposing experts.

When the exercise price is fair, courts tend to uphold crown jewel lock-up options. The fairer the price for the optioned asset, however, the less effective a deterrent the crown jewel option will be: unless the hostile bidder has a strategic need for the optioned asset, the bidder may be willing simply to proceed with its tender offer, allow the crown jewel option to be exercised, and attempt to acquire a company loaded with additional cash but stripped of its crown jewel.

Crown jewel options can raise questions concerning the need for shareholder approval under state law if the crown jewel(s) in question can be said to constitute all or substantially all of the target's assets.[1074]

1. Cases

Crown jewel lock-ups have not fared very well in recent cases. One of the leading precedents is *Revlon, Inc. v. MacAndrews & Forbes Holdings, Inc.*,[1075] in which the Delaware Supreme Court affirmed a Chancery Court ruling enjoining a crown jewel lock-up and finding that Revlon's board of directors had breached its duty of loyalty to Revlon's shareholders by granting the lock-up option to a white knight.

The case arose out of Pantry Pride's tender offer for Revlon. Pantry Pride had earlier approached Revlon with a "bear hug"—an ostensibly friendly acquisition offer that carries with it the threat of a hostile takeover if it is rebuffed—proposing a negotiated acquisition of Revlon at $42 or $43 per share. Pantry Pride also threatened to make a hostile takeover at $45 per share. The Revlon board met with the company's investment bankers, who advised them that Pantry Pride's offer was "grossly inadequate." The investment bankers estimated Revlon's

1074. *See, e.g.*, Del. Gen. Corp. Law § 271.
1075. 506 A.2d 173 (Del. 1986).

liquidation value to be $60 to $70 per share. The board therefore determined to oppose Pantry Pride's offer, adopted a "Note Purchase Rights Plan" (a form of poison pill), and authorized the repurchase by Revlon of approximately 16 percent of its own stock.[1076]

Pantry Pride launched its tender offer on August 23, at $47.50 per share. The Revlon board met and concluded that Pantry Pride's offer was still inadequate. Revlon therefore stepped up its defense by commencing an exchange offer, pursuant to which one-third of the company's outstanding shares were each exchanged for a senior subordinated note (of $47.50 principal, at 11.75 percent interest, due in 1995) and one-tenth of a share of $9 cumulative convertible exchangeable preferred stock, valued at $100 per share. The notes contained various shark repellent covenants that limited Revlon's ability to incur debt, sell assets, or pay dividends without approval of the "independent" (non-management) directors. The notes also provided that the board could waive the covenants to permit a sale at a fair price.

Pantry Pride had conditioned its $47.50 offer on Revlon's redemption of its poison pill. The board, however, declined to redeem the pill, and, on September 16, Pantry Pride announced a new tender offer at $42 per share, conditioned upon the tender of at least 90 percent of the outstanding shares. The Revlon board again rejected Pantry Pride's bid. Pantry Pride raised its offer to $50 on September 27, to $53 on October 1, and to $56.25 on October 27, subject to Revlon's redeeming the poison pills, waiving the note covenants, and electing three Pantry Pride nominees to the Revlon board.

Meanwhile, Revlon began negotiating with a white knight, Forstmann Little, for a leveraged buy-out of Revlon. Under the deal, each Revlon share would be converted into a right to receive $56, and Revlon would redeem the poison pill and lift the note covenants. Revlon also agreed to sell three of its divisions to help finance the offer. When the deal was announced, however,

1076. The Revlon poison pill is discussed in greater detail in § III.4.B(2)(b), *supra*.

the value of the notes dropped by almost 13 percent, and irate noteholders threatened litigation.

Pantry Pride increased its offer to $56.25 and announced its intention to engage in fractional bidding to top any Forstmann offer with a slightly higher one. In response, Forstmann increased its own offer to $57.25 and agreed to shore up the falling value of the Revlon notes, provided that Revlon (i) grant Forstmann a crown jewel lock-up option, exercisable if another buyer acquired 40 percent of Revlon's shares (ii) enter into a "no-shop" agreement precluding it from considering further bids from other parties,[1077] and (iii) pay Forstmann a $25 million "bust-up fee" if another bidder acquired more than 19.9 percent of Revlon's stock. After the Revlon board unanimously approved these arrangements, Pantry Pride (having previously sued to enjoin the issuance of the poison pill rights) filed an amended complaint and increased its offer to $58 per share for any and all Revlon shares, conditional on redemption of the rights, waiver of the note covenants, and issuance of an injunction against the exercise of the lock-up option. The Chancery Court enjoined the lock-up, no-shop, and cancellation fee provisions, and the Delaware Supreme Court affirmed.

Turning first, however, to the poison pill and to Revlon's original exchange offer, the Supreme Court held those measures to be protected under the business judgment rule. The board had been advised that "Pantry Pride was a small, highly leveraged company bent on a 'bust-up' takeover by using 'junk bond' financing to buy Revlon cheaply, sell the acquired assets to pay the debts incurred, and retain the profit for itself."[1078] The court therefore concluded that the adoption of the poison pill and the exchange offer constituted reasonable responses to the threat apparently posed by Pantry Pride's proposal.

But the Revlon board's responsibilities took on a different character "when Pantry Pride increased its offer to $50 per share, and then to $53, [and] it became apparent to all that the break-

1077. The Revlon no-shop agreement is discussed in § III.4.N., *infra*.

1078. 506 A.2d at 180–81.

up of the company was inevitable."[1079] At that point, "[t]he directors' role changed from defenders of the corporate bastion to auctioneers charged with getting the best price for the stockholders at a sale of the company."[1080] By granting Forstmann a crown jewel lock-up option and a no-shop agreement, Revlon essentially ended the auction, notwithstanding the minimal incremental increase in price and Pantry Pride's expressed determination to make a higher offer.

The court observed that Revlon's directors had favored the Forstmann offer principally because Forstmann had pledged to support the value of Revlon's notes. This commitment solved the board's problems with the noteholders, but only at the expense of the stockholders. Although the board argued that its actions properly were intended to protect a corporate constituency—the noteholders—the court concluded that the board should have been more attentive to the interests of the shareholders, to whom the board was primarily responsible, rather than to the noteholders, whose rights were fixed by contract. "Thus," the court held,

> when a board ends an intense bidding contest on an insubstantial basis, and where a significant by-product of that action is to protect the directors against a perceived threat of personal liability for consequences stemming from the adoption of previous defensive measures, the action cannot withstand the enhanced scrutiny which *Unocal* requires of director conduct.[1081]

Revlon thus raises serious questions—as do other cases such as *Edelman v. Fruehauf Corp.*[1082]—about the scope of directors' fiduciary duties when engaging in defensive tactics in the face of a hostile tender offer. These cases suggest that, once a board determines to sell the company, the directors must act as

---

1079. *Id.* at 182.

1080. *Id.*

1081. *Id.* at 184. For a further discussion of *Revlon* and *Unocal*, see *supra* § III.3.B(3).

1082. 798 F.2d 882 (6th Cir. 1986), discussed in § III.4.K., *supra*.

auctioneers, seeking the best possible price for the shareholders. In addition, once the auction is under way, the board may be on shaky ground if it attempts to use lock-up devices, poison pills, and other maneuvers that could block the bidding process, especially if it appears that the disfavored bidder is prepared to continue raising the ante.

The legality of lock-up options seems to depend largely on when they are granted. If a company grants a lock-up option to induce a new bidder to compete, the tactic will probably be considered a legitimate exercise of the directors' business judgment—at least if the tactic produces a bid materially higher than the original offer. But there seems to be substantial judicial antipathy to options granted after an auction has commenced, especially when the lock-up halts the bidding with only a marginal increase over the previous offer.

In *Hanson Trust PLC v. ML SCM Acquisition Inc.*,[1083] for example, the Court of Appeals for the Second Circuit held that a hostile bidder, Hanson Trust, was entitled to a preliminary injunction against the exercise of a crown jewel option granted by the target, SCM, to its white knight, Merrill Lynch. Although SCM's directors had fulfilled their duty of loyalty in opposing Hanson's offer and favoring Merrill Lynch's (the nine outside directors of the 12-member board unanimously approved the lock-up), the court concluded that the directors had failed to meet their duty of due care when they gave Merrill an option to buy SCM's most valuable subdivisions at a questionably adequate price.

The board's decision to grant the lock-up option had come in the midst of a "fast-moving bidding contest."[1084] Hanson initially had made an unsolicited cash tender offer for SCM at $60 per share. Merrill countered with a part cash, part debenture "junk bond" offer for a leveraged buy-out (in which SCM management would participate) valued at $70 per share, whereupon Hanson raised its bid to $72. Merrill then raised its own offer to $74 in

---

1083. 781 F.2d 264 (2d Cir. 1986).

1084. *Id.* at 267.

cash and debentures (but involving slightly less cash than had its prior offer) on the condition that SCM grant a crown jewel lock-up option entitling Merrill to purchase SCM's Pigments and Consumer Foods subdivisions for $350 million and $80 million, respectively, if any other party acquired more than one-third of SCM's outstanding shares.[1085] Hanson later announced its intention to make an all-cash tender offer at $75 per share, conditioned on the withdrawal or judicial invalidation of the lock-up. Hanson also filed suit, claiming that the grant of the lock-up option constituted a breach of the SCM directors' fiduciary duties, rather than a proper exercise of business judgment.

Noting that the use of a lock-up option "is not per se illegal . . . but it may nonetheless be illegal in particular cases,"[1086] the Court of Appeals declared that "the role of the court in an action to enjoin takeover measures is to allow the forces of the free market to determine the outcome to the greatest extent possible within the bounds of the law."[1087] "In this regard," the court continued, "some lock-up options may be beneficial to the shareholders, such as those that induce a bidder to compete for control of a corporation, while others may be harmful, such as those that effectively preclude bidders from competing with the optionee bidder."[1088]

The court proceeded to marshal the evidence showing that SCM's directors had failed to take the steps necessary to insure that the purchase price under the option for the company's crown jewels was fair and reasonable:

> [T]he SCM directors, in a three-hour late-night meeting, apparently contented themselves with their financial advisor's conclusory opinion that the option prices were "within the range of fair value," although had the directors inquired, they would have learned that Goldman Sachs had not calculated a range of

---

1085. *Id.* at 270.
1086. *Id.* at 273–74.
1087. *Id.* at 274.
1088. *Id.*

> fairness. There was not even a written opinion from Goldman Sachs as to the value of the two optioned businesses. . . . Moreover, the Board never asked what the top value was or why two businesses that generated half of SCM's income were being sold for one third of the total purchase price of the company under the second LBO merger agreement, or what the company would look like if the options were exercised. . . . There was little or no discussion of how likely it was that the option "trigger" would be pulled, or who would make that decision—Merrill, the Board, or management. Also, as was noted in *Van Gorkom*, the directors can hardly substantiate their claim that Hanson's efforts created an emergency need for a hasty decision, given that Hanson would not acquire shares under the tender offer until September 17 [*i.e.*, seven days after SCM's board approved the lock-up]. . . . The directors manifestly declined to use "time available for obtaining information" that might be critical, given "the importance of the business judgment to be made." In short, the SCM directors' paucity of information and their swiftness of decision-making strongly suggest a breach of the duty of due care.[1089]

The court stressed that directors' reliance on advice of counsel and investment bankers does not necessarily discharge the duty of due care; rather, "directors have some oversight obligations to become reasonably familiar with an opinion, report, or other source of advice before becoming entitled to rely on it."[1090] The court noted that, had the directors probed the basis of SCM's investment banker's advice, they "might have then discovered that the prices [under the option] represented lower valuations than their own experienced business judgment would allow them to approve."[1091]

The court addressed, in passing, the interesting issue of the extent to which any discount from fair value is appropriate in setting the price of an asset under a crown jewel option. Of course, absent some discount, the option has no value to its holder; at some point, however, the price can become too low to constitute a legitimate incentive.

1089. *Id.* at 275.

1090. *Id.*

1091. *Id.* at 276.

> Given this "working board's" considerable familiarity with SCM, we must question why it did not find the option prices troublesome in light of the considerable evidence—from Overlock, its own investment banker, and others, and from valuations made by SCM's management and Merrill—that the optioned assets were worth considerably more than their option prices. Indeed, given that the very purpose of an asset option in a takeover context is to give the optionee a bargain as an incentive to bid and an assured benefit should its bid fail, see Fraidin & Franco, *Lock-Up Arrangements*, 14 Rev. Sec. Reg. 821, 823, 827 (1981), one again might have expected under such circumstances a *heightened* duty of care. The price may be low enough to entice a reluctant potential bidder, but no lower than "reasonable pessimism will allow." *Cf.* Brudney & Chirelstein, *Fair Shares in Corporate Mergers and Takeovers*, 88 Harv. L. Rev. 297, 298 (1974). To ascertain that management's proposal has not crossed this critical line, the Board certainly should have subjected the proposal to some substantial analysis. Instead, we view the board as only minimally fulfilling, if not abdicating, its role.[1092]

This standard, obviously, is imprecise: it leaves directors to struggle, at their peril, with difficult judgment calls as to how low is low enough to provide an inducement to an otherwise reluctant potential bidder but not so low that a court might find that the board sold its company's crown jewels for inadequate consideration.

A crown jewel lock-up also was at issue in *DMG, Inc. v. Aegis Corp.*,[1093] in which the court declined to grant a preliminary injunction requiring an ultimately successful hostile bidder to honor a lock-up option that the target had granted to a white knight to induce it to enter the bidding. The terms of the option entitled the white knight to purchase a majority interest in a subsidiary of the target in the event that another bidder acquired 40 percent of the target's stock. After topping the white knight's bid and taking control of the target, the hostile bidder had amended the charter of the crown jewel subsidiary to

---

1092. *Id.* (emphasis in original).

1093. No. 7619 (Del. Ch. June 29, 1984).

prevent the white knight from assuming the control that it otherwise could have wielded upon exercise of the option.

The white knight sued to enforce its right under the option to take control of the subsidiary, arguing that the option agreement was enforceable because it represented a valid exercise of the board's business judgment at a time when the company was under siege. The hostile bidder, now in control of the target, attacked the validity of the lock-up, arguing that the grant of the option amounted to a waste of corporate assets and a breach of the fiduciary duties of the target's (prior) directors.

In declining to enjoin the bidder's actions, the court noted that the business judgment rule usually is invoked as a defense by directors who are being sued for an alleged impropriety; the rule is not an offensive weapon that a white knight can use to argue its own entitlement to an allegedly valid right that the target's board bestowed upon it.[1094] The court also expressed doubt about the adequacy of the consideration given for the crown jewel option:

> DMG is attempting to enforce the Wellcraft option, as well as certain other alleged contractual rights, for which it paid absolutely nothing. In the face of the Minstar tender offer Aegis sought a protective suitor. Enter DMG. But, in return for its agreement to merge with Aegis at a higher price per share to Aegis's shareholders than was then being offered by Minstar, DMG insisted upon certain things from Aegis. One was the requirement that all of its counsel fees and expenses in connection with the merger up to $1.25 million be paid by Aegis. Another was the requirement that Aegis pay it a fee of $1.5 million in the event that a third party acquired a 40% interest in Aegis prior to the completion of the merger. A third was the right to purchase 1.4 million shares of Aegis at an established price in the event that a third party acquired such a 40% interest. Finally, there was the requirement that DMG be permitted to purchase a 51% interest in Wellcraft [the crown jewel subsidiary] at a fixed price of $16 million in the event that a third party acquired a 40% interest in Aegis prior to the consummation of the merger.

1094. Slip op. at 9.

> For all of these purported contractual entitlements DMG did no more than obligate itself to obtain the financial commitments necessary to enable it to merge with Aegis at a price of $5.75 per share to be paid to the shareholders of Aegis. It neither paid nor promised to pay anything to Aegis itself for the additional rights it received in return. In particular, it paid nothing to Aegis as such for the two options, including the Wellcraft option.[1095]

The bidder therefore was allowed to amend Wellcraft's charter.

In *Thompson v. Enstar Corp.*,[1096] however, the same court that decided *DMG* upheld, on a motion for a preliminary injunction, a crown jewel lock-up in the form of a voting trust agreement. The case arose out of Roy M. Huffington's proxy contest for control of Enstar and the Enstar board's reaction to the imminent success of Huffington's efforts. Plaintiffs, including Huffington, challenged Enstar's last-minute agreement to a tender offer by a white knight, Unimar Co., coupled with a crown jewel lock-up in the form of a voting trust agreement that assured Unimar's voting control of Enstar Indonesia, Enstar's single most valuable asset.

The court denied the preliminary injunction and analyzed the decision to accept the Unimar tender offer as of the date that the decision was made. Although troubled by several aspects of the Enstar board's conclusion, the court held:

> While reasonable men may differ as to whether the offer was the best which might ever materialize, the plaintiffs have not met their burden of showing that it was unreasonable for the directors to conclude that, in their judgment, the offer of Unimar was the best which could be obtained under the circumstances and that it was possible it might be soon withdrawn, thus leaving the shareholders of Enstar to face the prospect of liquidation for a much lesser price and at some time in the distant future. The adoption of the lock-up provisions was a necessary prerequisite to Unimar making its tender offer and therefore it is probable that it was reasonable for the directors to accede to Unimar's demand.[1097]

1095. *Id.* at 5–6.

1096. No. 7641 (Del. Ch. June 20, 1984).

1097. Slip op. at 14.

The court relied in particular upon the facts that the board had received only one bona fide offer despite its attempts to obtain others, that the offer was contingent upon the granting of the lock-up, and that the tender offer price represented a substantial premium over Enstar stock's historical market value.

Lock-up options should be distinguished from sales of a target's subsidiaries, divisions, or other assets to a disinterested purchaser (*i.e.*, one not bidding for the target) as a takeover defense. In *Whittaker Corp. v. Edgar*,[1098] for example, the court declined to issue a preliminary injunction against the sale of a subsidiary in a transaction designed as a defense against an unwanted tender offer. The target had agreed to sell one of its key subsidiaries for a price substantially above the value that the hostile offeror had assigned to it. The offeror had made clear that it would withdraw its offer if the subsidiary were sold.

In analyzing under federal law (prior to *Schreiber v. Burlington Northern, Inc.*[1099]) the challenge to the proposed sale, the court reviewed the substance of the transaction under the then-valid precedent of *Mobil Corp. v. Marathon Oil Co.*[1100] (Although it may no longer be appropriate to analyze the substance of tender offer tactics under federal law, *Whittaker*'s observations about such a sale would be relevant to similar issues raised today under state law.) The court distinguished the sale of the target's subsidiary to a third party from the crown jewel lock-up rejected in *Mobil* and upheld the instant transaction. The court noted that the sale was not a lock-up device: it did not create an artificial price ceiling for the target's common shares, was not designed to block healthy market activity (indeed, the sale was "*part*" of healthy market activity), and did not threaten potential bidders with the loss of the subsidiary's value (although such bidders would have to bid for the target without the subsidiary).[1101] Thus, while the sale could be expected to

1098. 535 F. Supp. 933 (N.D. Ill. 1982).

1099. 472 U.S. 1, 105 S. Ct. 2458 (1985), discussed in § III.2.B(2), *supra*.

1100. 669 F.2d 366 (6th Cir. 1981), *cert. denied*, 455 U.S. 982 (1982), discussed in § III.2.B(1), *supra*.

1101. 535 F. Supp. at 949 (emphasis in original).

deter unwanted bids from Whittaker, which had expressed particular interest in the subsidiary that was sold off, it did not necessarily have the effect—unlike the lock-ups later disapproved in *Hanson Trust* and *Revlon*—of deterring other bidders.

The court also upheld the sale under Delaware law, finding that plaintiff had made an insufficient showing that the target's directors had fought the tender offer primarily to maintain control of the corporation. The presumptions of the business judgment rule therefore applied to the board's actions.

Moreover, the court ruled that the subsidiary did not constitute "all or substantially all" of the target's property or assets; it thus was unnecessary to obtain shareholder approval (under section 271 of the Delaware Corporation Law) of the sale of the subsidiary. The court held that, in order to constitute all or substantially all of the assets for purposes of section 271, the property in question must be " 'quantitatively vital to the operation of the corporation,' " and the sale must " 'strike at the heart of the corporate existence and purpose.' "[1102] The court concluded that "[t]he sale of an asset representing at least 26% and possibly as much as 50% of a corporation's total assets is not a sale of substantially all of the corporation's assets for the purpose of section 271. . . ."[1103]

GM *Sub Corp. v. Liggett Group, Inc.*[1104] also involved the sale of a target's crown jewel subsidiary to a non-bidder in response to a hostile tender offer. When Liggett announced the sale of its prize subsidiary for $97.5 million, the hostile offeror sued to enjoin the transaction. Although the sale clearly was a response to, and could be expected to deter, plaintiff's takeover attempt, the court did not find a sufficient basis for enjoining the sale.

The court's observations resembled those of the *Whittaker* court: the court noted that Liggett's investment bankers had solicited competitive bids for the subsidiary, that nine firms had

1102. *Id.* at 951 (quoting *Gimbel v. Signal Cos., Inc.*, 316 A.2d 599, 606 (Del. Ch.), *aff'd on other grounds*, 316 A.2d 619 (Del. 1974)).

1103. 535 F. Supp. at 951.

1104. No. 6155 (Del. Ch. April 25, 1980).

submitted bids, and that the company had accepted the highest bid. The winning bidder had offered a very favorable price, and plaintiff had produced no evidence to show that the sale was in any way so unfavorable to the target as to constitute a waste of corporate assets. Moreover, the sale did not prevent a change in control. Its essential effect was simply that "the asset [the subsidiary] . . . will have been exchanged for the asset, $97.5 million cash."[1105]

2. Guidance as to Lock-Ups

While the law in the area is unsettled, some guiding principles can be distilled from the cases on lock-up options:

(a) Lock-up options will be much harder to justify if management has an interest in the bidder—for example, when the bidder is a leveraged buy-out vehicle in which management is to have a percentage of the equity—than if management remains independent of the bidder.
(b) Lock-up options to buy shares of a target's publicly traded stock are easier to justify than are asset options because the subject of the option is easier to value and because the option is less likely (if limited to the customary 18.5 percent of the outstanding shares) to preclude further bidding.
(c) A lock-up is more likely to be upheld if it is reasonable in relation to the benefit conferred on the target's shareholders than if the shareholders gain little from the arrangement. Thus, a lock-up is more likely to survive judicial scrutiny if offered to induce a white knight to enter the fray (especially if the lock-up produces a substantial jump in the bidding) than if granted for a marginal increase in the bidding under circumstances suggesting that one of the existing bidders would have been prepared to offer approximately the same price in any event.

1105. Slip op. at 3.

(d) A cancellation fee should be defensible if it is reasonable for the target to compensate a bidder for the risks and costs (including the loss of alternative opportunities) involved in making a bid for the company.

N. No-Shop and Best Efforts Provisions

Whenever a target and a bidder (especially if that bidder is a white knight) enter into negotiations concerning a proposed takeover, it is quite likely that the bidder will request—or even demand—that the target execute a "no-shop agreement." No-shop provisions generally require target management not to "shop" the company—not to look around for other (and potentially better) acquisition offers—and, perhaps, not to negotiate or make any agreements with any other potential bidder. In addition, the parties might include in their agreement a "best efforts clause" requiring management to use its best efforts to obtain shareholder approval of the deal and to fulfill any other conditions necessary for consummation of the transaction.

No-shop and best efforts provisions might deter potentially interested bidders from making better offers; they also might return to haunt a board of directors that has approved what later appears to be something less than the best possible deal that the company could have obtained in the absence of such provisions. In addition, serious questions may arise when such agreements have been made in response to another, pre-existing offer or when a new offer later emerges: What are the duties and responsibilities of a target that has committed itself to a no-shop or best efforts provision? Must the company refuse to negotiate with a bidder that is willing to make an offer that is demonstrably superior to the one subject to the provisions?

The answers, as might be expected, depend at least in part on the precise terms of the agreement. No-shop and best efforts provisions are contracts; to the extent that they do not proscribe certain kinds of conduct, they do not impinge on the target's freedom to respond to events as they emerge. Moreover, targets often (and wisely) insist on the incorporation of a "fiduciary out" in no-shop and best efforts clauses, thereby preserving the contractual right to entertain competing bids when the board's fiduciary duty to the corporation and its shareholders so requires.

In addition, directors today may have an obligation to consider superior offers even if the no-shop and best efforts provisions do not contain a "fiduciary out." Several recent cases suggest that, at least under Delaware law, the board's responsibilities to the shareholders may override these contractual provisions and that directors who have decided to sell the company might have a duty actively to seek the highest possible offer for the shareholders, without regard to no-shop or best efforts restrictions in an existing merger agreement.

One of the leading cases dealing with this issue is *ConAgra, Inc. v. Cargill, Inc.*,[1106] decided under Delaware law. On September 28, 1978, MBPXL Corporation, the target company, entered into a letter of intent with ConAgra providing for the acquisition of MBPXL subject to further negotiations and the execution of a definitive merger agreement. Cargill also was interested in acquiring MBPXL and, despite its awareness of the September 28 agreement, contacted MBPXL and began formulating a takeover strategy.

After considerable negotiations over a no-shop clause, MBPXL and ConAgra approved and signed a definitive merger agreement on October 16. This agreement contained a best efforts clause with a "fiduciary out":

> "*Best Efforts.* The respective Boards of Directors and principal officers of each of ConAgra and MBPXL shall take all such further action as may be necessary or appropriate in order to effectuate the transactions contemplated hereby including recommending to their respective shareholders that the merger be

---

1106. 222 Neb. 136, 382 N.W.2d 576 (1986).

> approved; *provided, however, nothing herein contained shall relieve either Board of Directors of their continuing duties to their respective shareholders.*"[1107]

The agreement further provided:

> "The Board of Directors of MBPXL will duly call and use its best efforts to cause to be held a special meeting of the shareholders of MBPXL on December 15, 1978, or the earliest practicable date thereafter, and has directed that this Agreement and the Merger Agreement be submitted to a vote at such meeting, and will recommend that the shareholders of MBPXL vote in favor of approval of this Agreement and the Merger Agreement."[1108]

After the ConAgra-MBPXL merger agreement was signed (but before it was approved by the shareholders), Cargill entered into agreements with a number of large MBPXL shareholders to buy 21.9 percent of MBPXL's outstanding shares for cash and to acquire an additional 4.5 percent two months later. Cargill also committed itself to use its best efforts to make a tender offer for all remaining MBPXL shares at $27 per share, a price higher than that offered by ConAgra. When Cargill announced its tender offer, MBPXL retained an investment banker to analyze the new bid and to compare it with ConAgra's; when the investment banker reported that Cargill's offer was the superior one, MBPXL's board determined to continue to review that proposal.

Further negotiations between MBPXL, Cargill, and their representatives ensued, and, on December 5, 1978, MBPXL's board adopted a series of resolutions resolving that (a) in light of its fiduciary obligations, the board could not recommend to MBPXL shareholders that they vote in favor of the ConAgra merger proposal; (b) the shareholders' meeting scheduled for December 15 would be cancelled; (c) management should negotiate a mutual termination of the ConAgra merger

---

1107. 382 N.W.2d at 582 (emphasis in original).

1108. *Id.* at 582–83.

agreement; and (d) shareholders should accept the Cargill proposal.

ConAgra sued to enjoin Cargill from interfering with the ConAgra-MBPXL agreement and ultimately sought damages for breach of contract and tortious interference with contractual relations. The trial court granted partial injunctive relief and, in 1983, awarded ConAgra almost $16 million in damages, based on the difference between what Cargill had offered and what ConAgra had agreed to pay. The Nebraska Supreme Court reversed the judgment, holding that, under the circumstances, MBPXL's board had a fiduciary duty to withdraw its recommendation of the ConAgra proposal.

The court observed that the "fiduciary out" proviso to the best efforts clause constituted a recognition by ConAgra and MBPXL "that there was a continuing fiduciary duty owed by each board of directors to its respective shareholders which could not be contracted away."[1109] Moreover, the opinion's sweeping language suggests that the court might well have reached the same decision even in the absence of an express "fiduciary out." The court plainly expressed its unwillingness to sanction " 'agreements which have the effect of removing from directors in a very substantial way their duty to use their own best judgment on management matters.' "[1110] "In [this] regard," the court continued,

> we cannot imagine a greater duty owed to shareholders than advising them of the existence of a higher offer for their stock before asking them to approve a lower offer. The directors of MBPXL could not agree to assist ConAgra by pledging their best efforts if by doing so the directors of MBPXL violated their legal duties to MBPXL shareholders. . . .
>
> . . . .

1109. *Id.* at 587.

1110. *Id.* (quoting *Abercrombie v. Davies*, 35 Del. Ch. 599, 611, 123 A.2d 893, 899 (1956), *rev'd on other grounds*, 36 Del. Ch. 371, 130 A.2d 338 (Del. 1957)).

> When the MBPXL board resolved to cancel the shareholders' meeting at which the ConAgra merger proposal was to have been submitted and instead recommended shareholder acceptance of the cash-out Cargill offer, that was not a breach of the ConAgra merger agreement. Once the directors of MBPXL learned of the competing Cargill offer, the "best efforts" clause in the ConAgra proposal could not relieve the MBPXL directors of their duties to act in the shareholders' best interests. They had an obligation at that point to investigate the competing offer, and if, in the exercise of their independent good faith judgment, they found that the Cargill offer was a better offer for the MBPXL shareholders, they were bound to recommend the better offer.[1111]

ConAgra's holding—that corporate directors cannot, consistently with their fiduciary duty of loyalty, bind themselves to promote an inferior offer once a clearly superior (and, in this case, unsolicited) one has emerged—harmonizes with the Delaware Supreme Court's ruling in *Revlon, Inc. v. MacAndrews & Forbes Holdings, Inc.*[1112] *Revlon* grew out of a battle between a hostile tender offeror, Pantry Pride, Inc., and a white knight leveraged buy-out proposal sponsored by Forstmann Little & Co. for control of Revlon. After several rounds of skirmishes and defensive maneuvers, Forstmann demanded and received a crown jewel lock-up option and a no-shop provision in exchange for topping Pantry Pride's then-current bid. Pantry Pride, which had promised to engage in fractional bidding, eventually raised its offer and sued to invalidate the lock-up option and the no-shop clause.

The court affirmed an injunction barring enforcement of the lock-up option and the no-shop clause, holding that Revlon's directors had violated their duty of loyalty to Revlon's shareholders by thwarting Pantry Pride's attempts to make a superior offer. Once dissolution of Revlon became inevitable and the board's "primary duty [became] that of an auctioneer responsible for selling the company to the highest bidder," the directors could not make an agreement with Forstmann that

---

1111. *Id.* at 587–88.

1112. 506 A.2d 173 (Del. 1986), discussed in detail in § III.3.B(3), *supra.*

"ended rather than intensified the board's involvement in the bidding contest."[1113]

The *Revlon* court acknowledged that

> [f]avoritism for a white knight to the total exclusion of a hostile bidder might be justifiable when the latter's offer adversely affects shareholder interests, but when bidders make relatively similar offers, or dissolution of the company becomes inevitable, the directors cannot fulfill their enhanced *Unocal* duties by playing favorites with the contending factions. Market forces must be allowed to operate freely to bring the target's shareholders the best price available for their equity. Thus, as the trial court ruled, the shareholders' interests necessitated that the board remain free to negotiate in the fulfillment of that duty.[1114]

The court also implicitly criticized the Revlon board's decision, made even before agreeing to the no-shop provision, not to make financial data and other information available to Pantry Pride or to other prospective competing bidders.[1115]

Accordingly, *ConAgra* and *Revlon* strongly suggest that a court applying Delaware law would refuse to enforce a no-shop or best efforts clause intended to restrain the "active" role required of a board of directors once the board has decided to accept a proposed tender offer or other acquisition resulting in the sale or dissolution of the corporation. If a demonstrably superior offer emerges, the board probably has a duty seriously to consider it. (It is less likely, however, that the board may actively *solicit* new

---

1113. *Id.* at 184.

1114. *Id.* (footnote omitted).

1115. *See also Edelman v. Fruehauf Corp.*, 798 F.2d 882 (6th Cir. 1986), discussed in § III.4.K., *supra*. In *Fruehauf*, the target's board had agreed to a white knight leveraged buy-out that involved a no-shop clause. The court held that the directors had violated their fiduciary duties to the shareholders by favoring the leveraged buy-out group over the hostile bidder. Among other things, the court required the board to "make available upon reasonable notice to any potential bidder for Fruehauf all information concerning Fruehauf's business and properties (subject to such bidder agreeing to reasonable provisions to keep such information confidential) and to meet on mutually agreeable and reasonable terms with any potential bidder in good faith." *Id.* at 890–91.

offers after agreeing to a no-shop or a best efforts clause.) Moreover, courts applying Delaware law probably would construe a "fiduciary out" proviso to accord the directors broad flexibility to negotiate (if not to solicit) a higher bid for the target.

An earlier case, however, that showed greater judicial hospitality toward a no-shop clause is *Jewel Companies, Inc. v. Pay Less Drug Stores Northwest, Inc.*[1116] Jewel sued Pay Less Drug Stores Northwest ("Northwest") for tortiously interfering with an executed and board-approved merger agreement between Jewel and Pay Less Drug Stores ("Pay Less"). Articles 9.9 and 10.5 of the agreement obligated the board of each company to " 'use its best efforts to fulfill those conditions . . . over which it has control or influence and to consummate the Merger.' " Article 9 also required Pay Less neither to sell or transfer any of its properties or assets nor to enter into or terminate any contract other than in the ordinary course of business. Moreover, Pay Less could not " 'agree to, or make any commitment to' " effect, any sale, transfer, or extraordinary action prohibited by Article 9.[1117]

Following public announcement of this merger agreement, Northwest began to purchase Pay Less stock in open-market transactions and announced its intention to make a tender offer for Pay Less at $22.50 per share, conditioned on the Pay Less board's abandoning the merger with Jewel. When, pursuant to an agreement with Pay Less, Northwest raised its offer to $24 per share (which was considerably higher than Jewel's exchange offer, valued at $14.75 per share), the Pay Less board unanimously recommended that the company's shareholders accept Northwest's offer. The board also sent to all Pay Less shareholders a 29-page letter comparing the two offers.

Despite its recommendation of the Northwest offer, however, the board advised the shareholders that the stockholders' meeting scheduled to consider the Jewel offer would take place as

---

1116. 741 F.2d 1555 (9th Cir. 1984).

1117. *Id.* at 1557.

planned. The meeting was held, and Northwest, by then the majority Pay Less shareholder, passed a resolution rejecting the Jewel merger agreement. The district court granted Northwest's motion for summary judgment on Jewel's tortious interference claim, but the Court of Appeals for the Ninth Circuit reversed and remanded, holding that, under California law, a court may enforce clauses in a merger agreement that are designed to preclude a target's board from negotiating for or accepting a competing offer pending shareholder consideration of the initial agreement.

The Court of Appeals expressly recognized that "a board may not lawfully divest itself of its fiduciary obligations in a contract."[1118] "However," continued the court,

> to permit a board of directors to decide that a proposed merger transaction is in the best interests of its shareholders at a given point in time, and to agree to refrain from entering into competing contracts until the shareholders consider the proposal, does not conflict in any way with the board's fiduciary obligation.[1119]

The court remanded for further consideration of whether the parties actually *intended* that the Jewel-Pay Less agreement would require Pay Less to abstain from negotiating or executing a competing merger agreement.

Several aspects of the *Jewel* opinion merit particular attention. First, the case was decided under California law, which, unlike Delaware law (as expounded in *Revlon*), "does not adopt the auction model in regulating negotiated acquisitions."[1120] The laws of Delaware and California thus appear to be at odds on this point.

Second, the court observed that, even after committing itself to refrain from negotiating or accepting a competing bid, the target's board could not, "consistent with its fiduciary

1118. *Id.* at 1563.

1119. *Id.*

1120. *Id.* at 1562.

obligations to its shareholders, withhold information regarding a potentially more attractive competing offer."[1121] Instead, the board must pass on this information (presumably in a neutral fashion) to the shareholders, who "remain free to accept or reject the merger proposal presented by the board, to respond to a merger proposal or tender offer made by another firm subsequent to the board's execution of exclusive merger agreement, or to hold out for a better offer."[1122] As the Appellate Court of Illinois explained in a similar case (cited in the *Jewel* opinion), a no-shop or best efforts clause confers on the bidder an expectation only as to the performance of the target's board; it neither requires the shareholders to ratify the proposal nor restricts another corporation's freedom to make a competing tender offer directly to the target's shareholders.[1123]

Third, the *Jewel* court expressly declined to decide "whether upon the unsolicited receipt of a more favorable offer after signing a merger agreement the board still must recommend to its shareholders that they approve the initial proposal."[1124] This statement suggests that, even under California law, a target's board may have some room to back away from a merger agreement upon the appearance of a superior, unsolicited bid. How far the board can go in abandoning a merger that it had promised to use its best efforts to consummate, however, is uncertain. Perhaps the board may only refrain from recommending the inferior offer without actually supporting the superior one.

It is worth noting that Delaware law might not differ as much from California law as *ConAgra* and *Revlon* seem to suggest. In *Smith v. Van Gorkom*,[1125] which preceded *ConAgra* and *Revlon*, the Delaware Supreme Court appears to have concluded that,

---

1121. *Id.* at 1564.

1122. *Id.*

1123. *Belden Corp. v. InterNorth, Inc.*, 90 Ill. App. 3d 547, 45 Ill. Dec. 765, 413 N.E.2d 98, 102 (1980).

1124. 741 F.2d at 1564 n.13.

1125. 488 A.2d 858 (Del. 1985), discussed in detail in § III.3.B(2), *supra*.

once having pledged to use its "best efforts" to obtain shareholder approval of a proposed transaction, a board of directors must perform in accordance with the terms of the agreement or face liability for breach of contract.

Trans Union Corporation had entered into a merger agreement with GL; the agreement provided that Trans Union's board " 'shall recommend to the stockholders of Trans Union that they approve and adopt the Merger Agreement . . . and . . . use its best efforts to obtain the requisite votes therefor. GL acknowledges that Trans Union directors may have a competing fiduciary obligation to the shareholders under certain circumstances.' "[1126] An amendment to the merger agreement allowed Trans Union to terminate the agreement and abandon the merger only if, before the shareholders' meeting, the company had either consummated a merger (or an asset sale) with a third party or had entered into a "definitive" merger agreement more favorable, and for a greater consideration, than the proposed transaction with GL—subject only to shareholder approval.[1127]

Plaintiff shareholders challenged the adequacy of the merger price and argued that Trans Union's directors had acted with gross negligence in approving the merger agreement without fully considering the company's intrinsic value and the availability of alternative transactions. The directors countered that they had not bound, and could not bind, the company irrevocably to the agreement; that the best efforts clause itself contained an express "fiduciary out"; and that the board would have a chance to consider, and make a recommendation based on, all relevant factors before the shareholders actually voted on the proposal.

The Delaware Supreme Court ruled for the shareholders, holding that Trans Union's directors had breached their duty of care in approving the merger agreement and that they could not rely on the "fiduciary out" to cure their misconduct. Once they

---

1126. *Id.* at 879.

1127. *Id.* at 883.

had executed the agreement, the directors had two alternatives: they could proceed with the merger and the stockholders' meeting and continue to recommend the merger, or they could rescind the agreement, withdraw their approval, and cancel the meeting. This second alternative, however,

> would have clearly involved a substantial risk—that the Board would be faced with suit by Pritzker for breach of contract based on its September 20 agreement as amended October 10. As previously noted, under the terms of the October 10 amendment, the Board's only ground for release from its agreement with Pritzker was its entry into a more favorable definitive agreement to sell the Company to a third party. Thus, in reality, the Board was not "free to turn down the Pritzker proposal" as the Trial Court found. Indeed, short of negotiating a better agreement with a third party, the Board's only basis for release from the Pritzker Agreement without liability would have been to establish fundamental wrongdoing by Pritzker. Clearly, the Board was not "free" to withdraw from its agreement with Pritzker on January 26 by simply relying on its self-induced failure to have reached an informed business judgment at the time of its original agreement.[1128]

The court did not formally opine on whether subsequent developments would have justified a decision to exercise the "fiduciary out."

The import of *Van Gorkom* in the area of no-shop and best efforts provisions is unclear. First, the case was decided one year before *Revlon*, and the latter thus might be a better indicator of the current state of Delaware law. Second, *Van Gorkom*, unlike *Revlon* (and *ConAgra*), did not deal expressly with a board's ability to invoke its fiduciary responsibilities in order to withdraw from an agreement; rather, it addressed whether the directors had fulfilled their duty of care in approving that agreement, and it rejected the directors' attempt blindly to rely on a "fiduciary out" as a substitute for informed decisionmaking. It is entirely possible that the court's outrage at the directors'

1128. *Id.* at 888.

grossly negligent behavior led the court to adopt a less flexible view of the "fiduciary out" than would have been the case had the board acted in a more responsible manner. At any rate, however, *Van Gorkom* should be considered by anyone attempting to divine Delaware's law on best efforts and "fiduciary out" provisions.

Overlying the whole area of no-shop provisions, best efforts clauses, and tortious interference is *Pennzoil Co. v. Texaco, Inc.*,[1129] the basic facts of which may be gleaned from the related opinion in *Pennzoil Co. v. Getty Oil Co.*[1130] This lawsuit arose from Texaco's acquisition of Getty Oil after Getty and its controlling shareholders had entered into an agreement in principle to be acquired, in part, by Pennzoil.

On December 28, 1983, Pennzoil commenced a tender offer for approximately 20 percent of Getty at $100 per share. On January 2, 1984, however, Pennzoil entered into a Memorandum of Agreement with Gordon P. Getty, as Trustee of the Sarah C. Getty Trust (the "Trustee"), and the J. Paul Getty Museum (the "Museum"), which two entities together held 52 percent of Getty's outstanding shares. The agreement provided that Pennzoil would increase its tender offer price to $110 per share and would purchase up to 30 percent of Getty; that Getty would purchase the Museum's shares at $110 per share; that Getty would effect a cash-out merger at $110 to eliminate all shareholders other than Pennzoil and the Trustee; that Pennzoil and the Trustee would own Getty on a 3/7 – 4/7 basis and would work together to restructure the company; and that, failing agreement by December 31, 1984 on a restructuring plan, Pennzoil and the Trustee would liquidate the company and split up its assets on the basis of the three-to-four ratio.

The Memorandum, signed by Pennzoil, the Trustee, and the Museum, was submitted to Getty's board on January 2, and, after long negotiations, the board approved, on January 3, either a sale at $112.50 or the Memorandum itself with a revised price

1129. No. 84 – 05905 (Dist. Ct., Harris Cty, Tex.).
1130. No. 7425 (Del. Ch. Feb. 6, 1984).

of \$112.50 (depending on whether one believes Texaco's or Pennzoil's version of the meeting). The next day, January 4, Pennzoil and Getty issued identical press releases announcing that Getty, the Trustee, and the Museum had "agreed in principle" to a merger of Getty and a newly formed entity owned by Pennzoil and the Trustee. The press releases set forth the elements of the "agreement in principle" and stated that "[t]he transaction is subject to execution of a definitive merger agreement, approval by the stockholders of Getty Oil and completion of various governmental filing and waiting period requirements."

That same day, however, Texaco became very interested in acquiring Getty, and, by the next day, January 5, Texaco's board approved a tender offer at \$125 per share—\$12.50 more per share than Pennzoil was offering. On January 6, Texaco announced that it had agreed to buy the shares of the Trustee and the Museum, who promised to recommend the Texaco offer to the Getty board. The board approved the offer at \$125 (later raised to \$128) per share, and Pennzoil sued everyone in sight. The case ultimately ended up in the Texas courts, with Pennzoil pursuing a claim against Texaco for tortiously interfering with Pennzoil's agreement with Getty. In November 1985, a Texas jury, applying New York tort and contract law, awarded Pennzoil \$7.53 billion in compensatory damages and \$3 billion in punitive damages for a total award of \$10.53 billion—the largest award in human history.

Damages of that magnitude are bound to cause some concern in corporate boardrooms. In some respects, the verdict appears to fly in the face of *Revlon* and *ConAgra*, for the Getty board (whose fiduciary duties were prescribed by Delaware law) simply acted to maximize shareholder wealth—by \$15.50 per share.

Undoubtedly, there are serious inconsistencies between, on the one hand, *Revlon* and *ConAgra* and, on the other hand, *Pennzoil v. Texaco*. But there also are arguable distinctions between the former and the latter. First, *Revlon* and *ConAgra*, unlike *Pennzoil*, did not involve merger agreements that already had been approved (at least informally) by a majority of the target's shareholders. Second, unlike Texaco, the competing bidders in *Revlon* and *ConAgra* had entered the picture *before* the execution of the merger agreements at issue; indeed, Pantry Pride had expressly stated to Revlon its intention to outbid Revlon's "white knight." There thus was no question in those cases of the targets' having "shopped" for alternative suitors. Third, the *Revlon* court clearly had been concerned about the Revlon board's having entered into lock-up and no-shop agreements to protect the interests of certain noteholders (rather than those of the shareholders) and to save the directors from litigation threatened by those noteholders. Getty's board was presumably disinterested in its decision to approve the Pennzoil proposal. Fourth, *Revlon* involved a no-shop agreement that was granted in the heat of a bidding war and was designed to end the auction. When Pennzoil and Getty entered into their agreement, however, no other bidder was in sight, and the agreement thus did not deprive Getty shareholders of a foreseeable alternative offer.

Whether these distinctions make any real difference, and what that difference might be, is far more difficult to determine. The *Pennzoil* ruling currently is before the Texas Court of Appeals, and it remains to be seen whether the verdict will stand.

CHAPTER

5

STATE TAKEOVER LEGISLATION

During the 1960s, state legislatures and the Congress responded to the increasing use of cash tender offers by acquirors bent on taking over existing enterprises. Congress passed the Williams Act, which imposed new disclosure obligations designed to help target companies' stockholders make informed decisions about whether to tender their shares. The new law conformed to the federal tradition of promoting an informed market in securities transactions. At the same time, state legislatures developed a separate body of law rooted in the states' customary authority to protect local enterprises and investors and to regulate corporations chartered in their jurisdictions.

A. "First-Generation" Statutes

Beginning in 1968, some 37 states enacted laws now termed "first-generation" takeover statutes.[1131] Although the statutes varied from state to state, they tended to have common features: they required offerors, *prior* to commencing a tender offer, to make disclosures more extensive than those mandated by the Williams Act (which requires the offeror to disclose certain information *concurrently* with its offer); they authorized state securities regulators to conduct hearings concerning tender offers, to delay offers pending confirmation of the adequacy of disclosures, and even, in some states, to block offers entirely upon a finding of unfairness; and they broadly defined "target company" in ways that extended the states' authority to transactions between tender offerors and target shareholders residing in other jurisdictions.[1132] These state statutes obviously overlapped with the Williams Act, and the ensuing confusion resulted in many challenges to the "first-generation" statutes'

1131. The statutes are collected in Warren, "Developments in State Takeover Regulation: *MITE* and Its Aftermath," 40 Bus. Law. 671, 671 nn. 2–3 (1985).

1132. *Id.* at 677.

validity under the Supremacy and Commerce Clauses of the United States Constitution.[1133]

Attacks on these laws culminated in *Edgar v. MITE Corp.*,[1134] under which any current state attempt to regulate tender offer activity must be tested. The *MITE* case split the Supreme Court and failed to resolve the tension between state and federal law in this area. The nine Justices issued six different opinions, and only a bare majority of the Court supported the narrow ground of agreement. Two Justices did not reach the merits at all because they considered the case moot.

On January 19, 1979, MITE began a tender offer for all outstanding shares of Chicago Rivet & Machine Co. MITE was a Delaware corporation with its principal offices in Connecticut; Chicago Rivet was a publicly held Illinois corporation that conducted most of its business in Pennsylvania. MITE complied with the Williams Act by filing a Schedule 14D-1 with the SEC on January 19, but it openly defied Illinois' assertion of authority over the tender offer by suing for a declaratory judgment that the Illinois Business Take-Over Act was preempted by the Williams Act and unconstitutional under the Commerce Clause.

The salient features of the Illinois Act typified those of most "first-generation" takeover statutes. The Illinois law required a tender offeror to notify the Secretary of State and the target 20 days before the tender offer became effective. During this period, the target was free to communicate with its shareholders concerning the bid, but the offeror was barred from such contact. The statute defined "target" broadly to include any corporation in which Illinois shareholders owned ten percent of the class of securities subject to the offer or for which any two of the following were true: the corporation had its principal office in Illinois, was organized under Illinois law, or had at least ten percent of its stated capital and paid-in surplus represented within the state.

1133. *See id.* at 678 n.52 (citing cases in which "first-generation" statutes were invalidated under the Commerce and Supremacy Clauses).

1134. 457 U.S. 624 (1982).

The statute also required the offeror to register any takeover bid with the Illinois Secretary of State. A tender offer was considered registered 20 days after the filing of a registration statement, unless the Secretary of State exercised his authority to call a hearing to assess the fairness of the offer. The holding of a hearing during the 20-day period was mandatory if requested either by a majority of the target's outside directors or by Illinois shareholders holding at least ten percent of the class of securities subject to the offer. The statute further empowered the Secretary of State to block registration and thus end the offer if he found that the offeror had not disclosed all material information or that the offer was inequitable or fraudulent.

Justice White wrote an opinion, parts of which were joined by a majority of the Court, holding the Illinois statute unconstitutional under the Commerce Clause. The five Justices who adhered to this view based their decision on the principle, established in *Pike v. Bruce Church, Inc.*, that "[a] state statute must be upheld if it 'regulates even-handedly to effectuate a legitimate local public interest, and its effects on interstate commerce are only incidental . . . unless the burden imposed on such commerce is clearly excessive in relation to the putative local benefits.' "[1135] The *MITE* majority held that a statute allowing the Illinois Secretary of State to block a nationwide tender offer deprived shareholders throughout the country of an opportunity to sell their shares at premium prices, hindered the reallocation of resources to their most valuable uses, and reduced the incentive for incumbent management to perform well in order to sustain high stock prices.[1136] These burdens impermissibly outweighed Illinois' own interests.

Illinois sought to justify these nationwide effects by stressing its need to protect resident shareholders and its right to exercise its traditional authority over the internal affairs of Illinois corporations. The Court declared protecting local investors to be a reasonable state objective but held that Illinois had "no

---

1135. *Id.* at 640 (quoting *Pike v. Bruce Church, Inc.*, 397 U.S. 137, 142 (1970)).
1136. 457 U.S. at 643.

legitimate interest" in protecting nonresident shareholders.[1137] Moreover, the shareholder protection argument paled in light of the statute's exemption of a company's acquisition of its own shares. Chicago Rivet thus was able to make a competing tender offer subject only to federal disclosure law, while MITE had to comply with both federal and state law. Because the premise for the Illinois Act was the inadequacy of federal disclosure, the Court viewed this exemption for self-tenders as undermining the rationale that Illinois had presented to justify its burdening of interstate commerce.[1138]

The Court went on to find that the state statute afforded only "speculative" benefits to Illinois shareholders.[1139] Although the Illinois law required disclosures more extensive than those mandated by the Williams Act, the Court was not convinced that the extra information significantly increased shareholders' ability to make informed decisions about tender offers. Furthermore, although shareholders could benefit from the delays imposed by the Illinois Act, those possible benefits might "be outweighed by the increased risk that the tender offer [would] fail due to defensive tactics employed by incumbent management."[1140]

Finally, the Court rejected the argument that Illinois could justify the statute on the basis of the state's interest in regulating the internal affairs of Illinois corporations. Distinguishing the "internal affairs doctrine" as a conflict of laws principle designed to eliminate confusion as to which state is empowered to regulate the relationships among and between corporations and their officers, directors, and shareholders, the Court observed that, by contrast, "[t]ender offers contemplate transfers of stock by stockholders to a third party and do not themselves implicate the internal affairs of the target company."[1141] The Court found

---

1137. *Id.* at 644.

1138. *Id.*

1139. *Id.* at 645.

1140. *Id.*

1141. *Id.*

Illinois' reliance on the internal affairs doctrine "somewhat incredible" because the statute, as written, applied to any tender offer for a corporation in which Illinois residents held only ten percent of the outstanding shares. This low jurisdictional threshold clearly permitted application of the statute to corporations that were incorporated in other states and that conducted the bulk of their business elsewhere. The Court therefore declined to accept the state's alleged interest in preserving this traditional area of its authority as sufficient to justify the burden that the statute imposed on interstate commerce and the national securities market.[1142]

Only three of his colleagues (Chief Justice Burger and Justices Stevens and O'Connor) joined Justice White in further declaring that the Illinois statute constituted a *direct* burden on interstate commerce because it could be applied to some tender offer transactions occurring completely outside Illinois (for example, an offer involving a nonresident Chicago Rivet shareholder and a nonresident bidder). These four Justices recognized the traditional authority of state governments to enact "blue-sky" laws regulating securities transactions within their borders; indeed, a savings clause in section 28(a) of the Exchange Act[1143] is " 'designed to save state blue-sky laws from pre-emption.' "[1144] Blue-sky laws, however, by definition apply only when at least one party to the transaction resides in the given state; the Illinois statute, by contrast, could apply to interstate transactions taking place entirely outside Illinois.[1145] Thus, the four Justices focused on the physical setting of the regulated transaction rather than on the locations of the parties involved.

Justice Powell provided the critical swing vote for *MITE*'s holding that the Illinois statute imposed impermissible *indirect*

1142. *Id.* at 644 – 646.

1143. 15 U.S.C. § 78bb(a).

1144. 457 U.S. at 641 (quoting *Leroy v. Great Western United Corp.*, 443 U.S. 173, 182 n.13 (1979)).

1145. 457 U.S. at 641.

burdens on commerce. His concurrence specifically premised his willingness to join Justice White's opinion on his belief that the opinion's "Commerce Clause reasoning leaves some room for state regulation of tender offers."[1146] Justice Powell asserted that the Williams Act's neutrality assumed that tender offer contests would take place between corporate entities with relatively equal resources; in many contests, however, targets have faced bids from acquirors having sufficiently superior resources to undermine the rationale for the Williams Act's neutrality. In light of this reality, Justice Powell observed that the Act's policy "does not necessarily imply a congressional intent to prohibit state legislation designed to assure—at least in some circumstances—greater protection to interests that include but often are broader than those of incumbent management."[1147]

Only Justices White and Blackmun and Chief Justice Burger (three Justices did not reach the issue) considered the Illinois statute to be unconstitutional under the Supremacy Clause because it impermissibly conflicted with and thus disturbed the balance between incumbent management and tender offerors established by the Williams Act.[1148] These Justices recognized that, in enacting that legislation, "Congress did not explicitly prohibit states from regulating takeover offers" but instead left to the courts the determination whether a specific state statute impermissibly conflicts with, and thus is preempted by, the Williams Act.[1149]

The Williams Act was designed to protect investors not only by requiring tender offer participants to furnish them with information "but also by withholding from management or the bidder any undue advantage that could frustrate the exercise of an informed choice."[1150] Justices White and Blackmun and Chief Justice Burger opined that three features of the Illinois statute

---

1146. *Id.* at 646.

1147. *Id.* at 647.

1148. *Id.* at 634.

1149. *Id.* at 631.

1150. *Id.* at 634.

upset the balance that Congress had struck. First, the precommencement notice provision furnished incumbent management with too much additional time to take steps to resist the offer.[1151] Second, the discretion afforded the Secretary of State to call a hearing on the offer, with no deadline for completion, introduced unfair delay and assisted target management at the offeror's expense.[1152] Third, the Secretary's statutory authority to rule on the substantive fairness of the offer ignored the purpose of the Williams Act—namely, to furnish investors with sufficient information to enable them to make their own decisions about a tender offer's desirability.[1153]

Justice Stevens expressly refused to join this Supremacy Clause analysis. In a separate opinion, he observed: "I am not persuaded . . . that Congress' decision to follow a policy of neutrality in its own legislation is tantamount to a federal prohibition against state legislation designed to provide special protection for incumbent management."[1154]

In the wake of *MITE*, courts across the country invalidated many state takeover statutes already on the books, typically on Commerce Clause grounds.[1155] By the summer of 1986, at least 20 states had revised old laws or adopted entirely new measures in attempts to exercise the prerogatives to which Justice Powell had referred. These new state takeover statutes are referred to as "second-generation" statutes, in recognition of the obvious effects of *MITE* on their conception and execution.

1151. *Id.* at 635.

1152. *Id.* at 637.

1153. *Id.* at 639–40.

1154. *Id.* at 655.

1155. For discussions of post-*MITE* cases concerning first-generation statutes, see Warren, "Developments in State Takeover Regulation: *MITE* and Its Aftermath," 40 Bus. Law. 671, 686–94 (1985).

B. "Second-Generation" Statutes

Although different commentators have tried to define the "second-generation" statutes in their own ways, the most sensible distinction seems to be that the new laws, unlike their pre-*MITE* predecessors, tend to regulate takeovers through basic state corporation law rather than through state securities laws administered by state regulatory officials. The most useful way to analyze the post-*MITE* laws is to focus on the different provisions that they incorporate into traditional state corporation law in order to increase the difficulty of taking over local enterprises.

The first type of law, commonly referred to as a "control share acquisition statute," seemed discredited by the end of the summer of 1986, in light of federal court rulings invalidating such laws in five of the six states that enacted them and of Wisconsin's having repealed its own version.[1156] The apparent invalidity of control share laws might also cast doubt on the viability of other statutory approaches.

1. Control Share Acquisition Statutes

In 1982, Ohio enacted a statute that became the prototype for the control share approach.[1157] The law, which applied to tender offers and other purchases, required prior shareholder approval of "[c]ontrol share acquisitions"[1158] that would result in concentrations of ownership exceeding the 20-percent, 33-1/3 percent, and 50-percent levels (but not of purchases within those

1156. *See infra* § III.5.B(1); *see also Terry v. Yamashita*, 643 F. Supp. 161 (D. Haw. 1986) (declaring Hawaii Control Share Acquisition Act unconstitutional because it imposes direct and indirect burdens on interstate commerce, but refusing to reach Supremacy Clause issue).

1157. Ohio Rev. Code Ann. § 1701.831.

1158. *Id.* § 1701.01(Z)(1).

zones).[1159] The statute applied only to acquisitions of securities of any Ohio corporation that had 50 or more shareholders *and* that had its principal place of business, its main executive offices, or substantial assets in Ohio.[1160] Thus, by its terms, the law applied to acquisitions of securities of an issuer that had no shareholders living in Ohio, and it covered purchases from all shareholders, regardless of where they resided. The statute allowed the issuer's shareholders to vote to exempt their company from the law's constraints.[1161]

The Ohio statute further provided that the issuer's shareholders must approve any covered acquisition *both* by an absolute majority of the shares voted at a meeting called to consider a bid *and* by a majority of the shares voted by disinterested shareholders present at the meeting (thus excluding shares voted by the acquiror or by the target's officers or employee-directors).[1162] This provision introduced the possibility that insiders owning a majority of the issuer's shares could thwart a control share purchase approved by a majority of the shares controlled by disinterested shareholders. The target could schedule this special meeting, at its election, any time within 50 days after the purchaser furnished to the target an "acquiring person statement" disclosing the terms of the acquisition and other information.[1163]

The Ohio law, however, differed in several respects from the Illinois statute struck down in *MITE*: it did not include any precommencement filing requirements; it did not impose disclosure obligations more detailed than those prescribed by the Williams Act; and it did not provide for review by state regulatory officials of the fairness of the offer or the adequacy of the disclosure.

1159. *Id.* § 1701.831(E).
1160. *Id.* § 1701.01(Y).
1161. *Id.* § 1701.831(A).
1162. *Id.* § 1701.831(E)(1).
1163. *Id.* §§ 1701.831(B), (C).

On May 21, 1986, Fleet Aerospace, a corporation headquartered in and organized under the laws of Ontario, Canada, began a cash tender offer for any and all shares of Aeronca, Inc., an Ohio corporation having its principal executive offices in Charlotte, North Carolina, and its main business operations in Middletown, Ohio. On the same day, Fleet filed suit in federal district court to enjoin enforcement of the Ohio Control Share Acquisition Act and to obtain a declaration of the statute's unconstitutionality under the Commerce and Supremacy Clauses. The court struck down the Ohio statute on both grounds in *Fleet Aerospace Corp. v. Holderman*,[1164] and the Court of Appeals for the Sixth Circuit affirmed. The Court of Appeals adopted the reasoning of the district court's detailed opinion but questioned that court's conclusory statement that *MITE* " 'sounded the death knell for state control of federally regulated tender offers,' if the court meant by this statement that *all* state regulation regarding tender offers is foreclosed."[1165]

The district court ruled that the Ohio statute frustrated the objectives of the Williams Act and thus was preempted, under the Supremacy Clause, by the federal regulatory scheme. First, Ohio law allowed an issuer's management to delay tender offer purchases far beyond the period prescribed by the Williams Act. The SEC's regulations permit a tender offeror to begin buying shares as early as the twenty-first business day following commencement of an offer. The Ohio statute, however, prevented a purchaser from buying, and a shareholder from selling, shares in a control share acquisition without the approval of the issuer's shareholders, and management had the

---

1164. 637 F. Supp. 742 (S.D. Ohio), *aff'd*, 796 F.2d 135 (6th Cir. 1986), *appeal docketed*, No. 86–344, 55 U.S.L.W. 3175 (U.S. Sept. 2, 1986).

1165. 796 F.2d at 139 n.5 (emphasis in original) (quoting the district court's opinion). After the district court issued its ruling, Aeronca's directors accepted a revised Fleet proposal more generous to Aeronca shareholders and agreed to a subsequent merger. Because the Ohio securities regulators maintained that they still wished to enforce the statute, however, the Court of Appeals rejected the contention that the case was moot.

right to delay scheduling a shareholders' meeting for that purpose until 50 days after the purchaser furnished an "acquiring person statement." The law thus provided incumbent management with "a long period of delay in which defensive measures [could] be taken to thwart the acquisition of stock by the offeror,"[1166] and this delay "undermine[d] the basic policy of the Williams Act to maintain a neutral policy towards cash tender offers and tilt[ed] the carefully balanced scales in favor of incumbent management."[1167]

This defect was exacerbated by the requirement that the issuer's shareholders approve a covered acquisition by an affirmative vote, which requirement

> realistically converts a tender offer into a proxy contest before the offeror will be able to purchase tendered shares. Requiring an offeror to run the gauntlet of not only pursuing its tender offer but facing the probability of a proxy contest with its additional expense and potential for delays in announcing the shareholder vote, adjournments, vote challenges and similar procedural tactics, not only raises the possibility of an offeror being unable to complete the Ohio process prior to the 60 day withdrawal period [prescribed by the Williams Act], but may discourage offerors from pursuing tender offers and/or, at the least, imposes upon the offeror an additional costly and time consuming burden in connection with cash tender offers.[1168]

Again, Ohio's statute favored incumbent management and disturbed the neutrality that the Williams Act was designed to insure.

The court also noted that the Act was intended to assure that individual investors would receive information sufficient to allow them to make informed, personal decisions about whether to accept a tender offer.[1169] The Ohio statute's requirement that a majority of shareholders agree before any individual could sell a

---

1166. 637 F. Supp. at 757.
1167. *Id.*
1168. *Id.* at 758. (footnotes omitted).
1169. *Id.*

control share block left individual investors hostage to the group. For all of these reasons, the court declared Ohio's control share measure invalid under the Supremacy Clause.

The district court also held that the Ohio statute violated the Commerce Clause both because it constituted a direct regulation of interstate commerce and because the state interest in regulating control share acquisitions did not outweigh the burden that the statute imposed on interstate commerce. In defense of the statute, Ohio officials relied on the state's traditional authority to regulate the internal affairs of Ohio corporations and to protect the interests of those companies' shareholders. As the court noted, the state had elected to treat control of a corporation as a "corporate asset, the sale of which profoundly affects internal corporate affairs and corporate governance. . . ."[1170] Thus, defendants contended, Ohio had just as much of a right to control the disposition of this asset through tender offers as it did to regulate consolidations, liquidations, and other organic changes in corporate structure. Moreover, defendants argued, "the power to regulate the internal affairs of an Ohio corporation necessarily includes the power to regulate shareholders of an Ohio corporation, in their capacity as shareholders, regardless of where those shareholders reside."[1171] Finally, defendants asserted that the statute covered an area traditionally left to the state and that it only incidentally affected interstate commerce; it therefore did not violate the Commerce Clause.[1172]

In holding that the state statute directly regulated interstate commerce, the court noted that Ohio could apply the law to a tender offer for shares of Aeronca even if none of that company's shareholders resided in Ohio.[1173] Ohio thus was asserting the right to control, for example, the sale of one fifth of Aeronca's shares by a New York resident to a Californian. The court

1170. *Id.* at 759.
1171. *Id.*
1172. *Id.*
1173. *Id.* at 760.

concluded that the statute's impact on interstate commerce was "direct, intended and substantial" and "not merely an incidental effect of a general regulation of the internal affairs of Ohio corporations."[1174]

Nor did defendants succeed in convincing the court that the state's interests in adopting the statute outweighed the law's effects on interstate commerce. The court distinguished mergers and other types of voluntary corporate reorganizations from tender offers, which "do[] not of [themselves] change the nature of the corporate entity or alter its internal affairs."[1175] The right to regulate tender offers thus did not flow from the state's authority over Ohio corporations. Instead, the statute impermissibly reached out to regulate trading by shareholders (who might or might not be Ohio residents) and thus intervened in the process a step too soon—namely, at the stage when stock was traded, rather than at the stage when the acquiror of control attempted to use its new power to effect a change in the corporate entity or to alter its internal affairs.[1176] Relying on *MITE*, the court also held that Ohio had no legitimate interest in protecting nonresident shareholders.

Finally, the court rejected Ohio's argument that the statute served a legitimate state interest by protecting the state's business climate and the jobs of Ohio citizens from hostile tender offers.[1177] Defendants had adduced no evidence to support the proposition that a 20-percent or greater owner of an Ohio corporation would do something detrimental to Ohio, such as close a plant. Moreover, "any legislative attempt by Ohio to control or restrict the ownership of stock of a corporation by regulating the interstate sale of that stock in order to prevent a new owner from closing an Ohio plant or transferring assets elsewhere would clearly be an unconstitutional interference with

---

1174. *Id.* at 761.
1175. *Id.* at 763.
1176. *Id.*
1177. *Id.* at 764.

interstate commerce."[1178] The statute's failure to restrict existing management's authority to close or move a plant further belied the statutory purpose asserted by defendants.[1179]

The district court's treatment of the Ohio statute typifies the receptions accorded other control share statutes, regardless of the circumstances of their adoption. The fate of Missouri's anti-takeover statute, for example, resembles that of Ohio's.

In June 1984, the Missouri legislature adopted a Control Share Acquisition Statute[1180] similar to the one enacted in Ohio. Like the Ohio measure, it applied only to domestic corporations organized under Missouri law. On May 23, 1985, corporate raider Carl Icahn filed a Schedule 13D with the SEC disclosing his interest in TWA, a Delaware corporation headquartered in New York City. TWA conducted extensive operations in Missouri, using St. Louis as a flight hub and Kansas City as a training and repair center. In a desperate effort to block Icahn's acquisition of TWA, the Missouri legislature swung into action and, in a matter of days, adopted a provision applying the state's Control Share Acquisition Statute to foreign corporations that were common carriers employing over 7,500 people in Missouri and that had benefited from physical facilities financed by Missouri political subdivisions.[1181] There was only one such company: TWA.

Icahn immediately sued to enjoin enforcement of the statute against him in his bid for TWA, a foreign corporation merely doing business in Missouri. In *Icahn v. Blunt*,[1182] a federal district court held the statute unconstitutional, under the Supremacy and Commerce Clauses, as applied to foreign corporations. The court's opinion is notable for its strong reiteration of the *MITE* position that the location of the transaction(s), not the identities

---

1178. *Id.*

1179. *Id.*

1180. Mo. Rev. Stat. § 351.407.

1181. *Id.* § 351.575(2).

1182. 612 F. Supp. 1400 (W.D. Mo. 1985).

of the parties involved, is decisive when examining a control share statute's effects on interstate commerce.

The court ruled that the Missouri statute "differ[ed] substantially from state blue-sky laws in that [it] directly burden[ed] transactions taking place wholly outside the State of Missouri."[1183] In the instant case,

> Icahn, a resident of New York, seeks to gain control of TWA, which is incorporated in Delaware, by means of purchasing the common stock of TWA on the New York Stock Exchange. Under the provisions of H.B. No. 117, Icahn would be prohibited from purchasing shares from non-Missouri sellers until a supermajority of all shareholders approve. Similarly, all TWA shareholders regardless of where they live would be prevented from selling their shares to Icahn. If Missouri can so directly affect securities trading between non-residents on national exchanges, so too may other states. The interstate sale of securities on national and regional securities exchanges would be at the mercy of any state's parochial interests. Therefore, regardless of the local purposes prompting its enactment § 351.575 (H.B. No. 117) is an unconstitutional attempt to assert directly extraterritorial jurisdiction over persons and property.[1184]

The court further concluded that the statute's burden on interstate commerce outweighed Missouri's asserted interests in the state's economic well-being, the provision of air transportation for Missouri's citizens, the solvency of the state's political subdivisions, and the protection of resident Missouri shareholders.[1185] These state interests appeared particularly weak in light of the legislature's failure to include any statutory mechanism to insure that foreign corporations maintained any presence in Missouri and of the statute's exemption of management-approved control share acquisitions regardless of their effects on Missouri's economic interests.[1186]

1183. *Id.* at 1415.

1184. *Id.*

1185. *Id.* at 1416 – 17.

1186. *Id.* at 1417.

Minnesota had been the first state to have its post-*MITE* control share acquisition statute invalidated. In *APL Ltd. Partnership v. Van Dusen Air, Inc.*,[1187] a federal district court applied the *Pike* balancing test and found that the statute's benefits to Minnesota did not justify the burden that the law imposed on interstate commerce. The court observed that

> [a] state may have a legitimate desire to accomplish a certain objective. That desire represents an interest of the state. However, to the extent that a statute which burdens interstate commerce fails to further the state's desired result, that statute will not result in any local benefits to a state.[1188]

Thus, a state must demonstrate not merely that its approach was designed to further a valuable state interest but that it in fact does so.[1189]

The court also rejected, as a basis for the control share approach, Minnesota's reliance on its traditional right to regulate the internal affairs of domestic corporations: "The acquisition of shares does not implicate the internal affairs of the target corporation. The use of that power *once the shares have been acquired* may well be a proper subject of state regulation, but that is not what the [statute] regulates."[1190]

Following the *APL* ruling, the Minnesota legislature revised its control share statute in an attempt to meet the court's objections. But even this milder version of the law recently was invalidated in *Gelco Corp. v. Coniston Partners** as imposing an indirect burden on interstate commerce and as violating the Supremacy Clause.

The court admitted that the 1985 and 1986 amendments to the Minnesota statute removed some of "the most onerous

---

1187. 622 F. Supp. 1216 (D. Minn. 1985), *vacated as moot*, No. 85-5346 (8th Cir. Nov. 25, 1985).

1188. 622 F. Supp. at 1221.

1189. *Id.*

1190. *Id.* at 1223 – 24 (emphasis in original).

*Civil No. 3-86-847 (D. Minn. Nov. 10, 1986).

burdens" of other control share laws: the Minnesota revision did not disqualify "interested" shares held by an acquiror from voting in the shareholder referendum on the control share transaction, and it mandated that such a vote be held within 20 business days of receipt of the acquiror's required disclosures. Nevertheless, the court held, the statute burdened interstate commerce. The shortened time frame for the vote did not alter the fact that the vote requirement itself had "an extremely coercive effect": in this case, for example, it forced stockholders to choose between the target's unconditional exchange offer (valued at $21 – $24 per share) and Coniston's independent tender offer (of $26 per share), which was contingent on a shareholder vote that might not be finalized until after the exchange offer closed.

The court also questioned whether the statute's shortening of the formal period for a shareholder vote guaranteed against delays in vote tallying and other procedures that might prevent a bidder from beginning to acquire shares at 12:00 a.m. on the twenty-first business day following commencement of the offer, as allowed under the Williams Act. Moreover, the court rejected the internal affairs doctrine as a justification for the law and noted that the statute was not narrowly tailored to apply only to Minnesota residents, as is its "legislative cousin," the disclosure-based Minnesota Corporate Take-Over Act.**

In addition, the court held the control share statute invalid under the Supremacy Clause. Although it noted that the statute could delay a bidder's ability to purchase shares (despite the 20-day deadline for the shareholders' vote on the transaction), the court was more disturbed that the law required shareholder approval of certain tender offers but not of others. This feature "in effect converts a tender offer into a proxy contest—with additional expense and potential for delay." "There is a vast difference," declared the court, "between requiring disclosure of information to allow investors to make informed decisions and requiring a vote using that information. The Williams Act

---

***See infra* § III.5.B(2) (discussing Minnesota Corporate Take-Over Act).

requires the former. The Minnesota Act goes considerably further by requiring both." The court held that the statute's "depriving individual shareholders of the right to make independent decisions regarding offers to sell" impermissibly conflicted with the objectives of the Williams Act and thus violated the Supremacy Clause.

Wisconsin, Minnesota's neighbor, reacted to the 1985 *APL* decision both by repealing the control share acquisition provisions added to the Wisconsin Business Corporation Law in 1984[1191] and by amending the Voting Rights section of the Corporation Law. The revised statute reduces to 1/10 (or 10 percent) the voting power of a public corporation's shares held by any party owning more than 20 percent of the issuer's outstanding shares,[1192] unless a majority of shares represented at a specially called shareholders' meeting votes to remove this disability.[1193]

The promoters of the new Wisconsin approach advanced several bases for their strategy.[1194] Unlike the control share acquisition statutes, Wisconsin's law relates to voting rights, an area exclusively and traditionally within the province of state corporation law. Moreover, the new approach does not prevent the acquisition of shares; indeed, the law specifically provides that a party *proposing* to acquire more than 20 percent of a target's stock may ask for a shareholders' vote to prevent dilution of voting power.[1195] (However, the issuer need not schedule the shareholders' meeting until 50 days after receiving this request.[1196])

The proponents of the statute also claimed that the law constitutes nothing more than the flip side of supermajority

---

1191. Wis. Stat. § 180.69 (repealed).

1192. *Id.* § 180.25(9)(a).

1193. *Id.* § 180.25(9)(d)(3).

1194. The discussion here is drawn from 13 Wis. Sec. Bull. (Office of the Commissioner of Securities, Madison, Wisconsin) at 7 (No. 7, Dec. 1985).

1195. Wis. Stat. § 180.25(9)(c)(6).

1196. *Id.* § 180.25(9)(d).

voting rights provisions adopted by several states and included as "shark repellents" in the charters and bylaws of hundreds of corporations. In second-step mergers (occurring after an acquiror has obtained a majority, but less than all, of an issuer's shares), supermajority voting requirements grant greater voting power per share to shares held by minority shareholders. By contrast, the Wisconsin statute reduces the voting power of shares held by a 20-percent (or greater) holder in the first stage of gaining control of a corporation. Advocates of the Wisconsin statute have noted that supermajority voting provisions in state statutes and corporate charters have regularly withstood challenge.

The recent decision in *Dynamics Corp. of America v. CTS Corp.*[1197] may cast doubt on the validity of Wisconsin's revised statute. In *DCA*, the Court of Appeals for the Seventh Circuit struck down Indiana's control share acquisition statute, which did not bar the acquisition of shares but instead provided that the acquired shares would lose all voting rights unless the acquiror obtained the approval of a majority *both* of all shares and of "disinterested" shares voted at a special shareholders' meeting called to consider the issue.[1198] The court held that the Indiana statute violated both the Supremacy and Commerce Clauses.[1199]

Of special interest was the court's unwillingness to defer to the state's usual authority to prescribe rules relating to voting rights. In its Supremacy Clause analysis, the court declared:

> Cleverly drafted though the statute is to skirt judicial holdings that forbid states to delay tender offers beyond the period required by the Williams Act, the cleverness is fairly transparent. The effect of the Indiana statute is both to impose a 50-day delay on tender offers at the option of the target firm and to make it far more difficult for tender offers to succeed even if delay is not an impediment. The offeror dare not accept the tendered shares till

---

1197. 794 F.2d 250 (7th Cir.), *probable jurisdiction noted*, 107 S. Ct. 258 (1986).

1198. Ind. Code §§ 23 – 1 – 42 – 1 through – 11.

1199. 794 F.2d at 262 – 64.

> the stockholders' meeting is held, since if he loses the vote on voting rights he will end up with nonvoting shares and will not be able to control the corporation—the main purpose of most tender offers.[1200]

This skepticism toward the Indiana statute's reliance on the state's traditional authority in the realm of corporate governance extended to the court's Commerce Clause discussion. The court admitted that "[w]e may assume without having to decide that Indiana has a broad latitude in regulating [the internal affairs of Indiana corporations], even when the consequence may be to make it harder to take over an Indiana corporation. . . ."[1201] But this acknowledgement of Indiana's plenary authority over corporations did not automatically insure that its statute complied with the Commerce Clause: "The law in question is an explicit regulation of tender offers; that the mode of regulation involves jiggering with voting rights cannot take it outside the scope of judicial review under the commerce clause. Any other conclusion would invite facile evasions of the clause."[1202]

2. Other State Approaches

Although the federal courts have shown great skepticism toward post-*MITE* state statutes, a notable exception suggests that there might still be room for state takeover legislation. When Minnesota adopted its control share acquisition statute (which was invalidated in *APL Ltd. Partnership v. Van Dusen Air, Inc.*[1203]), the legislature also enacted other amendments to conform state law to *MITE* and its progeny.[1204] The amendments provide that an offeror must file a registration statement no later than the day

---

1200. *Id.* at 261.

1201. *Id.* at 264.

1202. *Id.*

1203. 622 F. Supp. 1216 (D. Minn. 1985), *vacated as moot*, No. 85-5346 (8th Cir. Nov. 25, 1985), discussed in § III.5.B(I), *supra.*

1204. Minn. Stat. §§ 80B.01 – 03.

on which the offeror begins its tender offer.[1205] Within three calendar days of this filing, the Minnesota Commissioner of Commerce may suspend summarily the effectiveness of the tender offer, but only as to Minnesota residents, if he finds that the statement either does not include the required information or fails to disclose all material information regarding the tender offer.[1206] The Commissioner must then hold a hearing within ten calendar days of the suspension and decide, within no more than three days after the hearing concludes and, in any event, no more than 16 calendar days after the suspension, whether to suspend the offer permanently in Minnesota.[1207] The Commissioner's authority permanently to suspend the offer is subject to the offeror's right to correct the inadequate disclosure or other deficiencies that the Commissioner identifies.[1208]

This revised Minnesota statute is the second-generation statute that most closely resembles a pre-*MITE* measure.[1209] However, in *Cardiff Acquisitions, Inc. v. Hatch*,[1210] the Court of Appeals for the Eighth Circuit upheld the law as facially constitutional even though the court ruled that the Commissioner had applied it unconstitutionally in certain respects.

The court distinguished the Minnesota statute from the Illinois law struck down in *MITE*: the Minnesota Act requires no precommencement notification, permits only the Commissioner (and not the target) to ask for a hearing, does not delay the tender offer process beyond the time period established in the Williams Act, and permits the Commissioner to rule only on the quality of the disclosure, rather than on the fairness of the offer.[1211] The court also pointed out that the Minnesota

---

1205. *Id.* § 80B.03(1).

1206. *Id.* § 80A.03(4)(a).

1207. *Id.* § 80B.03(5).

1208. *Id.*

1209. Block, Barton, and Roth, "State Takeover Statutes: The 'Second Generation,' " 13 Sec. Reg. L.J. 332, 340 (1986).

1210. 751 F.2d 906 (8th Cir. 1984).

1211. *Id.* at 910 – 11.

statute applies only when 20 percent of the target's shares are owned by Minnesotans and when the target owns or controls "substantial" assets in the state; moreover, any suspension ordered by the Commissioner affects only Minnesota residents. The statute thus imposes only an indirect burden on interstate commerce, and only when Minnesota's interests are at stake.[1212]

In addition, the court ruled that the benefits to be balanced against this intrusion on interstate commerce were "not illusory."[1213] The disclosures required under the Minnesota law for the most part parallel those mandated by the Williams Act; the court approved the simultaneous enforcement of the statutes partially because the "SEC apparently lacks the resources to police the thousands of schedule 13(d) reports and amendments filed each year."[1214] Moreover, the additional disclosure required by the Minnesota statute relates primarily to a proposed takeover's impact on Minnesota residents and thus helps them to appraise the value of the offer.[1215] Finally, the court held that the Commissioner's statutory authority to review the adequacy of disclosure and to suspend a tender offer if he finds the disclosure inadequate does not conflict impermissibly with the Williams Act and thus does not violate the Supremacy Clause.[1216] However, the court struck down provisions of the Minnesota statute granting the Commissioner the discretion to require an offeror to disclose additional information beyond that specifically prescribed by the statute.[1217]

As 1986 ended, control share acquisition statutes had been largely discredited by the federal courts. The statutes' demise raised the deeper question whether the post-*MITE* technique of regulating tender offers through basic state corporation law was the route that Justice Powell had envisioned when he joined

---

1212. *Id.* at 911.

1213. *Id.*

1214. *Id.* at 912 (footnote omitted).

1215. *Id.*

1216. *Id.* at 913.

1217. *Id.* at 914.

Justice White's opinion in *MITE* on the assumption that it left room for a state role in takeover regulation. *Cardiff Acquisitions* suggests that statutes tailored to protect a specific state's own shareholders are the least constitutionally suspect.

A number of states have adopted a different—and as yet untested—approach and have followed the post-*MITE* fair price model first enacted in Maryland. In essence, the Maryland law presents an offeror with a draconian choice: either buy out stockholders in the second stage of a two-tier "business combination" involving a Maryland issuer at prices equal to or higher than those paid for similar securities in the first tier of the deal, or, in the alternative, secure supermajority approval (80 percent of the issuer's outstanding shares *and* two-thirds of the shares held by stockholders not considered "interested," as defined) to execute the second-tier purchase without paying the higher price.[1218] The statute defines a "business combination" as a merger, consolidation, or share exchange with an "interested stockholder" (defined as any person, other than the issuer or a subsidiary, who owns or has owned ten percent or more of the issuer's voting securities at any time within two years prior to the relevant date), unless the transaction does not change the contract rights, or convert any of the outstanding shares, of the stock.[1219] Thus, the statute applies only to the second step of a two-step tender offer.

The Maryland statute represents an obvious attempt to conform to the Supreme Court's pronouncements in *MITE*. Because the Court there declared that tender offers themselves are not part of the internal affairs of corporations, legislatures now focus on regulating those corporate internal affairs that inevitably affect tender offers. As cases involving control share acquisition statutes demonstrate, this solution is not foolproof. The fair price statutes adopted by Maryland and more than ten other states may yet prove vulnerable when challenged in court, both as measures that make tender offers more difficult to

---

1218. 79 Md. Corps. & Ass'ns Code Ann. § 3 – 602.

1219. *Id.* §§ 3 – 601(E) and (J), 3 – 603(B), 3 – 202.

complete (and that therefore burden interstate commerce) and as disturbers of the neutrality principle that the Williams Act purports to embody.[1220] For example, the Maryland statute would affect second-tier prices paid to stockholders regardless of where they resided. Nevertheless, because the Maryland law focuses on a later stage in the takeover process, rather than on the initial acquisition of shares, it may receive a more favorable judicial reception as a purer effort to regulate the internal affairs of Maryland corporations.[1221]

The Pennsylvania Shareholder Protection Act,[1222] enacted in 1983, is very similar to the Maryland law in its requirement of a majority vote of stockholders (except interested ones) for approval of a second-step merger or consolidation.[1223] An acquiror can escape this mandate only by obtaining a majority vote of directors independent from the acquiror or by paying, in the second tier, consideration equal to the highest amount per share (of the same class) that the acquiror paid for the stock that it already controls.[1224] The Pennsylvania law also expressly alters the fiduciary duties of directors and officers in evaluating tender offers by allowing those persons to consider an array of factors other than price, including effects on employees, suppliers, and customers of the corporation as well as on the communities where the corporation is located.[1225]

The other distinctive feature of the Pennsylvania statute is its adoption of the United Kingdom takeover model, under which an offeror who acquires a 30-percent stake in a target may have

---

1220. Block, Barton, and Roth, "State Takeover Statutes: The 'Second Generation,'" 13 Sec. Reg. L.J. 332, 353 (1986).

1221. The Maryland statute recently was challenged by Dart Group in its bid for Safeway Stores; the issue was never resolved, however, because a white knight deal ended the battle.

1222. Pa. Cons. Stat. Ann. §§ 408, 409.1, 910. The Maine legislature passed a measure that in some ways resembles the Pennsylvania statute. Me. Rev. Stat. Tit. 13A, § 910.

1223. Pa. Cons. Stat. Ann. § 409.1(C)(1).

1224. *Id.* § 409.1(C)(2).

1225. *Id.* § 408(B).

to purchase all the remaining shares outstanding after the tender offer.[1226] The statute requires an offeror to notify the remaining shareholders once the offeror has purchased 30 percent or more of the target's shares.[1227] The offeror must pay, to any shareholders demanding to be bought out, the cash value of those holders' shares, which equals the fair value of each voting share on the day prior to the occurrence of the control transaction. (The statute also allows shareholders to use the standard procedure established for dissenters seeking their appraisal rights in other settings.) The statute specifically provides for consideration of "an increment representing a portion of any value payable for acquisition of control of the corporation" in establishing the value of the stock on the day prior to the control transaction.[1228] This provision means that the 30-percent owner probably will wind up paying, to all remaining stockholders who wish to be bought out, the highest premium paid in acquiring any portion of the 30-percent stake. As do most second-generation statutes, the Pennsylvania statute allows a corporation to enact a charter amendment declining to accept the protections available under Pennsylvania law.[1229]

The Pennsylvania statute may be subject to constitutional attack on several grounds. First, the provision allowing the independent directors to accept a merger and thus to sidestep the majority approval requirement may upset the neutrality established by the Williams Act. Second, the majority approval and the forced buy-out features may make tender offers for Pennsylvania corporations more difficult to complete and thus may burden interstate commerce by unduly interfering with the rights of those companies' shareholders throughout the country.

In the midst of this ferment, legislators in New York responded with a seemingly different tactic. In August 1985, Governor Mario Cuomo vetoed a bill that included provisions typical of

---

1226. *Id.* § 910(D), (E).

1227. *Id.* § 910(C).

1228. *Id.* § 910(E).

1229. *Id.* § 910(A).

the control share acquisition approach because the bill posed constitutional problems. The legislature tried again, and the Governor signed a bill, effective December 16, 1985, that added section 912 to the New York Business Corporation Law ("BCL").

Section 912 attempts to address judicial objections to post-*MITE* statutes that have regulated the actual trading of shares. In order to establish the state's interest, the legislature directed the statute only at "resident domestic corporations," which not only must be incorporated under New York law but also must have "principal executive offices" and "significant business operations" in New York; in addition, at least ten percent of those corporations' shares must be "beneficially" owned by New York residents.[1230] The new law imposes a five-year ban on any "business combination" between a "domestic corporation" and any "interested shareholder," defined as a holder of 20 percent or more of the issuer's stock.[1231] Such "business combinations" are broadly defined and include mergers, consolidations, and sales, leases, exchanges, or other measures through which assets of the issuer having a market value greater than ten percent of the issuer's total assets, outstanding stock, earning power, or net income change hands.[1232] The law does not apply to business combinations with persons other than 20-percent shareholders or their associates; agreements with white knights are allowed.

The statute provides that a would-be acquiror can avoid the five-year ban on business combinations by obtaining approval from the issuer's board, before becoming a 20-percent holder, for either the business combination itself or for the acquisition of more than 20 percent of the stock.[1233] If the board does not grant such approval, and if the acquiror acquires a 20-percent (or

---

1230. N.Y. Bus. Corp. L. § 912(a)(13). Several other states have passed similar measures: Kentucky (Ky. Rev. Stat. § 271A.397(b)(3)); Indiana (Ind. Code §§ 23 – 1 – 43 – 1 through – 19); New Jersey (New Jersey Shareholders Protection Act, Ch. 74, L. '86, to be codified) (effective Jan. 23, 1986) (includes sunset provision for expiration on January 12, 1988, unless renewed).

1231. N.Y. Bus. Corp. L. §§ 912(b) – (d).

1232. *Id.* § 912(a)(5).

1233. *Id.* § 912(c)(1).

greater) stake, the five-year ban takes effect unless the disinterested shareholders approve a bylaw amendment rendering section 912 inapplicable to the issuer. Even in such a case, however, the bylaw would not take effect until 18 months later.[1234] Once the five-year ban has ended, the acquiror still suffers a disability: it may consummate a business combination only by gaining the approval of a majority of the stock held by disinterested shareholders or by paying a premium under a fair price approach similar to the Maryland model.[1235]

The law also requires the board of directors of a domestic corporation to respond in writing within 30 days (or such shorter period as may be prescribed under the Securities Exchange Act) after receiving a good faith business combination proposal and to give its reasons for approving or disapproving the proposal. Failure to respond is deemed to constitute disapproval.[1236]

The New York statute might be challenged some day by a hostile tender offeror bent on acquiring a New York corporation.[1237] The statute allows a target's board effectively to veto business combinations necessary to an interested shareholder who wishes either to use the target's assets to finance his bid or to take complete control of the corporation through a merger. Moreover, the law does not provide for a vote of disinterested board members to lift the restrictions on business combinations. The statute thus may tend to protect incumbent management's efforts either to continue to run the corporation or to mount a management-sponsored leveraged buy-out or freeze-out; it also may tend to limit shareholders' ability to tender their shares.

The board's discretion to block a tender offer, however, is not unconstrained. In deciding whether or not to approve a

---

1234. *Id.* § 912(d)(3).

1235. *Id.* § 912(c)(2), (3).

1236. *Id.* § 912(b).

1237. This discussion of the potential constitutional objections to the New York statute relies heavily on Pinto, "Constitutionality of N.Y.'s New Takeover Statute," Nat'l L.J., Feb. 24, 1986, at 17, 30, 31.

proposed transaction and thus to exempt it from the statutory scheme, the target's directors most likely will still have to satisfy the duties of care and loyalty that would apply to a board's decision whether or not to redeem a poison pill in the face of a particular tender offer. Moreover, the New York statute purports to regulate only those business combinations over which the state traditionally has been able to exercise authority. These distinctions might prove strong enough to protect the law from invalidation on Supremacy Clause grounds. After all, an offeror still can seek to buy the shares of a New York corporation and can wage a proxy fight to gain board approval of the tender offer if the transaction involves leveraging or a second-stage business combination.

Other constitutional issues might arise under the Commerce Clause. First, the statute imposes restrictions on an interested shareholder's ability to consummate business combinations and acquisitions involving the target and its securities. Second, although the statute purports to regulate only the capacity of corporations to merge or conclude similarly significant dispositions of assets, a court might look behind that literal purpose to the legislative goal of inhibiting hostile takeovers. The law's limits and its five-year ban on business combinations mean that the statute could affect the movement of assets among states and the concomitant ability of shareholders to receive the premiums that their shares might command in a free market. Nevertheless, the narrowness of the class of corporations governed by the statute might insure that the statute will apply only to those takeovers that necessarily affect New York interests, and this fact could assist a target in defending the statute's constitutionality under the Commerce Clause.

The debate continues over whether takeovers constitute techniques for monitoring management or destroyers of local businesses. If a court were to view the New York statute as an attempt to regulate an economic evil, that court might question the applicability of the internal affairs doctrine, which normally is justified only by the state's traditional role in regulating relationships among shareholders, officers, and directors. Even if applied, however, this principle probably would not insulate from constitutional scrutiny an unreasonable, indirect burden on interstate commerce not justified by a tangible state benefit, as distinguished from a state interest in impeding takeovers. Thus, a court may have to decide whether New York's focus on the business combination itself, instead of on the acquisition of shares, suffices to save the statute from constitutional invalidity.

C. Conclusion

Since the 1982 *MITE* decision, the debate over the proper role of states in regulating tender offers has continued to rage in arenas other than state legislatures and the federal courts. In 1983, the SEC Advisory Committee on Tender Offers made numerous recommendations that would have limited the state presence in this area.[1238] The Committee suggested that states should be allowed to regulate only when local companies are involved and that state laws should be preempted "to the extent necessary to eliminate abuses or interference with the intended function of federal takeover regulation. . . ."[1239] The SEC, however, voted to reject recommendations that would involve preemption of state corporation law or would ban charter and bylaw provisions limiting changes in corporate control.[1240]

When faced with a post-*MITE* attack on a pre-*MITE* statute, the Court of Appeals for the Tenth Circuit wondered aloud about the question that now dominates state attempts to regulate takeovers: "It is less than clear as to what room is left for state regulation. . . ."[1241] Some pre-*MITE* state statutes remain on

---

1238. SEC Advisory Comm. on Tender Offers, *Report of Recommendations*, [Special Report No. 1028, Extra Edition] Fed. Sec. L. Rep. (CCH) (July 15, 1983).

1239. *Id.* at 17 – 18 (Recommendations 9(a), (b)).

1240. *See* 16 Sec. Reg. & L. Rep. (BNA) No. 11, at 496 (March 16, 1984).

1241. *Mesa Petroleum Co. v. Cities Serv. Co.*, 715 F.2d 1425, 1430 n.8 (10th Cir. 1983).

the books, awaiting the first serious tender offer battles in the relevant jurisdictions. Their fates under such challenges seem predictable. Even in states that have responded to *MITE*, many citizens and officials feel vulnerable to plant shutdowns and to the perceived indifference that new managements often bring to local problems. The recent decisions involving the post-*MITE* statutes leave these people to ponder whether the room for state regulation that Justices Stevens and Powell once foresaw actually exists. For advocates of state legislation, the issue remains what role, if any, the state that grants a corporation its legal birthright may play in the subsequent transformation of that company.

TABLE OF CASES

INDEX